Praise for *Experience-Driven Leader Development*

"There is a wealth of experience presented in this volume that is both cutting edge and grounded in leader development research and theory. It is highly recommended reading for anyone interested in state-of-the-science leader development."

> **David Day**, Ph.D., Woodside Chair of Leadership and Management, The University of Western Australia Business School

"CCL pioneered research on experience-based leadership development, and now this book showcases a wealth of tried-and-true practices that transform research into reality. Leadership developers can access and adapt tested advice, models, organizational practices, and tools to their unique circumstances. Finally—some ready-to-use answers to how informal experience-based learning can be developed, designed, and supported in ways that boost performance for leaders and their organizations!"

> **Victoria J. Marsick**, Ph.D., Department of Organization & Leadership, Columbia University, Teachers College

"*Experience-Driven Leader Development* is a comprehensive resource rich in examples, models and practical advice. This is a must read for anyone interested in developing leaders to achieve personal or organizational goals."

> **Marcia J. Avedon**, Ph.D., senior vice president, Human Resources and Communications Ingersoll Rand, Board of Governors., Center for Creative Leadership

About This Book

Why Is This Topic Important?

Learning from experience is *the* number one way that leaders develop. If you are reading this book, you probably already know this. It's evident in the research you follow. It's plain from your own observations and experiences in organizations. Despite the overwhelming evidence, however, experience-driven leader development receives considerably less attention and organizational resources compared to formal education, training, and coaching. Thus, there are untapped opportunities to optimize the value of experience for leader development.

What Can You Achieve with This Book?

For the greatest impact, you want to harness the power of experience for leadership development. The way to do this doesn't lie in a formula or a step-by-step process. Rather, you can find different ways to answer that challenge using the array of tools, techniques, interventions, initiatives, and models collected in this volume. These are not simply ideas that ought to work. They come from practitioners like you, people who are enhancing experience-driven development in organizations and communities, in many different ways and with a wide variety of audiences. Whatever your approach, you can find in this book the tools and practices that will help you develop the best possible talent in organizations while having a positive and powerful effect on people's lives.

How Is This Book Organized?

The book is organized into four sections, each targeting a critical element of experience-driven development.

In the first section, *Developmental Experiences: More Intentional for More People*, you will find ways to help more people access leadership experiences to target their particular development needs.

Section 2, *Leaders: Better Equipped to Learn from Experience*, addresses the fact that an experience does not guarantee learning. In these pages you will see how you can enhance leaders' ability to learn from their experiences so that they extract the maximum developmental value.

Section 3, *Human Resource Systems: Designed for Experience-Driven Development*, looks at the formal systems and processes for managing talent that many organizations have put into place. The contributions in this section describe how to build experience-driven development into those processes.

Section 4, *The Organization: Enabler of Experience-Driven Development*, takes on the shared values, the behaviors, and beliefs of employees, and processes and routines found in organizations. Rather than allowing those attributes to get in the way, you can use the knowledge in this section to influence an organization in ways that enable rather than inhibit experience-driven learning.

We have tagged each contribution based on whether it shares a tool (a specific activity or technique), an organizational practice (a formal process or initiative), a model (a conceptual framework that guides thinking and action), or advice (an overview of a topic with insights based on expertise or research).

Experience-Driven Leader Development

Models, Tools, Best Practices, and Advice for On-the-Job Development

Cynthia D. McCauley
D. Scott DeRue
Paul R. Yost
Sylvester Taylor

WILEY

Cover design: JPuda
Cover images: (model) © browndogstudios/istock; (wrench) © scottdunlap/istock; (checklist) © scottdunlap/istock; (info) © runeer/istock

Published by Wiley

One Montgomery Street, Suite 1200, San Francisco, CA 94104-4594
www.wiley.com

For additional copies/bulk purchases of this book in the U.S. please contact 800-274-4434.

Wiley books and products are available through most bookstores. To contact Wiley directly call our Customer Care Department within the U.S. at 800-274-4434, outside the U.S. at 317-572-3985, fax 317-572-4002, or visit www.wiley.com

Wiley publishes in a variety of print and electronic formats and by print-on-demand. Some material included with standard print versions of this book may not be included in e-books or in print-on-demand. If this book refers to media such as a CD or DVD that is not included in the version you purchased, you may download this material at http://booksupport.wiley.com. For more information about Wiley products, visit www.wiley.com.

CIP data is available on file at the Library of Congress.
ISBN 978-1-118-45807-5(hbk)
978-1-118-76765-8 (ebk)
978-1-118-76784-9 (ebk)

Printed in the United States of America

HB Printing   10   9   8   7   6   5   4   3   2   1

Contents

SECTION 2. Leaders: Better Equipped to Learn from Experience 141

List of Exhibits, Figures, and Tables

Foreword

A Quarter Century and Counting: Getting Serious About Using Experience to Develop Talent

Morgan W. McCall, Jr.
University of Southern California

LONGER AGO THAN I care to admit, my colleagues and I set out to understand how experience shaped leadership talent. Back in those days we talked about managers and executives, reserving the term *leader* for something else, though it is common today to use the terms interchangeably. Also back in those days, *executive development* referred almost exclusively to programs, usually training programs, in house or out of house, designed and delivered by human resource professionals or academics. To be sure, there were experience-based practices such as career paths (for example, IBM's famous two years line, two years staff), rotational assignments, and *assistant to* positions, but conversations about systematically using online experience for development seldom got past "throw them in the fire and see who comes out the other side." Ironically, our effort to understand development through experience began in a place that, appropriate to the time, strove to be a premier leadership training center.

The product of our initial research into experience, *The Lessons of Experience* (McCall, Lombardo, & Morrison, 1988), almost never made it into print. We had interviewed and surveyed successful executives about their experiences and what they had learned from them, and we hoped that by analyzing their stories we would change how development was viewed. But the original contract was with a major publishing house that seemed intent on a book with titillating stories about celebrity executives. Although we had plenty of tales to tell, they weren't about people you would have heard of. They were the stories of talented but regular people educated in the metaphorical "school of hard knocks" and by "learning in the trenches." Fortunately, a small publishing house picked up the book, which is still in print, and over time interest grew in using experience more systematically.

Fast-forward through the years as additional research accumulated on experience, what it can teach, and how it might be used more effectively to develop talent (see, for example, McCauley, Ruderman, Ohlott, & Morrow, 1994; McCall, 1998; McCall, 2010; McCall & Hollenbeck, 2002; Spreitzer, McCall, & Mahoney, 1997). But even though interest in the concepts increased, putting the ideas into practice stumbled forward in fits and starts. For the reasons so beautifully articulated in the introductory chapter of this book, the knowing-doing gap (Pfeffer & Sutton, 2000) persists. True, the companies *Fortune* considers "most admired for their leaders" do more than others to use experience for development (Colvin, 2009), but experience-driven leadership development, despite some heroic efforts to implement it (see, for example, McCauley & McCall, in press), has not yet created a paradigm shift.

It is with delight that I discovered that there has been an insurgency building all along. Sung—but mostly unsung—heroes, operating in all kinds of organizations, quietly have developed tools and practices that make it possible to *do* experience-based talent development. Instead of trying to change the world, they have been trying to nudge, twist, cajole, prod, and otherwise influence practice. Not only that, these bricoleurs are willing to share the results of their efforts with anyone facing similar issues. But it took tenacity and insight to pull all of these pieces together and make them accessible, so hats off to McCauley, DeRue, Yost, and Taylor for providing this compendium of raw material.

Making experience-driven development work is not as easy as it sounds, and that's why the tools, practices, and advice found in this book are so important. At first glance using experience seems straightforward: identify someone with leadership potential, put her in a stretch assignment, repeat several times, and voila—a leader. Even if it were this simple, to actually do it one would still need some way to identify potential, a way to identify the stretch assignments and choose the appropriate one, and some way to assess and track development across repeated trials.

But it isn't that simple. How do you match people to experiences? What do you do to get the right person into the right experience at the right time—especially if the "right" assignment involves crossing an organizational boundary? Because people don't always learn what an experience offers, what can you do to increase the odds of actually learning the lessons in the experience? What can you do if the needed experience isn't available, either because it doesn't exist or because it is being blocked by a solid performer? What happens if you make a mistake and put someone in an assignment that is over his head? Perhaps even more daunting, how can effective use of experience be embedded in an organization's core so that it is a natural act rather than a peripheral one?

These are just a few of the practical questions that doing experience-based development raises, and for which answers will come only by trying things out and seeing how well they work for learning through experience. As Mary Catherine Bateson observed, "Insight, I believe, refers to that depth of understanding that comes by setting experiences, yours and mine, familiar and exotic, new and old, side by side, learning by letting them speak to one another" (Bateson, 1994, p. 14). And that's what this book is, at its heart: eighty or so experiments that will give you things to try out, to chew on, and that I hope will inspire others to follow suit in developing appropriate tools and sharing their accumulating wisdom.

References

Bateson, M. (1994). *Peripheral visions*. New York, NY: HarperCollins.

Colvin, G. (2009, December 7). How to build great leaders. *Fortune, 160*(10), 70–72.

McCall, M.W., Jr. (1998). *High flyers: Developing the next generation of leaders*. Boston, MA: Harvard Business School Press.

McCall, M.W., Jr., (2010). The experience conundrum. In N. Nohria & R. Khurana (Eds.), *Handbook of leadership theory and practice* (pp. 679–707). Boston, MA: Harvard Business School Press.

McCall, M.W., Jr., & Hollenbeck, G.P. (2002). *Developing global executives: The lessons of international experience*. Boston, MA: Harvard Business School Press.

McCall, M.W., Jr., Lombardo, M.M., & Morrison, A.M. (1988). *The lessons of experience: How successful executives develop on the job*. Lexington, MA: Lexington Books.

McCauley, C.D., & McCall, M.W., Jr. (Eds.) (in press). *Using experience to develop leadership talent*. San Francisco, CA: Jossey-Bass.

McCauley, C.D., Ruderman, M.N., Ohlott, P.J., & Morrow, J. (1994). Assessing the developmental components of managerial jobs. *Journal of Applied Psychology, 79*(4), 544–560.

Pfeffer, J., & Sutton, R. (2000). *The knowing-doing gap: How smart companies turn knowledge into action*. Boston, MA: Harvard Business School Press.

Spreitzer, G., McCall, M.W., Jr., & Mahoney, J. (1997). Early identification of international executive potential. *Journal of Applied Psychology, 82*(1), 6–29.

Acknowledgments

IT IS IMPOSSIBLE to name all the people who have played a role in developing and advancing experience-driven approaches to leader development. However, we want to acknowledge Morgan McCall, Mike Lombardo, and Bob Eichinger, each of whom has played a major role as thought leaders and champions of on-the-job leader development. The field owes much to their pioneering work.

This book would not have been possible without the many authors who joined us in this endeavor. We are enthusiastic about the models, tools, and practices they have crafted and grateful for the advice and lessons learned that they shared, as well as their willingness to respond to rounds of feedback and editing. We also appreciate the organizations that were open to having their tools and practices published as resources for others.

Finally, we want to thank Shaun Martin, Steve Rush, Peter Scisco, Taylor Scisco, and Martin Wilcox from the publication staff at the Center for Creative Leadership. Special thanks to Elaine Biech for sharing her expertise early in our process, and to Jill Pinto for helping to organize the disparate pieces of the book into an orderly manuscript (and doing it with a smile).

Introduction

NDIVIDUALS BROADEN AND deepen their leadership capabilities as they do leadership work. In fact, there are good reasons to believe that learning from experience is *the* number one way that leader development happens.

As a leader development practitioner you know this. You know it from the research-based professional knowledge you consume and from your own observations and experiences in organizations. Yet the field continues to focus considerable time, money, and resources on the other two major sources of growth and development for leaders: (1) education and training, and (2) relationships for learning. U.S. companies spend an estimated $13.6 billion annually on formal leader development (O'Leonard & Loew, 2012). The vast majority of this investment goes toward education and training. On average, another 20 percent or so of an organization's leader development solutions are relationship-based (for example, formal coaching or peer networks). In contrast, the average percent of experience-driven leader development solutions range from 9 percent for first-level supervisors to 14 percent for senior managers (O'Leonard & Loew). The number one driver of leader development gets the least attention in leader development systems.

How can organizations rectify this imbalance and better harness the power of experiences for leader development? In our search for answers to this question, we connected with practitioners who had taken up the challenge of enhancing experience-driven development in organizations and communities—in many different ways and with a wide variety of audiences. We did not discover a formula or a step-by-step process, but rather an array of tools, techniques, interventions, initiatives, and models. We invited these individuals to share their work. The result is a compendium of resources that you can use to jump-start, guide, and stimulate your own efforts to use experience more intentionally to develop leaders.

Let's first return to the imbalance and understand why it happens. A number of forces draw your attention and energy away from experience-driven development and toward coursework and relationship-based development:

- The field is part of a larger society that takes for granted that learning is something that happens in the classroom, yielding knowledge and skills that are put to use later in one's career or back on the job or in some other aspect of one's life. This cultural mindset is pervasive. Classroom language is even used when describing learning outside of that realm (for example, "the school of hard knocks" or "leaders teaching leaders"). Putting experience-based development ahead of formal education and training is countercultural—not just for leader development professionals but for their customers, too.

- Practitioners have developed a wealth of knowledge and expertise about how to design and deliver effective programs, coaching initiatives, and formal mentoring processes. Done well, these practices do make a difference—they impact the development of leaders in important ways. It is no surprise that people focus on what they know how to do well, particularly when they can point to the positive impact of their work. There is much less knowledge in the field about how to best use experiences to develop leaders.

- Experience-driven development is messy. Programs have a beginning and an end, specific objectives, and design elements that support those objectives. They can be managed, evaluated, and continuously improved. On-the-job experiences are unfolding and unscripted. Teasing out the impact of a particular experience on a leader is tricky. When training or coaching, the practitioner is right there guiding and encouraging the learner. Give a leader a stretch assignment, and he or she is in charge of any learning that happens.

- Experience-driven development is less visible. It is hard to quantify and, when done really well, is a natural part of business and organizational processes. The closer you come to embedding leader development into the ongoing work of the organization, the less visibility you have for your work. In fact, a real success means that leaders themselves will own and take credit for the development of leaders in the organization.

But it's not as if the field has been devoid of experience-driven development practices. Job rotation programs are common at entry levels in organizations. Organizations often move high potential managers through a series of assignments to broaden their knowledge and skills in preparation for higher-level leadership responsibilities. Apprenticeship models of learning and development are standard in numerous professions. Action learning is in the toolkit of many practitioners.

Yet we sense a shift in the field. Not a shift away from coursework and relationships as important modes of learning, but rather a move to make learning from experience a more central part of the practice. What's the evidence for this shift?

- *Increased visibility for the concept of experience-driven development.* You can find more publications on the topic. The topic shows up more in conferences and practitioner forums. More research—some of it published in top academic journals—is available. In human resource circles there is even a catchphrase, "70–20–10," to describe leader development that puts more emphasis on job experiences (the 70) than relationships and training (the 20 and 10). Popularized by one consulting firm (Lombardo & Eichinger, 1996), the phrase is now used regularly in the field.

- *More sophistication in established experience-based practices.* For example, action learning projects that are part of leadership development programs increasingly engage participants in demanding work with real consequences for the organization (rather than safer study-and-recommend projects that might simply end up on a shelf somewhere). Take expatriate assignments as another example. Organizations are now more likely to carefully select candidates, prepare them prior to the assignment, coach them during the assignment, and capitalize on the expatriates' gained insights, connections, and skills in their next assignment.

- *Ongoing experimentation with new practices.* As awareness and understanding of experience-driven development has grown, practitioners have been at the forefront in designing new ways to make it happen and to support it throughout the organization. If you are like us, as you read about the models, tools, and practices in this book, you'll be excited—and sometimes surprised—about innovation in the field.

- *Practices that link and integrate experiences, relationships, and coursework for learning.* One of the criticisms of the 70–20–10 concept is the implication that these three ways of learning represent separate paths. However, what we see in practice is the integration of these three approaches within the same initiative or practice to get the biggest boost for the investment.

This book is about how individuals in the field are making this shift happen. Before you jump in to learn directly from these individuals, we want to accomplish two things in this Introduction: (1) provide you with a brief overview of the stream of research that helped fuel the shift and (2) orient you to the content of this book.

The Research Catalyst

A significant stimulus for the shift toward more focus on experience-driven leadership development happened in 1988 with the publication of *The Lessons of Experience: How Successful Executives Develop on the Job*, authored by Morgan W. McCall, Jr., Michael M. Lombardo, and Ann M. Morrison. The book became a catalyst, moving the focus away from what distinguishes effective leaders to how leaders are developed. As a result, experience-driven development emerged as a new focus for organizations and leader development professionals.

The book was based on qualitative data from 191 executives who were asked to reflect on their career and identify three key experiences that had led to a lasting change in the way they managed. The executives described their experiences in detail, including the skills and perspectives they gleaned from these experiences. The analysis of the executives' stories yielded five categories of key developmental experiences:

- *Challenging Assignments*: A job or a task within a job that stretched the executive because it was new, complex, or demanding. Examples include being responsible for turning around an operation in trouble and moving from a line to a staff position.

- *Other People*: Positive and negative role models—primarily bosses and others higher in the organization—who strongly influenced the executive's approach to management.

- *Hardships*: Setbacks and failures that generated a sense of loss and aloneness. Examples include business mistakes, demotions and missed promotions, and personal life traumas.

- *Coursework*: Formal training and academic programs.

- *Personal Life Experiences*: Experiences that occurred in the family, in school, or in the community, and that varied in nature from difficult situations to inspirational ones.

A majority of the experiences (56 percent) were challenging assignments, and for the most part, the other people and hardship experiences were also happening on the job.

That people learn a great deal from their experiences was certainly not a new discovery. Learning from cycles of action and reflection is a familiar concept in the field of adult learning. What was galvanizing about *Lessons of Experience* was threefold. First, it grounded this abstract concept of learning from experience in the vivid, real-world experiences of executives. It's like the idea of "seeing is believing"—the stories provided the depth and texture that compelled the reader to believe that the concept was significant. Second, it went beyond saying "people learn from their experiences." The research pointed out what kinds of experiences developed executives, what drove the learning in these experiences, and which capabilities were most associated with which experiences. This more detailed examination of developmental experiences created knowledge that could more readily be used by practitioners. Finally, another piece of data from the study was eye-opening. Of the 616 key experiences described by executives in the study, only thirty-eight (6.2 percent) were coursework experiences. This small percentage made people in the program-centric leader development profession pause.

Lessons of Experience spawned a new stream of leader development research. Because the participants in the original study were almost entirely white American males in senior executive roles, the research was replicated in more diverse samples, including senior women executives, African-American executives, middle managers, global executives, and executives in each of several Asian countries (Douglas, 2003; McCall & Hollenbeck, 2002; Morrison, White, & Van Velsor, 1987; Yip & Wilson, 2010). In some of these studies, the percentages of other people or hardship experiences were higher than the original study (and the percentage of challenging assignment experiences was lower)—making it clear that 70–20–10 should not be understood as a one-size-fits-all solution. However, the same overall pattern was clear: On-the-job experiences are a significant driver of leader development, particularly experiences that challenge leaders to lead in novel and diverse environments, to create change in high stakes situations, and to work across organizational and cultural boundaries.

Researchers also began building evidence that leaders who have a broad range of challenging leadership experiences are more effective than those who do not, for example, they are more competent at strategic thinking and are rated by others in the organization as more promotable (De Pater, Van Vianen, Bechtoldt, & Klehe, 2009; Dragoni, Oh, Van Katwyk, & Tesluk, 2011). And they explored individual and situational factors that influence who learns the most from developmental experiences. The leader's level of learning orientation (for example, the motivation to gain new skills and master tasks) is one factor that influences the impact of developmental experiences, and access to feedback can offset the diminishing returns associated with high levels of developmental challenge (DeRue & Wellman, 2009; Dragoni, Tesluk, & Oh, 2009).

Lessons of Experience was more than a summary of a research study. It began to lay out a workable approach that organizations could use to better harness the power of experiences for developing management and leadership talent. This approach included identifying developmental jobs, creating a talent pool, helping people learn from experience, and clarifying line management's responsibility for the development process. It identified foundational building blocks necessary to make this approach work, for example, a strong corporate identity, the willingness to take risks, and a culture that supports learning. Practitioners began to find ways to make elements of this approach work in their organizations, themselves learning by trial and error and by sharing with and learning from their like-minded colleagues.

Sharing the Practice

Today researchers are generating new insights about learning from experience. Organizations are creating tools, processes, and practices that enable them to more intentionally use experience for development. So what's missing from this picture? From our perspective, what is missing is the documentation and dissemination of these tools, processes, and practices. They are being invented, designed, tested, implemented, and embraced—but there is little systematic and widespread sharing. You hear about a tool or practice here or there in presentations or through your professional network, or you may read about a particular process in a trade magazine, but there is no central resource for finding out what practitioners are actually doing. Filling that gap was our motivation for creating this book.

We drew on our own experiences, networks, and reading to find people who had material to share—things they actually used in their practice or that their organizations had put into place. Thus, although we are confident that this approach yielded useful contributions, we make no claims of being systematic or exhaustive in our search. We were intentional about only including models, tools, and practices that you are free to borrow (and we encourage you to do so). There are commercially available tools, publications, and other materials that are used to support experience-driven development in organizations, and these are mentioned in several of the contributions, but our goal was to share what practitioners can do in their own settings, not to provide a compendium of things you can purchase.

We were also intentional about only including practices that are consistent with research on effective leader development and about capturing applications from a wide variety of organizations and sectors—corporate, nonprofit, government, education—and in different parts of the world. Some of the processes and practices described in the book are still in early stages of experimentation and refinement while others are well-established. They range from tools that can fit on a single page to major initiatives in organizations. And even though we use the phrase *experience-driven development* to label this field of practice, we welcomed and preserved the various labels used by others, including learning from experience, on-the-job development, experience-based development, and real-world development.

The book is organized into four sections, each targeting a critical element of experience-driven development:

1. *Developmental Experiences: More Intentional for More People.* Many people do get on-the-job developmental experiences—stretch assignments, new responsibilities, unexpected obstacles—without any sort of intervention from leadership development professionals. Yet how can you help more people gain leadership experiences that target their particular development needs?

2. *Leaders: Better Equipped to Learn from Experience.* Having a stretch experience does not guarantee learning from that experience. How can you enhance leaders' ability to learn from their experiences so that they extract the maximum developmental value?

3. *Human Resource Systems: Designed for Experience-Driven Development.* Most organizations have formal systems and processes for selecting and developing leadership talent. How can you build experience-driven development into these processes, embedding it in the organization's DNA?

4. *The Organization: Enabler of Experience-Driven Development:* Many aspects of an organization—its shared values, the behaviors and perceptions of its employees, its processes and routines—can either support experience-driven development or get in its way. How can you influence the organization more broadly to enable rather than inhibit experience-driven learning?

We have also visually tagged each contribution based on whether it shares a:

- *Model:* a conceptual framework or typology that guides thinking and action.

- *Tool:* an activity or technique that leadership development professionals can put to use.

- *Organizational Practice:* a specific process, program, or initiative that an organization has put into place.

- *Advice:* an overview of an important topic with insights based on expertise or research.

You might choose to read this book from cover to cover to gain a broad view of what is happening in the field, starting with how to create more experiences for more people and ending with how to influence the organization in ways that support experience-driven development. You might just pull it out when you have an immediate need, finding those pieces that are most relevant for you in the moment. You might want to read it with your colleagues, getting together along the way to share ideas that it has stimulated for your own work. Whatever your approach, our aspirations are that these tools and practices provide you with resources to accomplish the critical goal of developing the best possible talent in organizations—and that through leader development, you enable positive change in people's lives, in organizations, and in society overall.

References

De Pater, I.E., Van Vianen, A.E.M., Bechtoldt, M.N., & Klehe, U. (2009). Employees' challenging job experiences and supervisors' evaluations of promotability. *Personnel Psychology, 62,* 297–325.

DeRue, D.S., & Wellman, N. (2009). Developing leaders via experience: The role of developmental challenge, learning orientation, and feedback availability. *Journal of Applied Psychology, 94,* 859–875.

Douglas, C.A. (2003). *Key events and lessons for managers in a diverse workforce: A report of research and findings.* Greensboro, NC: Center for Creative Leadership.

Dragoni, L., Tesluk, P.E., & Oh, I. (2009). Understanding managerial development: Integrating developmental assignments, learning orientation, and access to developmental opportunities in predicting managerial competencies. *Academy of Management Journal, 7*, 731–743.

Dragoni, L., Oh, I., Van Katwyk, P., & Tesluk, P.E. (2011). Developing executive leaders: the relative contribution of cognitive ability, personality, and the accumulation of work experience in predicting strategic thinking competency. *Personnel Psychology, 64*, 829–864.

Lombardo, M.M., & Eichinger, R.W. (1996). *Career architect development planner*. Minneapolis, MN: Lominger.

McCall, M.W., Jr., & Hollenbeck, G.P. (2002). *Developing global executives: The lessons of international experience*. Boston, MA: Harvard Business School Press.

McCall, M.W., Jr., Lombardo, M.M., & Morrison, A.M. (1988). *The lessons of experience: How successful executives develop on the job*. Lexington, MA: Lexington Books.

Morrison, A.M., White, R.P., & Van Velsor, E. (1987). *Breaking the glass ceiling: Can women reach the top of America's largest corporations?* Reading, MA: Addison-Wesley.

O'Leonard, K., & Loew, L. (2012). *Leadership development factbook® 2012: Benchmarks and trends in U.S. leadership development*. Oakland, CA: Bersin & Associates.

Yip, J., & Wilson, M.S. (2010). Learning from experience. In E. Van Velsor, C.D. McCauley, & M.N. Ruderman (Eds), *The Center for Creative Leadership handbook of leadership experience* (3rd ed., pp. 63–96). San Francisco, CA: Jossey-Bass.

Section 1

Developmental Experiences: More Intentional for More People

Equipping Employees to Pursue Developmental Experiences

Leveraging Existing Experiences for Learning

Creating New Developmental Experience

Section Introduction

One of the first questions that you will grapple with as you work to use experiences more intentionally for leader development is this: *How can the organization help more people get the leadership experiences they need for development?* In thinking about this question, keep in mind the three basic ways that people gain an on-the-job developmental experience:

1. They take on a new job that stretches them in new ways.

2. They add different challenges to their current set of tasks and responsibilities.

3. They more deliberately focus on learning from some aspect of the work that they are already engaged in.

In this section, contributors share the models, tools, and organizational practices that encourage and support these "experience-gaining" tactics. Their interventions seek to:

- Equip employees to pursue developmental experiences,

- Better leverage existing experiences for learning, or

- Create new types of developmental experiences.

A major way to equip employees to pursue developmental experiences is to provide them with models and frameworks that describe the kinds of experiences they should seek to develop as leaders. You can make use of a number of research-based developmental assignment typologies (see Corporate Executive Board, 2009; Kizilos, 2012; Lombardo & Eichinger, 2010; McCauley, 2006; Van Katwyk & Laczo, 2004; Yip & Wilson, 2010). The content of these typologies overlaps a great deal—choosing which one to use is a matter of assessing the best fit to your organizational context. In this section, you'll find descriptions of three typologies and how they can be put to use in pursuing developmental assignments (see *Intensity and Stretch: The Drivers of On-the-Job Development, A Leadership Experience Framework*, and *Identifying Development-in-Place Opportunities*). There is also value in creating assignment typologies that are based on in-company research and thus are customized to your own organizations (see *Leadership Maps: Identifying Developmental Experiences in Any Organization* and *Building Organization-Specific Knowledge About Developmental Experiences*). A second important way to equip employees to pursue developmental assignments is to create processes that aid their search for a specific type of assignment (see *Expression of Interest: Making Sought-After Roles Visible, Designing Part-Time Cross-Functional Experiences*, and *Creating Project Marketplaces*).

You can also seek to capitalize on the developmental potential of naturally occurring experiences inside and outside of your organization, working to better leverage these experiences for learning. You'll find examples of how practitioners frame certain assignments as developmental and provide resources for learning during the experience (see *Leveraging the Developmental Power of Core Organizational Work* and *Learning Transferable Skills Through*

Event Planning), how they facilitate the matching of new assignments with individuals who most need the learning opportunity offered by that assignment (see *Pinpointing: Matching Job Assignments to Employees*), and how they encourage development through leadership experiences outside the workplace (see *Learning from Personal Life Experiences*).

Finally, you can create new types of developmental experiences for employees. Often these experiences are targeted for high potential leaders in the organization—individuals being developed to move up in the organization and take on broader leadership responsibilities. The assignments are typically temporary, full-time assignments outside of the individual's current work setting. And they are aimed at broadening individuals' perspective on the business, developing their strategic thinking capability, or deepening their global leadership skills (see *Strategic Corporate Assignments to Develop Emerging Market Leaders*, *Full-Time Strategic Projects for High Potentials*, and *A Personalized Rotation Program to Develop Future Leaders*). Increasingly, organizations are also looking to company-sponsored service projects in nonprofit and community organizations as a leader development strategy (see *Corporate Volunteerism as an Avenue for Leader Development* and *Developing Socially Responsible Global Leaders Through Service Projects*). Action learning projects are another avenue for creating new developmental assignments; more on the action learning approach can be found in Section 3 of this book.

At the other end of the continuum are very short and focused experiences for development. These include experiences that expose individuals to the challenges of working at higher levels in the organization (see *Stretch Assignments to Develop First-Time Supervisors* and *Executive Shadowing*), "micro-assignments" that can be carried out in an hour or two and encourage a "learn every day" mindset (see *Leadership Fitness Challenge: Daily Exercise of the Leadership Muscle*), and opportunities to tackle a job dilemma or business issue in a collaborative learning environment (see *Using a Video-Case-Based Collaborative Approach in Leader Development* and *Cross-Company Consortiums: Tackling Business Challenges and Developing Leaders Together*).

The practices described in this section go beyond simply getting people into a stretch assignment. Other aspects of the learning-from-experience process are embedded in many of the practices—for example, matching assignments and individual development needs; enhancing development from assignments by building reflection, feedback, coaching, learning partners, or formal training into the experience; and overcoming organizational obstacles to experience-driven learning. These elements will be revisited and take center stage in subsequent sections of this book.

References

Corporate Executive Board. (2009). *Unlocking the value of on-the-job learning.* Arlington, VA: Authors.

Kizilos, M.A. (2012). *FrameBreaking leadership development.* Chanhassen, MN: Experience-Based Development Associates.

Lombardo, M.M., & Eichinger, R.W. (2010). *Career architect development planner* (5th ed.). Minneapolis, MN: Lominger.

McCauley, C.D. (2006). *Developmental assignments: Creating learning experiences without changing jobs.* Greensboro, NC: Center for Creative Leadership.

Van Katwyk, P., & Laczo, R.M. (2004). *The leadership experience inventory technical manual.* Minneapolis, MN: Personnel Decisions International.

Yip, J., & Wilson, M.S. (2010). Learning from experience. In E. Van Velsor, C.D. McCauley, & M.N. Ruderman (Eds.), *The Center for Creative Leadership handbook of leadership experience* (3rd ed., pp. 63–96). San Francisco, CA: Jossey-Bass.

1

Intensity and Stretch: The Drivers of On-the-Job Development*

Mark Kizilos

Experience-Based Development Associates, LLC

MY COLLEAGUES AND I have worked with a number of organizations to develop *experience models* that describe the most critical development experiences for their leaders (see *Building Organization-Specific Knowledge About Developmental Experience* on page 37 of this book). Our work was motivated by the realization that, while experience is acknowledged to be a powerful source of learning, leadership development professionals are generally not able to provide more than the most basic guidance to aspiring leaders who seek answers to two simple questions: "Which experiences do I need to be successful in my organization?" and "What should I learn from those experiences?"

Our client work provided company-specific insight into the most important developmental experiences and the lessons that they teach. However, the approach was resource-intensive—it took a great deal of time and care in each organization. Through the process, we created experience models for several organizations. To do this, we interviewed and held group discussions with more than two hundred highly successful leaders and analyzed nearly 250 hours of interview transcripts.

---

*Note: Part of this contribution is adapted from the author's book *FrameBreaking Leadership Development*, published in 2012 by Experience-Based Development Associates, LLC.

After looking back at the extensive data that we collected on the career experiences of highly successful leaders, our team posed a new research question: "What common dynamics are at play across all of the developmental experiences we have documented?" Rather than seeking to list the content of various specific developmental experiences, we now sought to understand the developmental potential of *any* experience. We distilled the essential dynamics of all of the experiences from leaders in our sample down to two fundamental dimensions: *Intensity* and *Stretch*. These dimensions are conceptually distinct measures of the developmental potential of an experience, and they combine to form the FrameBreaking™ Model.

Intensity is the extent to which an experience involves higher performance demands than an individual has faced in prior career experiences (see Exhibit 1.1). High-intensity experiences have the potential to be developmental because they push the individual to perform at a higher level, requiring full engagement and learning in order to handle difficult challenges under pressure. One must *thrive* to survive in such situations, hence the acronym THRIVE is used to summarize the dimensions of intensity.

Exhibit 1.1. Defining Intensity—THRIVE

Time pressure—Requiring action within specific, aggressive time constraints and with high costs for delays, versus being open-ended with no time constraints

Holistic responsibility—Involving responsibility for an entire outcome or set of outcomes, versus participation as one of many contributors to an outcome

Risk—Involving high financial, reputational, or other stakes and a moderate risk of failure, versus low stakes and low risk of failure

Impact—Involving results that are critical for business survival, profit, growth, or other success metric, versus being a discretionary activity yielding nice-to-have results

Visibility—Involving visibility at the highest levels and to a large population, versus being private or visible to only a small, local population

Expectations—Degree to which others expect success versus have no or low expectations for results.

Stretch describes the extent to which an experience pushes one outside an area of expertise, background, or preparation (see Exhibit 1.2). For example, if you asked an IT manager to participate in a sales call that might be routine for a sales professional, the IT manager would likely feel pushed outside of a familiar comfort zone: "How do I act on a sales call? What does the customer want to know? What do I need to know about what we are selling?"

These and other questions would likely be raised because the IT manager's frame of reference lacks information applicable to the new situation. One must *reach* to master these new situations, hence the acronym REACH is used to summarize the dimensions of Stretch.

Exhibit 1.2. Defining Stretch—REACH

Relationships—Involving the need to interact with people who hold differing perspectives, outlooks, or viewpoints

Expertise or knowledge—Involving the need to develop expertise or knowledge in an unfamiliar area in order to be successful

Adaptability—Involving the need to handle more ambiguity than one is used to

Context—Involving the need to work within a different function/department/area or culture

How-to skills—Involving the need to spend time doing things he or she doesn't know how to do

---

The FrameBreaking Model combines the Intensity and Stretch dimensions. The four quadrants of the model describe four broad, but distinct, types of experiences (see Figure 1.1):

1. *Delivering*—using already developed capabilities;
2. *Mastering*—taking on greater challenges within an already-established area of experience or domain;
3. *Broadening*—taking on new types of work or relating to new types of people and situations; and
4. *FrameBreaking*—handling both higher levels of challenge and new types of work or people and situations.

The FrameBreaking Model is a subjective, dynamic, descriptive, and developmental lens for thinking about experiences.

- *Subjective:* Intensity and Stretch are not objective properties of a developmental opportunity, but properties of the interaction between the opportunity and the individual. Exhibits 1.1 and 1.2 describe an illustrative range of values for each dimension of Intensity and Stretch. However, the important factor for understanding the developmental potential of an experience for an individual is the *individual's subjective experience* of each Intensity and Stretch dimension.

Figure 1.1. The FrameBreaking Model

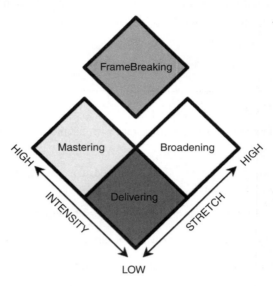

- *Dynamic:* Throughout a career, most people will spend time in each of the four types of experience. A typical career arc will involve a wide range of situations, some of which involve utilizing well-established skills on familiar ground while others push the individual to develop in new ways. Moreover, any given assignment may involve a mix of the familiar and the new.

- *Descriptive:* No one type of experience is better than the others. Although the model is referred to as the FrameBreaking Model, that is not to suggest that FrameBreaking is a "better" type of experience for leader development than Delivering, Mastering, or Broadening. FrameBreaking experiences offer the greatest developmental potential, but they also present the greatest risk for failure. And it may not be necessary for an aspiring leader to take such risks to achieve desired career goals.

- *Developmental:* The model reflects growth of capabilities over time. Think of the size of the Delivering quadrant as one's level of proven capability. Early in a career, the Delivering quadrant is relatively small. The young professional has not acquired a very large or broad repertoire of experiences and cannot make large contributions to an organization. Early on, many work activities are experienced as Mastering, Broadening, or even FrameBreaking, because they are almost all outside the small, but growing, Delivering zone. Over time, as a young professional engages in various Mastering, Broadening, and FrameBreaking experiences, the size of his or her Delivering zone grows and the capacity to contribute increases.

The FrameBreaking Leadership Development Process

You can use the FrameBreaking Model in a five-step process to help leaders reflect on the developmental patterns in their careers and construct a robust, experience-based development plan aimed at achieving both short-term results and long-term career goals. The process described below has been implemented through workshops (half-day, full-day), coaching engagements, and as self-paced instruction (with the support of a suite of online tools). In all cases, the support and involvement of others in the organization (for example, one's manager, a sponsor, a mentor, or a coach) are especially important to achieving results.

Step 1: Gain Insight from Prior Experiences and Understand Development Needs

The first step highlights the types of experience an individual has had and the key learning the individual has gained. Ask individuals to start by identifying a long-term career goal. This helps to ensure that reflection about where they have been in the past will be done in the context of where they want to go in the future. With this career goal in mind, have individuals document each step of their careers (even jobs that seem unrelated to the career goal), along with a few key pieces of information about each job: (1) key experiences in the job, (2) significant learning from the job, (3) an assessment of the type of experience that best characterizes one's time in the job (Delivering, Mastering, Broadening, or FrameBreaking), and (4) an assessment of the THRIVE and REACH dimensions that were most salient.

Next, have individuals create a visual display of the information they have just generated:

- Write each job on a sticky note using a specific color to indicate the type of experience the job represented (red = Delivering; blue = Mastering; yellow = Broadening; green = FrameBreaking).

- For each job, write the significant lessons learned on a separate white (or other contrasting color) sticky note.

- On a sheet of flipchart paper draw an x-axis at the bottom and label it "time"; draw a y-axis on the left side and label it "level of responsibility."

- Organize the first set of sticky notes onto the chart to reflect when the job occurred and the level of responsibility it entailed. Early jobs would start in the lower left corner, and subsequent jobs would progress upward to the right corner.

- Place each learning note next to its associated job.

If you conduct this exercise in a classroom setting, individuals can share their visual career summary in pairs, triads, or small groups. Each person should explain the experiences and key lessons on his or her flipchart and enlist input from others in the group in thinking through possible patterns: Are some experience types missing or over/underrepresented? Are there other things that may have been learned from a key experience that the individual has not considered? What type of trajectory is the individual on?

Step 2: Draft a Career Story and Understand a Personal Development Arc

With the perspective gained from reflecting on the key experiences in one's career and insights gained from those experiences, ask individuals to organize their career highlights into a story with a beginning, middle, and end (in this case, the career goal). This simple and intuitive structure helps individuals discern important patterns that have influenced their careers, understand the development arc they are on, and identify the types of experiences still needed to reach their career goals. Beyond the self-awareness gained from understanding how the pieces of one's career fit together, being able to concisely tell one's story is useful preparation for discussing personal development with a manager whose support they may need.

Step 3: Identify Potential Development Experiences

In the third step, individuals use the FrameBreaking Model to identify the *right* development experiences needed for continued career progress. Ask individuals to generate possible development experiences they could pursue and to reflect on each experience using the THRIVE and REACH dimensions to compare the development potential of each. They can use the form in Exhibit 1.3 to rate an experience on each of the dimensions. An experience that involves more of a dimension (for example, time pressure) represents a greater opportunity for development than one that involves a level of the dimension that has been successfully managed in the past.

As a second part to this step, encourage individuals to consider the potential risks that may be involved in taking on development activities that will push them on an underdeveloped dimension. For example, what should they watch out for if an experience will involve a higher degree of visibility than one has had previously?

Step 4: Create an Experience-Based Development Plan

Once individuals have gone through the first three steps, they are prepared to formalize their development plans. In fact, the hard work of creating the development plan is already done because the preceding steps have guided the developing leader through the identification of a long-term career goal, the development needed to make progress toward that goal, an appropriate development experience given the need, the specific learning sought from the activity, and a number of potential risks to be managed. At this point, the formalization of the development plan merely involves reviewing those elements and identifying resources or support that may be needed.

Exhibit 1.3. Evaluating Your Development Experience

My development experience:

Think about the development experience relative to past experiences you have had in your career. Will this experience involve Less, About the Same, or More of each dimension below than your prior experiences have involved? Circle your responses in the space below. Items that involve More of a dimension represent potential learning opportunities.

Time pressure	Less	About the Same	More
Holistic responsibility	Less	About the Same	More
Risk	Less	About the Same	More
Impact	Less	About the Same	More
Visibility	Less	About the Same	More
Expectations	Less	About the Same	More
Relationships	Less	About the Same	More
Expertise/knowledge	Less	About the Same	More
Adaptability	Less	About the Same	More
Context	Less	About the Same	More
How-to skills	Less	About the Same	More

For any item rated "More," ask the question: What can I learn by the way I will be pushed on this dimension in this particular experience? Write your answers below.

Step 5: Use Ongoing Reflection to Gain the Most Out of Experience

As individuals engage in a developmental experience, it is important for them to keep focused on their learning agenda. A simple, structured set of questions for reflection on the experience and what they learned is a powerful tool to ensure that learning is kept top-of-mind. Advise individuals to regularly schedule conversations to review development progress with a manager, sponsor, coach, or mentor, and prepare for those conversations with these simple questions:

- What challenge or issue have I faced?
- Is what I am doing to handle it working?
- If what I am doing is working, why? If not, why not?
- Where else can I apply what I am learning?

The key to making this routine successful is *never* skipping the last question. This is where individuals mentally rehearse the application of newly generated insights to new situations—a critical step for making what is learned useful in the future.

Additional Applications of the FrameBreaking Model

The FrameBreaking Leadership Development process outlined here is the most comprehensive and robust application of the FrameBreaking Model. However, the model itself can be a useful tool for discussing experiences with leaders. The simple and accessible language of the model provides an intuitively appealing lens for leaders to think about where they have been and where they need to go in their careers.

The model can also be introduced quickly, so it's ideal for use in leadership development programs or talent reviews to guide thought-provoking discussions about a range of topics:

- What types of experiences are the people in a particular group or function having?

- Are too many people in Delivering experiences?

- Are top talent individuals being given the kinds of development experiences that they need to prepare them for the future?

- Which leaders are having FrameBreaking experiences, and what is being done to support them?

- Does the organization encourage siloed development by rewarding Mastering experiences and discouraging Broadening experiences?

Resources

Kizilos, M.A. (2012). *FrameBreaking leadership development: Think differently about work experiences to achieve more, faster*. Chanhassen, MN: Experience-Based Development Associates.

More information about the FrameBreaking model can be found at http://framebreaking.com/

2

A Leadership Experience Framework

Paul Van Katwyk, Joy Hazucha, and Maynard Goff
Korn/Ferry International

THERE ARE TWO reasons to assess a leader's experience. The first is to judge job qualification: A leader's experience is a critical component of his or her readiness for a future role and for identifying positions that would be a good fit. The second is to use the assessment as a development tool: Experience is a key vehicle for converting potential into readiness, and understanding a person's current state helps plan next steps in experience.

Although line and HR managers recognize the importance of experience for effective job performance, the vocabulary for describing an individual's leadership experience is sparse. Typical variables for evaluating experience are amount, function or industry, and culture (for example, "five years of experience in sales management in the fast moving consumer goods industry" or "fifteen years of experience, and experience in a challenging, fast-paced environment"). However, both amount and type of experience are complex. A leader could have had the same one year of experience fifteen times, or could have continuously built on his or her experience each year. A sales management job could require rolling out a change in strategy, weathering a recession, or driving fast growth. Clearly, a framework is needed. Note that, in addition to describing leaders' qualifications, better clarity in describing key leadership experiences is useful in creating success profiles that capture the requirements of leadership roles.

The Leadership Experience Framework

To better define leadership experience, we based our original Leadership Experience Framework, created in 1995, on an analysis of personal history forms for managers, as well as a review of the literature. The data from these sources were content analyzed by four management experts, who identified sixteen categories of experience. These categories reflected the content of the job, the context of the experience, and self-development and extra-curricular activities. We developed a tool, the Leadership Experience Inventory (LEI), for assessing a person's experience across the categories (Van Katwyk & Laczo, 2004). Testing and refinement of this tool led to our current Leadership Experience Framework that delineates twenty-three categories of experience in four broad arenas (see Exhibit 2.1):

- General Management Experiences
- Overcoming Challenge and Adversity
- Risky or Critical Experiences
- Personal and Career-Related Experiences

Exhibit 2.1. Categories of Leadership Experience

General Management Experiences

- *Strategy development:* Experience defining, planning, or shaping initiatives that set key strategic direction for the organization.

- *Project management and implementation:* Experience related to the management and implementation of key projects (for example, technology upgrade, new facility).

- *Business development and marketing:* Experience in developing a business or marketing.

- *Business growth:* Experience growing a new or existing business (for example, new product line, new market).

- *Product development:* Experience developing new or enhanced products.

- *Start-up business:* Experience managing a start-up or new business.

- *Financial management:* Experience involving financial management (for example, P&L responsibilities, budget management).

- *Operations:* Experience related to core operations (for example, procuring resources and facilities, scheduling production, delivering or servicing products/services for customers, maintaining and improving the quality of customer products/services).

- *Support functions:* Experience where the main responsibilities are to provide functional support (for example, HR, IT, marketing, finance) to key organizational operations through both assigned roles and temporary assignments.

- *External relations:* Experience representing the organization externally (for example, to customers, government, community).

Overcoming Challenge and Adversity

- *Inherited problems and challenges:* Experience taking over a situation with significant problems or challenges to be resolved.

Exhibit 2.1. Categories of Leadership Experience (*continued*)

- *Interpersonally challenging situations:* Experiences that are challenging because of strong interpersonal components (for example, adversarial, involving strong emotions).

- *Downturns or failures:* Experience managing through a downturn or responding to a failed initiative or failure in the business.

- *Difficult financial situations:* Experience dealing with difficult, challenging, or complex financial issues.

- *Difficult staffing situations:* Staff related experiences that are challenging and/or adversarial in nature (for example, poor performance, layoffs).

Risky or Critical Experiences

- *High-risk situations:* Experience with responsibility for situations that, although possibly promising significant returns, are very risky in terms of potential failure, costs, or negative impact on the organization.

- *Critical negotiations:* Experience that includes negotiations in which the outcome is extremely important for the organization's future.

- *Crisis management:* Experience responding to and managing an expected or unexpected crisis.

- *Highly critical/visible assignments or initiatives:* Experience in being responsible for assignments or initiatives that are seen as highly critical and visible and have the attention of senior leaders or the public.

Personal and Career Experience

- *Self-development:* Experience focused on developing oneself.

- *Development of others:* Experience focused on developing others.

- *International/cross-cultural:* Experience that involves working with those from other cultures or physically working in other countries.

- *Extracurricular activities:* Experience gained outside of the job or organizational context.

Our research using the LEI confirms that leadership experience matters. For example, although leaders with more intellectual capability, assertiveness, and curiosity are stronger strategic thinkers, the amount, depth, and breadth of a leader's experience also contributes to strategic thinking skills (Dragoni, Oh, Van Katwyk, & Tesluk, 2011; PDI Ninth House, 2011). And we found that experiences are most developmentally effective when they occur several times and progress through levels of complexity, for example, from contributing to the execution of a project, to assuming managerial responsibility, to strategically leading the effort by setting overall direction and maintaining ultimate responsibility.

Experiences Across Organizational Levels

One application of the Leadership Experience Framework is the identification of experiences leaders are more likely to encounter at critical transitions in their careers. Using our

Leadership Experience Inventory database, we identified the top five experiences that differentiated leadership roles at three transition points: from first-level leader to mid-level leader, from mid-level leader to business-unit leader, and from business-unit leader to senior executive (PDI Ninth House, 2012).

The top five experiences that differentiate mid-level leadership roles from first-level roles are:

1. *Difficult staffing situations.* Mid-level leaders face difficult staffing situations, such as firing someone for poor performance or dealing with layoffs. In this experience, they are responsible for making decisions and carrying out required actions.

2. *Financial management.* Mid-level leaders likely create and manage expense budgets, set and manage revenue goals, and hold responsibility for different aspects of financial management for their groups.

3. *Interpersonally challenging experiences.* Mid-level leaders need to manage emotionally charged relationships in the workplace. For example, they might work with a boss who is controlling or unsupportive, or work with a direct report or peer who is uncooperative or short-tempered, with repercussions for the group.

4. *Managing a function.* They manage responsibility for a support function such as HR, IT, marketing, or finance. This experience might come through a permanent assignment or a temporary assignment, such as serving on an advisory group for a new performance appraisal system or conducting a study on technology.

5. *Dealing with inherited problems and challenges.* In this experience, mid-level leaders take over a situation with existing problems. For example, they might lead a group with historically low morale or low productivity, perhaps having succeeded an ineffective leader.

The top five experiences that differentiate business-unit leadership roles from mid-level roles are

1. *Strategy development.* Business-unit leaders define plans, shape initiatives, and set strategic direction for the business unit, consistent with the organization's strategy. This reflects a distinct change in responsibility, from executing strategy to shaping it.

2. *Highly visible or critical assignments.* Business-unit leaders work on assignments that have the attention of senior leaders or the public. For example, they might make a highly visible decision in which failure would cause financial losses for the organization or payroll terminations. Or they may be responsible for a large change project that affects how much of the organization operates.

3. *High-risk situations.* They are responsible for situations that promise significant returns, but carry the risk of failure in terms of financial costs or negative impact on the organization. For example, a business-unit leader might initiate a large-scale technology change in a manufacturing plant that has the potential to increase production, but carries the risk of failure and loss during implementation.

4. *Critical negotiations.* Business-unit leaders negotiate with individuals or groups that are extremely important for the organization's future, such as labor and important customers or suppliers.

5. *External relations.* These leaders represent the organization externally. For example, they might serve as spokespersons to customers or represent the organization's interests with regulatory agencies or public interest groups.

The top five experiences that differentiate senior executive roles from business-unit leadership roles are

1. *Strategy development.* Senior executives set strategic direction for the whole organization, based on customer trends, the competitive landscape, and the unique value the organization has to offer. The strategy at this level may include dramatic changes in the organization's priorities and plans, such as getting into or out of specific markets.

2. *Start-up or new business experience.* They might manage a start-up or new business, such as setting up an organizational unit in another country or starting up a function or division that did not previously exist in the organization. This senior executive experience is unique to the top five transition experiences.

3. *Highly visible or critical assignments.* Like business-unit leaders, senior executives have a greater breadth and depth of highly critical or visible assignments. While business unit leaders are visible within the organization, senior executives represent the organization externally, with the public and the media.

4. *High-risk situations.* Senior executives are involved in a greater variety and frequency of high-risk situations, such as mergers and acquisitions, which can lead to significant returns but also carry a serious risk of failure. They are also the point persons in a crisis, such as a large-scale accident or a significant financial loss.

5. *Interpersonally challenging situations.* Although this skill is important for the transition from first-level leader to mid-level leader, senior executives are likely to experience a greater variety of these situations and to be in them more frequently. In addition to facing challenging interpersonal situations with employees, they experience them with senior executives from other organizations, the media, external funding agencies, and the like.

Conclusion

Understanding the experiences that leaders will encounter at different levels of the organization is useful on several fronts. First, individuals can be better prepared for new leadership roles. Development programs can be tailored to develop the competencies needed to deal effectively with the challenging experiences at the next level. Assignments can expose leaders to experiences similar to ones they will encounter as they move up in the organization. Second, learning from the new situations encountered at each level can be more intentional. Leaders can be encouraged to approach these experiences as opportunities to stretch and grow, and organizations can provide support for learning, such as coaches and peer networks. Finally, the degree to which leaders master the top experiences at a particular organizational level can serve as an indicator of their readiness for higher-level responsibilities.

References

Dragoni, L., Oh, I.-S., Van Katwyk, P., & Tesluk, P.E. (2011), Developing executive leaders: The relative contribution of cognitive ability, personality, and the accumulation of work experience in predicting strategic thinking competency. *Personnel Psychology, 64*, 829–864.

PDI Ninth House. (2011). *Are strategic leaders born or made?* Minneapolis, MN: Author. Retrieved from www.pdinh.com/thought-leadership/research/are-strategic-leaders-born-or-made

PDI Ninth House. (2012). *Transitions in leadership experience: How experiences shape leadership at every level*. Minneapolis, MN: Author. Retrieved from www.pdinh.com/thought-leadership/research/transitions-leadership-experience-how-experiences-shape-leadership-every

Van Katwyk, P., & Laczo, R.M. (2004). *The Leadership Experience Inventory technical manual*. Minneapolis, MN: Personnel Decisions International.

3

Identifying Development-in-Place Opportunities

Cynthia McCauley
Center for Creative Leadership

MAJOR JOB MOVES are often the most developmental experiences in a person's career. However, relying on job moves as the primary strategy for getting stretch assignments is problematic. Such moves don't come along that often and obtaining them is often outside the individual's control.

On the other hand, ongoing development as a leader can be pursued using the concept of *development in place*—adding challenges to current work and non-work pursuits in ways that broaden the individual's portfolio of leadership experiences. Three common strategies for creating development-in-place assignments are reshaping the job, taking on temporary assignments, and seeking challenges outside the workplace.

Ask individuals to work through the three steps outlined below to help them be more intentional about development in place. Individuals can work through the steps on their own, with a coach or boss, or as part of a facilitated workshop.

Step 1: Identify the Kinds of Experiences You Need to Add to Your Leadership Portfolio

Review the ten key challenges shown in Exhibit 3.1. Each represents a characteristic or feature of job assignments that can stimulate leader development. You should seek to experience each of these challenges multiple times during the course of your career. To pick a challenge to add to your current work, ask yourself:

- Which of the challenges have I had the least exposure to?

- Are there some challenges that I haven't experienced in a number of years?

- Are there any challenges that my current job rarely provides?

Exhibit 3.1. Ten Leadership Challenges

1. *Unfamiliar Responsibilities*: Handling responsibilities that are new or very different from previous ones you've handled.

2. *New Directions*: Starting something new or making strategic changes.

3. *Inherited Problems*: Fixing problems created by someone else or existing before you took the assignment.

4. *Problems with Employees*: Dealing with employees who lack adequate experience, are not highly competent, or are resistant to change.

5. *High Stakes*: Managing work with tight deadlines, pressure from above, high visibility, and responsibility for critical decisions.

6. *Scope and Scale*: Managing work that is broad in scope (involving multiple functions, groups, locations, products, or services) or large in sheer size (for example, workload, number of responsibilities).

7. *External Pressure*: Managing the interface with important groups outside the organization, such as customers, vendors, partners, unions, and regulatory agencies.

8. *Influencing Without Authority*: Influencing peers, higher management, or other key people over whom you have no authority.

9. *Work Across Cultures*: Working with people from different cultures or with institutions in other countries.

10. *Work Group Diversity*: Being responsible for the work of people of both genders and different racial and ethnic backgrounds.

Step 2: Generate Ideas About Where You Can Find These Experiences

Pick a couple (or even three) of the challenges you are seeking and start generating specific ideas about how you could add these challenges to your job. Consider each of these three strategies for accessing new experiences (see Table 3.1 for examples of each):

Reshape your job. Add new responsibilities to your job on a more or less permanent basis. These could be responsibilities moved from your boss to you (or exchanged among peers). Or they may be responsibilities that no one currently owns in your group or organization. Another way of reshaping your job is to focus more on an aspect of your work that is not receiving the attention it needs.

Take on a temporary assignment. Seek out tasks or responsibilities that are bounded by time: projects, task forces, one-time events, or assignments that can be rotated among team members.

Seek challenges outside the workplace. Take on leadership responsibilities in community, nonprofit, religious, social, or professional organizations.

Table 3.1. Examples of Three Development-in-Place Strategies

Challenge	Reshape Your Job	Temporary Assignment	Outside the Workplace
Unfamiliar Responsibilities	Ask your boss to delegate one of his or her job responsibilities to you.	Take on part of a colleague's job while he or she is on temporary leave.	Volunteer for a task that you've never done before in a community organization.
New Directions	Be responsible for a new project or new process in your group.	Join a project team that is plowing new ground in your organization.	Start a new group, club, or team.
Inherited Problems	Be responsible for dealing with dissatisfied customers or difficult suppliers.	Redesign a flawed product or system.	Join the board of a struggling nonprofit organization.
Problems with Employees	Coach employees with performance problems in your group.	Resolve a conflict with a subordinate.	Coach a sports team.
High Stakes	Manage an annual organizational event with high visibility.	Do a tight deadline assignment for your boss.	Work on a political campaign.
Scope and Scale	Serve on multiple project teams simultaneously.	Join a team managing a large-scale project.	Serve as an officer in a regional/national professional organization.
External Pressure	Add external interface roles to your job.	Take calls on a customer hotline.	Take a media relations role with a community organization.
Influencing Without Authority	Manage projects that require coordination across the organization.	Represent concerns of employees to higher management.	Serve as a loaned executive to a nonprofit organization.
Work Across Cultures	Serve as the liaison with a business partner in another country.	Work in a short-term assignment at an office in another country.	Serve as a host family for a foreign exchange student.
Work Group Diversity	Train regularly in your company's diversity program.	Lead a project team with a diverse group of members.	Join special-interest networks that attract a diverse group of people.

Note: An organization can help individuals generate ideas by adding more examples to this table that are customized for its own context.

Don't just rely on yourself to generate these ideas. Ask co-workers and friends for their ideas.

Step 3: Create a Plan

A practical next step is to narrow your options and pick one developmental assignment to undertake. Talk to your boss and other stakeholders: What's practical? What's doable? What would be most beneficial to your organization? What would be most motivating to you? Once you have decided on an assignment, you need a formal plan for maximizing your learning from the assignment:

- Be clear on the ways in which the assignment can help you grow as a leader.

- Think through the skills, behaviors, and actions you'll need to practice in the assignment.

- Identify the kind of support you'll need from others (for example, ongoing feedback, advice, or encouragement) and seek out people who can provide this support.

- Identify and commit to other strategies that will help you focus on learning from the assignment (for example, keeping a journal, reading on a particular topic, or interviewing others who have had similar assignments).

Resources

McCauley, C.D. (1999). *Job Challenge Profile: Participant workbook*. San Francisco, CA: Jossey-Bass.

McCauley, C.D. (2006). *Developmental assignments: Creating learning experiences without changing jobs*. Greensboro, NC: Center for Creative Leadership.

4

Leadership Maps: Identifying Developmental Experiences in Any Organization

Paul Yost
Seattle Pacific University
Joy Hereford
Yost & Associates, Inc.

[Handwritten margin notes: "Point 2: what is it?" "Purpose →" "How to build leadership maps:"]

THE LEADERSHIP MAP is an evidence-based process that organizations can use to build a list of the strategically important developmental experiences for leaders in an organization, the lessons learned from those experiences, the personal strategies that leaders use to develop from the experiences, and the situational catalysts that allow (or force) learning to occur. The leadership map provides a way for organizations to make experience a pillar in an organization's talent-management process that is as important as competency models.

We have now used the process with six diverse organizations (large and small, for profit and not-for-profit, and from a variety of countries). The process is simple and is designed as an intervention itself—helping leaders reflect on their own learning and building a list of key developmental experiences that are research-based and tailored to the strategic needs and language of the organization. Building an organizational leadership map includes four steps:

1. *Interviewing senior executives.* Conduct interviews with ten to twenty senior executives to identify the key experiences, lessons learned, personal strategies, and situational catalysts to promote learning that are critical for future leaders in the organization.

2. *Conducting leadership workshops.* Conduct leadership workshops to finalize the definitions and collect information that will allow you to link the experiences with the lessons, personal strategies, and situational catalysts.

3. *Mapping the linkages.* Conduct analyses to link each of the experiences with the lessons, personal strategies, and situational catalysts.

4. *Building the toolkit.* Create an on-the-job development (OJD) toolkit of resources, checklists, and tools that can be integrated into your organization's talent-management processes.

In the following sections, we'll describe each of the steps in more detail, discuss why they are important, and provide tips on how to make them successful.

Interviewing Senior Executives

The first step in building your leadership map is to conduct interviews with at least ten senior executives to discover the experiences that have been most important in their development, the lessons they have learned, the personal strategies they used to learn in the events, and the situational catalysts that helped them grow, plus the experiences that they believe will be most critical for future leaders in the organization. Each interview should take about sixty minutes to complete. The information collected during the interviews is written down by the interviewer during each executive interview. The interviews can be captured in notes (recorded and transcribed, but this adds a level of detail that is seldom necessary because the goal is to capture categories that emerge across all of the interviews). A sample interview guide is provided in Exhibit 4.1.

Exhibit 4.1. Senior Executive Interview Guide

When you think over your career as a leader, certain events or episodes probably stand out in your mind, things that led to a lasting change in your approach to leadership. Please identify at least three key events in your career—things that made a difference in the way you lead others.

- What happened?

- What did you learn from this event (for better or worse)?

Personal Strategies

- What was it about *you* that allowed you to learn and grow from this event? (Other leaders might have gone through this event without growing from it. What was it about you that allowed you to grow?)

Exhibit 4.1. Senior Executive Interview Guide (*continued*)

Situational Catalysts

- What was it about the situation that allowed (or forced) you to learn and grow? (What was different about this situation from other situations in your life that made it such a powerful leadership growth experience for you?)

  Think about two leaders you know who have great potential to be future leaders in this organization.

- What are three positions you would rotate these future leaders through?

- Why did you identify these as critical developmental assignments? What were the elements of these assignments that made them so developmental?

Note: For an expanded set of questions, see P.R. Yost & M.M. Plunkett, *Real Time Leadership Development.* London, UK: Wiley-Blackwell, 2009.

The interviews are important for three reasons. First, they are a great way of engaging senior leaders in the process (the final products will be based on their stories and are a very salient way for the leaders to realize the significant role that on-the-job experience has played in their own development). Second, the interviews ensure that you are capturing the experiences in the language of the organization. And, third, the interviews will explicitly tie the leadership map that you create to the future needs of the business.

Once the interviews are concluded, you will conduct a content analysis to build draft taxonomies of the (1) key experiences, (2) lessons learned, (3) personal strategies, and (4) situational catalysts (see Exhibit 4.2) and you will draft definitions for each. To conduct a simple content analysis, read about 20 percent of the interviews. Create a draft list of key experiences, lessons, personal strategies, and situational catalysts. You will want to have about ten to twenty themes in each category. Each category should include a name and a short definition (see Exhibit 4.3). Once you have identified an initial list of themes, read 20 percent more of the interviews and see if they can be coded with your initial themes. If not, modify the definitions or add more categories if needed. Continue to do this until you are not adding any more themes. To make this an even more rigorous process, have two people code the same interviews and see how well their ratings match. Any areas of disagreement can be discussed and the definitions changed. This step will ensure that all of the categories are clearly defined and mutually exclusive. You might even be able to combine some categories to simplify the final tools!

Exhibit 4.2. Example of a Leadership Map

Experiences	Lessons Learned	Personal Strategies	Situational Catalysts
Business Experiences Start-up business Turning a business around Cross-company initiative **Functional Experience** Corporate staff role Brand management Operations Finance **Leadership Experiences** Good/bad role models External relations and training Failures/mistakes	**Running the Business** Thinking strategically Driving results Business acumen **Managing People** Building a team Directing and motivating others Managing conflict Developing others **Working Across the Business** Building coalitions Working with senior executives Negotiating with others Managing external relationships	**Learning Focus** Seizing opportunities Seeking feedback Learning from mistakes **Thinking Like a Leader** Seeing the big picture Bringing an entrepreneurial spirit Making tough decisions **Building Relationships** Building a network Respect and caring for others Leveraging the talent of others Developing other people **Personal Characteristics** Drive for results Persisting through difficulties Acting with integrity Bringing patience and humility	**Taking on New Challenges** Proving yourself High autonomy High stakes Leading without authority **Drawing on People** Working for a challenging and supportive boss Leading a talented team Leading a dysfunctional team Managing diversity **Managing the Business** Managing multiple stakeholders Managing customer relationships Managing external relations Dealing with time pressures

Exhibit 4.3. Examples of Definitions

Key Experiences

Turning a Business Around: Turning a business around includes taking over a business, product, or service that is failing. The most powerful experiences require fixing a problem that is critical to the organization's success, where the leader will be held responsible for the success or failure of the turnaround, and complex problems require the leader to consider and work with multiple stakeholder groups.

Global Experience: Taking an assignment that requires the leader to live and work outside of his or her home country. Other global experiences, though less powerful, might include managing products or services with a global customer base from one's home country, managing a global supply chain, or leading a project with global team members.

Lessons Learned

Strategic Thinking: Learning to rise above day-to-day operations to take a more holistic view and gain a broader perspective.

Exhibit 4.3. Examples of Definitions (*continued*)

Building Teams: Building a team where people hold each other accountable and learn from each other, fostering collaboration, cooperation, and trust.

Personal Strategies

Seeing the Big Picture: Taking a systems-thinking perspective with a long-term focus and making connections across content areas, situations, and divisions.
Reflection: Taking time to consider how one is doing in the job and making an honest assessment of one's learning, personal strengths, and weaknesses along the way.

Situational Catalysts

High Stakes: Clear deadlines, pressure from senior leadership, high visibility, and responsibility for success or failure in the job is clearly evident.
Leading Outside Your Expertise: The leader is required to manage work where people have talents and expertise the leader doesn't possess. The leader has to depend on their expertise and talent.

To help develop your initial set of themes, you can draw on the resources in this book and previous research. Your goal is to build a list of experiences, lessons, personal strategies, and situational catalysts that is consistent with what is known from research and is in language that is tailored to the unique needs of your organization.

Leadership Experiences

The key experiences that the senior executives identify will likely include (1) several of the experiences that were identified in the original research on the lessons of experience (for example, start-ups, turning a business around, line to staff switches), (2) key functions in the organization (for example, engineering, manufacturing, customer facing roles), (3) business units (for example, commercial, defense, retail), and (4) key geographies (for example, North America, Asia, Europe).

Lessons Learned

The lessons are the knowledge, skills, abilities, and competencies that are developed in the experiences. If the organization has a competency model, this will provide a natural link into the current talent management system. You also will likely want to go beyond just the competencies to also create a list of more specific lessons that are learned in each of the experiences (for example, working with senior executives, how to deal with poor performing employees).

Personal Strategies

Personal strategies are the learning strategies that people use to develop knowledge, skills, and abilities from their key experiences. Similar concepts include learning tactics, learning agility, and learning potential. See the contributions on *PARR* (page 151), *GPS•R* (page 157), and *Identifying and Assessing for Learning Ability* (page 309) for examples of taxonomies that can be used to build a list of personal strategies.

Situational Catalysts

Situational catalysts represent the elements of the environment that support and challenge leaders to learn. These will include both positive catalysts, such as a supportive boss, and challenging catalysts that force learning to occur (for example, inherited problems, time pressures).

General Advice

As noted, your goal should be to identify about ten to twenty categories in each of the four dimensions. Any more than this and the lists start to feel overwhelming. If you need to include more, consider grouping them into subcategories. The one exception to this rule might be the lessons taxonomy, where capturing more specific lessons can be valuable.

As you define the dimensions, make sure the definitions are broad enough to apply to multiple leadership levels (for example, define what a "turning the business around" experience will look like for senior leaders *and* for first-level managers). This will increase the value of the leadership map for leaders throughout the whole organization and increase its dissemination. Your ultimate goal is to develop all leaders and ensure a strong leadership pipeline for the future.

Conducting Leadership Workshops

The next step in the process is to conduct workshops with leaders who are one or two levels below the senior executives. The broader group of leaders will allow you to ensure that the taxonomies can be applied broadly and to collect data to link the experiences to the lessons learned (for example, to determine which experiences develop which lessons). The information can be collected via interviews or workshops. The latter is preferable because you can collect a great deal of information in less time. The workshops can be conducted within existing leadership development programs in the organization. For example, you might want to leverage a corporate high potential program or collect the information in one of your leadership training and development programs. Alternatively, special workshops might be organized by inviting leaders who are nominated by the executives who participated in the initial interviews. Whatever approach is used, collect information from about seventy leaders who represent all of the key business lines, functions, and geographies. You want to be confident that results generalize across the whole organization. In the workshops or interviews, collect three experiences from each person. This will give you data on 210 leadership experiences from a broad range of leaders in the organization.

A sample outline for the workshop is provided in Exhibit 4.4. In the workshop, you will ask the leaders to jot down three key experiences in their development, the lessons that they learned, the personal strategies they used to capture the lessons, and the situational factors that allowed (or forced) them to learn. Then, you will provide packets with (1) the list of key experiences, (2) the lessons learned, (3) the personal strategies, and (4) the situational catalysts that you developed in the first step and ask participants to code each of their experiences using each of these lists (see Exhibit 4.5 for an example of a coded experience). Participants should be encouraged to review the definitions and add any dimensions that are missing.

These workshops are more than just data collection. They serve as powerful developmental interventions in their own right. Participants are exposed to a new way to think about their development. They reflect on their journey and will see experiences they have not had yet. Like the executives, the leaders become co-developers, increasing their commitment to the outcome because the final list of experiences and lessons will be based on their journeys and their stories.

Exhibit 4.4. Leadership Workshop Outline

1. Overview of leadership experiences mapping and the current project (20 minutes)

   - Overview of importance of experience-driven development (on the job is where people *really* develop).

   - Project overview.

   - Outline the critical role that they will play to build the leadership tools.

2. Leaders reflect on their own development (20 minutes)

   - Leaders write three key experiences in their development (including event itself, lessons learned, situational catalysts, and personal strategies).

3. Leaders self-code the three experiences that they identified (30 minutes)

   - Leaders code the three experiences and code the lessons, situational catalysts, and personal strategies learned for each experience using the draft taxonomies that were developed from the senior leader interviews.

4. Open discussion (15 minutes)

   - How well did the information provided in the taxonomy match and capture your experiences?

   - What, if anything, is missing?

   - How, if at all, would you change the definitions?

5. Wrap up (10 minutes)

   - Next steps in the project.

   - Thank you and conclusion.

Exhibit 4.5. Example of Coding Leadership Experiences

Key Experiences in Your Development

Directions: To begin, jot down the first of your three key events—things that left a lasting change in the way you approach leadership. In your description, include: (1) the key experience (what happened); (2) lessons learned (what you learned from this event, for better or worse); (3) personal strategies (what it was about *you* that allowed you to learn and grow from this event); and (4) what it was about the *situation* that allowed (or forced) you to learn and grow.

> *Launching XYZ Service Division. The company where I worked only manufactured the product, but in 1996 they wanted to launch a service business as well. I was put in charge of the new initiative. I had to develop the strategy from scratch, defining the market, selecting/hiring the team, and getting off the ground within 1 year. I learned how to lead when you don't know all the answers and motivate a team when we didn't really know what we were doing. We were just making it up as we went along. I love working in that kind of environment. I knew the potential customers. I am more of a service person than a manufacturing person, so I liked getting to know the customers and solving their problems. The experience was developmental because I had to deliver—everyone was watching. I also had a great mentor and a very talented team.*

Directions: In the following section, think about your *first* experience and mark with an X all the categories that apply.

Experiences (Choose one)	Lessons Learned (Mark all that apply)	Personal Strategies (Mark all that apply)	Situational Catalysts (Mark all that apply)
Business Experiences	**Running the Business**	**Learning Focus**	**Taking on New Challenges**
_X_ Start-up business	_X_ Thinking strategically	_X_ Seizing opportunities	_X_ Proving myself
___ Turning a business around	_X_ Driving results	___ Seeking feedback	___ High autonomy
___ Cross-company initiative	___ Business acumen	_X_ Learning from mistakes	_X_ High stakes
Etc.	Etc.	Etc.	Etc.

Mapping the Linkage

The third step in the process is to combine all of the information collected in a matrix that maps the key experiences as rows and the key lessons in the columns. For each person, you will identify the experience and then mark the lessons that he or she learned. When this is done for all of the leaders, the matrix will show a pattern of the lessons that were identified as most common for each experience. The mapping task will also highlight any experiences and lessons that are not identified very often and should be dropped or combined with other categories. The same process can be used to map experiences to personal strategies and situational catalysts. This will tell you, for each type of experience, what personal strategies are most likely to be used and which situational catalysts are most relevant. From this output, three matrices are created: Experiences by Lessons, Experiences by Personal Strategies, and Experiences by Situational Catalysts. You will likely want to convert the numbers into a *Consumer Reports*-type chart that identifies the primary and secondary lessons with symbols (see Figure 4.1). To determine which symbols to use, you might decide to use cut-off scores based on natural breaks in the frequency counts or more formal statistical techniques (for example, binomial tests) to identify lessons that are named beyond chance levels.

The final taxonomies and matrixes form the basis for a wide variety of experience-driven leadership development tools that can be built and integrated into your organization's talent-management processes.

Figure 4.1. Key Experiences and the Lessons They Develop

	1. Running the Business	Thinking Strategically	Innovative Problem-Solving	Learning How the Business Works	Under standing the customer	Shouldering Full Responsibility	2. Managing People	Engaging and Directing others	Building a Team that Works Together	Relying on Others' Talents and Expertise	Developing Others	Understanding Other's Perspectives	Managing Through Multiple Levels	3. Working Across the Business	Collaboration & Cooperation	Dealing with Conflict	Political Savvy	Working with Senior Leaders	Strategies of Negotiation
1. Setting the Stage																			
Early Work Experience		O	◆	◆	O	◆		O	O			◆	◆		◆	◆			
First Supervisory Experience		◆		O				◆	◆	◆	O	◆			◆	◆			
2. Leading on the Line																			
Starting Something from Scratch		◆	O	◆				O	O										
Turning a Business Around		O		◆				◆	◆	◆	O	◆				◆			
External Relations		O	◆		◆			◆	O						◆	◆			◆
Global Experience					◆					O	O	◆	◆		◆			◆	
3. Leading by Persuasion																			
Project/Task Force Assignment		◆	O					◆	O	◆					◆			◆	
Functional/Staff Role		O	O					O			◆						O		O
Integration Role		◆		O				O				O							
4. Other																			
Good & Bad Role Models		O						O											
Career Hardships																			
...cation			O	O															

◆ = A primary lesson in this experience

O = A secondary lesson in this experience

Building the Toolkit

Some of the leadership development tools that can be created with the information that you generate in the first three steps might include:

A Leadership Dashboard. Turn the four categories into a dashboard (see Exhibit 4.2) that leaders can use to self-assess and identify areas for future development.

Leadership Experiences and the Lessons They Teach. Create a development guide that includes the key experiences and the matrixes. The definitions and matrixes can be used to help leaders identify: (1) the key developmental experiences and the lessons they should learn by looking across the rows and (2) the lessons they want to learn and the experiences that are most likely to teach them by looking down the columns (see Figure 4.1). You might also want to create reports that identify how people can navigate the key experiences, including information about the personal strategies and situational catalysts for each of the experiences.

What Is Your Learning Potential? Use the personal-strategies taxonomy to create a self-assessment for leaders to complete and identify the personal strategies that they are using to navigate developmental challenges and areas that are underutilized (see Exhibit 4.6).

What Is Your Job Stretch? Use the situational catalyst taxonomy to create a self-assessment for leaders to evaluate the developmental potential of their jobs. Users with low scores can use the feedback to identify the ways that they can increase the stretch in their jobs by identifying the areas that were rated low (see Exhibit 4.7).

The development tools can be put online so they are available to all leaders and easily integrated into other HR processes. Some of the resources can be made more interactive

---

Exhibit 4.6. What Is Your Learning Potential?

Directions: Not everybody who goes through a developmental experience necessarily comes out a stronger leader on the other side. You need to ensure you are capturing the lessons that experience can teach. Take a few moments to assess your learning potential. Rate each item on the following scale:

1 = Almost Never   2 = Sometimes   3 = Often   4 = Very Frequently   5 = Almost Always

Sample Items

Learning Focus

_____ I am curious and always looking for something new to learn.

_____ I look for role models who can provide examples on how to do things well.

Thinking Like a Leader

_____ People describe me as someone who sees the big picture.

_____ I am willing to make tough decisions and take the heat if I am wrong.

Exhibit 4.7. What Is Your Job Stretch?

Directions: Almost any job can be developmental if it contains the right elements. Below is a list of the situational catalysts that make a job more developmental. Rate each item on the following scale to assess which ones are true of your job and help you determine the developmental potential of your job.

1 = Almost Never   2 = Sometimes   3 = Often   4 = Very Frequently   5 = Almost Always

Sample Items

Taking on New Challenges

_____ I feel pressure to show others that I can handle this job.

_____ Success or failure in this job is highly visible and critical to the success of the company.

Managing the Business

_____ I have profit-and-loss (P&L) responsibilities in my current role.

_____ I am responsible for launching a new process, project, or business in the company.

(for example, let leaders pick the lessons they want to learn and then have the online tool provide them with a map of the experiences that would best provide development in these areas). The Learning Potential and Job Stretch checklists can also be put online, providing people with a score and advice in their feedback.

Lessons Learned

Several lessons have emerged as we have worked with organizations:

- Starting with the senior executive interviews is a powerful hook to engage them in the process and make it personally meaningful.

- Find an internal champion. Identify a champion inside the organization to sponsor and drive the work. The champion will provide the momentum to sustain the project through all four steps and can help ensure the taxonomies and tools "fit" the organizational culture.

- Keep senior executives involved along the way. For example, after you have concluded with the senior interviews, report back your results. You also might ask them to assign a high potential leader to serve on a steering committee that can review the work as it progresses.

- The tools and resources that are developed should be simple, easy to implement, and immediately relevant to business leaders.

- Design your tools for "pull"—that is, leaders would be crazy not to use them and then "push"—find an HR system or process where they can immediately be used. For example, include the experiences as part of the succession-planning slates (you might have leaders identify the experiences that succession candidates have had and ones that should be targeted for future development). In your development-plan guidelines and forms, add links to the taxonomies and checklists so leaders see them and naturally reference them just in time. Or include the topic in your next high-visibility leadership training program.

5

Building Organization-Specific Knowledge About Key Developmental Experiences

Paul R. Bly
Thomson Reuters
Mark Kizilos
Experience-Based Development Associates, LLC

AT THOMSON REUTERS, we knew from various needs analyses that it was important to build our bench strength. We also knew that the organization has an abundance of on-the-job experiences in which key skills for business leadership can be developed. Therefore, we launched an initiative to help our current and aspiring leaders take advantage of the developmental potential of these experiences.

Our first step was to create a model of high-impact developmental experiences for our current business leaders. The model was not intended to describe every experience that could be helpful or to say that any particular experiences are required for success as a business leader. Rather, it describes fifteen experiences that leaders at Thomson Reuters found to be highly developmental for them (see Figure 5.1).

Our next steps were to develop multiple approaches for sharing this information with our current and aspiring business leaders. We wanted to have a scalable way to provide guidance to our employees to help them think through their choices about what career challenges to take on in order to develop their skills, and to provide helpful information

Figure 5.1. Key Developmental Experiences

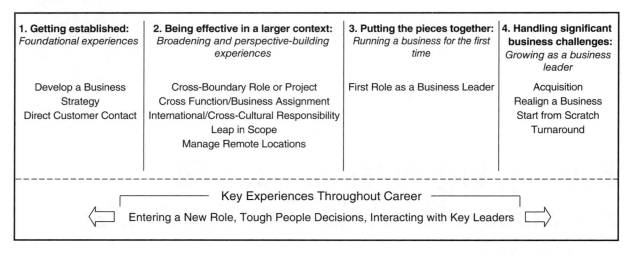

about how others successfully dealt with similar challenges. We did this by writing a book describing the key developmental experiences in the model, creating a series of podcasts to share the same information, and developing two forms of workshops to help our talent learn how to maximize the development available from whatever experiences they have in their careers.

Creating the Model of Key Developmental Experiences

We interviewed a representative sample of more than thirty business leaders from across the company, asking them to describe the experiences they found to be the most formative in the development of their general management skill sets. We then analyzed the interview data to create the model of key developmental experiences at Thomson Reuters. Below are the main steps we followed.

Engage stakeholders. We shared our plans and goals with the HR leaders in our business units and gained agreement on the plan from the CEO. We also involved a small number of the HR leaders in the project, both for support and to help with buy-in.

Identify executives to interview. Two sets of interviews were conducted. One was with the chief strategy officers and CEOs of our major business units, getting their views on the experiences that will be most critical for our future business leaders to have as part of their development. The second set of interviews was with other leaders who were currently successful general managers at a level below the business unit CEOs.

Invite executives. To schedule the interviews we sent the executives a short note explaining that we would be looking for time to interview them and briefly explaining what the interview was about. Closer to the interview date we sent a second e-mail with more information to help them prepare, advising that we would ask them to tell us about the experiences they had found to be most developmental in their careers.

Interview executives. Interviews lasted two hours, had two interviewers in attendance, and were done in person when possible. One interviewer led the discussion and the other took notes. The interviews started with the executive providing a brief summary of every job he or she had had. Then we transitioned to gather more detail about the experiences the executive found to be most developmental. For each of the key experiences, we asked questions to understand where the person was in his or her career when the experience had occurred, the key challenges faced, what was learned, and advice that the executive would give to others entering a similar experience.

Transcribe interviews. We recorded each interview so we could focus on the discussion with the executive and also ensure that afterward we would have access to everything said. Following each interview we gave the recording to a transcription company that sent us a Word document with the entire contents of the interview.

Code the transcripts. Each interview transcript was read by two members of the project team. The reader was to identify all the experiences mentioned during the interview, the challenges faced, and advice provided. The two people who read the transcript then met to compare notes and agree on the final coding of the transcript.

Enter transcripts in qualitative analysis tool. The transcripts were loaded into software for conducting qualitative data analysis (we used Atlas.ti); the final codes were entered. Having all the transcripts loaded and coded in a single software tool enabled us to pull the subsets of information we needed from across the transcripts for analysis. For example, we could create a list of all the experiences mentioned and print a document with every quote from the interviews related to a specific type of experience.

Integration meeting. The final step was an integration meeting where the team reviewed all the experiences mentioned in the interviews and decided which ones should be part of the final model. Ninety-six experiences were coded from the interviews, so the integration meeting was about reducing that number to a smaller set of the most meaningful experiences. This was done in part by combining the experiences that were coded with different names but were similar (for example, agreeing that "gaining customer insight" and "working directly with customers" could be combined into one experience). Another element of creating the final model was to decide which experiences had the most support in the data. Some experiences were developmental for a few executives but were not included in the final model because they were mentioned less consistently across the interviews.

Information Contained in the Book

Once the model of key experiences was created, it was time to put that information into a format that could help others develop in their careers. We began by writing a book to describe the experiences, lessons learned, and advice. We made no assumption that anyone would, or should, read the book cover to cover. It contains an introduction with some overview information followed by fifteen stand-alone chapters, one chapter for each of the key experiences. There is no conclusion chapter.

We wrote the book in such a way that readers can pick it up, flip to the chapter most relevant to them, and find the information they need quickly. We emphasized that point in our discussions about the book, knowing that it was most likely to be used if it was quick, easy, and helpful for the reader. For the same reason, we avoided being highly formal in the book, preferring to use a light style.

The introduction is only six pages long. It describes the value of experience-based development, explains how we created our model of fifteen key developmental experiences at Thomson Reuters, lists the experiences, and provides recommendation for various ways to use the book. Appropriately, it is the shortest chapter in the book.

Each chapter follows the same format:

- There is an introduction defining the experience and listing the key developmental dynamics. That is, it explains what it means to be in an experience (for example, what a leap in scope is) and the aspects of having that experience that made it developmental for our leaders.

- Best practices are cited, as suggested by our business leaders. This section summarizes the recommendations most frequently made by our leaders for others to consider when entering a similar experience. For example, in the experience of dealing with tough people decisions, the recommendations included practices such as, "DO: Look into options for dealing with people who are currently not on track to be part of a team that helps you achieve your objectives" and "DO NOT: Hesitate to remove or change responsibilities for people when it is clear that they are not going to meet the business's needs."

- Insights from our leaders are presented. This section contains representative quotes about what made experiences developmental for leaders or advice they would give to others. We used exact quotes to the extent that we could, but we edited them for readability and confidentiality. This is a compelling part of the book because the quotes allow the emotion and reality of the experiences to come to life for the reader. In another example from the experience of dealing with tough people decisions, one quote is, "You have got to make tough decisions. Firing somebody is not easy, but part of being successful is being able to move people out. . . . It's not just about assessing people; I believe my assessments were correct. Those skills I had. What I didn't do was move on my assessments quickly enough. My breakdown was not moving on what I knew."

One of our business units publishes books for professionals, so we contracted to have the book printed internally. We used an external graphic artist to design a cover. These days, an author could use a service like logocontest.com or 99designs.com as a low-cost way to obtain a variety of design recommendations.

Converting the Book to Podcasts

Our purpose for structuring the book the way we did was to make it easy and quick for a reader to access the content. We knew that some employees would be more likely to review the content if it was in audio format rather than written, so we converted the book to a series of podcasts. The book structure lent itself to this approach because each chapter could be readily converted to a single podcast about that experience that made sense on its own without any additional context. A listener could benefit from any podcast from the book without having to listen to podcasts of preceding chapters.

Appropriately, an internal instructional designer took on the project of converting the chapters to podcasts as a development experience for herself. She rewrote each chapter into a script, so it would sound natural when read aloud, and divided the content into sentences that would be read by three different "characters" in the podcast: a narrator and two leaders.

The narrator read the introduction and such sections as key developmental dynamics, and the two leaders spoke the quotes included in the book. Instead of having a separate section of quotes, as in the book, the podcasts wove the quotes into the other segments of each chapter to help avoid monotony from listening to a single narrator's voice for too long. For example, in one podcast the narrator said, "When you accept a new position that represents a leap in scope, you must be prepared to become a different leader than you were in the past." Then one of the leader voices said, "This role was very different in the sense that in both of my two prior roles, I came in on the ground floor, building the business as I went along. Now, all of a sudden, I'm being handed this large group." The voice of the leader provided color commentary, in the form of our leaders' quotes, to highlight the main points made by the narrator.

A local talent agency provided the voice talent to use for our three characters in the podcasts. We hired a local recording studio to manage the process of recording the audio and converting it to the audio files needed for the podcasts. For two days the voice talent came to the studio to read their lines. We were there to answer questions and to do rewrites of the script when something didn't sound right as it was being read.

How the Book and Podcasts Are Being Used

One of our major office locations hosted a series of "Meet the Author" events in which authors would come to discuss their books with our employees. After our book about experience-based development was printed, we used that series to officially launch the book.

That was nice for us, and everyone who attended received a free book, but that is not where most of the value was derived. The books and podcasts were used more broadly through our intranet and workshops and by our HR business partners.

We created a page dedicated to experience-based development on our intranet. The site contained a variety of content, including general information about learning from experience, video clips of thought leaders discussing experience-based development, and links to the content of the book. Users could see all the experiences described in the book and download either a PDF copy of the relevant book chapter or access the associated podcast. This enabled easy global distribution of the content that could be accessed as users needed it. There was also a link for e-mailing the authors with a request for a printed copy of the complete book, which was given to employees at no cost upon request.

The book content was also leveraged by integrating it into development workshops. For example, our MBA graduate rotation program regularly holds development events for program associates. We created a module to help the associates think about the experiences they've had in their careers and the lessons learned from those experiences and then to assess future opportunities based on the learning they are likely to have from each opportunity. We also created a two-day workshop dedicated specifically to the topic of learning from experience, but the workshop proved to be too much. The content was better received in shorter modules.

Various HR business partners chose to use the book as part of programs they ran. Examples include sharing the book as part of manager training aimed at developing employees, providing the book to all new employees at or above a certain level in the company as a part of orientation, and making the book a topic for meetings of mentoring groups.

Lessons Learned

As should be the case, we learned numerous lessons in our experience of creating and utilizing the book. In the order of the steps we followed, our advice includes:

Keep the leader interviews anonymous. In part, anonymity encourages leaders to be more open about the challenges they have faced and where they struggled. It also helps protect the shelf life of the content. Over a period of time the interviewed leaders will start to leave the company. The advice they gave is still valid, but it can lose some luster if readers know a quote is from a leader who is no longer with the company.

Record the interviews. Even with one interviewer dedicated to taking detailed notes, that person would struggle to capture all the comments accurately, and you never know until long after the interview which quotes from a leader you are going to want to use later. The recording is also impartial and does not depend on what an interviewer chose to write down, misheard, or wrote in error during the interview.

Use a qualitative analysis software tool. We used Atlas.ti; others are available as well. Coding the transcripts within the software allowed us to pull quotes related to specific experiences and lessons learned as needed, and to revise the codes readily as our model of experiences was developed.

Have convergent thinkers in the integration meeting. In the meeting where the interviews and their preliminary codings are being reviewed in order to create the model of experiences, the task is to synthesize a large amount of data into a smaller set of experiences. Those tasks are more complicated when too many team members are divergent thinkers who are inclined to identify the many ways in which the quotes could be interpreted. It's not that there is only one correct model that could be derived from your qualitative data, but you need to arrive at a single model, and the process can be drawn out if the team members spend too much time exploring all the options.

Deliver the content in short segments. It worked well not to assume that the book would be read cover to cover, or that anyone would listen to several hours worth of content about developmental experiences. Our book content lent itself to this format, but with the other experience-based development curricula we developed we also found that trying to cover too much ground at once quickly runs into the law of diminishing returns.

Create worksheets or other tools. Our book did not include any worksheets or tools for helping readers think through the experiences in their careers. The worksheets we developed for use in workshops were very useful, and it would have been good to include some version of them in the book. For example, we developed a two-sided worksheet where one side described five steps for identifying a developmental experience for oneself or a direct report, and the other side provided a format for documenting the decisions to be made in each of the five steps.

6

Expression of Interest:
Making Sought-After Roles Visible

Tanya Boyd

Payless Holdings, Inc.

AFTER CONDUCTING OUR employee engagement surveys at Payless, it became evident that career development was a key area for improvement. Associates across the organization, but particularly salaried associates below manager level, gave low ratings on questions related to career development conversations and opportunities. In follow-up focus groups, we learned that people narrowly defined career development as promotion. If people weren't being promoted or didn't see promotions around them, they did not feel that career development was happening.

While we recognize that promotion is one component of career development, we also believe that career development is much broader than that. Clearly, we needed to change people's understanding of career development. We approached this challenge with a combination of education and action—teaching people about the different kinds of career development available (many of which they can control and drive themselves), and showing them using a program to increase lateral developmental moves. We call this program "Expression of Interest" and piloted it within the human resources department.

The Approach

As part of our ongoing commitment to associate development, each associate has a profile that includes demographic information, performance information, strengths, opportunities,

Figure 6.1. Sample Associate Profile

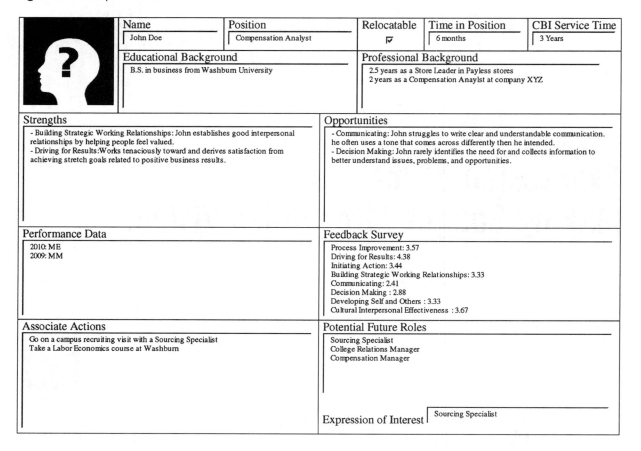

Name	Position		Relocatable	Time in Position	CBI Service Time
John Doe	Compensation Analyst		☑	6 months	3 Years

Educational Background
B.S. in business from Washburn University

Professional Background
2.5 years as a Store Leader in Payless stores
2 years as a Compensation Analyst at company XYZ

Strengths
- Building Strategic Working Relationships: John establishes good interpersonal relationships by helping people feel valued.
- Driving for Results: Works tenaciously toward and derives satisfaction from achieving stretch goals related to positive business results.

Opportunities
- Communicating: John struggles to write clear and understandable communication. he often uses a tone that comes across differently then he intended.
- Decision Making: John rarely identifies the need for and collects information to better understand issues, problems, and opportunities.

Performance Data
2010: ME
2009: MM

Feedback Survey
Process Improvement: 3.57
Driving for Results: 4.38
Initiating Action: 3.44
Building Strategic Working Relationships: 3.33
Communicating: 2.41
Decision Making : 2.88
Developing Self and Others : 3.33
Cultural Interpersonal Effectiveness : 3.67

Associate Actions
Go on a campus recruiting visit with a Sourcing Specialist
Take a Labor Economics course at Washburn

Potential Future Roles
Sourcing Specialist
College Relations Manager
Compensation Manager

Expression of Interest | Sourcing Specialist

actions that higher management has committed to in support of the person, and actions that the HR management team suggests that the associate commit to for his or her own development (see Figure 6.1). These profiles include a space for the senior HR leadership team to identify roles that they see the person potentially moving into (which may or may not be shared with the individual). We added an option for the associate to indicate areas or positions of interest, either within HR or cross-functional roles outside of HR. We also developed a career mapping tool to facilitate a discussion between an associate and his or her manager to help understand how an associate sees his or her career developing over time. Using the map, associates mark the box of their current position and then draw lines to other areas or positions they are interested in. If an associate draws only a vertical line, this can trigger a conversation with his or her manager about the benefits of lateral moves.

Any time that an associate adds an Expression of Interest to his or her profile, it is also added to a master list that is managed by the senior leadership team in HR. This way the senior leaders are knowledgeable about people's interests and can consider them when opportunities arise, or they can consider creating an opportunity that would allow an associate to fulfill an Expression of Interest. Sometimes these are permanent changes, such as if an analyst in compensation is interested in a recruiting role, and a recruiter is interested in learning about compensation, the HR leaders may decide to just switch the two individuals in those roles. Another possibility is if a person goes out on maternity leave, the leaders may choose a person who has expressed interest in that role to fill it temporarily. Yet another common occurrence is for special projects. For example, our compensation team had a special project to evaluate international compensation levels. This was going to require additional personnel above their regular team members, but instead of hiring a temp, the compensation leaders found a person in organization development who had expressed interest in compensation. The compensation team worked with this person's current manager to see whether it was feasible to take on an additional project while the associate remained in his or her current role.

As well as developing a master list of associates who have expressed an interest in a different area or role, the HR leadership team meets regularly to review the profiles of the individual contributors and managers in HR. At this time they also discuss any Expressions of Interest that these associates may have. The associates are not in these meetings, but their managers represent them and ask questions of the other directors and VPs in HR to find out whether the Expression of Interest is supported and being considered actively, or if instead these leaders think that the associate needs to gain additional skills or experience before being placed in a lateral rotation. The manager takes this feedback back to the associate and works with him or her to gain any additional skills or knowledge that has been identified as necessary.

In this way, managers help their associates to be prepared for taking on a special project role or a rotational position. Also, because an associate's profile identifies strengths and opportunities, current managers as well as new managers associated with a lateral rotation are aware of the associate's strengths and opportunities. The managers can use that information to construct learning goals linked to specific projects. The managers can also consider how much overlap time to plan for in shifting an assignment from one person to another.

Some associates express an interest in working in a different function. In this case, the senior HR leadership team works with the senior leadership of the other function to identify opportunities that might make it possible either for a short-term assignment, a trade (where HR would take an associate from that function in exchange for the one coming out of HR), or a permanent career track change.

Benefits and Challenges

This approach of using planned lateral moves to enhance career development benefits associates in HR as they begin to see that career development is more than climbing a ladder. They can appreciate that development can come as a result of their own interests and how they would like to grow. The approach also benefits the organization because it can better plan lateral moves so that people are more prepared for the roles they are taking. The result is many more cross-trained associates who have knowledge of HR areas outside their particular area of expertise. These are also the people who will be tapped to become future generalists because they have been able to gain a wide variety of experiences across HR.

The main challenges with this program come when associates express an interest in an area for which they do not currently have any skills or knowledge, and if they are not known to be adaptable and quick learners. However, these individuals are often very motivated to develop the skills they need because they have identified the area of interest themselves. The regular meetings of the senior HR leader and his or her management team provide an opportunity for feedback to be shared with these associates about what they still need to do in order to be considered for an Expression of Interest rotation.

Another challenge is gaining manager buy-in for the program. With this program comes many more moves than is common in organizations, which means many more people are not experts in their roles. It is tough for the manager in compensation who has an analyst with five years of experience in that role to let that person move into a new role and to take on a new associate without the years of experience. Even though we can plan for overlap time to allow for knowledge transfer, the manager still has to commit to spending extra time to ensure a smooth transition. This program is only successful if the most senior leader in HR is a proponent and is willing to provide managers with the understanding and support they need to support new associates who are learning new skills. It is important that the commitment to development be clear, which requires patience in regard to the mistakes that inevitably occur when people are learning new skills and gaining new experience. One way to somewhat manage this aspect of the process is to be careful about the number of moves made at any one time, and to consider what else is going on in the organization before making a move.

7

Designing Part-Time Cross-Functional Experiences

Nisha Advani

Genentech, a member of the Roche Group

Senior Leaders Need broad business knowledge and a systems perspective of the organization—knowledge and perspective that are aided by cross-functional experiences. The dilemma is how to provide such experiences more regularly earlier in the career track. At Genentech, we have been experimenting with a solution: part-time cross-functional assignments with a strong network of support.

We recognized a particular need to enhance cross-functional perspectives and business knowledge in our director-level population—the feeder pool for senior leadership roles. We were also experiencing increased turnover at this level, and a survey of this population called out a need for broader understanding of Genentech and help navigating the culture. In response we created Director Development Pathways (DDP), a process in which participants spend about 10 percent of their time over six to nine months in a host function. Their experiences could include job shadowing, observation, special projects, committees and taskforce participation, and entrée into decision-making meetings. Each participant also receives critical development support from his or her manager, a functional advisor in the host function, and a coach.

We knew that a director's developmental path needed to include exposure to and first-hand experience in other functions to gain an understanding of how the other functions contribute to the business overall and how they impact decisions in his or her own area. And for this level of leaders, building cross-functional networks was just as important as understanding other functions. However, it was not feasible to provide cross-functional experiences for directors primarily through job moves or even through temporary full-time assignments. Given that directors are mid-senior leaders, usually with deep expertise and with jobs of large scope, finding "back fills" would have been hugely challenging. DDP was thus mindfully designed to be a flexible, part-time solution.

After a piloting phase, DDP is now a self-managed process available to our entire director population. The DDP website describes a basic five-step process and provides a suite of resources and tools for carrying out each step. Each process step is summarized on a single page (see Figure 7.1 for the Step 1 page). In addition, the website houses guides for the director's manager, functional advisor, and coach.

Figure 7.1. Process Step Summary Page

WHAT IS THE DDP PROCESS?

STEP ONE–ASSESS

The first step in the process involves assessing your current skills, competencies, and development needs. It also includes reviewing your interests and aspirations. In this step, you will need to synthesize this information, discuss with your manager and then determine how to leverage cross-functional opportunities to assist you in your development.

DDP includes a number of tools to help you effectively assess your development needs and aspirations. It is a good idea to keep in the forefront your development goals and learning objectives and update them as you continue on your development path.

Key questions to ask yourself in this step are:

- What are my strengths and development areas?
- What are my aspirations/interests?
- What do I want to focus on?
- Are increased cross-functional exposure or knowledge high priorities for my development?

ACTIONS AND KEY TOOLS:

1. Review your current job description and, if available, development profile for your current role
2. Review your recent PPR data, 360 data, and multi-rater feedback
3. Summarize key take-aways on Assessment Summary
4. If you have a coach, ask him/her to assist you with the synthesis of this information and drafting of your Development Goal and possible learning objectives.
5. Summarize your findings and prepare notes for a meeting with your manager (the Assessment Summary can help you do this)
6. Schedule a focused development conversation with your manager (use the Assessment Discussion Script to help you conduct this conversation) to determine whether a cross-functional development experience will be valuable for you at this time.

ADDITIONAL DEVELOPMENT TOOLS:

- Leveraging a Coach
- Sample Development Goal

SUMMARY:

INPUTS: PPR data, current development plan, 360 Degree Feedback, Multi-rater data, feedback from your manager or others, job description development profile for your current role, your interests and aspirations.

DECISIONS: Does a cross-functional development opportunity make sense for me?

OUTPUTS: Agreement with my manager to pursue a cross-functional development opportunity and the cross-functional area(s) I will focus on through DOP

Step 1: Assess Strengths, Needs, Interests, and Aspirations

Directors first assess their current skills, competencies, and development needs, as well as their interests and aspirations. The Development Profile is an important starting place for this assessment. Similar to a job description, this profile describes key success factors, how success in the role is typically measured, example job responsibilities by position, and specific types of development that would benefit job incumbents. A core tool in this step is an Assessment Summary that guides the director in reflecting on developmental interests and aspirations, reviewing recent performance and development feedback, listing strengths and development areas, drafting development goals, and listing preliminary ideas on which functions might be valuable to gain exposure to. Having synthesized the assessment information, directors plan and structure their development conversations with their managers, leveraging the second tool for this step, an Assessment Discussion Script.

Step 2: Investigate Possible Cross-Functional Opportunities

Directors next determine the specific types of experiences that will benefit their development. They review information about each function in the Genentech Function in a Box (gFIB) tool. Built by subject matter experts in each area, the tool includes an overview of the function, key focus areas and priorities, organizational structure, leadership and governing bodies, primary events, and links to select resources (for example, websites, articles, and podcasts) that help explain the purpose and activities of the function. Directors are also advised to leverage their networks (and their managers' networks) to conduct informational interviews to learn more about possible opportunities. The primary tool for this step is the Investigative Summary (see Exhibit 7.1), used to consolidate information about developmental activities in other functions and people who can help them accomplish their objectives.

Exhibit 7.1. Investigative Summary

Use the DDP Investigative Summary to explore possible functions, opportunities, and activities. With this information, revise your Learning Objectives and finalize your Development Goal.

1. List the functions (and departments or groups within each function) that would provide you the targeted perspectives and knowledge you would find valuable. (See gFIBs.)

2. List types of opportunities or potential activities that are available in your function(s) of interest. Note with whom and the approaches you would use to implement each activity.

3. Review and, as appropriate, revise your learning objectives, incorporating information related to potentially available opportunities and activities. Update your development goal if necessary.

Step 3: Create a Detailed Action Plan

Having identified goals and explored opportunities, directors create a targeted and specific action plan. An Action Plan template captures the specifics of their selected activities and events and the names of people who will support their development. Directors are advised to be realistic about the time these activities will take and the obstacles they may encounter and to proactively identify people they can leverage if needed. They are also encouraged to review their plans, listing new activities as they learn more, and to plan a systematic midterm review of their plans. An additional tool, the Action Plan Script, provides tips for conversations with their managers and functional advisors so that they can enlist the important support needed for success (see Exhibit 7.2).

Exhibit 7.2. Action Plan Script

This script may be useful to help you finalize your plan with your manager.

Beginning

- State the purpose for today's meeting.

  "As we agreed, the purpose of today's meeting is to review and finalize my Development Action Plan so that I can start to execute it."

- Summarize development goals and learning objectives.

  "As we discussed previously, my goals are to build cross-functional breadth, increase business knowledge, and work on building my cross-functional network. Toward those goals, I have listed three specific learning objectives, and I'd like to discuss activities to target for each of these."

Middle

- Review your draft Development Action Plan with your manager.

  "So, as you recall, previously I was investigating options and thinking through initial opportunities and activities. Now, I have fleshed out more details and would like to discuss those with you."

- Review final learning objectives and activities targeted for these.

  "Here are the activities that I have listed to help me address learning objective X. For each activity, I have specified time to complete and also required resources. Do you have any other feedback or input regarding this plan?"

  "Do these activities, timing, and resources make sense to you? Do you think I am missing anything?"

  "In order for me to have the time to complete these activities, I will need to rearrange my calendar. One of their key meetings conflicts with your LT meeting. Will it be alright if I do not attend your LT meetings for the next three months, or can we figure out some other alternative?"

- Confirm your manager's input.

  "Okay, so you feel this plan is feasible and appropriate for my development goals. Is that correct?"

Exhibit 7.2. Action Plan Script (*continued*)

"I believe we also agree that before I start to execute against this plan, I would talk with John about transitioning one of my current projects to him. I was thinking I would give him X starting as of [date]. This will give John a good learning experience, too. Does this make sense?"

- Incorporate your manager's input and check in for other inputs.

  "I will update you after I meet with John this week. This will likely mean I start my development activities in about two weeks."

  "Is there anything else you recommend that I do at this time?"

End

- Discuss next steps.

  "I was thinking it would be good to meet every two weeks during DDP to discuss my progress. Does this seem reasonable?"

  "I will go ahead and schedule these debrief meetings for us every two weeks for the next six months."

- Thank your manager for his/her time, input, and support.

Step 4: Execute Action Plan

Directors spend the majority of their time in this step learning about the target function. The Action Plan serves as a map; however, directors are encouraged to be flexible and seize unplanned learning opportunities that may present themselves. Several other tools support this step: an Ongoing Discussion Script that offers suggestions for discussing progress with one's manager, functional advisor, and others; a Meeting Notes template; and a Journal template for recording observations, insights, and challenges, as well as applications back to their current jobs. These notes serve as useful memory jogs for directors in their meetings with their managers, functional advisors, and coaches.

Step 5: Debrief, Reflect, and Apply

The final and crucial step is for directors to solidify their insights and determine how to translate what they have learned back to their day-to-day work. Self-reflection plays a large role for each director here, with assistance from the manager, functional advisor, and coach. In completing a Learning and Insights Summary, directors write about their key insights and lessons from the DDP experience, identify three to five opportunities to apply these insights and lessons back on the job, and note the cross-functional contacts they have added to their network.

Lessons Learned

Director Development Pathways is a self-serve solution for a large director population. When using a website for self-guided development, critical factors for successful outcomes include: equipping directors with the guidance and tools for creating a customized and flexible development plan that fits their situations, creating a support network that meets their needs, and ensuring that they hold and leverage important conversations with their managers and other key people.

Overall, the DDP approach has been well received and seen as relevant. The business need for directors to have solid business knowledge, cross-functional perspectives, and broad networks is ever more critical in today's complex, fast-moving, and global environment. However, it was very clear that the size and complexity of directors' roles make it difficult for them to leave their jobs for development, even for short durations. This lends further support for a customized and flexible self-paced solution, enabled by easily accessible, clearly organized online tools and support, rather than a cohort program. In addition, at Genentech we believe that over a period of time this kind of part-time, assignment-based solution could be more broadly implemented with less-senior managers or individual contributors.

8

Creating Project Marketplaces

Cynthia McCauley
Center for Creative Leadership

A COMMON PROBLEM that employees encounter, when looking for opportunities to tackle a new challenge or to gain experience outside their current jobs, is not knowing what opportunities are available. Enter *project marketplaces*. Housed on an organization's intranet, a project marketplace is a space for managers to post projects looking for help on certain tasks or in need of particular skills, short-term assignments, jobs needing to be filled on an interim basis, and job rotation openings. By posting to the project marketplace, the manager lets others know that he or she has work that needs to be accomplished and is willing to have that work need met by someone who would learn and grow from the experience.

An example of a project marketplace is IBM's Blue Opportunities (Davis, 2007). Created in response to an expressed desire from employees at all levels of the organization for greater access to more and varied experiential learning, Blue Opportunities offers stretch assignments, cross-unit projects, job rotations, and on-site job shadowing to employees worldwide. For example, a Brazilian employee contributed his coding skills to a manager in Ireland, and in the process learned about another business unit without leaving his home office. Employees with diverse backgrounds regularly volunteer to serve as instructors in the organization's employee orientation session, receiving training and regular practice in facilitation skills. The Blue Opportunities program allows employees to broaden their organizational perspective and gain skills they may otherwise have missed.

Other organizations have designed project marketplaces within functional groups such as marketing or finance, or have put restrictions on the scope of the projects that can be posted. For example, one organization uses its marketplace for short-term part-time assignments only, allowing only postings that would require no more then three to five hours of work a week for twelve weeks.

Individuals who have created and managed project marketplaces offer this advice on how to establish such a program in your organization:

- Pilot the program with small, targeted populations. This will demonstrate to the business that employees and their managers can be creative in finding ways for employees to participate without putting critical work at risk or jeopardizing the productivity of the unit.

- Survey managers who post and fill opportunities to learn how they have benefitted and share the results widely in the organization.

- Require employees who seek assignments via the project marketplace to indicate how the experience supports their development goals.

- Encourage employees who have completed a project or assignment to share the insights and skills gained with their co-workers.

- Create a learning contract template that the host manager and the employee can use to document agreed upon learning goals, expectations, and timelines.

- Have both the employee and the host manager evaluate the experience. Employees should assess what they have gained from the experience and how they can use the gained knowledge or skills in their current jobs. Host managers should evaluate the employee's performance, learning, and additional benefits to the organization.

Reference

Davis, N.M. (2007, November). One-on-one training crosses continents. *HR Magazine*, pp. 55–56.

9

Leveraging the Developmental Power of Core Organizational Work

Patricia M.G. O'Connor
Wesfarmers

EFFECTIVE MANAGERS CONTINUALLY seek opportunities to increase the return on every project they oversee. Couple this driver with what is known about the power of accelerating leader development through challenging experiences, and you begin to see work practices in a new light. If you take a developmental lens to "naturally occurring" work that the business is already engaged in and committed to, the number of potential developmental opportunities, and thus returns to the business, grows exponentially. The following outlines how one such practice—integration teams—can be more intentionally refined to accelerate leadership development and deliver higher overall value to the business.

Context

Wesfarmers Ltd. is a conglomerate that was founded as a farmers' cooperative in 1914 and grew into one of Australia's largest and most successful companies, with approximately two hundred thousand employees. The company includes nine divisions operating in diverse industries, including retail, industrial, and insurance. The objective of the company is to deliver satisfactory return to shareholders, and it does so by taking a long-term investment perspective, buying underperforming businesses, embedding more rigorous standards and systems, and creating greater value for shareholders, employees, and the communities within which the businesses operate.

Much has been argued about whether conglomerate structures deliver value, with the prevailing belief being that the requirements for effectively leading and monitoring diverse businesses are simply too demanding for any one CEO. Wesfarmers' total shareholder return (TSR) since listing in 1984, however, has demonstrated that this structure can indeed deliver value if (1) clear expectations for business and leadership performance are set, (2) robust financial and human capital systems are embedded, and (3) divisions are given the autonomy as well as the accountability to deliver results.

The Practice

To ensure that these three success factors are built into each new acquisition, the company forms and deploys an integration team. Although the integration process is a complex one, with unique requirements for each acquisition, there are consistencies across all acquisitions. Overall, the charter of each integration team is to work closely with the new business to embed the Wesfarmers culture and values (that is, "the Wesfarmers Way"), integrate "pure corporate" functions (for example, investor relations, tax, treasury, company secretary) into Wesfarmers, enhance (or where necessary create) financial and human capital systems to standard, conduct major project reviews of critical areas for rationalization, facilitate the review and group managing director approval of any new structures, and ready the new leadership team to operate as an autonomous business within the guiding principles of the Wesfarmers portfolio.

The primary challenge with all integration work is to conduct it in such a way that it does not distract the business from operational imperatives. To take on this important and challenging leadership work, individuals are temporarily reassigned from their current roles to deliver full time as integration team members. A senior executive is appointed as the team leader, but each member also takes responsibility for a functional or operations work stream, requiring each to deliver as both an individual contributor as well as a leader.

Accelerating Leader Development

The integration team experience is a rich one, with all former members of these teams reporting significant leadership insights that they believed equipped them to be even more effective going forward. Post-experience, most of the team members either took on greater responsibility in their current roles or moved into new, more challenging roles. So while the practice is viewed post-hoc as developmental, there is an opportunity to more intentionally leverage the developmental power of the work by introducing enhancements to several of the work elements (see Figure 9.1): role positioning, team composition, team member preparation, flow-on development, developmental check-ins, after-action review, post-experience placement, and evaluation.

Figure 9.1. High Leverage Work Elements

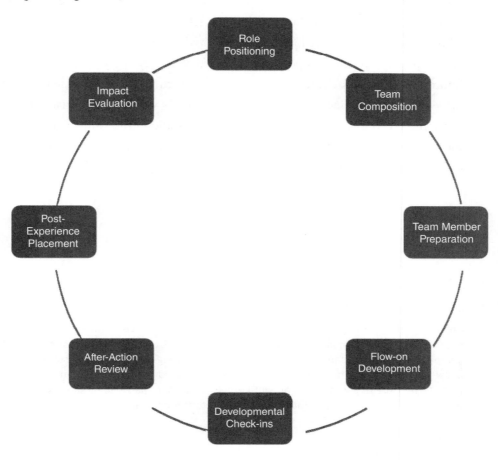

Role Positioning

The opportunity to serve on an integration team is viewed as a plum assignment. It is an opportunity to engage in important and highly visible work that is also fairly rare, given the relative infrequency of acquisitions. An improvement to this element is to be explicit about the developmental expectation in the positioning the assignment. That is, team members should be expected to focus on developing their leadership capabilities while delivering on the team's work, and thus return to their businesses better equipped to address complex businesses challenges as a result of this experience. Involvement of and alignment with the individual's manager in the positioning is central to its effectiveness.

Team Composition

The team leader and members are chosen from across the existing businesses, representing the array of functions and knowledge required to successfully integrate the new company. This includes possessing a practical understanding of the Wesfarmers Way, as well as demonstrating themselves as strong performers. Further, as these individuals represent the first exposure the employees of the acquired business have to the new parent company, it is essential they personally model the Wesfarmers values and principles. Individuals who fit these criteria as well as being recognized as ready for a new challenge are in some cases tapped; in other cases people are selected after they apply for a role on the team. An improvement to this element is to ensure that each individual selected is both ready to deliver immediate value to the integration process as well as be materially stretched by the experience. This can be achieved through an application process involving a personal statement that gives the employee an opportunity to demonstrate the readiness, self-awareness, commitment, learning orientation, and intentionality required for the assignment (see Exhibit 9.1).

Exhibit 9.1. Sample Integration Team Assignment Application

Thank you for your interest in the Wesfarmers Ltd. Wonder Division Integration Team opportunity. The first step in the process is formally registering your interest through the completion of this personal statement, including securing your manager's support. This will allow the selection committee to more clearly understand your readiness, motivation, and overall fit as to the role requirements. You will be notified within one week of submission whether your application has been successful, advancing you to the interview stage.

Name:
Current title and business:
E-mail:
Mobile phone:

What is your understanding of the role requirements and demands of an Integration Team member?

Why is this opportunity attractive to you at this particular point in your career?

What relevant skills, knowledge, abilities, and experience would you bring to the team?

What do you specifically seek to learn, develop, or test through this experience?

What practical difference would the application of these learnings make to your back-home team and broader business?

I [your manager's full name and title], fully support and endorse [your name] in her/his application to serve on the Wonder Division Integration Team.

Signature:
Date:

Team Member Preparation

In addition to the reflection prompted as part of the application process, successful applicants should begin readying themselves for the assignment in a number of ways. First, they should sit down with their managers and identify areas for individual capability growth as well as organizational capability growth. As to the latter, what might the individual learn and bring back that will benefit and improve the business? For example, the person may inform the business's approach to driving rapid and complex change, which is essentially what integration work seeks to accomplish. Second, interviewing former integration team members will help transfer advice and guidance from those with experience in the assignment. Finally, readying direct reports and other stakeholders who will be affected by the secondment ensures a smooth transfer of responsibilities and management of expectations during the assignment.

Flow-on Development

As individuals leave their current roles to join the integration team full-time, an opportunity is created for either another individual to step into the vacated role or the individual's manager to restructure the team's work, assigning new stretch responsibilities to a number of members. To the degree that the flow-on effects can be designed as material and meaningful professional opportunities, the business benefits from a very low cost development investment. Further, the disappointment of others who may have been unsuccessful applicants for an integration-team role are mitigated to some degree.

Developmental Check-ins

Significant energy and attention are required to deliver on complex, high stakes leadership work. Keeping the developmental objective top of mind for team members is challenging, if not impossible, while they are engaged in the work itself. Building in planned developmental check-ins with both the team leader as well as the individual's manager provides essential support for accelerating the intake, understanding, and application of new insights. These need not be long or complicated discussions, but regularity is important. These insight-focused sessions will not only stimulate the individual's longer-term leadership capability but generally also yield immediate benefits to the current work deliverables.

After-Action Review

Immediately upon completing the assignment with an integration team, each member should engage in both individual reflection and journaling, as well as a team debriefing about the leadership implications of the experience. Like any other meeting, preparation is key to an effective after-action review (see *After-Event Reviews* on page 221 of this book). It is suggested that each team member spend time prior to the session addressing a set of questions that serve to accelerate the acquisition and transfer of key lessons from the integration-team experience (see Exhibit 9.2).

Exhibit 9.2. Sample After-Action Review Pre-Work

As preparation for the upcoming Integration Team after-action review, please reflect on and respond to the following questions:

What were my primary learnings from this work experience?

Which of those am I ready to apply now and which do I need more time or guidance to discern the relevance to me or my business?

What aspects of the work required me to operate outside of my comfort zone, and how did I fare in that space?

Can I re-create aspects of this developmentally challenging environment back into my team?

Did my understanding of my developmental priorities change throughout the experience, and if so, how?

How did this experience change how I understand my business? Wesfarmers Ltd?

What do I now feel more equipped and confident to take on in my business?

What insights can I pass forward to my team members, peers, or the business at large?

What support do I require going forward to attain the highest return from this experience?

Post-Experience Placement

Most integration team members return to their original businesses after the assignment, but there is a ripe opportunity to assess roles across the portfolio of business in order to identify where each individual is now equipped to make the biggest contribution. Although up-front promises of transfers or promotions cannot be made, as these would need to be guided by business needs, sharing the members' profiles with the senior management team for consideration can net more leveraged post-experience placements.

Evaluation

Six months from the dissolution of the integration team is an ideal time to conduct follow-on interviews with the team members, their managers, their teams, and other key stakeholders about demonstrated changes in leadership capability, mindset, and approach, and the difference those changes produced for themselves, their teams, and the business. For those who were placed in new teams or businesses, the interviews would focus more on what distinct contributions the individual brought to the team, and tangible examples of the impact of those contributions—for example, more timely delivery of major project milestones or more effective management of key stakeholders.

Applying This Approach to Your Organization

My overall advice about leadership development is, first and foremost, to resist the temptation to create new assignments, structures, practices, processes, or programs in order to accelerate it. Most organizations would deliver greater value by intentionally integrating leadership development into a few organizational practices and avoiding the accretion of development initiatives that stand apart from naturally occurring work.

Second, if you are not already familiar with the practices that are core to your company's success, inform yourself now. In other words, identify the practices whose absence, if they were removed tomorrow, would almost certainly result in a serious and negative impact to company reputation or results. These work practices represent the most fertile ground for accelerating leader development.

Third, avoid overdesigning the developmental elements of the work. Be realistic about the intensity and resources that work core to company success already requires, as well as your organization's relative sophistication, and thus readiness, to take a more developmental approach.

Finally, design and position the developmental elements as an intrinsic part of the work charter. That is, they should generate a higher return by delivering on business imperatives while simultaneously building leadership capability to be more effective in the future.

10

Learning Transferable Skills Through Event Planning

Kenna Cottrill and Kim Hayashi
Leadership Inspirations

OVER THE PAST twenty years, high schools have relied on and have spent hundreds of thousands of dollars on event-planning companies to plan their dances. After years of watching dance committees hand over their event responsibilities to these companies, one of us (Kim) decided to create an integrative program whereby students could learn and have control over the outcome of their event. Instead of simply selecting a theme and colors and making posters for publicity, this program sought to provide students skills they could use in the future: for instance, understanding group development, working through conflict constructively, understanding how to read contracts, and making budgetary decisions. It became a great opportunity for building skills and experience during an actual major school event—the prom!

In many ways our event-planning process is similar to what you would find at any event-planning company. We maintain working relationships with venues and vendors, negotiate contracts, and handle day-of-event management. Where we differ is that managing the more intricate details, budgeting, and decision making becomes a part of the student process. While guided by an experienced leadership coach, students are given the opportunity to discuss, determine, and decide what is best for the outcome of their event, based on goals they have set.

This process has two phases. Phase 1 occurs a year to eighteen months before the event, and focuses on finding a venue. Students are tasked with finding locations that fit their size and budget and will be the best fit for the student body. After visiting the sites, their coach provides input and direction while the group discusses the pros and cons of each location to reach a decision on a mutually agreed on site. This phase has many intricacies, as often the students choosing the location are not the students who end up planning it, which makes the facilitation of a big picture view very important.

Once the big picture has been determined and the venue set, Phase 2 of the process occurs in the months preceding the event, right up to the event itself. Student planning groups have six meetings with their coach—five times before the event and one time after the event. These meetings focus on group development, goal setting, brainstorming and creativity, action planning, accountability, discussing challenges and successes, evaluation, and feedback. The meetings last about an hour and are outlined below and summarized in Exhibit 10.1.

The first meeting has an emphasis on group norms. The students have already worked together for several months, but this is often the first time they are working with a professional event planner and are introduced to some of the tools we use. A leadership style assessment is given to help the group understand the strengths and challenges of individual team members, and the dynamics of the results are discussed within the group. Since the students have been working together, they assess what they already do well as a team and what areas they can improve, and we refer back to this information consistently throughout the process. The team develops goals to set the foundation for its process and brainstorms all the tasks it has to complete to make the event a reality. To ensure the event-planning process is occurring in between meetings, students are given homework, including a SWOT (strengths, weaknesses, opportunities, and threats) analysis, calendaring of tasks, and individual goal-setting.

In the second meeting, homework is reviewed, particularly the SWOT analysis, as it helps us understand the school culture as well as connect to their individual and group strengths. A budget and expense-tracking system are developed by and for the students, which they use to continually monitor where they stand financially, examining the different ways in which expenses affect their profit. Their task list is reviewed in the context of their strengths, which provides a foundation for a more effective delegation strategy based on those strengths. Finally, in preparation for the next meeting's site visit, we provide students the location contract and policies, encourage them to visit the website, and ask them to prepare questions for the venue.

The third meeting is primarily a site visit, in which the students visit the location, often for the first time. The coach works to stay behind the scenes of the visit so that the students feel empowered to ask the questions they deem most important; however, the coach guides the students toward any questions they may leave out. The students also must consider the layout for their event and assess how many security guards will be needed. This requires

Exhibit 10.1. Focus of Planning Team Meetings

Meeting Content	Homework
Meeting 1 _____	**Homework**
Introductions	SWOT analysis
Schedule	Job descriptions
Group norms	Personal goals
Leadership style assessment	Contract for feedback
Event goals	Set deadlines for tasks
Brainstorm event task list	
Meeting 2 _____	
Review homework	Review location contract
Budget	
Review task list	
Delegate responsibility based on strengths	
Meeting 3 _____	
Review homework	Floor plan (including security locations)
Visit site	Discuss additional entertainment/activities
Review floor plan and facility policies	
Discuss publicity strategy	
Meeting 4 _____	
Review homework	Secure volunteers and staff
Finalize theme	
Review vendor contracts	
Finalize floor plan and publicity strategy	
Meeting 5 _____	
Review homework	
Finalize event schedule	
Practice coronation speech	
Final budget	
Meeting 6 _____	
Evaluate event and event planning process	
Discuss final report	
Discuss rewards and recognition	

students to consider safety and any possible inappropriate behaviors that could occur during the dance, which is not a typical issue that they consider.

In the fourth and fifth meetings, the bulk of the work to prepare for the event is discussed, including alternative activities for attendees, and vendors the students would like to bring in to their event. Vendor contracts are reviewed, the publicity strategy is discussed and evaluated, and the budget is updated. Typically, in these meetings we begin to hear about conflicts that have occurred, either within the team or with other members of the student government. Conflict-resolution coaching and resources are provided to help students address their concerns and move forward in the planning. The fifth meeting is typically less than two weeks before the event and is the last opportunity to review the final schedule of the event, as well as the setup and cleanup.

Within two weeks after the prom, the coach meets with the group one last time to evaluate the event and the event-planning process. A discussion is facilitated about the aspects of the event that could be repeated in the future, as well as understanding mistakes that were made that could be avoided in the future. In discussing the event-planning process, we examine how the students worked together and what they can learn from their group's experience, as well as how well they worked together in accomplishing their goals. We discuss whether their goals were accomplished, and if not, what prevented them from happening and what the students can learn for future goal setting. We also discuss their strategies for getting feedback from the student body and student government class. Details of the content of their final report are outlined, which they complete in the following weeks. This final report is used to keep a record of the event and the planning process for future committees planning the same event. When we work with the school on next year's prom, one of the first things the students do is review the previous year's binder to become familiar with the overarching process and lessons learned by previous groups.

In the end, the students who participate in this process develop a better knowledge of how an event is produced and how a group functions. Instead of relying on someone else to do the work for them, students are engaged, involved, and empowered to make important decisions, learn, and create. Previous participants have reported feeling more confident in their abilities to plan an event and feel their events are more successful (in attendance, profit, and overall atmosphere) when using this process.

This process—combining the work of organizing an event with activities that enhance the knowledge and skills needed to effectively plan and implement an event—is transferable to many other settings. Think of all the events that organizations plan—from United Way campaigns, to sales meetings, to trade shows. Organizing events is an ideal way for employees to learn and apply skills such as goal setting, comprehensive planning, monitoring progress, evaluating performance, and group problem solving.

11

Pinpointing: Matching Job Assignments to Employees

Jeffrey J. McHenry
Rainier Leadership Solutions

AN HR COLLEAGUE and I were having a discussion with one of our vice presidents about providing on-the-job learning opportunities for some key individuals in his organization. "Of course, I support developing high potentials and giving them stretch experiences," he assured us. "But I've got a business to run. Our goals this year are incredibly challenging. On top of that, we have at least ten key projects we need to complete this year in order to have half a chance to make our numbers next year." He paused, then smiled a bit skeptically. "If you can figure out a way I can develop my key people and still meet my numbers, I'll support it." A week later, we came back to him with an approach he liked a lot. We call it *Pinpointing*.

Everyone knows that the best way to develop employees is to provide them with challenging experiences similar to those that they will encounter in future, more senior job assignments. Through these experiences, they develop the capabilities needed to be successful as they progress in their careers. The challenge most companies face is how to match the experiences that employees need against the business challenges and priorities facing the organization (more specifically, the part of the organization where the employee is working) at a particular point in time. Often organizations invent interesting assignments that match the experiences employees need but are not relevant to the business. As a result, these assignments fall to the bottom of the employee's priority list and lack the urgency required to truly catalyze learning. The goal of Pinpointing is to provide experience-based development that is rooted in and takes advantage of the business's priorities and execution plans. Pinpointing can be used in partnership with a senior-leader attempt to create development plans for his or her direct report team, or with a leadership team that is working on development plans for the high potentials in the organization.

Pinpointing Steps

Essentially, the flow of pinpointing is to take stock of the organization's business priorities and assignments that need to be filled, make a list of development priorities for each individual, match the business assignments with the employee development needs, and follow up to ensure that employees are learning from their job assignments and experiences. I offer some tips on specific steps below.

Step 1: Develop a List of Possible Assignments

Use the organization's business plans to generate a list of the key initiatives the organization will be undertaking during the upcoming business cycle (typically six to twelve months). Identify initiatives where help is needed, the type of help required, and time requirements. For example: develop a product plan to launch a new product line in Asia; need someone who can work with product development on how existing products need to be adapted for Asia in support of project lead; 25 percent time for next six months. This becomes a list of possible assignments.

Step 2: Triage Employees Based on Learning Stage in Their Current Jobs

A very simple assessment is recommended (see Figure 11.1):

- Developing—new to job and/or still on a steep learning curve with limited capacity to take on additional work (could be someone who has been in the role a while but is struggling). No further action is required for these individuals because the job itself is currently providing all the challenge they need to learn and grow.

- Full—fully or nearly fully capable of performing on the current job, not yet ready for a move but capable of taking on additional work.

- Exceptional—fully capable of performing the current job, already routinely taking on special projects and assignments, very soon or currently ready for a new job.

Step 3: List Capability and Experience Gaps for Each Employee

Identify the most likely next career move (one to three most likely scenarios) for employees at the full or exceptional stage of the learning cycle for their jobs. Then list two or three

Figure 11.1. Job Learning Stages and Recommended Development Approach

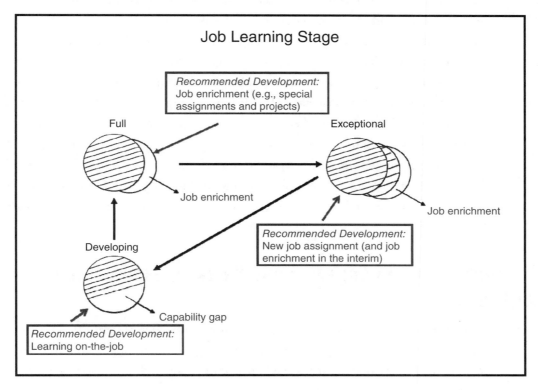

capabilities they have not yet demonstrated that will be critical to their next jobs (for example, needs to demonstrate that he or she can lead a cross-functional team, needs to demonstrate that he or she can work effectively outside his or her home country, needs to demonstrate that he or she can create and communicate product strategy). The best approach is to think like a prospective hiring manager. "If I were considering this individual for her likely next job(s), what gaps would worry me when I reviewed her résumé, and where would I probe when I interviewed her?"

Step 4: Match Job Assignments to Employees

For example, one of the projects may be to work with corporate headquarters on launching a new product to a customer segment. This assignment might be matched to someone who needs experience working with corporate headquarters or who needs experience working on a cross-functional team or who needs experience developing a business plan for and launching a new product.

Step 5: Determine Additional Development Support for Each Employee

The goal is to help ensure that employees are successful in and learn from their stretch assignments. What additional development support will be useful to each employee? At a minimum, it should include a conversation with the employee about why he or she was selected for the assignment, what success looks like, and what the person can and should expect to learn from the assignment. It also may be useful to assign a mentor or coach, send the employee to training, provide the employee with a list of key stakeholders to meet, provide air cover that helps the employee navigate tricky political issues, and so on.

This is also a good opportunity to have a conversation about next career moves for employees at the exceptional stage of their job learning cycle. What steps will be taken to help them identify and secure their next jobs? This might include creating opportunities for them to get exposure to prospective hiring managers or sponsors in the hiring organization (for example, through mentoring relationships, attendance at business meetings, job shadowing, or informal one-on-one conversations) and making sure that these individuals are listed as future job candidates in talent reviews and succession planning conversations.

Making Pinpointing an Engaging and Valuable Experience for Senior Leaders

One of the keys to the success of Pinpointing is leader engagement. The degree to which leaders enjoy and are engaged by the Pinpointing conversation is a good predictor of the quality of the development plans the leaders create, how well those plans are executed, and how much employees learn from their assignments.

One factor that affects leader engagement is the amount of preparation work that is done in advance. One approach is to come to the meeting prepared with a list of potential assignments (Step 1) and an assessment of each employee to be discussed (Steps 2 and 3; see Exhibit 11.1 for an example). A draft list of potential assignments can usually be generated relatively easily from the organization's business plan, typically in partnership with the leader's business manager/chief of staff or the head of strategy for the division.

If a draft list is completed and circulated in advance to the leaders participating in the Pinpointing exercise, it typically takes no more than fifteen to twenty minutes to clarify and finalize the list during the meeting. Similarly, a draft employee assessment (see Exhibit 11.1) can be completed in advance by interviewing the managers of each employee (or possibly their line HR business partners). Generally, preparing the list of potential assignments in advance enhances leader engagement in Pinpointing because it makes for a faster-paced conversation.

The employee assessment is another matter, especially when the Pinpointing conversation includes a senior leader and his or her leadership team, and the focus of the conversation is a group of key employees (for example, high potentials) within the organization. Typically, there will be several leaders who have exposure to and valuable insights about each key employee. When a draft assessment is completed and handed out to leaders in advance of the Pinpointing exercise, in general the leaders have been less willing to share their opinions

Exhibit 11.1. Employee Assessment

Employee Name	Current Job	Job Learning Stage	Likely Next Career Move(s)	Key Capability Gaps
Sanchez, Charles	Director, Product Marketing	Full	Regional Sales Director, Regional Business Development Director	Field sales and marketing (very limited experience), New product launch (no experience)
Yu, Alice	Director Product Development	Developing	N/A	N/A
Wilder, Rosa	Senior Director Supply Chain	Exceptional	GM Regional Operations	International operations (very limited experience), Cross-functional partnerships outside Operations (limited experience), Regional P&L–planning, budgeting, management (very limited experience)
Carloni, Peter	Senior Director Manufacturing, Industrial Products	Full	Senior Director Supply Chain, Senior Director Country Operations, Senior Director Manufacturing (different product line)	Emerging markets (limited experience), Business operations outside Industrial Products (very limited experience)

and insights; they tend to accept the draft assessment as a "done deal." Typically, a better approach is for each leader to come prepared to discuss his or her key employees at the Pinpointing meeting, with time then reserved to finalize the assessment together. One additional benefit of this approach is that it improves leaders' assessment skills—it helps them become more clear and concise about the capabilities and development needs of the people who work for them and with them.

Another way to increase leader engagement is to physically involve them in the matching task. An easy way to do this is to record each assignment and each individual assessment on a sticky note (one color for assignments, another for assessments), stick the notes on a wall or whiteboard, and kick off the matching exercise by asking participants to go up to the board together and make a preliminary match of assignments to their key employees (see Figure 11.2). This leads to energetic and sometimes very creative conversations between

Figure 11.2. Example of Sticky Notes for Pinpointing Exercise

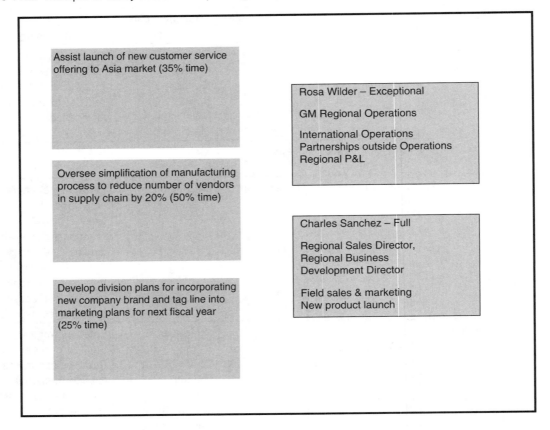

leaders as they make their matches together, and also causes them to feel more ownership of the assignments made for their key employees.

Follow Up

The effectiveness of Pinpointing, like any planning activity, is only as good as the execution. At the end of the exercise, it's critical to send the senior leaders who participated in the Pinpointing discussion a summary that includes the assignments and the additional development support to be given to each employee, action items for each senior leader (for example, communicating assignments to employees, launching employees in their new assignments), and the timeframe. A review of Pinpointing progress should be completed every six to eight weeks, so that adjustments can be made if assignments are not working as planned or additional development support is needed for some employees. Typically, assignments last four to six months, so most organizations will find it useful to go through a Pinpointing exercise twice a year—often at the beginning of a fiscal year as new projects are being launched, and again at midyear as the organization begins planning in earnest for the upcoming fiscal year.

When done well, Pinpointing results in experience-based development plans that address critical capability gaps, and it enables employees to progress in their careers. It also helps the organization do critical work by assigning the most critical work to key employees. Finally, Pinpointing helps grow leaders' capability to develop future leaders by improving their assessment skills and engaging them in the leadership development process. Pinpointing can be a powerful tool for enhancing leadership capability in an organization.

12

Learning from Personal Life Experiences*

Marian N. Ruderman and Patricia J. Ohlott
Center for Creative Leadership

MANAGERS AND EXECUTIVES too often discount what can be learned from experiences outside of work. And the popular media consistently portrays the intersection of work life and personal life as fraught with career peril. Although non-work roles and responsibilities can limit and interfere with performance at work, there is another side to this story that is much richer in possibilities and rewards. Interests, roles, and responsibilities outside of work can also serve as creative and supportive sources for learning how to be a more effective leader.

It is important for people to see that ordinary non-work activities such as organizing a fundraising event, coaching a youth sports team, and even advocating for a community cause are not irrelevant to or disconnected from work activities. Such activities provide both the practical skills and psychological support that can enhance a leader's effectiveness on the job. As a leadership development practitioner, you can help individuals discover the developmental nature of non-work experiences by engaging them in the following reflective exercise.

---

*Note: This contribution is adapted from the authors' book *Learning from Life: Turning Life's Lessons into Leadership Experience*, published in 2000 by the Center for Creative Leadership.

A Reflective Exercise

There are three important ways in which private life encourages and enhances leadership development. The first is by providing opportunities to develop psychological strength. No doubt you've noticed that events in your personal life can from day to day have different effects on your outlook and concentration. Your personal responsibilities and relationships contribute to your general sense of how strong, secure, confident, and capable you feel. A second way is through the support of family relationships and friendships, which can encourage and advise you. A final way is through learning opportunities. The roles you play off the job can be your laboratory for mastering management and leadership skills. Let's examine how non-work activities can strengthen your own leadership capability by providing psychological strength and support and by motivating skill development.

Psychological Strength

Think about the activities you have outside of work, the ones that really recharge your batteries. They don't have to be high action pursuits. You might enjoy gardening or reading; others might enjoy a sports activity or attending a concert. Everyone has a place of refuge that can be used to gain perspective. That place of refuge can be a literal place, like a favorite room or a house of worship. Or it can be more abstract, like a favorite book or movie. Whichever you choose, such an activity can provide a buffer from the stress of work.

Action: Make a list of those sources of refuge that can serve as a buffer when the challenge of work is high. Can you give any more time to any of those activities to provide an even stronger buffer?

Another kind of psychological resource your private life can provide to you is confidence. For example, have you addressed a large crowd in your private life, successfully negotiated with a difficult vendor, or held an office in a community organization? Success in your personal life can contribute to a reservoir of confidence that supports you at work.

Action: Make a list of leadership challenges that you have successfully faced in your non-work life. What did you learn that you can translate to your on-the-job challenges?

Personal Relationships for Support

To successfully meet challenges at work, it helps to have a support network from which you can get feedback, try out ideas, and learn new skills. But you can also build a support network among the people you know outside of work. Family, close friends, neighbors, and community partners can all be drawn on as support, and you can transfer the benefits of that support to your work.

   Action: Make a list of family members, friends, and others you can count on to encourage your learning and growth. Who among that list is a good sounding board for ideas and plans? Who has some relevant experience for the kind of challenges you face at work? Who do you trust to give you completely honest feedback? Who can you count on for a boost when you feel discouraged?

Opportunities to Learn

Experiences outside of work are rich opportunities for learning practical management and leadership skills. Sometimes these learning opportunities come without warning, as in a hardship. More often than not you can choose experiences that build specific leadership skills. Take a look at the list in Exhibit 12.1 of roles and experiences people often encounter outside of work and the leadership skills that can be gained from each of these.

   Action: Use the list to stimulate your own thinking about the potential learning opportunities in your outside roles, responsibilities, and experiences. What leadership skills are you trying to learn or improve now? Which of your non-work activities could help you develop those skills? What have you already learned in a non-work domain that you can bring to bear on your current work challenges?

Connecting to On-the-Job Development

Once people are more aware of the developmental opportunities embedded in their non-work roles and activities, they can begin to more intentionally use those opportunities in their formal development plans. You can design development planning resources and templates to remind them to think broadly when crafting plans for achieving goals. For each development goal, they can be encouraged to include non-work roles and responsibilities as places to practice the skills and behaviors needed to reach their goals and to include personal-life relationships as resources to support their efforts to achieve goals. And you can encourage managers as part of developmental conversations with their direct reports to invite discussion of off-the-job development that individuals are experiencing and how their growing skills and knowledge can be best used in the workplace.

Resource

Ruderman, M.N., & Ohlott, P.J. (2000). *Learning from life: Turning life's lessons into leadership experience.* Greensboro, NC: Center for Creative Leadership.

Exhibit 12.1. Matching Experiences to Skills Development

Outside Roles and Experiences	Leadership Skills
Parenting	Interpersonal competence Coaching Appreciation of individual differences
Stepparent	Managing a project that started out as "someone else's baby" Dealing with business situations that have other active shareholders
In-law roles	Appreciating cultural differences Appreciating individual differences Maintaining good relationships
Marriage/significant relationship	Collaboration Negotiation Listening
Selling season tickets for a nonprofit arts organization	Marketing and sales experience Selling a concept, purpose, and mission
Advocating for a social or environmental cause	Crafting the case for a proposal or plan Dealing with the opposition
Volunteering at a crisis hotline	Handling emergencies
Leadership role in a community organization	Practice skills in a different context See how others react to your leadership style
Planning an important social event	Project management
Coaching a team	Developing others Motivating people Building and leading a team
Traveling abroad	Operating with incomplete information Dealing with other who are very different from yourself Becoming more comfortable handling ambiguity
Exercise program	Discipline Goal setting
Gardening	Learning from mistakes Patience
Spiritual experiences	Perspective
Managing family responsibilities	Juggling multiple tasks Setting priorities Resolving conflicts Planning and scheduling
Difficult neighbor	Conflict resolution Negotiating and compromising skills

13

Strategic Corporate Assignments to Develop Emerging Market Leaders

Anita Bhasin
Sage Ways, Inc.
Lori Homer
Microsoft
Eric Rait
Honeycomb Development

MANY EMERGING MARKETS are growing rapidly, and organizations with operations in these markets are finding they do not have the talent needed in-country to meet the rising demand for managers. As we at Microsoft looked at this challenge, we wanted to ensure that high potential talent from key emerging markets had the opportunity to engage in a powerful learning experience while also applying their expertise to the complex issues of a large, global organization—issues typically worked on at the corporate headquarters. The goal of the resulting initiative—the Sales, Marketing, and Services Horizon Immersion Program (SHIP)—is to accelerate the development of leadership talent for our fastest-growing markets by providing on-the-job experiences that immerse participants in corporate business practices. A secondary goal is to have participants bring back new perspectives, approaches, and ways of doing business, and to share them with the subsidiary teams.

The Approach

At an early stage, those involved in designing the initiative decided that these learning experiences needed to be full immersions in temporary assignments with actual work accountabilities—real work on real projects, not a passive job shadowing or a tourist-like experience. We started with a six-month window to ensure that the experience was long enough to be immersive but also short enough that the subsidiary could figure out how to get by without one of its high potential leaders. As mentioned at the end of this piece in the Lessons Learned section, we have since shortened this window to three months, a decision based on our first few experiments in which we saw that three months could still drive learning and six months was a bigger hit to the subsidiary and to the individuals than we wanted to cause.

Each assignment includes two elements. One is a project that allows participants to use their extensive knowledge of how the field organization works by helping their colleagues at corporate prepare a business initiative to be rolled out globally to the field. The other element is related more directly to each individual's development needs. Let's look at the process of nomination and highlight some of the tools that have been helpful in matching development needs to the assignment in the business.

Nomination and Preparation

To be eligible to participate, individuals must be nominated by the subsidiary country manager and confirmed by the subsidiary leadership team. Nominees must be considered top high potential talent for the subsidiary and must have been in their current roles for eighteen months or more. They are typically managers, but can also be senior-level individual contributors. All are serious contenders in succession planning conversations.

We collaborated with our network of HR Business Partners (HRBPs) in the field and together we identified four process steps, including:

Step 1: Select nominees. HRBPs help identify talent for movement. This is typically done at the beginning of the fiscal year, soon after the performance review is complete. Our guidance to HRBPs is that these assignments are best suited for those leaders who have a low level of international experience, have identified leadership gaps, or need to build a network at corporate. They then also complete a profile of the nominated participant that includes personal data, such as length of time at the company, previous history, their roles in succession plans, their career plans and ideal next moves, and their strengths, areas of development, and specific experience to be gathered from the assignment.

Step 2: Select assignment opportunities. We then share each participant's information with the HRBPs in a targeted host organization and ask them to craft an immersion opportunity profile tailored to the individual (see Exhibit 13.1).

On the opportunity profile we require a brief description of the assignment, who the sponsor and day-to-day manager will be, articulation of key business outcomes, ideal timing and duration, experience to be gained, and competencies to be developed. Many groups within Microsoft feel that the organization's planning window presents great learning opportunities, which often means all participants are at corporate in a similar timeframe. A critical element of success in this step is that we identify real business projects.

Exhibit 13.1. Example of an Immersion Opportunity Profile

Nominated Individual: John Doe

Role/Project Description

Leverage field experience to amplify XYZ team results. Projects include:

- Help drive best practices
- Build consumer-marketing scenarios
- Develop messaging for global sales conference

Host Manager: Alice Smith

Timing and Optimum Duration

Mid-February through July (pending manager approval)

Business Outcomes

- Improve marketing return on investment and effectiveness by optimizing marketing approaches for key consumer segments
- Actionable content to enable field experience to be gained

Experience to Be Gained

Exposure to corporate planning, foundational marketing skills and experiences, and experience with operations at the headquarters level

Leadership Competencies to Be Developed

Business and strategy leadership, executive maturity, integrated marketing excellence, impact and influence, and cross-organization collaboration

Step 3: Finalize assignment details. In this step we facilitate a call between the host manager and the participant to discuss and agree on the assignment. This mutual contracting to understand the scope of the work and set expectations is important to ensuring a strong start. It is also when both parties agree on the best timing for the assignment to start and for the participant to be absent from his or her normal role.

Step 4: Logistics kickoff. Once we are clear on assignment details we kick off the visa and relocation discussions and outline the benefits that the participant will receive while on assignment. At this stage we also may bring in our compensation and benefits team to support the transition. To relieve the participants of as much administrative burden as possible, we assign a program coordinator to expedite the process and liaise with legal, tax, travel, housing, and benefits.

During the Assignment

While on assignment, participants are encouraged to focus on three support elements to ensure a positive learning experience. These include:

1. *On-Boarding.* At the start of the assignment a peer mentor is identified and key stakeholders are introduced. If needed we also offer cross-cultural training and local orientation services. At this stage it is also useful to identify local training that may be scheduled while the participants are on assignment, as it can be a very enriching experience to attend a workshop with other peers from across the corporate headquarters.

2. *On-Assignment Coaching.* In addition to regular one-on-one meetings with the host manager, we arrange for an external professional coach to conduct a monthly check-in. Each check-in serves a particular purpose:

   • *Setting the Stage:* The purpose of this session is for the coach and participant to get to know each other and identify the key learning intentions for each of the assignment objectives. Typical follow-up will be an e-mail with relevant resources for the participant to explore.

   • *Midpoint Check-in:* During this second session the coach reviews how things are going and probes to determine whether there are areas that require additional support. The coach also encourages the participant to begin reflecting on what he or she has learned. This is important, as many will focus on getting the work done and less time on extrapolating the learning.

   • *Final Session:* This entails a full discussion of the impact of the alignment, lessons learned, and how the participant can take them forward into their current and future roles when they return to their home teams.

3. *Re-Entry.* Typically, participants will return to their previous roles in the subsidiary, but occasionally there may have been organizational changes afoot while they were away on assignment. In these special circumstances we will take a proactive role in engaging with the home country human resource director and manager to ensure re-entry is smooth. Regardless of the role a participant goes back to, we encourage a broad presentation of their lessons learned to the subsidiary leadership team and peers.

There are multiple layers of benefit of this approach for each participant as summarized in Exhibit 13.2.

Impact

We measure the impact of the program directly after the experience and then track promotion velocity and career moves for all participants. The power of the learning experience is often immense and leaves participants with a much stronger appreciation of what it takes to operate in the complex setting of a corporate headquarters, for example, the scale at which one needs to think, the broader perspective that has to be taken, and the capability

Exhibit 13.2. Benefits of Participation in SHIP

For the Participant

- Provides leaders with a global perspective
- Generates accelerated and focused learning and perspective-building experience
- Provides access to senior corporate leaders
- Develops valuable personal network of relationships and resources

For the Corporate Host Organization

- Provides a way to "train" top talent in critical markets
- Builds a deep connection to those markets and stronger field collaboration
- Provides field perspective and influence on major projects

For the Home Country

- Increases knowledge and understanding of doing business at Microsoft at scale
- Provides an avenue to test the potential of talent in an unfamiliar environment
- Models a talent development mindset for critical talent

needed to "connect the dots." One participant was able to build consumer marketing scenarios, strategies, and activities for consumer segments and another was asked to operationalize a new services-sales strategy and prepare for global rollout. Regardless of the different experiences the participants went through, they are in unanimous agreement that the program will 100 percent support their future career advancement.

Host managers also find the experience rewarding and are willing to take on future participants, as they also benefit from a new team member with a different perspective. Effective assignments provide high potential talent with opportunities to step outside of their comfort zones and challenge themselves while implementing solutions to real problems. These stretch assignments accelerate their development, especially when they are exposed to different functions within the company or a different business group entirely.

Key business outcomes include personnel in emerging markets being able to build a strong network with their corporate-based peers, in addition to increased global fluency and a deeper understanding of the field at corporate. There is also a stronger leadership pipeline, with many participants taking key roles within twelve months of their return.

Lessons Learned

Following are a number of decision points and tips that may be helpful for practitioners, based on our experience:

Logistics can make or break the program. Make sure you have tapped into company resources that can support your needs for tax treaty advice, visa applications, relocation, and benefits. For example, we learned that the tax treaties between nations can affect how long someone is allowed to be on a work assignment. We also were able to gauge through the advice of immigration lawyers how long to allow for visa processing in each of the target countries, which can vary considerably.

Length of assignment is a key decision point. Work out what is best for your company culture; over the past few years we have gone from six- to three-month assignments, as we have found that the longer participants are away from their home country, the harder the re-entry.

Invest in an on-site coach to help maximize the participant learning. Quite often the participants are absorbing so much new information as they fulfill their deliverables that they need support to create some time to facilitate their reflection and maximize their learning. We create this time through both an individual coach and also through peer roundtable sessions, so participants can learn from each other.

Centrally funding the program, with no cost to the host organization, facilitates obtaining immersion opportunities for the participants. This funding covered travel, including one home trip during assignment, car rental, lodging, per diem meals, gym membership, driving and language lessons (if needed), as well as tax and visa assistance. The home country maintains payroll for the participant.

Where possible, maximize the participants' experience by helping them gain visibility to senior leaders in different settings. We manage this through tying the timing of the temporary assignments to key company events or processes.

We require that participants agree to return to their home subsidiary, whether it's to their original role or to a new role, at the end of the assignment. We stipulate this to allay the concerns of home-country managers who worry they may lose their employees to the corporate offices.

Use the coach to preempt any issues related to reintegration. It is the coach who may hear about pending changes in the home organization, which becomes an indicator for additional follow-up. It is also a great time for the subsidiary leader to schedule a one-on-one.

The position the participant is leaving behind also opens up a developmental opportunity for someone else on the team. Thus, managers are encouraged to think about how they can use this temporary absence to allow someone else to try a stretch assignment. Being able to leave your current role also says a lot about a participant; for example, one sales manager was able to demonstrate his ability to delegate by leaving his team to manage in the last quarter of the year.

Encourage peer learning. Because many participants are at corporate in a similar time-frame, we have been able to set up peer-learning sessions, which have presented a rich environment for reflection and learning.

The HRBPs are an invaluable resource. When brokering talent with assignment opportunities, they are the ones who are able to identify the target organization and the right host manager.

Full-Time Strategic Projects for High Potentials

Paul Orleman
SAP

I N 2006, SAP initiated a High Potential Fellowship Program. It has been notably successful in offering high potentials powerful real-world development opportunities. The fellowship program provides the opportunity for high potentials to step out of their roles for six months and work full time on strategic projects, usually in a different functional area or country. At the conclusion of a fellowship, the participant returns to his or her original role.

Initially, the concept was a hard sell. It went something like this: "We'd like to take away one of your most talented resources for six months. You will continue to pay his or her salary and bonus, and the individual will stay on your cost center. This person will continue to be counted as a headcount on your team, and you can't replace the missing headcount. The individual will return after six months." Despite this, six forward-thinking managers agreed to this development opportunity for individuals on their teams. Since then the program has grown steadily. As of October 2012, more than one thousand colleagues have served a fellowship.

The Process

Two six-month fellowship cycles are run each year—January through June and July through December. Several months before each cycle, managers are asked to identify fellowship "seats" (that is, opportunities in their areas for a fellow). The guidelines for defining a fellowship include: (1) a fellow should be assigned responsibility for a key project or subproject appropriate in scope for a six-month timeframe, and (2) someone on the receiving team must commit to serve as a manager/mentor who will manage, coach, and support the fellow during the assignment (with respect to both the project deliverables and the fellow's developmental goals).

The receiving team is given a job description template that helps it describe the mission, vision, and responsibilities of the sponsoring organization; the objectives and deliverables of the fellowship role; the background, skills, and experience a candidate should have; and the knowledge, skills, and competencies the fellowship assignment will help to build. For each fellowship position an HR contact is identified who will support the fellow and the manager/mentor.

A receiving team has several options for defining a fellowship. Some roles are defined as virtual; they can be performed by anyone from his or her home location. Other fellowship seats are based at a specific location and open only to candidates at that location. Certain fellowships are based at a specific location but open to global candidates. The receiving team determines whether they have the budget to fund relocating a fellow from another country. If they do, the receiving team assumes all costs associated with relocation: lodging, transportation, visa and work permits, per diems, and two trips home during the six months. Typically, 40 percent of the posted fellowships offer this option. The costs vary greatly depending on the home and host country combination. The range suggested to receiving teams is between $30,000 and $60,000 USD.

Fellowships are offered across all functional areas and cover a diverse range of projects. Exhibit 14.1 provides some examples.

Any manager has the option of defining a fellowship role. In the last cycle there were more than 450 fellowship opportunities posted. Some of the functional areas appoint a

---

Exhibit 14.1. Examples of SAP Fellowships

- Design and implement a plan to educate the field sales team on a key new product.
- Create an active community of executive thought leaders within the SAP customer base.
- Build mobile apps on different devices and tablets for the next generation of CRM application in the cloud.
- Work as part of the learning team and in partnership with the various SAP internal universities to insure there is a role-based curricula in place for all employees.
- Plan and run a competition to "bubble up" the creative demo ideas from all areas of SAP, identify the best, and promote them for re-use.
- Manage the projects and programs to execute the Middle East-North Africa regional growth plan strategy.

coordinator to screen all fellowship jobs to ensure they align with the functional area's strategic goals. Others opt to allow any manager to submit a job description directly to the fellowship program team. Fellowship job descriptions are collected by the program team and posted in SAP's internal eRecruiting system, in a restricted area accessible only to high potentials.

Once all the job requisitions are created, the cycle is launched via an e-mail to all high potentials, announcing the launch of the fellowship application cycle. Any high potential, at any level, has the option of considering a fellowship opportunity. Interested high potentials talk to their direct managers to determine whether a fellowship supports their development goals and to discuss how their home responsibilities could be covered during a six-month absence.

Teams have identified a number of creative ways to cover a fellow's absence. In some cases, the work is divided among other team members. Consultants may begin a fellowship when a customer engagement concludes. Some teams that are "losing" a high potential will offer a fellowship seat to cover their fellow's absence.

If the high potential and the direct manager agree that a fellowship opportunity aligns with the individual's development goals, the high potential can apply. Manager/mentors at receiving teams accept online applications, determine whether to interview an applicant, conduct interviews, and then make offers to viable candidates. When a fellowship seat is filled, the job posting is withdrawn from the eRecruiting system.

As a fellowship cycle is about to begin, information is provided to help ensure success for fellows and receiving team manager/mentors. For example, fellows have live and recorded info-sessions; manager/mentors and fellows receive on-boarding guides; and there are kick-off lunches at sites with large fellow populations.

One tool that has proved particularly beneficial is an online fellowship community on SAP's intranet. The community is open to past, present, and future fellows. Those who are beginning fellowships can ask questions to colleagues who have been through the experience. Fellows, both past and present, use the community to network, arrange lunch meetings, and share information and ideas. The fellowship-program team uses the site to get information to strengthen the program. For example, it has asked, "What makes an attractive (and an unattractive) fellowship?" The responses were used to create guidelines for managers who want to offer fellowship seats.

As a fellowship begins, the fellow and the receiving team manager clarify performance objectives for the fellowship and the learning and development goals for the fellow; a simple template is provided for this. At the year-end performance review, the receiving manager/mentor serves as an "additional appraiser" to ensure the individual's contributions during the fellowship are taken into account.

At the conclusion of their assignments, fellows write reports summarizing their accomplishments and lessons learned. The reports are shared with the fellowship manager/mentor and home-team manager. Many fellows choose to share these reports with a broader audience: the fellowship team, home team, and other fellows (via the online fellowship community).

A Highly Selective Process

The recruiting process is highly selective on the part of both the applicants and the receiving team managers. In each cycle quite a few positions do not receive a single application, while others receive dozens. In each cycle the jobs that generate high interest and those that generate no interest are monitored. This information is communicated to all managers at the start of the subsequent cycle in order to give guidance for crafting interesting positions. For example, fellows were asked what they looked for when considering a fellowship opportunity. Their responses included the following: (1) responsibility for a key project or subproject; (2) a role that extends one's understanding of SAP; (3) the chance to work in a different country or culture; (4) wide business exposure (across a region, management, and teams); (5) a manager/mentor who spends time coaching and helping one to succeed; (6) the ability to exercise and refine existing skills, and to add new ones as well; (7) a position that offers the potential for a new job opportunity; (8) a high-visibility project in terms of strategic impact, and the opportunity to work directly with a senior leader; (9) the chance for intensive networking, with customers, partners, SAP colleagues, and locals; and (10) a deep exposure to a different functional area.

Fellows also were quite clear about positions that were less appealing. They didn't want a position that has all the tasks that other members of the team don't like; a position that is too broad, covering a lot of activities with no clear strategic impact; a role that sounds like being somebody's helper at a desk for six months rather than being a driver and making new things happen; and a role with a manager who does not spend any time with the fellow and provides little guidance or direction. In the last cycle, 25 percent of the 450 posted positions had no applications.

The process is also selective in terms of the choices that receiving team manager/mentors make. Receiving manager/mentors have very high standards and expectations when it comes to candidates. Out of the 338 jobs that received applications, only 179 offers were made, and 157 of those offers were accepted by candidates. Based on the experience with the past few cycles, I would expect SAP to fill about 160 fellowships each cycle.

Benefits and Return on Investment

A fellowship can provide multiple benefits. The fellow gains breadth of knowledge and builds new skills by working in a substantially different arena, focusing on key strategic topics. The assignments stretch fellows. They often describe the experience as challenging and very powerful, and use adjectives such as *amazing, incredible, fantastic, extraordinary, energizing,* and *life-changing.*

The receiving team benefits from a talented resource that often brings new approaches and ideas and makes a strong contribution toward strategy execution. Receiving manager/mentors often cite the refreshing perspective, passion, and eye-opening ideas a fellow can bring.

The sending manager gives up a key resource for six months, but a returning fellow brings new knowledge and connections back to the home team, which often has a strong payoff. As one manager put it, "The fellow returned with new skills, knowledge, confidence, and connections that have paid off for our organization countless times."

From an organizational perspective, the fellowship program helps break down silos and provides high potentials with a broader perspective of the global organization. For some it is their first time working outside their native country. Others experience life outside their usual functional worldview; a developer may experience things from the sales perspective, benefiting from the chance to work with external customers extensively. A fellowship can provide a valuable experience for someone on a general manager development track.

In a recent survey, fellows were asked what happened in terms of their career following their fellowship assignment. See Table 14.1 for their responses.

Continued Experimentation

SAP is experimenting with fellowship projects outside of the organization. In conjunction with our Corporate Social Responsibility department, three fellows were sent to support Ghanaian farmers producing shea butter, primarily women, with mobile technology delivered in the cloud, to provide a more secure income. Shorter-term "social sabbaticals" have also been piloted. Recently, nine high potentials were sent to Belo Horizonte, Brazil, where

Table 14.1. Fellows' Post-Fellowship Careers

	I returned to my previous job and I am currently in that role.	20 percent
	I returned to my previous position but have taken on significant additional responsibilities.	17 percent
Relative to the role you had before your Fellowship, where are you now?	I was promoted to a higher-level position in my home organization or line of business.	14 percent
	I moved to an additional role in my original line of business.	11 percent
	I moved to a different role in a different line of business (but not connected to my fellowship).	20 percent
	I have accepted an offer from my fellowship team and have joined that organization.	17 percent

they worked in teams with three NGOs—an association of garbage collectors, an organization that empowers people with disabilities, and an institution that supports artisans by exporting their products internationally. Finally, SAP sponsored a high potential fellowship exchange with a customer, sending one of its high potentials to work for six months in the customer's organization, and offering a six-month assignment within SAP to one of the customer's high potentials.

Keys to Success

I would offer the following advice to any organization considering a similar program:

- Start small, assess results, and improve things each cycle.

- Carefully plan the communication required for all stakeholders: candidates, the managers of candidates, receiving team manager/mentors, HR business partners who will support each fellowship team, and global-mobility specialists who will support the relocation for fellows.

- Define the roles and clarify the expectations for all players.

- Investigate and communicate the benefits realized. This helps market the initiative.

- Work to build executive sponsorship for the initiative. Many managers will welcome the opportunity to create a fellowship role and benefit from a talented resource for six months; fewer managers initially will be willing to give up their best players while continuing to pay their salaries. Emphasize that this is a developmental opportunity for someone flagged as having the capacity for bigger and broader leadership. Enlist the executive sponsorship to emphasize the long-term value of the short-term cost.

- Connect past fellows with current fellows. Having lived through the experience, the former provide the best answers and advice for the latter.

15

A Personalized Rotation Program to Develop Future Leaders

Bela Tisoczki and Laurie Bevier
General Electric

TWO YEARS AGO, General Electric (GE) launched a leadership development program that brings a new approach by combining the strengths of structured rotational programs with customized individual development. In this contribution, we describe the context, the program structure, and the early experiences with the program.

Context

For a long time, job-rotation programs have been a key method for developing employees at GE. In a number of the organization's functional areas, rotational programs for newly hired college and professional school graduates are well regarded and attract a high number of applicants (for example, the company's Financial Management Program). Rotational programs are also used to develop more experienced employees. A primary reason that job rotations are such a central feature of GE's development system is the strong belief across the organization that development comes from experience. These programs are well accepted and supported by management, and they provide an integral part of functional talent pipeline development. About 48 percent of the members of the Corporate Executive Committee, GE's top leadership team, have graduated from a rotational program.

A typical job rotation program design at GE entails a set of defined-length assignments within the given functional area. For example, the Financial Management Program consists of four six-month rotations across different finance jobs and may take place across diverse business units. The goal of these programs is to develop the future leadership pipeline within the given function.

One of the most important experienced-level development programs in the company has been Corporate Audit Staff (CAS), the internal audit function of GE. Employees who join CAS work there two or more years full-time. They participate in four-month audits, both financial and process ones. These assignments spread across the globe and cover all the divisions of GE from the industrial businesses to the financial services arm of the company. The assignments provide an excellent opportunity and a steep learning curve to gain knowledge about the business as well as the organization. High performance is expected from participants; however, it is also enabled by frequent assessment, feedback, and training. Typically, CAS graduates take management positions when they move back to the business and keep rising afterward.

In recent years GE senior management started to recognize an emerging need. CAS has been excellent for growing finance-minded leaders in the company who looked at the business through a strong, financials-driven analytical lens. Over time CAS conducted fewer process audits, and the finance focus was represented more heavily. Senior management recognized that GE also needed an additional pipeline that comes from a different background and would look at business processes from a different perspective. They recognized a need for leaders with deeper domain expertise in technical and business knowledge. Although CAS remains a key leadership pipeline for leaders, a new program, Corporate Leadership Staff (CLS), was created to build a pipeline of business leaders with industry expertise.

The new program was launched with the objective to provide talent with operational, commercial, and technical expertise with opportunities similar to those provided by CAS. Its aim is to accelerate the development of high potential talent in these non-finance-related fields and enable them to lead business units in the future within the company. CLS took over many best practices from the existing programs, but it moves rotational programs to the next level: It combines previously used program elements with a personalized development approach.

Program Design

Similar to other leadership programs, members are carefully selected. Nominations happen through GE's annual succession planning and talent review process. A candidate must have a bachelor's degree (or equivalent) in an engineering, business, or technical field and at least four years of work experience in GE with an exceptional track record of performance that has already demonstrated achievement in the commercial, technical, or operations function.

The person has to be seen as high potential with demonstrated ability to manage multiple responsibilities, including rigorous assignment, training, and project work. Geographic mobility and willingness to live outside one's home country is also a condition.

Several key design features were built into the program:

1. *Full-time cross-functional assignments.* Although there are other GE full-time, assignment-based rotational programs, most of them operate within a specific function. The specialty of CLS is that, while participants stay in their industry segment (that is, business division), they work in roles in different functions.

2. *Individualized development.* A major novelty of the new program in comparison to the previous ones is that CLS is highly customized to the participants. This recognizes the fact that program members have diverse backgrounds and operate in very different business segments. The high-priority business assignments are selected according to the development needs of the individual, and even the lengths of the rotations are customized. As a consequence, the duration of the program is not the same for everybody. Program members remain on CLS for two to five years, and program completion is dependent on demonstrating leadership capabilities, rather than on spending a certain time in the program or on completing a number of defined length assignments. In effect, the program consists of a series of full-time jobs that develop the program participants and broaden their horizons. The jobs include rotations in multiple functions. For example, one participant with an operations background moved to work in a position in sales and later in product management. Since developing a global mindset is also a key objective, participants go through an international assignment, too, if they have previously missed such an experience.

3. *Capability assessment framework.* The consistency across the program is provided by a capability assessment framework, which focuses on five areas: growth, leadership, operational excellence, capital efficiency, and domain expertise. It includes capabilities in these areas that have been identified as required for successful GE business leaders (see Figure 15.1). For each capability a behavioral definition and a required proficiency level is set. Furthermore, information is provided on possible assignments, projects, and training that can help in developing a selected capability. The same framework is used to assess the skill gaps of the participants as well as evaluating their progress. Finally, it also serves to evaluate if participants are ready to graduate from the program.

4. *Leveraging relationships.* Another important element of the individualized development approach is that, while in the program, each participant is paired with a senior manager who acts as an executive coach. These senior managers have strong track records as leaders as well as talent developers. When the

Figure 15.1. Capability Matrix

CORPORATE
LEADERSHIP
STAFF

CAPABILITY	DEVELOPMENT ASSIGNMENTS			TRAINING	PROJECTS
	PROD. MGMT	SALES/MKTG	OPERATIONS		
GROWTH					
Go to Market	✓	✓		✓	
Strategy and Innovation	✓	✓		✓	✓
Technology	✓			✓	
OPERATIONAL EXCELLENCE					
Processes and Quality Systems	✓		✓	✓	
Supply Chain	✓		✓	✓	
Financial Performance	✓		✓	✓	✓
Risk Management			✓	✓	
CAPITAL EFFICIENCY					
Capital Allocation	✓	✓	✓	✓	
Cash Generation	✓	✓	✓	✓	✓
Inorganic Growth	✓	✓	✓	✓	
LEADERSHIP					
Growth Values	✓	✓	✓	✓	
Managing People			✓	✓	
Managing the Matrix	✓	✓		✓	✓
Communication	✓	✓	✓	✓	
Change Management	✓	✓	✓	✓	
Project Management	✓	✓	✓	✓	

program starts, they go through a joint workshop with the participants. The senior managers are trained in coaching, and the program participants have the opportunity to establish a relationship with their coaches. At the same event the executive coach helps the participant build an individual development plan—including assignment and project options—based on the capability gaps and the career interest of the participant. Following the kick-off workshop, the pairs keep frequent contact (many of them talk every two weeks) to discuss challenges, learning, and progress. Regular feedback and assessments are an integral part of the program and happen both in connection with the individual assignments as well as the program seminars. The individual development plans are continually reviewed and adjusted in the light of this feedback.

Integrated with the Business

Launching a new assignment-based leadership development program is not easy. If it is not supported by the key stakeholders and the overall organization, it is doomed to fail. Although CLS is managed by corporate resources, it is designed as a program that happens in a given business and it was created to serve the needs of that business. In order to integrate CLS from the beginning with the organization, the program has been developed and managed together with a group of business stakeholders. From each of the six GE businesses there have been business champions as well as program managers appointed. They, together with the corporate team, shape and manage CLS. The idea is to accomplish a balance between business ownership and corporate program management.

Although program participants belong to a corporate program, they maintain a strong alignment to their business units. They are nominated and sponsored by their businesses while on program. They do their rotations in their businesses, and that is also where they are expected to move into their first off-program job to take a senior position. On the other hand, all of them participate in the same program structure and are part of the program participant network and online community. Furthermore, they attend the joint program seminars twice a year. Based on the participants' feedback, this peer network is one of the most valuable elements of the program. The members utilize the cross-functional and cross-business expertise of this highly capable group and they leverage each other when they face challenges or need help in a new functional area during their assignments. As a result of this embedded approach, CLS participants benefit from the support and interaction with corporate leadership, an extensive peer network, business assignment managers, business champions, business program managers, and dedicated business coaches.

Initial Insights

Although the program has been running only for a short time relative to the time that is required to make full impact, some lessons have already been learned from it.

First, because the CLS program was new, there wasn't an IT system to provide a platform to manage it. In fact, there is a doubt to what extent there could be. In a certain sense the CLS program philosophy goes against the current industry trend of standardizing (and so automating) talent management processes. The program has to be highly individualized. The participants come with different backgrounds, they operate in different domains, and they have different development needs. The underlying philosophy is that individualization of the learning experience brings the highest impact. This poses a significant challenge for program administration. As a program manager put it, "It is like running a mini-college program with individuals taking individual tracks."

Although the processes are difficult to standardize and they remain labor-intensive, the program management saw an opportunity to automate the development plans and have therefore developed a tool to track the individual assignments, training, and projects. That said, the emphasis remains on ensuring the appropriate return on the effort by keeping the program very selective and focusing on the quality of the candidates, the support provided, and the assignments.

Second, the program has been launched globally and based on a global participant pool. This pool is very diverse and includes participants from different functions, industries, and geographies. Although the capabilities framework has proven to be effective for creating a standard approach to capability building, there is an emerging need to accommodate the specificities of different market contexts. The challenge is particularly visible in growth markets. In those regions, such as China, India, Latin America, and Middle East, the market realities are completely different. The rotation opportunities are different, the business challenges are different, and candidates have different profiles compared to the more developed markets. To bring full benefits for the local business organizations, the program needs to reflect this diversity. It needs to do more than merely adjust the profile of the candidates or the management of the assignments. It must also help participants develop some market-specific leadership skills. Even a strong alignment with an industry may not be enough. In some cases the exposure has to be more regional and not limited to one industry in order to enable building the desired skill set or career path.

This raises the point that certain experiences may be more important for participants, depending on which market they are coming from. To give an example, in China the company operates through many joint ventures. Effectively managing a joint venture is key for future leaders in China, while it has little importance in other markets. In fact, in this market it is a *must-have* skill. The current capability model already recognizes the mix of leadership skills that future leaders need, depending on whether they operate in a growth, stable, or shrinking market. However, the regional specificities are not yet reflected to the desired level. If the program fails to build the market-specific capabilities, it may undermine its future success.

To date, more than 120 high potentials have participated in the program. Their experience with the program is very positive. They feel that it is highly developmental and that it opens new perspectives for them. As one expressed, "The program moves me into areas I would have never thought of." Of course, participant feedback is just one aspect of program assessment. The ultimate results will show over time as program participants take on, and succeed in, senior management positions.

16

Corporate Volunteerism as an Avenue for Leadership Development

Shannon M. Wallis
Arrow Leadership Strategies
Jeffrey J. McHenry
Rainier Leadership Solutions

EXPERIENTIAL LEARNING IS one of the most impactful ways to develop leaders. However, finding meaningful experiences that provide real world challenges outside the workplace, where developing leaders may feel more comfortable and safer practicing new skills, can be daunting. Enter corporate volunteerism programs, a growing trend in leadership development. Corporate volunteerism programs are skill-based volunteer programs that are usually aligned with a firm's Corporate Social Responsibility (CSR) initiatives. Although not exclusively, many programs are focused on nongovernmental organizations (NGOs), social enterprises, and educational institutions found in emerging markets.

According to CDC Development Solutions (2012), the annual growth rate of corporate volunteerism programs since 2006 is 52 percent. In fact, the number of countries visited by these volunteerism programs has grown from four countries in 2006 to sixty-two countries in 2012.

Corporate volunteerism programs bring many benefits to a firm, including increased staff motivation and retention, professional skill growth, better understanding and increased knowledge of opportunities and challenges in emerging markets, substantive improvements in communities where the organization has projects, and enhancement of the firm's image both internally and externally. If done well, the benefits for leaders are substantial. Corporate volunteerism programs enable leaders to build a more global perspective, develop an understanding of national competitiveness, and demonstrate a commitment to corporate citizenship.

Projects come in many varieties. IBM's Corporate Service Corps consists of teams of eight to fifteen high potential leaders who work with government, business, and civic leaders in emerging markets to help address high-priority issues over a one-month period (Litow, 2012; see *Developing Socially Responsible Global Leaders Through Service Projects* on page 107 of this book). In comparison, Microsoft's award-winning Front Lines™ program teams two to three high potential Microsoft executives with a similar number of executives from selected NGOs, social enterprises, and government agencies to solve urgent business problems during a three-day immersive and six-week follow-up virtual experience ("Global impact," 2011).

While there are many ways to develop leaders through these experiences, a key factor in the success of volunteerism programs is securing appropriate internal and external partners for the experience itself. Leadership development professionals struggle with how to identify and select both internal and external partners as well as business challenges that best serve the objectives of their programs. While organizations such as United Planet, Emerging World, and CDC Development Solutions have strong connections to potential agencies, they don't necessarily know the agencies that are best aligned with a firm's strategic objectives or the learning objectives of the firm's leadership development programs. Decisions about internal and external partners must be made by the firm's leadership development team.

Identifying and Selecting Partners

The following steps can help leadership development professionals identify and select the partners who are the best fit for their firm's program.

Step 1: Determine Learning Objectives for the Program

Before any work is done identifying and screening potential partners, the firm must establish learning objectives for the development experience. This may seem like an obvious step, but we have observed organizations get so carried away in their excitement about working with a particular development agency or executive education partner that they fail to take the time to determine whether that partner is a good fit for their learning objectives.

Here are some questions that may be useful to organizations seeking to clarify the learning objectives for their development program:

- What leadership competencies should the program help build (e.g., cultural awareness, interpersonal skills, customer insights)?

Figure 16.1. Selecting a Target That Meets the Firm's Learning Goals

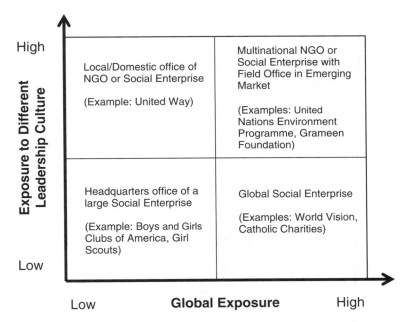

- What critical developmental experiences should leaders gain through the program (e.g., run a business where the leader has little or no business/functional expertise, work in a staff role, work outside one's home country)?

Typically, one of the learning goals of a volunteerism program is to broaden the way that leaders approach business and organizational challenges by exposing them to work in a very different culture. Thus, a key question facing program designers is what cultural boundaries they want leaders to cross as part of their volunteerism experience. For example, do they want to expose leaders to a nonprofit organizational culture, where the motives and values of the organization and its workforce likely differ significantly from the motives and values of those working in a for-profit firm? Or do the program designers want to expose leaders to people or a culture outside their home country in the hopes that it will make the leaders more globally aware? Figure 16.1 shows how the answers to these questions will help to identify the potential partner organizations that are best fit for a firm's program.

Step 2: Establish Criteria for Evaluating and Selecting Partners

The learning objectives in Step 1 lead directly to the most important criterion for evaluating and selecting partners: To what extent will this partner help and enable the organization to achieve the desired learning objectives for the volunteerism program?

It's important to specify at this point whether the volunteer experience should (or should not) be relevant to the firm's core businesses. Some firms choose to provide volunteerism experiences that are completely unrelated to the company's businesses because they want leaders to operate in an environment that is completely new and different. Others prefer or focus exclusively on projects that relate to the firm's core business. For example, every volunteer project selected for Microsoft's Front Lines™ program includes an information technology (IT) component. This makes the projects more engaging and job-relevant for participants, enhances senior leader support for the program, makes it easier to recruit very committed internal partners (see Step 3), and has the side benefit of helping participants learn more about IT challenges in emerging markets.

Beyond this, there may be other practical and logistical considerations in selecting a partner (e.g., the scope and duration of the volunteerism assignment, travel time and expenses, and the number of volunteers the partner is able to successfully "manage" and deploy).

Step 3: Identify and Select Potential Internal Partners

Internal partners are typically found in three areas of the business: Corporate Social Responsibility (CSR) groups, sales organizations, and research and development groups responsible for new product introduction.

CSR groups, usually housed within a Corporate Affairs department, are often in an excellent position to partner. CSR groups typically focus their attention on local communities near the firm's headquarters location or in other locations where the firm has a very large number of employees, but some CSR groups in large multinational firms are engaged in global issues and are involved in CSR work all around the world. CSR programs generate positive press coverage and good relationships with local authorities, and CSR staff are well-versed in how to manage any situations that might result in sudden damage to the firm's reputation. CSR program administrators are familiar with the CSR objectives of the firm and know the types of agencies or initiatives that have been targeted for strategic purposes. The CSR group's relationships with these targets enable the CSR group to better assess the need within those agencies and the types of problems that might be present. They can work with leadership development professionals to match the objectives of the CSR program with the objectives of the leadership development experience to help ensure that participants have a beneficial learning experience.

Sales organizations are another option to consider, especially those based in the BRIC countries (Brazil, Russia, India, and China) or emerging markets in Latin America, Africa, and Asia. If the firm has a particular focus for its CSR and corporate citizenship activities (e.g., health care, affordable education, or technology), that focus usually will be cascaded down to the firm's regional and national sales subsidiaries. The subsidiaries will be engaged in local CSR initiatives that serve their local markets and highlight the firm's brand and commitment to the community. Regional and national subsidiaries will likely welcome the opportunity to work with a volunteerism program if it will enable the subsidiaries to make progress on their CSR initiatives or provide a "value added" service such as "free consulting from a team of our high potential leaders" to their customers and CSR partners. It is an easy way for them to differentiate their organization from the competition. Another possible partner within the sales organization is a vertical sales team focused on NGO customers. The NGO sales team may already be helping their customers who are involved in work that lends itself readily to volunteerism projects (e.g., economic development, health care, energy conservation, environmental protection). Like sales subsidiaries, they may jump at the opportunity to partner with a leadership development program that will enable them to provide their customer with free consulting and attention.

Finally, research and development (R&D) groups can be an excellent internal partner option. Continually seeking new product ideas and ways to innovate, R&D groups may be interested in sending or sponsoring a team of leaders to travel to an emerging market to do volunteer work and simultaneously conduct ethnographic observations that spur creative thinking about possible R&D ventures. They may have strategic R&D partners or customers headquartered or deeply embedded in emerging markets who are interested in helping design and support a leadership development project.

The criteria developed in Step 2 can be used to help evaluate and select the internal partners who can best support and contribute to the success of the volunteerism program.

Step 4: Secure External Partners

Securing external partners requires as much if not more attention than selection of internal partners. Once the firm identifies internal partners, those partners will want to be involved in the selection of external partners.

It's useful to step back at this point and have a discussion with the internal partners about the criteria (Step 2) that will be used to evaluate and select targets. There may be some additional criteria the firm considers in choosing external partners, such as their capability and capacity to engage in a project of this nature, and whether they have a real and urgent business problem to solve. We have heard a number of stories about prospective nonprofit partners who are doing outstanding work, but don't have the experience or know-how required to use a team of senior-level leaders effectively on a volunteer project, and have not given adequate thought to the problem they would like the leaders to help them solve. Useful questions for evaluating external partners include:

- Does the external partner have senior leaders who would welcome and promote this type of partnership?

- Does the external partner have leaders who need development in complementary areas?

- Does the external partner have associates with the capacity to engage in this type of project?

- Does the external partner have a real and urgent business problem to solve?

Of all these considerations, selecting the business problem should be of utmost concern. Firms should avoid selecting problems that are already being worked by another team inside the firm or the external partner. If there is another team already working on the problem, either find a different problem or find a way to include the volunteerism program participants in the team already working the problem. The risk of having two separate teams "owning" the problem is that the leaders participating in the volunteerism program may decide that they are "dispensable" and invest little effort in their problem. This minimizes the urgency and does not create the best learning environment for participants because they have no "skin in the game."

Ideally, there will be a "problem owner" in the external partner organization who feels a real and urgent business need to solve the problem—it should be part of the problem owner's job description or one of his or her annual objectives. It's even better if the problem owner has made little to no headway yet on the problem. The problem should be critical to the target organization's success, a matter of passionate interest to its leaders, and within the target organization's accountability and scope of impact.

Another consideration may be whether the external partner is involved in work that is directly relevant to the firm's strategic business objectives. For example, is it possible that cooperation with a particular external partner on a volunteerism program could lead to new business opportunities or growth in an existing business, to better relationships between the firm and key government officials, or to goodwill or recognition that helps the firm achieve its CSR goals regionally or in a specific country?

Again, once a list of prospective external partners has been identified, the criteria from Step 2 and the additional considerations and criteria listed above should be used to select the best target(s) for the volunteerism projects.

Step 5: Conclude Project and Follow Up with External Partners

The main work of the project begins following Step 4. If all goes well, participants will immerse themselves in a deep understanding of the problem and work with the external partner to develop and help implement solutions that enable the external partner to better achieve its organizational mission.

Once most project work has been completed, it's important to follow up with the external partner to gather feedback and decide on any next steps. To begin, the project team should determine whether the external partner was satisfied with project outcomes and how the project was conducted. For example:

- Was the work completed appropriately, and were the deliverables in line with the external partner's expectations?

- Were the various phases of the project—contracting, planning, problem solving, and implementation—completed efficiently and effectively?

- Were there any unpleasant surprises along the way?

- What was the quality of partnership between project team and external partner staff?

- What advice would the external partner have for the future?

- Would the external partner be interested in doing something like this again, if the right opportunity arose?

Second, the project team should inquire whether the external partner might be a positive reference for the firm. Can the external partner give a clear account of how their organization and the stakeholders they serve benefited from the project? Would the external partner be willing to share their experience with the news media, be cited in press releases and articles, or provide reference to other prospective partners? It's very useful to include the firm's Corporate Affairs or CSR staff in these conversations.

Third, the project team should examine whether the project revealed any new business opportunities for the firm with the external partner, with a government agency, or with another organization. The account representative who supports the external partner should be very involved in these conversations, possibly along with one or more staff working in the country where the work was done. We know some leadership development professionals become uneasy at the idea that their firm might "exploit" a corporate volunteerism project to increase sales and profits; however, our experience is that external partners are very appreciative of these conversations. Their chief interests are serving their clients and achieving their mission. They will be delighted if the corporate volunteer project points to ways that they can do this more effectively by doing more business with the firm.

Conclusion

When firms follow these five steps to selecting great partners and business problems, the learning experience for leaders can be exceptional. The most impactful learning and development experiences happen on the job because the problems are real and challenging and the stakes are high. Corporate volunteerism projects with NGOs, social enterprises, and educational institutions in emerging markets are a great alternative approach to professional and leadership skill development because the learning experience has very similar urgency to on-the-job learning. By providing meaningful options for development that involve real-world challenges and an opportunity to practice new skills outside the workplace in a relatively safe environment, volunteerism projects prepare leaders for future success as they do good work for society.

References

CDC Development Solutions. (2012). *International corporate volunteerism benchmarking study 2012.* Washington, DC: CDC Development Solutions.

Global impact submission: Front lines—partnership between Microsoft and Emerging World. (2011). *Global Focus: The EFMD Business Magazine, 5*, 25–28.

Litow, S. (2012, November 14). Global volunteerism is good for business. *The Atlantic.* Retrieved from www.theatlantic.com/international/archive/2012/11/global-volunteerism-is-good -for-business/265166/

17

Developing Socially Responsible Global Leaders Through Service Projects

Mathian Osicki and Caroline Smee
IBM

IN 2007, IBM was immersed in a period of great change. The CEO at the time, Samuel Palmisano, expressed the desire to advance the company into the new era of globalization. IBM was a multinational company, but it needed to act as a globally integrated enterprise, not simply an American company with offices scattered in other nations, and it needed to function in a more globally savvy and responsible way. Palmisano initiated several programs to further IBM's globalization goals, but felt there was still more to be done. He consulted the Corporate Citizenship and Corporate Affairs team (CC&CA) about possible additional efforts. Led by Stanley Litow, this internal group develops strategies to further business goals in a socially and environmentally responsible manner. They pinpointed the need for a corporate citizenship project where employees could develop skills and have global experiences while advancing business objectives. The group reached out to IBM's employees and asked how globalization affected them. A large amount of feedback and suggestions were generated but none as promising as the Corporate Service Corps.

In its simplest form, the Corporate Service Corps involves a small group of IBM employees from around the world getting to know each other and gaining training and development virtually through social media and online learning for a three-month period. This primary development all leads up to the group traveling to a developing nation, where they spend thirty days doing pro bono work for an underprivileged community. After that month in the field, the IBM employees return to their day jobs and share what they learned with their colleagues.

Kevin Thompson, a thirty-four-year-old manager at IBM, came up with this dynamic idea that fit CC&CA's tall order. He envisioned a program where exceptional IBM employees traveled to developing countries to share their skills in short-term service projects. The idea was primarily inspired by two programs Thompson had taken part in. The Peace Corps, a nonprofit organization that sends Americans to remote locations globally to serve communities in need, was the first major source of inspiration for Thompson (Mirvis, Thompson, & Gohring, 2012). Their mission is to achieve world peace and make friendships; this mission helped to generate the global service aspects of the new IBM program. The Outdoor Leadership School inspired the leadership development aspect, which would become central to the new program's mission. The Outdoor Leadership School is an organization that companies send their employees through to promote leadership skills. Participants are sent into nature for a few days and are expected to work together, make decisions, do activities, and explore. The natural environment and uncertain terrain is perfect for leadership development. Team building is strong because participants spend all their time together. The "no electronics" rule gives participants peace and clarity to reflect and think forward (Kanengieter & Rajagopal-Durbin, 2012). These two innovative programs were the major inspiration behind the Corporate Service Corps. This cultivation of leadership in a socially responsible and business minded way was the innovative idea IBM needed to help pursue its mission of becoming a globally integrated enterprise.

From the inception of his idea, Thompson worked hard to put the Corporate Service Corps into action. Initially, there was the challenge of figuring out how to convince the leadership team of a publically traded company that a program with no immediate economic benefit was a good use of shareholder dollars. It was the popularity of the program that eventually sold itself. Thompson convinced the rest of the company that the Corporate Service Corps was essential to leadership development at IBM, and this bottom-up approach was successful and led to upper management accepting the idea. After Thompson figured out plans such as the format, selection process, NGO partnerships, pre-work, and logistics, the program was announced in July of 2007. It was geared to the youngest third of IBM's workforce. They expected approximately five hundred applications for the first assignment in 2008. In the end, 5,500 people applied, which was the first sign of the great success the program would have.

Program Design

In the program, ten to fifteen high-performing IBM employees are placed into developing parts of global growth markets to share their knowledge and skills in the betterment of the community. For instance, people have been sent to Calabar in the Cross River State of Nigeria, Davao City in The Philippines, and multiple areas across Ghana. Each project extends six months in three parts. The first part involves three months of prep work. Teammates are introduced and encouraged to get to know each other through social media and videoconferencing. Biweekly meetings are held to plan and prepare for their task. Fifty hours of materials are allotted with information on the culture of the community, nature of the project, travel plans, team building, and consulting tactics. These are received through a learning software delivery platform (Mirvis, Thompson, & Gohring, 2012).

The next step is the in-country portion of the assignment, which lasts one month. Typically, two weeks are used to gather information from stakeholders, and the remaining two weeks are spent making plans and executing them. The team is usually sent to the client location to work among the clients for the month they are in country. The ten to fifteen IBM employees are broken into groups of two or three people, with their own assignments and client sets. At the end of the thirty days, the small teams each make presentations to their clients on their recommended actions.

The final step of the full assignment consists of two months of follow-up where employees share what they have learned with their peers and begin to enact the skills they have acquired and sharpened. These two months generally lead to a lifetime of impact on each of the potential future leaders selected.

Benefits

The list of benefits that result from instituting a program like the Corporate Service Corps is extensive, with one of the main rewards being the cultivation of future leaders. The demanding situations these employees are put into are ideal for the development of many leadership skills, including:

- *Dealing with uncertainty:* For instance, consider the uncertainty of being placed in a remote village with a team of people you just met and with the task of bettering a community. This kind of situation pushes people out of their comfort zones. They learn to make decisions in ambiguous situations and to be comfortable taking risks. They also learn from the inevitable mistakes made in such situations. And the situation encourages teammates to learn to lean on each other.

- *Team skills:* Participants undergo living, working, and eating with other team members. This element of the experience fosters bonding among them. The global networks they build will serve them well in future roles and leadership positions at IBM.

- *Diversity sensitivity:* Learning to work with and for people with diverse backgrounds is another major leadership skill honed in the Corporate Service

Corps. Being a leader at IBM requires global knowledge and experience. The time spent with such team members and in emerging market cultures is extremely beneficial for a future leader to call on.

- *Getting to know the business:* With 400,000 plus employees in IBM, it is difficult to know what every corner of the company is responsible for. This program helps expose future potential leaders to some of the other work that takes place globally in different parts of the organization.

Another critical aspect of the program is that there is no defined leader in the project groups, which is based on an aspect of the Outdoor Leadership School that forces every member to take responsibility and step up at different times and in different ways. Participants also learn when to divert leadership to another person, a skill that becomes clear in times of uncertainty and should be replicated in day-to-day business. Because participants are less connected in terms of texting and reliable Internet, they have the ability to be in the moment with greater clarity (Kanengieter & Rajagopal-Durbin, 2012). This is a gift that many participants will not experience again in their lifetimes.

Aside from the extensive benefits in leadership development, the Corporate Services Corps positively impacts IBM, the community, and the individual in other ways. Across the world, remote parts of growth market countries receive free IBM services. A few examples of projects include the implementation of free health care to reduce the mortality rate in the Cross River State of Nigeria, the development of an online marketing service and a potential investment database in The Philippines, and the realization of an eco-tourism industry in Tanzania. These projects have changed and saved lives.

IBM employees get joy and a sense of satisfaction and accomplishment from knowing how meaningful their efforts are. Participants are able to experience new cultures, serve others, and make new friends in addition to the important goal of developing skills essential for future leadership. IBM as a company gains more than just great leaders. They are giving their employees an experience that makes them appreciative and more loyal, which leads them to stay at IBM longer. Not only does IBM retain talent through the Corporate Service Corps, but the publicity of the program attracts new talent (Gordon, 2011). IBM is promoting their brand name in emerging markets, critical areas for potential future business. Many villages where projects occurred hadn't heard of IBM until the team arrived. Furthermore, IBM is showing the world that they are a socially responsible company. For the children whose lives were saved with the help of Corporate Service Corps volunteers in the Cross River State, potential was instilled in those children to do great things for their villages or country. Someday they may join IBM and participate in their own Corporate Service Corps assignment. The Corporate Service Corps costs IBM around $250,000 to $400,000 per project (Gordon, 2011), however—as we have illustrated above—its benefits far outweigh the costs. We hope other major corporations will follow IBM's successful model to develop their own leaders in a socially responsible way.

Advice for Others

The Corporate Service Corps initiative demonstrates that developing leaders can be done in a socially responsible way, with business objectives in mind. However, careful selection and preparation of participants and the selection of reliable partners are critical to the success of the initiative.

One of the major success factors of the program is the strong application rate. Every year, up to ten thousand IBM employees from more than sixty countries apply for only a few hundred spots (Gordon, 2011). This large pool allows the acceptance process to be highly selective and rigorous. Globally, there are nine application review boards that are responsible for their respective regions. The selection process needs to be rigorous to ensure the right people are sent on the mission, since it is a cost that must be explained to the shareholders. These are future potential leaders who will represent IBM in each of the areas they enter, which is a big responsibility. In order for an employee to be considered, he or she must have been at IBM for at least two years and have received consistently high performance ratings. Those chosen have leadership potential, previous predilection for service, and are extremely motivated (Weiner, 2013).

Taking effective selection one step further, it is also important to ensure the selected candidates are given the appropriate tools, skills, and knowledge needed for the in-country experience. The three months of preparation prior to leaving is critical to success on the mission. This time gives participants an opportunity to get to know each other prior to spending twenty-four hours a day for thirty days in close company. Additionally, it is critical to get to know the country or region the group is being deployed into—the political context, cultural customs, language, etc., in order to effectively work with the local people. Logistical training increases bonding among team members, preparedness, and the understanding of the type of situation they are entering into—immunization shots, work visa needs, living arrangements, etc. Last, some basic consulting, negotiation, and team development skills help with any of the assigned missions.

A somewhat sensitive area of the program design is choosing nongovernment organizations to partner with. These partnerships are crucial to the success of each project. NGOs help with logistics like lodging, travel accommodations, and visas. The Corporate Service Corps partners with NGOs like CDC Developmental Solutions, Digital Opportunity Trust, and Australian Business Volunteers. It is important to pick these organizations carefully to ensure the safety of the participants and the fluidity of the projects. The logistics partner should be an organization recommended by others, and a group with a global presence, a positive track record, and local contacts in the country the employees are entering. (For additional advice on choosing partners, see *Corporate Volunteerism as an Avenue for Leader Development* on page 99 of this book.)

We believe that many more organizations can reap the benefits of adapting programs similar to the Corporate Service Corps. Leadership development, talent retention and attraction, publicity, and service are just a few of the advantages to this corporate social responsibility initiative. In creating your own program, you will be one more organization working toward a mission of creating the next generation of global citizens.

References

Gordon, A. (2011). How to win friends and train leaders in global markets? Just follow IBM. *Forbes*. Retrieved from www.forbes.com/sites/adamgordon/2011/12/14/global-leadership-ibm/

Kanengieter, J., & Rajagopal-Durbin, A. (2012). Wilderness leadership on the job: Five principles from outdoor exploration that will make you a better manager. *Harvard Business Review, 90*(4), 127–131.

Mirvis, P., Thompson, K., & Gohring, J. (2012). Toward next-generation leadership: Global service. *Leader to Leader, 64,* 20–26.

Weiner, S.P. (2013). Corporate philanthropy and the role of industrial-organizational psychology. In J.B. Olson-Buchanan, L.L. Koppes-Bryan, & L. Foster Thompson (Eds.), *Using industrial-organizational psychology for the greater good: Helping those who help others* (pp. 148–175). New York, NY: Routledge.

Resources

Aguinis, H. (2011). Organizational responsibility: Doing good and doing well. In S. Zedeck (Ed.), *APA handbook of industrial and organizational psychology* (Vol. 3, pp. 855–879). Washington, DC: American Psychological Association.

IBM Corporation. (2011). IBM corporate responsibility report. Retrieved from www.ibm.com/ibm/responsibility/2011/ceos-letter/index.html

IBM Corporation. (2011). IBM's Corporate Service Corps: A new model for leadership development, market expansion and citizenship. Retrieved from www.ibm.com/ibm/responsibility/corporateservicecorps/pdf/IBM_Corporate_Service_Corps_Essay.pdf

IBM Corporation. (2009). IBMers use their passion for a smarter planet to save lives in Nigeria. Retrieved from www.ibm.com/smarterplanet/us/en/healthcare_solutions/article/corporate_service_corps.html

Marquis, C. (2009). *IBM Corporate Service Corps external evaluation.* Cambridge, MA: Harvard Business School. Retrieved from www.ibm.com/ibm/responsibility/corporateservicecorps/press/2009_05.html

18

Stretch Assignments to Develop First-Time Supervisors

Sally A. Allison and Marsha Green
Duke University

A FINANCIAL ANALYST who was participating in our First Time Supervisor program had a difficult assignment: leading a working group through the creation of a financial operations procedures manual in his department during the busiest time of the year. "I had to go to the folks I work with, people who didn't report to me, and say 'Can you do a little bit more than what we are already swamped with?'" said the participant. This broadening of project management and interpersonal skills is common during a stretch assignment, a critical part of the First Time Supervisor program offered by Duke University and Health System's Professional Development Institute (PDI).

PDI is a center dedicated to providing tailored development programs to foster career growth for targeted employee groups and to support Duke's staffing needs. Developing the skills and talents of current Duke staff to fill critical job needs through internal promotion or transfer has several advantages over hiring external candidates. Some of these advantages include quicker productivity and proficiency because incumbents are familiar with the Duke culture, increased loyalty and retention due to investment in our own workforce, increased staff satisfaction with more career development opportunities, a more diverse workforce throughout Duke's organization, and cost effectiveness gained through reduced turnover and improved productivity.

The First Time Supervisor (FTS) program is a ten-month program that focuses on developing project and people management, budgeting, and other supervisory skills while participants continue their regular jobs. Duke covers the training costs and managers adjust schedules to allow employees to attend classes and complete projects. This program is a priority for "growing our own" front-line supervisory staff at Duke.

The program contains key elements for success: classroom instruction, experiential learning, mentors, coaching, department support, career guidance, and job search assistance. In exchange for the investment Duke makes on behalf of participants, individuals in the class agree to remain at Duke for at least two years after completing the program. Taking the class doesn't guarantee a promotion. However, 75 percent of graduates have advanced at Duke since the program began in 2006.

Stretch Assignments

Stretch assignments are a key component of the program, providing a participant with learning opportunities in functions or areas beyond the participant's past experiences and current level of competency. Stretch assignments occur within the participant's current department while the participant is in his or her current job, yet involve increased or new duties for the participant. Managers are expected to work with the First Time Supervisor participant to identify assignments in the department that would help develop supervisory skills such as budgeting, team leadership, program design, and project management.

The purposes of a stretch assignment are to:

- Address development needs identified in the participant's professional development plan

- Build supervisory competencies

- Develop project planning skills

- Develop new competencies and skills

- Work as an individual contributor

- Stretch into a new role in the participant's department

Participants choose their assignments through discussions with their department supervisors. These choices can be current department initiatives, future projects, or ongoing department operations. A list of potential stretch assignments is provided to participants and supervisors to stimulate their thinking (see Exhibit 18.1). Once an assignment is agreed on, participants complete a Project Approval Form to ensure that there is a clear articulation of the assignment, the goals and objectives of the assignment, and the action steps needed to complete the project (see Exhibit 18.2).

Both the participant's PDI coach and his or her supervisor monitor assignments. Both the supervisor and the participant complete formal evaluations and judge the assignment

Exhibit 18.1. Possible Stretch Assignments

- Complete a communication planning project
- Create a procedures manual
- Participate in an individual/buddy orientation for new employees
- Create a department recognition program
- Revise or update the department's website
- Enhance all job descriptions within department
- Create a process for handling outdated materials
- Develop an electronic filing system for department
- Develop a departmental orientation
- Create a promotional document for the department
- Map the departmental work flow
- Facilitate focus groups to identify organization needs
- Complete a training gap analysis, assessment, and design
- Manage staff meetings

Exhibit 18.2. Stretch Assignment Project Forms

Stretch assignments provide participants with learning opportunities in functions or areas beyond the participant's experiences and current level of competency. It is expected that the manager will work with the employee to identify an assignment. Each participant will work one-on-one with his or her manager to complete an assignment in his or her work area. The stretch assignment is individualized based upon department need, participant's skill gap, and the development areas and competencies. The stretch assignment requires ongoing discussion and collaboration among the First Time Supervisor (FTS) participant, his or her supervisor, and PDI coach.

Use the forms below to complete the following steps:

1. Stretch assignment (what the FTS participant is to accomplish)

2. Outcome/Goals (the supervisory competency the FTS participant will develop by completing this stretch assignment)

3. Objective (measurable accomplishments in support of the goals)

4. Action Steps (steps to accomplish objectives; include time, cost, resources, etc.)

Stretch Assignment: _____ **Due Date:** _____ **Status:** _____

Describe the assignment and how exactly it will stretch you:

Outline the scope of the assignment:

Draft a general timeline of the assignment, building check-ins with manager and PDI coach throughout assignment:

Exhibit 18.2. Stretch Assignment Project Forms (*continued*)

Outcome/Goals

(**Level 1** = no experience, no knowledge; **Level 2** = some experience, performs independently in routine situations; **Level 3** = extensive experience, can give expert advice and lead others to perform)

Supervisory Skill/ Competency	Current Level (1–3)	Planned Level (1–3)	Target Date	Status

Objectives/Action Steps

Objectives	Action Steps and Resources Needed	Target Date	Date Completed	Evaluation Method

Signatures

FTS Participant: _____ Date: _____

FTS Supervisor: _____ Date: _____

FTS Coach: _____ Date: _____

according to how well the original objectives were met. (See Exhibit 18.3 for the supervisor evaluation form.) Each participant is required to make an individual presentation of five to seven minutes to his or her classmates about the assignment.

Using stretch assignments as a development tool has proven to be successful for this Duke program. Below is some advice on coordinating this type of experiential learning:

- Provide detailed instructions for participants and their supervisors, including forms. This creates consistency for each participant experience and ensures better communications between supervisors, participants, and PDI coaches.

- Routinely monitor the experience. PDI staff perform periodic check-ins with managers, class check-ins with participants, and presentation rehearsals. These activities ensure that participants are staying on track and meeting deadlines.

- Provide an opportunity for structured evaluation. This allows managers a way to concentrate on the assignment and how well the participant performed.

- Require each participant to present information about the stretch assignment to classmates. A class presentation by each participant allows them to show the results of the assignment, the importance to the department, the lessons learned, and the next steps. Making the presentation provides an opportunity for participants to practice clear, concise communication, an important supervisory skill.

Exhibit 18.3. Evaluation from Manager

Please rate the FTS participant's Stretch Assignment using the following rating scale:
1 = Needed improvement

2 = Fully met expectations

3 = Exceeded expectations

1 2 3 Value of assignment to the department

1 2 3 Use of resources inside and outside the department

1 2 3 Adherence to established timelines of assignment

1 2 3 Ability to manage regular workload and/or customer/patient load along with stretch assignment

1 2 3 Ability to manage interpersonal relationships with co-workers

1 2 3 Development of competencies identified in this assignment

Please provide comments for the following questions:

1. What were the FTS participant's major achievements while working on this stretch assignment?

2. How well did the FTS participant get along with co-workers during the stretch assignment? Did you see any role change as the FTS participant assumed more supervisory responsibilities?

3. Please identify areas of performance (behaviors and results) and competencies on this stretch assignment that have improved.

4. Based on your experience observing the FTS participant complete this stretch assignment, what are the key competency areas for future development?

Title of Assignment: _____

FTS Participant: _____

Manager: _____ Date: _____

In evaluations of the stretch assignment component of the program, participants often comment about the importance of sufficient supervisor input in choosing the project and in creating time for assisting with and managing the assignment. It is vital for supervisors to consider carefully the breadth and competencies of the participant and the breadth and detail of the assignment. For example, one participant may stretch to handle only one aspect of a budget presentation, while another participant can be asked to manage an entire budget.

First Time Supervisor class members routinely identify stretch assignments as key to their successful growth and completion of the program. During a recent graduation ceremony, our vice president of the Office for Institutional Equity congratulated employees for their hard work and commitment and reminded them that they represent a special segment of Duke's workforce. "We often talk about recruiting the best and brightest employees to come to Duke," he said, "but there is something very special about developing our own."

19

Executive Shadowing

Ritesh Daryani
Expedia, Inc.

A FEW YEARS back, we developed an executive shadowing program in response to research that suggested a large number of executives derail when they move from management to executive positions. Executive shadowing experiences not only provide managers with an overview of the role, but also a sense for whether they would like to consider an executive path in the future. The experience provides managers with the opportunity to spend time with an executive leader, observe the executive performing his or her role, and ask relevant questions.

Our program identified high potential managers and matched them with executives based on the manager's interest and career aspirations. During the program, we gave managers the opportunity to shadow an executive for a day and learn by observing, asking questions, and applying the learning later in their respective roles. We instructed executives beforehand to choose a day that was varied in terms of meetings and activities, to educate their assigned managers on various aspects of their work, to solicit questions, and to provide an overview of their executive roles.

The program planning started with an executive sponsor and was followed by a project plan (see Exhibit 19.1). The first step in rolling out the program was to create a web page on the company intranet that provided all the details about the program to both executives

Exhibit 19.1. Checklist for Launching an Executive Shadowing Program

- ❏ Identify an executive sponsor for the initiative
- ❏ Create an overview of the program to share the details with the sponsor
- ❏ Get buy in for the program from the sponsor and the executives
- ❏ Identify the executives to participate in the program
- ❏ Identify high potential managers to participate in the program
- ❏ Create teaser e-mails to generate curiosity about the program
- ❏ Create a mailbox for this program named "Executive Shadowing Program"
- ❏ Send out teaser e-mails and final invites to target audience
- ❏ Create videos of senior leaders talking about the importance of the program
- ❏ Match executives with participants based on self-selection
- ❏ Block the calendar of the executives and the participants
- ❏ Create candidate preparation material
- ❏ Make travel arrangements and obtain respective manager approvals
- ❏ Design process to capture learning from the participants and executives
- ❏ Launch the actual program

and high potential managers. The web page included a video of senior leaders describing the importance of the program, profiles of all the executives, the objective of the program, an outline of the program, articles on the importance of executive development, and also an opportunity for the managers to provide their preference in choosing an executive. We posted articles to educate the managers and build some theoretical foundation in the area of executive development.

The participants in the program were high potential managers located in the Pacific Northwest who were eighteen to twenty-four months away from an executive role. We encouraged these managers to participate via e-mail flyers on the importance of the program and how it could potentially help the managers to know more about executive roles. The executive sponsor and the immediate managers of potential participants in the program also drove participation.

We identified executives who were in the Pacific Northwest and who had been in executive positions for at least two years across units. The executive sponsor facilitated participation by sending an invitation to the executives encouraging them to get involved in the program. In addition, the culture of the company has always encouraged leaders to develop employees as part of their executive responsibilities. In fact, executives typically have a goal that is associated with development of employees in the company. We communicated these expectations and responsibilities to the executives via an e-mail during the program.

The participants had the opportunity to choose an executive to work with based on the participants' aspirations and skill sets. The participants visited the web page created for the program, went through the profiles of executives, and then chose three executives in order of preference. Giving a self-selection opportunity to the participants was important in making them feel part of the program. Self-selection also helped the participants to align their career aspirations with the learning they wanted from the executives.

Matching the participant and the executive was an important step in the executive shadowing program. Research has shown how specific characteristics, such as work styles, work interests, values, demographic background, personalities, non-work interests, proximity, and rank, can facilitate or reduce the effectiveness of the relationship (Allen, Finkelstein, & Poteet, 2009). Matches based on work style, personalities, and non-work interests have shown favorable results in the relationship. The matching strategy would depend on the culture of the organization, needs of the program, commitment of the senior leaders, and availability of resources.

Once the matching was completed, we sent an e-mail to all the participants and the executives. The executives received their participants' profiles, career aspirations, and resumes. We asked the executives to identify a day when they could provide an overview to the participants in areas such as people management, client relationships, stakeholder management, and new program or product development. We also instructed the executives to keep a gap of at least thirty minutes between meetings to provide the participants the opportunity to ask specific questions related to a meeting or a conference call. Additionally, we advised executives to share their thoughts on the objectives and outcome of the specific meeting. It was imperative for the executives to process the information immediately after the meeting to enhance the participants' learning.

We sent a similar e-mail to participants containing a detailed profile of the executives and their experience history. There were also details on how a participant could enhance learning during executive shadowing sessions by observing and by asking the right questions. We included sample questions the participants could use to extract maximum learning out of the scheduled session (see Exhibit 19.2). These questions encouraged the participants to learn from the executive's experience; the answers could also provide insight on learning that could be imitated by the high potential managers. We told the participants to go well prepared into the session to get the best out of the shadowing experience; for example, they should read the executive profile, go through the portal to read about the program and its benefits, and prepare questions that they could ask the executive. There was also information on the venue, timings, and articles related to leadership development.

Lessons Learned

Once the executive shadowing session was completed, we collected survey data to understand the effectiveness of the program, and then compiled and shared feedback with the

Exhibit 19.2. Sample Questions for Participants to Ask Executives

- What experiences helped you to grow as an effective executive?
- What has been the most challenging assignment in your career? What skills did you develop while working on the assignment?
- What characteristics are required to be a successful executive?
- Who are your role models and why?
- How do you leverage your mentors to perform your role effectively?
- Share an assignment or a project that was unsuccessful from your perspective. What was your learning?
- Why do you think many executives derail?
- What is your advice to managers who aspire to be an executive?
- What have you learned to be effective ways to balance personal and professional life?
- Would you recommend any specific roles that could help in becoming a successful executive?

leadership team. Overall, the feedback indicated the value the participants saw in helping them envision the executive roles. The top concern was the duration of the executive shadowing program, as participants requested more than a day of shadowing.

One of the key lessons we learned was that, even though our executive pool seemed diverse, it did not completely represent all the skills and backgrounds that were needed to best match all the high potential managers' needs. Therefore, in future programs we have to expand the executive pool to include additional skills and executives with more diverse backgrounds. Another lesson was the importance of positioning the program as a valuable piece of the organization's overall leadership development strategy. Some of the participants felt that executive shadowing was "bolted on" versus "built in." Even though management felt as though they were adequately showcasing the executive role, they had not built the program as part of a strategic development plan. It is unlikely, however, that an executive shadowing program can exist in isolation, not aligned with the overall talent strategy.

Reference

Allen, T.D., Finkelstein, L.M., & Poteet, M.L. (2009). *Designing workplace mentoring programs: An evidence-based approach*. Oxford, UK: Blackwell-Wiley.

20

Leadership Fitness Challenge: Daily Exercise of the Leadership Muscle

Laura Ann Preston-Dayne
Kelly Services, Inc.

IN 2011 THE Leadership Development and Talent Management Team at Kelly Services was looking to increase awareness of the value of using experience-based development throughout the organization. Yet a major obstacle existed: How could a team of three meaningfully connect with a full-time employee base of more than eighty thousand? There were several internal communication vehicles to consider (for example, daily digest e-mails, intranet articles, SharePoint sites, virtual or self-paced training), but none seemed to embody the "go out and do something" spirit of experience-based development.

The idea of using a social media approach to engage a wider audience was crystallized after a team member attended a presentation by Accenture during Bersin & Associate's 2011 IMPACT conference. During this session Accenture described how its internal social media platform was allowing employees all over the globe to share ideas and tools, discuss trends, brainstorm, and benchmark to provide more innovative approaches for their clients. The speaker also highlighted how some of the users were developing a Facebook-like "following" because they regularly contributed thoughtful content to the learning portal. After the conference we wondered whether anyone would want to follow our team and, if so, why? Within days of IMPACT, the team launched an internal leadership development group on Kelly's social networking platform and began posting links to relevant articles and industry reports and providing personal commentary on the topics of leadership, talent, and development. Yet, very few people knew the team was even out there and, subsequently, it was impossible to generate momentum. After interviewing the platform's administrators and several internal marketing experts, the team realized that it needed to have a formal (and preferably novel) campaign to draw people to the site.

These conversations led directly to the creation of the Leadership Fitness Challenge (LFC), a social media–enabled, experience-based, leadership development experiment that piloted during the summer of 2011. Using Kelly's internal social-networking platform, employees around the world were invited to join the Leadership Development Team in "exercising" their leadership muscle by engaging in a specific five- to ten-minute activity each day for a thirty-day period. Each day's development activity was unique (see Exhibit 20.1 for examples).

Exhibit 20.1. Sample Fitness Challenge Activities

- Do you have a selective listening problem? Most people are capable of being good listeners (not interrupting, paraphrasing, asking thoughtful questions, and so on) when they slow down and take the time, yet with too much to do in not enough time this critical skill is often forgotten. Take a moment to read this article about the importance of listening, learning, *and* leading and then ask a person you don't know to tell you a little about him- or herself and his or her work. Use this time to practice your listening skills.

- While leadership rightfully receives a much deserved amount of attention, followership seems to receive very little. The leadership-followership dynamic is a critical and fragile partnership that makes or breaks organizations and careers. What are you doing that productively enhances achievement of a goal that you and a leader agree together is worth attaining? What could you do to be an even better follower? Identify and commit to changing one aspect of how you follow during the upcoming week.

- Ram Charan, a world renowned business author and keynote speaker, developed his business acumen sensibility from working in his parents' shoe shop in India. Take a few minutes to listen to him discuss the five core building blocks of business and then answer his three closing questions for yourself; share your answers with your team as appropriate: www.youtube.com/watch?v=s8aGEU9hgk8

- Want to be more innovative, but not sure how to begin? Research has shown that just being exposed to new ideas, concepts, and novel applications can help jump-start your own creativity. For a fresh perspective on the world, we suggest listening to a TED Talk. (TED is a nonprofit organization that showcases great ideas across the areas of technology, entertainment, and design.) Take a few minutes today to explore the variety of topics available at www.ted.com/themes

- Everyone has heard about creating SMART goals to clearly outline what they are trying to achieve, yet targets lacking energy, passion, ambition, or personal aspiration are all too often relegated to a file folder until it's time for My Career discussions. Take a minute to review the Beyond SMART Goals worksheet and choose to "ramp up" at least one of your business goals (bonus points if you can do this for a shared team goal).

- A key element of leadership is the ability to inspire others to follow you. Unfortunately, many managers try to influence solely through hard data, numbers, and metrics and forget to appeal to others' hearts and passions. Today we challenge you to identify one project or initiative that could use a motivational boost and determine how you can employ some change-leadership "see-feel-change" strategies to re-engage your team/audience.

Here are the steps and guiding principles that the team followed to plan, implement, and assess this effort.

Step 1: Identify a Desired Outcome

The purpose of the LFC was to engage leaders and individual contributors in simple and practical experience-based development activities while reinforcing competencies from Kelly's Leadership Blueprint (a graphical depiction of the competencies necessary to be a successful leader at Kelly). Since the LFC was a new initiative on a relatively new platform, a modest participation goal was set of one hundred individuals by the end of the challenge.

Step 2: Create the Brand

Inspired by a number of Weight Watcher and Curve commercials that were promoting health and wellness programs in preparation for the summer season, the team selected a "fitness challenge" theme with a stick-figure weight lifter as our mascot. It was important that the initiative have a lighthearted tone that encouraged participant experimentation, sharing, and openness to development experiences. Potential participants were invited to take part with the following pitch:

> Interested in refining your leadership skills? Looking for opportunities to incorporate development into your daily work routine? Want to hear how other Kelly leaders are living the Leadership Blueprint? Then join the Leadership Development Fitness Challenge. The Leadership Development Team will be hosting a thirty-day campaign of five- to ten-minute daily activities that will allow you to build your leadership muscle. This activity is open to ALL Kelly employees, and you can join by "following" the Leadership Development group.

Step 3: Generate Ideas

In order to create sufficient content to support the six-week challenge, each member of the Leadership Development and Talent Management Team (including our summer interns) was instructed to draft at least five potential ideas for the challenge that would each take less than ten minutes to complete and would drive leadership development. (The directions were intentionally left ambiguous in order to encourage creativity in the writing and content.) Based on the initial content generated, the team was quickly able to highlight consistent themes; "people" competencies such as collaboration, influence, and communication came up across all of the drafts. By comparing these items to the Leadership Blueprint, the team was able to call out additional areas that required further attention with respect to experience-based development.

Step 4: Organize and Refine Content

The team knew it needed to embed social, collaborative, and on-demand learning approaches to the format of the challenge itself to keep things interesting. Through several iterations of writing, reviewing, and editing, varied learning mediums were incorporated into the daily challenges, including weekly videos from topical experts (for example, Dan Pink and John Kotter), downloadable how-to worksheets, links to popular leadership articles and blogs, and member best-practice discussions.

Step 5: Build in Transfer of Training or, in This Case, Development Opportunities

Because IBM's Parallel Learning and Coaching Model, PARR (prepare, act, reflect, and review; see *PARR: A Learning Model for Managers* on page 151 of this book for more on this model) was emphasized, it was important to embed it into the LFC—making it possible to further promote the "R" concepts (something people traditionally struggle with) as well as to enhance learning. Therefore, the challenges issued every Friday during the LFC were dedicated to reflecting and reviewing. Participants were asked to think about what they had learned over the course of the week and determine how they could share these items with colleagues during the upcoming week. They were also given instructions on how to transfer the learning into their daily routines. Interestingly, participants indicated (usually with surprise) that this was one of the most helpful components of the LFC, as it unified the daily challenges and reinforced the importance of applying learning versus "checking the box."

Step 6: Determine How to Measure Success

The final step in preparing the LFC content included outlining how to know whether the initiative was successful. As stated above, a preliminary target of one hundred users was set. After some early promotion, that number was hit several days prior to launching the program. Once it was clear that there was an appetite for something new and developmental, the team challenged itself to look at the overall quality of the experience. It was possible to track participant activity through their contributions to the site and the number of times challenge content was accessed. An after-action review was scheduled with the most active users in order to debrief the LFC and to document lessons learned. Yet the most meaningful and reaffirming feedback came from informal interactions with other Kelly employees during the challenge. The team regularly heard people in the hallways discussing the topic of the day, saw individuals completing worksheets and reading recommended articles, and had executives asking to see a preview of coming attractions so they could support the daily challenges within their groups. The buzz generated from the program at all levels in the organization far exceeded original expectations for a voluntary development pilot and reinforced the interest employees had in managing their career development.

Step 7: Communicate (and It Helps to Have Some Evangelists)

Most development programs typically include a formal communication element in their project planning, but because this was a soft social launch, the team relied more on word of mouth to draw participants to the experience. Several broad messages were sent to the "all Kelly" universe of social media users as the content was being developed, and from there several highly credible and visible individuals gave their unsolicited endorsement for the LFC. Once leaders outside of the HR space touted the value of the challenge, there was a noticeable uptick in adoption in both the field and corporate centers. Subsequently, it was realized that the role of a credible online communicator in the success of this program is similar to that of executive sponsorship for traditional leadership development activities. Looking to the future of LFC, the team plans to recruit these knowledgeable or well-known individuals in advance so they can help evangelize the effort and provide thought leadership for subject-specific daily challenges.

Step 8: Launch and Monitor Progress

The entire process was executed with an overall investment of eighty hours spread across the team (approximately seventy hours of prep work and ten hours actually implementing the pilot). When it came to launching the LFC, it was found that having established content proved to be extremely advantageous, and I would strongly recommend this approach to others versus building the challenges in real time. Having the content already in the queue ensured a consistent tone and flow of the daily exercises and allowed the team to focus on responding to blog commentary, facilitating discussion, answering questions, and trouble-shooting technical difficulties as they arose.

Lessons Learned

At the conclusion of the LFC there were 280 participants (nearly three times the number originally estimated), and the goal of raising awareness of experience-based development had been accomplished. The after-action focus group indicated that brevity and variety were the keys to success—participants were initially drawn to the challenge because of the unique nature of the event and maintained interest because of the varied content and format. These findings, as well as the experience with social media, have helped shape the thinking at Kelly about adult learning and have influenced the organization to further incorporate informal and blended learning solutions into its leadership development and talent management offerings. Moreover, preparations for the second annual LFC are currently being made, and it will include several enhancements:

- It will launch with a formal kick-off message from Kelly's chief human resource officer that describes the connection between challenge participation and the My

Career process (Kelly's blended performance management and career development process).

- It will address bandwidth and connectivity concerns that limited participants' ability to access external resources.

- It will have experts weigh in on certain challenge days (for example, a brand manager will blog about new products in Kelly's pipeline on an innovation-focused day).

- It will close with a video message from the CEO that will introduce a global Leadership Blueprint contest.

21

Using a Video-Case-Based Collaborative Approach in Leader Development

Nate Allen

U.S. Army, National Defense University

CONSIDER THE FOLLOWING experience of a front-line U.S. Army leader serving in Iraq:

> We were headed out to a pretty easy mission. My front truck reports that there's a dead body under a car in the middle of the road subsequent to a roadside bomb explosion. At this point the gunner from my lead truck noticed a double-decker bus that had stopped. And there was a guy up on the top deck who appeared to have a blue video camera, and he was just hanging out the window videotaping the attack. . . . I looked down my sight and noticed that same thing. The gunner looked through binos and noticed the same thing.

The above scenario was shared by Ben, a young leader in combat, during a conversation in which he described some of his most challenging experiences as a leader—what some would describe as *critical incidents*. Ben's video interview was edited to fit within the framework of the web-based Leader Challenge platform and is made available to young officers preparing for combat. These leaders watch Ben sharing his presenting dilemma. And without knowing the decision he made, they describe and vote on how they would handle the situation. Then, after they've expressed what actions they would take, they observe a second video in which Ben shares what he actually did.

So let's pause for a moment and reflect. If you were Ben, what would you, reader, do in this situation? What emotions are you experiencing, what are your options, and what do your soldiers need from you? And, importantly, what are the short- to long-range, and tactical to strategic, implications of your decision?

In this particular incident, Ben directed his team to use restraint and to secure and unload the bus. In doing so, he created space to further develop the situation. In that process what his team found was not an insurgent with a video camera. Rather, they discovered a boy who had a boom box held up to his ear—what from a distance and within that context looked like someone videotaping the attack.

What a powerful way to demonstrate the chaos, complexity, and fog of combat! In fact, in situations like this, things are often so complex that one might "see" what one is looking for. And this is the exact tendency that novice leaders need to be aware of. Furthermore, the worst time for young leaders to initially consider how they will approach sense-making and decisions in chaotic and complex environments is when they are physically in a situation like Ben's—which in combat can be guaranteed.

One way to think about leader development is in terms of the key experiences that leaders will have in their unique context, and then to design learning resources around those experiences. This is a different approach from one taken with traditional competency frameworks, in which the essential knowledge, skills, and abilities for a job are codified and trained. In fact, directing a novice leader to an outline of competencies that guide his or her behavior isn't always helpful. The person will lack the concrete experience to know what a list of abstract concepts might look like in action. For example, directing the leader to "make sound and timely decisions" is not helpful in guiding action in a situation like Ben's. However, if that leader can have the opportunity to engage with a set of concrete experiences that he or she will likely encounter, the transfer of learning to practical application and effectiveness is far more likely. This is where the Leader Challenge approach can have significant impact, providing novice leaders who lack the experience they need to do their jobs with a set of vicarious experiences that is grounded in the lived experience of their more seasoned colleagues.

The Leader Challenge is a case-based, experiential learning approach to leader development. A leader, such as Ben, shares the narrative of a specific challenge he faced in combat. The video story is spliced immediately after the presenting dilemma, so the novice leader watching the video is presented with a common challenge and then asked what he or she would do to address such a challenge. The developing leader then has the opportunity to interact with fellow practitioners either face-to-face or online across the organization in a conversation about the presented dilemma. Upon the novice sharing how he or she would react, the rest of the story in terms of what the protagonist did is made accessible. Finally, after participating in the Leader Challenge, the developing leader is presented with analysis and resources that provide additional insights.

With this in mind, a Leader Challenge initiative for your organization might consist of the following elements:

1. Analyze the specific practice you are focused on and develop a portfolio of experiences that it is highly probable every leader in that practice will face. In fact, it might even be said that a leader is missing something developmentally if he or she hasn't had this set of experiences. Examples of such experiences might include making a determination whether to fire or develop a poorly performing employee or making a decision to enter or leave a particular market.

2. Interview seasoned practitioners around these experiences, capturing stories, decision points, and critical assumptions made. Additionally, for each situation develop a range of possible responses.

3. Edit the interview so that there is a video in which the protagonist describes the presenting dilemma and a video in which he or she shares how the situation was addressed; these can be separate files made available on your web-enabled platform.

4. Package the online resource as a progressive web-based experience in which the participant might: (1) watch a video of the presenting dilemma; (2) write out in a text box how he or she would address the situation; (3) interact with colleagues in an online discussion thread about the scenario (participants should be able to mark submissions as helpful, comment on submissions, and post responses); (4) watch a video about the rest of the story, in which the protagonist describes how the challenge was actually addressed; and (5) access additional resources relevant to the situation, for example, related articles and videos of diverse leaders sharing vignettes of similar experiences (see Figure 21.1).

5. Once a Leader Challenge is created, it can be used in multiple venues. For example, a challenge developed for junior officers can be made available within an online professional forum such as *CompanyCommand* (see *CompanyCommand: A Peer-to-Peer Learning Forum* on page 279 of this volume). It can also be used in face-to-face venues, such as in front-line leader development programs, and with cadets at West Point or in the Reserve Officer Training Corps. In face-to-face venues, the lead facilitator plays the initial video for participants, and then novice leaders are matched up with their more seasoned colleagues at round tables to discuss how they would address the scenario while exploring alternative points of view. After a rich table-based dialogue, the video of the rest of the story is played and followed by further discussion about the experience and others like it.

Conclusion

The Leader Challenge approach grounds an organization's learning curriculum in the experience of current practitioners—a sort of living curriculum that is continuously being renewed

Figure 21.1. Online Leader Challenge

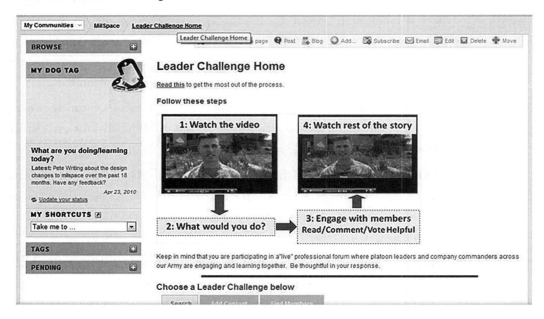

by contemporary leaders in the field. This is especially impactful for a large organization, like the Army, that is distributed globally and operating in a constantly changing environment. For such organizations, what is taught in the schoolhouse will naturally lag behind the realities on the ground. Thus, an approach that proactively grounds curriculum in current practitioner experience enables both the field and the schoolhouse to learn collaboratively. Furthermore, this has the effect of scaling out localized pockets of excellence across the organization, allowing the organization to learn as individual practitioners at the edges of the enterprise develop and learn.

22

Cross-Company Consortiums: Tackling Business Challenges and Developing Leaders Together*

Yury Boshyk
The Global Executive Learning Network

THERE IS A growing realization that executives gain considerable development and learning, as well as business insights, when they engage with other business people *outside* of their organizations, and share their experiences and dilemmas in a systematic and focused way. This realization has led to a growth of self-managed *cross-company consortiums*, sometimes called business-to-business or B2B consortiums, which involve non-competing companies and leaders.

A cross-company consortium is a group of companies that come together to learn from each other and to explore common business challenges. Such consortiums allow companies to accelerate the development of their senior leaders through peer group interaction while sharing the costs of such development. Although companies in the past have relied on business schools to initiate and manage cross-company consortiums, companies now self-organize and self-manage their own consortiums.

*Note: This article is a summary of lessons learned from over a decade of experience with self-managed cross-company consortium programs throughout the world. Others have also provided their perspectives, and I would, therefore, like to acknowledge the following individuals: Stefan Bauer, Karl-Georg Degenhardt, Aruna Krishnan, Chantal Fleuret, Stephen Mercer, Celeste Messina, Julie Powell, Ake Reinholdsson, Tony Russell, and Jan Wilmott.

One early pioneering example was the Boeing-initiated International Consortium Program (ICP) (2001–2004) that involved ABB, ABN Amro Bank, BHP Billiton, and later the Benfield Group, Standard Bank from South Africa, and Tata from India (see *Better Together: Building Learning Communities Across Organizations* on page 433 of this book). Following on the heels of the ICP was another consortium, the Global Consortium Program (GCP) that included Alcan, Allied Domecq, First National Bank (South Africa), Honeywell, and PanAsia Paper. Today, there are several other consortiums, including the Global Learning Alliance with Eli Lilly, L'Oreal, Rio Tinto, Schneider Electric, and Wipro. And there are also local, that is, national self-managed B2B consortiums. For example, in India seven companies have come together to implement a senior leaders program involving the Aditya Birla Group, Colgate Palmolive, Dr. Reddy's, Genpact, HDFC Bank, Mahindra & Mahindra, and Wipro.

Cross-company consortium programs share some common characteristics. They tend to be modular and run for a total of less than three weeks over a six-month time span. The programs include a business challenge provided by their respective top management, while also incorporating sessions on leadership and other business topics chosen by participating company representatives. In general, the programs involve four to seven companies, sending no more than eight participants each, with fewer than forty participants for each program. The level of participants varies, but most are focused on engaging senior executives and, separately, high potential talent. In the case of the Indian consortium, participants are three levels below the top executive team but with work experience of between fifteen to twenty years and an average age of between forty and forty-five. In the case of the Global Learning Alliance, participants, in general, are selected from those who report directly to the board or executive committee. It is often important that all participants are peers and deal with similar degrees of complexity in their roles.

Today's consortiums tend to be self-managed by a steering committee, on which all companies have a representative and work in partnership with an external provider. Usually, a steering committee plays an active role in the design and implementation of the program, along with the outside advisors. In most cases the program directors also participate actively in their respective company teams during the program as well. When it comes to venues, these are usually organized either at a member company's learning center or where a location serves the common business interests of the consortium companies. Finally, cost is on a per company basis. A company is charged the same whether it sends four or seven participants, thus ensuring cost sharing equality and the optimization of attendance.

Cross-Company Consortium Objectives and Benefits

Participating companies believe that international and local consortiums accomplish several objectives and needs. For instance, consortiums:

- Accelerate the development of global executives who can gain knowledge and understanding of global business practices, cultures, and shared leadership dilemmas from executives in other global companies

- Enhance and accelerate a deeper understanding of trends in business and society on a global level

- Provide a platform to build external orientations and networks for their leaders

- Encourage leaders to learn alternative perspectives on problem solving from other companies

- Ensure greater customization of design and contents for the program, designed and managed by learning partners to serve the needs of a specific population of executives and be easily aligned with business priorities

- Make possible an obvious cost advantage; for example, sharing the cost of world class global inputs and premiere faculty reduces costs for all participating companies

Not surprisingly, participants also add that consortiums help them:

- Relate better to theory when participants see it being practiced by peers from other industries

- See their own business challenges through the lens of these peers, providing a completely different perspective to business challenges and hence more innovative solutions

- Generalize leadership competencies and behaviors through interaction with peers from different industries who are facing similar leadership challenges, albeit in different environments and industries

- Develop many long-lasting business and personal relationships as the program provided a "safe" platform whereby trust and honesty were established

What to Consider When Starting a Consortium

Companies that would like to launch and implement cross-company consortiums should consider the following steps and issues:

1. There should be a "champion" company or a core group of companies that have the backing of their top executive leaders to initiate and implement such a consortium.

2. A consortium requires resources both in terms of time and funds. The initial clarification of objectives, discussions with potential partners, and alignment and

agreement of consortium members takes several months, longer than most people think.

3. Managing the administration and logistics of a program are far more complicated and time-consuming than companies originally assume. And when consortium programs are fully self-managed, that is, without the assistance of outside providers, ensuring uniform quality of experience when a module or program moves from one consortium partner to another is not easy, making it important to establish clear guidelines and standards.

4. The reasons for selecting consortium partners can vary widely, so there should be clear selection criteria. For example, the following may be taken into account: non-competing industries and companies, number of employees, size of annual revenues, the global reach or "footprint" of the company, reputation and brand, depth of innovation, membership in the Fortune Global 500 or the Financial Times Global 500, assets under management, and so on.

    Strategic objectives and realities drive learning objectives and hence partner selection criteria. Boeing, for example, was looking to globalize their senior executives as quickly as possible in order to compete more effectively internationally. Most of their people were U.S.-based, with a smattering of Australians, and had little or no exposure to the global business environment. As a result, Boeing sought out companies that had their home bases in various regions of the world, such as India, Africa, Europe, Australia, and had either an obvious regional or global presence, or both. The reasoning behind this was to expose Boeing's executives to leaders who had very extensive international and regional experience and were willing to share their knowledge and lessons learned. Flexibility was as important as exclusivity in the minds of the Boeing organizers, and so size often was not as important as the depth of possible learning and openness to learning and sharing.

    Most companies in international consortiums tend to be on both the Fortune Global 500 or the Financial Times Global 500, but sometimes a small yet dynamic company has been invited into a consortium on a rotational basis, since it would not, due to its size, have a large enough pool of top executives to participate in a consortium over a longer period of time than other members. In the end, however, flexibility is more important that exclusivity when considering new company partners.

5. Also vital is the active participation and engagement of a steering committee made up of representatives from the consortium companies. One program director viewed a steering committee as the "heart and soul" of a consortium program and compared it to "somewhat like a marriage—but one without any

type of legal contract." Although his consortium also had a charter, its real strength lay in "the members' personal pledges to work together, communicating openly and honestly, supporting the program through thick or thin, and devoting the energy and resources necessary to the consortium's growth and success. Trust and teamwork were the essential ingredients. We spent many hours together developing plans, strategies, and just getting to know one another." Participants must also respect their steering committee member so they can more easily "trust the people and trust the process."

6. The steering committee members representing their companies in a consortium should be influential and respected in their organizations, with considerable self-confidence to deal effectively and easily with the very top senior executives at board level, as well as with other line managers in their company. Steering committee members should be able to help their internal senior executive sponsors craft and assign important strategic business challenges for participants to work on, ensure a balanced appreciation of a focus on business results, and promote learning that is of significant benefit both for the organization as well as for individual participants. Steering committee members must also be able to command the respect of peers in other companies, since it is their role to recruit new companies into a consortium.

7. Having a charter or agreement among the consortium companies is essential both for the efficient running of a consortium as well as for providing guidance and clarity to potential company partners. One such "charter" covered the following topics:

- Principles and objectives of the consortium
- What is required of a consortium member company
- What is required of a steering group member
- Financial arrangements
- Steering committee processes and organization
- Participants from partner companies (number, levels of responsibility, profiles, and responsibilities during the program)
- Cancellation and postponement
- Use of company facilities/location for modules
- Appropriate number of participants and participating companies
- New participant companies
- Program design (and timelines)
- Relationship, processes, fees, and roles of outside advisor/providers

8. A website for a program is essential because it allows participants to capture information and share knowledge well beyond a specific program's duration, thus also building an effective alumni network.

9. Careful consideration should be given to the program venues. Some consortiums select venues based on criteria that are not just cost-effective, as described above. For example, in one consortium, locations for the programs are also chosen for the importance to the respective company businesses, and in another example, a two-module program venue selection is based on selecting a representative venue for an emerging economy and then for a mature economy.

10. Effective consortiums turn into ongoing communities of practice, with participants and program directors going beyond learning and sharing on matters during the program. In the best cases, larger dilemmas and issues are discussed even after the program ends.

11. When it comes to content in the consortium programs, it is important to keep in mind the nature of adult learning, and to respect the maturity of participants. To paraphrase one pioneer of executive learning, the best curriculum is in the experience of participants in the room and the best teachers are the participants themselves. Lectures, case studies, and simple simulations should be kept out of a consortium program or kept to a minimum. They tend to be more in the domain of MBA and other business studies. Almost all participants have already been through these approaches and this career phase. In most cases, these traditional tools are not helpful as the realities and issues encountered by senior executives are far more complicated, where there are no right answers. Encouraging participants to see themselves as "partners in adversity" and creating as many opportunities as possible in order for them to share, clarify, and discuss their business and leadership challenges is the true contribution any cross-company consortium should strive to achieve.

The Future of Self-Managed Cross-Company Consortiums

The future of cross-company consortiums lies in the lessons learned from past experiences. The best learning and business results come from people tackling unfamiliar problems in an unfamiliar setting. The consortiums discussed above can be described as settings in which participants tackle familiar problems in a somewhat unfamiliar context. In the 1960s and 1970s some pioneers of executive development and education went further. Among the things they initiated were consortiums that included participation from public- as well as private-sector organizations, participants working on the business challenges of *other* organizations, and participants implementing their recommendations on the business challenge in the other organizations—truly unfamiliar problems in an unfamiliar setting. For example, one participant, an engineer from a manufacturing company, worked on a major business challenge in a bank and was then responsible for implementing his recommendations inside that organization. Who is doing this today? And why not?

Cross-company consortiums are clearly of value to participating leaders and their organizations. With a little more effort and imagination, and guidance from past experiences, even more can be achieved by going "back to the future" in one way, and in another way recognizing the benefits of working together in our increasingly collaborative world.

Resources

Bellon, D., Dilworth, R.L., & Boshyk, Y. (2010). National level experiments with action learning: Belgium and beyond. In Y. Boshyk & R.L. Dilworth (Eds.), *Action learning: History and evolution* (pp. 96–113). Basingstoke, UK: Palgrave Macmillan.

Boshyk, Y. (2009). Developing global executives: Today and tomorrow. In D. Dotlich, P. Cairo, S. Rhinesmith, & R. Meeks (Eds.), *The 2009 Pfeiffer annual: Leadership development* (pp. 108–126). San Francisco, CA: Pfeiffer.

Revans, R.W. (1971). *Developing effective managers: A new approach to business education.* New York, NY: Praeger.

Wilmott, J., & Wilkinson, L.C. (2003). *Developing global leaders: The international consortium program.* Retrieved from www.gel-net.com.

Section 2

Leaders: Better Equipped to Learn from Experience

Organizing Frameworks

Learning Strategies and Tactics

Reflection and Retention

Learning Communities and Support

Section Introduction

Leadership is learned through experience, and the ability to learn from experience is what separates high potentials from everyone else. Most people rush from meeting to meeting and project to project, checking e-mail all the time, jumping on and off phone calls, and putting out fires. Their definition of victory is another task being checked off the to-do list. For these people, life is a series of events that go undigested. But there is that rare person who is intentional and deliberate about extracting every ounce of learning value from his or her experiences. Even in times of uncertainty and extreme complexity, these people have an ability to balance their desire to perform with a hunger for personal growth. They have the ability to surround themselves with people who provide consistent, reliable feedback, and the courage to seek out feedback. They have the ability to slow down, capture the lessons of each and every experience, and apply those lessons with laser-like focus to future experiences. For you, the fundamental question is: *How can you develop this ability to learn in leaders throughout the organization?*

In this section of the book, a diverse group of thought leaders, practitioners, and experts in the field of management development share their models, tools, and practices for improving individuals' ability to learn from experience. Several authors present their frameworks for improving the ability to learn from experience (see *Mindful Engagement: Learning to Learn from Experience*; *PARR: A Learning Model for Managers*; *GPS•R: A Tool for Assessing Learning Readiness*; and *Asking Questions to Foster Learning from Experience*). Two themes are common across these frameworks. First, the timing of learning strategies is important. There are specific actions that people can implement prior to, during, and after their experiences to maximize their learning. Second, these frameworks point to actions that both individuals and organizations can implement to improve the ability to learn from experience. Organizational support for learning is necessary, but individuals must also take responsibility for their own development.

In addition to these frameworks, there are also a number of specific strategies and practices that you can implement to help your employees learn from challenging, developmental experiences. First, individuals must maintain an orientation toward learning despite a natural bias for action and the extraordinary performance demands placed upon them (see *Using the Classroom to Create a Learning Orientation*; *Establishing a Learning Mindset*). It is also vital that individuals engage in specific strategies and tactics that enhance learning from experience (see *Tactics for Learning from Experience*), seek and receive constructive feedback (see *Proactive Feedback Seeking: The Power of Seeing Yourself as Others See You*; *Micro-Feedback: A Tool for Real-Time Learning*; *Feedback: Who, When and How to Ask*), and regulate their emotions in ways that help learning from experience (see *Narrating Emotions to Enhance Learning*). In addition, managers must surround themselves with a network of trusted advisors who can help guide them through challenging experiences, provide emotional and social support, and offer constructive feedback (see *Building a Board of Learning Advisors*). Both during and after experiences, individuals must also engage in a reflection process where they digest their own and others' actions, the consequences of these actions, and the fundamental lessons of experience (see *Leadership Journeys: Intentional Reflection Experiences; After-Event Reviews: How to Structure Reflection Conversations; Scaffolding Reflection: What, So What, Now What?; Life Journeys: Developing for the Future by Looking at the Past; Strategies for Facilitating Learning from Experience; Teachable Point of View: Learning to Lead by Teaching Others; Implementation Intention: A Refinement to Leadership Development Goal Setting;* and *Twelve Questions for More Strategic Work and Learning*). Finally, the ability to learn from experience is not an individual act. Rather, the best learning often comes vicariously, or as people talk through experiences with others who have shared or are going through similar experiences. We highlight a number of unique and novel approaches for building and leveraging communities of practice and learning networks in organizations (see *Building a Learning Community Through Reflection and Experimentation; Using Communities of Practice to Cultivate Leaders of Integrity; CompanyCommand: A Peer-to-Peer Learning Forum;* and *Virtual Roundtables: Using Technology to Build Learning Communities*).

The first section of this book discussed how you can identify and create experiences that offer the potential for learning and development. The strategies, tools, and practices described in this section explain how you can turn this potential learning into actual learning—by improving individuals' ability to learn from the experiences they are having each and every day. Teaching people how to lead is necessary but insufficient—you must also teach them how to learn to lead.

23

Mindful Engagement: Learning to Learn from Experience

D. Scott DeRue and Susan J. Ashford
University of Michigan

TALENT PROFESSIONALS SPEND countless resources identifying and securing developmental roles for high potentials. Whether it is a rotation program that exposes managers to diverse areas of the business, or stretch assignments that require executives to drive change and innovation, they know a lot about what fosters executive development. Experiences that are novel and require agility and adaptation, involve interpersonal and cultural diversity, and span across organizational boundaries and functions all help in leadership development.

Unfortunately, much less is known about how to help executives learn from these experiences. Indeed, executives going through the same developmental experience can learn vastly different amounts. Executives should bend but not break as they are stretched beyond their current capabilities, but learning from experience does not occur naturally. Learning can be risky, requires effort, and asks people to accept that they might not be perfect or have all the answers. In fact, high-potentials often are the least likely to learn from experience because of their own biases and the pressures to perform. To help executives learn, unlearn, and relearn as they go through high-challenge, high-risk experiences, we have developed a framework called *mindful engagement* (see Figure 23.1). It is organized into three phases: approach, action, and reflection, and it identifies critical mindsets and behaviors to maximize learning.

Figure 23.1. A Model of Mindful Engagement

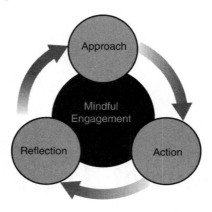

Approach

The ability to learn from experience begins even before the experience itself. It begins in the planning and on-boarding process where high potentials receive coaching on how to prepare for their new roles. In the approach phase, there are two objectives. The first is to stimulate a learning orientation, and the second is to set specific learning goals.

Stimulate a Learning Orientation

In any experience, what people see depends on which "window" they look through—their mindset. Research in psychology highlights two possible windows: a learning orientation or a performance orientation. People with a learning orientation view experiences as opportunities for learning, whereas people with a performance orientation focus on proving or demonstrating their ability. Those with the latter tend to avoid difficult tasks and seek to prove how "perfect" they are to others. In contrast, people with the former are more willing to take risks, and they see experiences as opportunities for learning and personal growth.

Of course, every person is a mix of both mindsets. Everyone wants to perform well *and* grow skills. The problem is that a strong orientation toward performance can actually get in the way of learning. High potentials with a strong performance orientation become preoccupied with what others think, overly concerned with image, and often fail to see how they impact others. They do not ask questions for fear of looking stupid and they become overly concerned with doing things right. As a result, they miss opportunities to try new things or stretch beyond their comfort zones.

In contrast, people with a strong learning orientation see risk taking as an essential element of growth and innovation, readily admit areas of uncertainty as a strategy for gaining new information, and understand setbacks are part of the learning process. The results are clear: People with a learning orientation are less stressed, learn more from their experiences, and, ironically, perform better in stretch experiences than people with a strong performance orientation.

How can you help instill a learning orientation in high potentials, who are where they are today because of their past *performance* achievements (and often a past performance orientation)? Work to create a culture where admitting uncertainty is expected and modeled by others. Emphasize that the purpose of a stretch assignment is learning and that the organization understands that there will be times when the person is over his or her head. Establish incentive systems to reward taking risks and learning, not just performance. The aim here is not to deemphasize performance but rather to emphasize and reward risk taking and learning. And the first time people make a mistake, ensure that they are coached and supported—not judged and discredited. You have to consistently reinforce a learning culture and a learning mindset in your top performers.

Set Learning Goals

Goals drive behavior. If you want people to learn from an experience, ensure they have specific goals for what they need to learn from the experience. Everyone has a learning "edge," something about him or her personally and his or her behavior that needs to be improved. Whether it is the ability to work cross-functionally or cross-culturally, to cope with complexity, or to inspire others, setting learning goals directs people's attention toward specific needs and objectives and provides a foundation for coaching, assessment, and feedback.

These goals need to be SMART: **s**pecific about the skills and knowledge that are expected to be learned; **m**easureable through assessment and feedback; **a**ttainable given the person's starting skill base; **r**ealistic given the experience's demands and challenges; and **t**ime-bound with clear milestones.

Action

The pace of executive life is like a speeding train: The train barrels forward—down tracks that are sometimes straight, sometimes curvy, and sometimes change from one to the other—and past new landscapes that can appear every few seconds. Many high potentials are caught up in simply trying to do everything they can to keep the train on the tracks. We have identified three tactics that help high potentials not only direct the train but also maximize the value of the ride for their own development. Learning from experience requires that individuals actively experiment, seek feedback, and regulate their emotions.

Active Experimentation

Louis Boone, an emeritus professor of business, once said, "Don't fear failure so much that you refuse to try new things. The saddest summary of a life is: could have, might have, and should have." If you do the same things in the same way, you rarely learn anything new. A planned strategy of active experimentation helps push people beyond their comfort zones and into the learning zone.

Before someone enters his or her next stretch assignment, have that person identify and commit to at least two different experiments that will be tried during the assignment. The experiments could be new behaviors that he or she wants to try out, or even a new attitude or mindset. Have the person talk about exactly how he or she plans to conduct the experiments, when they will occur, who will be involved, and how these particular experiments align with specific learning goals. Regular meetings to examine progress on the experiments and to identify new ones can help keep the learner on track. By repeating cycles of experimentation, people begin to develop a habit of active experimentation that will not only advance their own learning but also model learning oriented behavior for others.

Feedback Seeking

Everyone knows that learning requires feedback. People need consistent feedback on their performance, how they can better leverage their strengths, and what they can do differently to improve on their weaknesses. The problem is that power, politics, and fear often make others reluctant to give feedback, particularly when that feedback would be directed to people parallel to or above them in the organizational hierarchy. By actively seeking feedback, leaders can overcome these barriers to learning. Seeking feedback communicates openness to others' input and helps uncover feedback that might otherwise go unshared.

There are multiple strategies and approaches to seeking feedback (see *Proactive Feedback Seeking: The Power of Seeing Yourself as Others See You* on page 195 of this book). People can indirectly seek feedback by monitoring how others react to them, and more directly by inquiring about their performance with key stakeholders. Learning is enhanced when seeking occurs close to the events in question and when people seek not only from their bosses but also from their peers, subordinates, customers, and even people outside of their normal work day. Seeking feedback from a broader array of people enhances creativity and innovation. Finally, it is important to reinforce that people must understand that seeking feedback will not always be comfortable and that sometimes they will learn things that were unexpected—but they can take comfort in knowing that people see feedback-seekers as more committed to learning, more open to others' input, and having greater potential for more senior roles.

Emotion Regulation

Both leadership and learning can be anxiety-inducing activities. Leadership is risky because success or failure is often attributed to the "leader." Learning might be even riskier, as people must accept that they are not perfect, break old habits, and try new approaches. Both activities put individuals' behaviors and performance on display and can rouse emotions. Yet, to learn from experience, people must maintain equilibrium and not become overwhelmed. Extreme emotions, whether positive or negative, hurt the learning process (see *Narrating Emotions to Enhance Learning* on page 187 of this book).

Emotion regulation first involves leaders naming, understanding, and coping with the various feelings that might arise during an experience. Such coping might involve them discussing their emotions with others, or seeking out ways to reduce negative emotions, or keeping positive emotions in perspective. In fact, seeking feedback can help with both negative and positive emotions. It helps reduce uncertainty about others' impressions, thus reducing anxiety, and it also helps leaders gain perspective on where they still need to improve. Leaders who experience extreme positive emotions can often become complacent with the status quo and fail to see new opportunities for learning; seeking feedback helps reduce that complacency. In order to enhance learning, in addition to regulating his or her own emotions, a leader can help regulate others' emotions. Making others feel less anxious about, say, giving feedback will result in receiving more timely and accurate feedback from others, and this will help identify opportunities for learning and ways to improve performance.

Emotion regulation is not easy. Emotions are scary for many people, and society is rife with norms against recognizing or talking about emotions. Many leaders find their learning goals to be beneficial in regulating emotions effectively. Revisiting those goals, assessing progress with the assistance of a coach, and recommitting to those goals are all strategies that help leaders process emotions and keep them in perspective. The worst possible strategy for managing emotions—which we commonly see among high potentials—is to hide behind positive emotions or pretend that negative emotions will go away if ignored. Leaders must be encouraged to find appropriate outlets for recognizing and discussing their emotions in service of learning from experience.

Reflection

In our mindful-engagement workshops with high potentials, we often ask participants whether they have fifteen years of experience or one year of experience fifteen times over. The key differentiator is whether executives are able to digest, synthesize, and draw patterns across their experiences and whether they are able to reflect on and identify the key lessons of their experiences. Unfortunately, many executives claim to not have time for reflection. Busy schedules, competing demands, and routine crises keep people focused on their most current tasks, not their most important tasks. The result is that people are *going through* experiences, but they are not actually *having* experiences. They are always looking forward without realizing that the best path forward might be revealed by looking back.

At the University of Michigan we have developed a structured process for executive reflection based on a concept first developed by the military called *after-event reviews*, or AERs (see *After-Event Reviews: How to Structure Reflection Conversations* on page 221 of this book). After important developmental milestones and throughout key stretch assignments, managers use this AER process to develop an accurate picture of what happened in a given experience, what might have happened if they had behaved differently, and what the implications are for future behavior change. Our research demonstrates that this structured reflection process minimizes the biases that get in the way of learning and results in more personal growth and development than traditional forms of reflection. Over time, as managers use the AER process to structure reflection conversations with employees, AERs become part of the culture and help build a learning organization.

Concluding Thoughts

Our model of mindful engagement organizes how people should approach, go through, and reflect on developmental experiences in order to enhance their ability to learn. The tool is relatively inexpensive, can be easily scaled, and can be used by individuals or teams. Effective implementation requires attention, time, and a disciplined effort, but the payoff is significant. If experience is a leader's best teacher, mindful engagement puts learners in the best position to benefit from those lessons.

24

PARR: A Learning Model for Managers

Laura Ann Preston-Dayne
Kelly Services, Inc.

AS KELLY SERVICES began its transition from a traditional performance management process to a ratings-free business and professional development conversation in 2008, two things became very clear: Employees were eager to have meaningful career conversations, yet neither they nor their managers knew how to have them. Although both parties were open to thoughtful discussions, tradition, culture, and incumbent skill/comfort level limited the overall number and quality of these interactions. The challenge for the Talent Management and Leadership Development Team was to create an environment in which it was acceptable (and even encouraged) to share one's professional interests, goals, and aspirations, and to introduce tools that could facilitate the process.

To help support the emerging blended performance-management and career-development process, which we call My Career, a new instructor-led training course entitled Leader as Coach (LAC) debuted in 2009. Its goals are to help participants understand the expectations Kelly has for them as leaders and to enable them to select and execute meaningful development for themselves and their employees, thereby driving employee engagement and retention. During the early sessions, a development paradox emerged: When leaders were asked to describe the most impactful development experience in their careers, the responses were almost always centered on specific experience-based development (EBD) opportunities (for example, working in a particularly challenging business environment, taking on a start-up assignment, or receiving performance support/coaching from a trusted leader). Yet when

Figure 24.1. PARR Learning Model

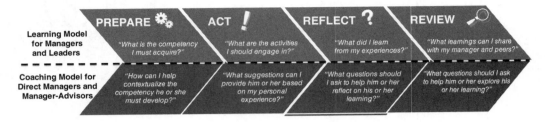

asked how they developed their own staff, most defaulted to easily available generic resources (for example, having them read books or participate in virtual courses). This led us to adopt IBM's Parallel Learning and Coaching Model, PARR, as a development aid to describe how to drive development.

The PARR Model

PARR (an acronym for prepare, act, reflect, and review) is a framework for experience-based development. Its four-step approach (see Figure 24.1) helps employees select, execute, and transfer learning from developmental opportunities. Moreover, this model provides managers guidelines on how to support employee development through questioning, encouraging reflection, and supporting the transfer of knowledge back to the job.

Prepare

Both the employee and his or her manager must be clear on the development targets and which competencies it will take to get there. The best way to do this is to begin with the end in mind, asking the following kinds of questions: What do you want to achieve? What competency is required for you to achieve your goal? If you improve a given competency and put it to use, what will that enable you to do? What are the results you can expect?

Act

Once both parties have agreed on the goals and needed improvements, they must identify the possible development activities and methods that would enable the employee to meet the prescribed goals. This is often a frustrating challenge for employees. After all, if you are not good at doing something, then how can you know how to improve? It is the role of the manager to push employees to select and execute development options with the greatest return on investment.

For example, what would be more beneficial: reading a book on influencing people or coming up with a strategy to approach someone you want to influence and execute it? Development experts would say the answer is clear—take action—yet a novice employee may not feel comfortable doing so. In this scenario, the manager can help maximize the development experience by encouraging the employee to acquire new knowledge (through reading) while pairing it with a real-world opportunity to try out those skills. Questions that can help guide these kinds of conversations include the following: What are some possible development activities to engage in? Which development method would best help you meet your goal? What activity or activities will you select, and when will you begin? What is your plan to use what you are learning? How can I help? The answer to the last question might include helping brainstorm development activities.

Reflect

Beyond going out and doing something, reflecting on one's experience is a critical post-act step that facilitates learning transfer. Employees who think about how the activity went, what they learned, and how they might apply those insights at a later date are more likely to do so. An example of reflection is a typical project postmortem debriefing. Moreover, involving the manager in the reflection phase reinforces the importance of sustainable ongoing development progress ("Wow my boss asked me what I learned, so next time I better have something to say") and can foster employee engagement ("My manager is supportive of my pursing both business and professional-development goals").

Simple questions can spur the reflection process: What did you learn from the activities? How effective was your experience in helping you reach your goal? Next time would you do things differently? How will you use what you have learned and determine how you will know it is working?

Review

The final step in the PARR process is reviewing what you have learned with others. Although you may have shared some concepts with your manager during the reflect step, review goes further to include teaching the principles to others. As most educators or facilitators will attest, communicating to novices requires the employee to have greater fluency and mastery of the content than just listening to it; in addition to knowing the core material, good instructors prepare for audience questions, integrate real-world examples, and incorporate their own perspectives. And in many cases, the act of teaching the information can lead to future "act" opportunities for the teacher or the listener.

Questions to help close out the PARR process include: How did you apply what you learned and what impact did your efforts have? What did you learn that you can share with others? Who might benefit from this information and how? Are there things you would recommend others do differently and why?

Implementing PARR at Kelly Services

In the years since PARR was introduced during the LAC live training sessions, it has been incorporated into a number of Kelly's talent and development processes. For example, the PARR training module from the LAC sessions has been translated into an instructor-led virtual version available to all Kelly full-time employees; this course provides first-time leaders with an orientation to their role in employee development and serves as a good refresher for others preparing for the My Career process. In addition, the "R" components of PARR have been incorporated into a variety of existing learning resources. And where appropriate, specific support materials and guidance are being given to participants in traditional development courses as well as those crafting individual development plans to ensure they are applying what they have learned from the development activity and regularly sharing progress with their manager—that is, regardless of the development method, employees are increasingly being asked to do something with what they have learned/experienced.

From a leadership development function perspective, we have been able to use PARR as a way to hold senior leaders more accountable for developing others. During annual talent planning discussions, leaders discuss their team members' strengths, areas for further growth, and potential next roles and give a personal commitment regarding each individual's development. We document this information and then follow up with those leaders to discuss year-over-year development progress, creating the climate for sustained development attention and momentum.

Finally, the PARR framework is being used to drive the blended learning architecture for an internal talent pipeline development program will launch soon. Given the interest in PARR to date, we expect continued traction in the rollout and further penetration into other human capital practices as we go forward.

Potential Risks, Roadblocks, and Unintended Consequences

The PARR rollout has not been without its detractors or naysayers. Discussions regarding the assumptions underlying PARR have illustrated a change in Kelly's entire development philosophy. Before, development was measured by the number of actions completed or the checkmarks recorded on one's development plan. Today it's not about quantity; rather it's about the impact of the development. While we recognize that there are different development methods (training, networking/social exchange, independent study, coaching/mentoring, and EBD), we are also willing to say that not all development is created equally. We emphasize that the majority of one's development occurs through doing the job and that development plans should reflect this, and that when other development methods are being employed, there still should be a plan in place to take action on those lessons. Moreover, this approach requires that both employees and managers be invested in development. Employees cannot wait for their managers to develop them, and leaders cannot just send employees to training classes and expect them to come back developed. For meaningful development to occur, a supportive partnership needs to exist, and employees and their managers must be comfortable discussing career aspirations, strengths, and areas for future growth—not an easy cultural shift from a strict business goals performance discussion!

Why PARR?

Even considering these cultural challenges, we still view PARR as the best way to guide learning transfer at Kelly. PARR is intuitive, has resonated at all levels within the organization, and can be easily incorporated into one's daily work life. Moreover, it provides a straightforward structure that applies to any development method—from reading a book, to taking a class, to practicing new skills on the job. Anecdotal feedback we have received from LAC training has also indicated that the approach increases the variety of development methods and actions outlined in individual development plans. And perhaps most importantly, it clearly delineates the dual responsibility of the employee and the manager in development.

As Kelly has restructured its PMP process and further clarified leadership accountabilities, PARR helped us clearly articulate the roles and responsibilities of both parties. Employees are able to work linearly through the model, showing developmental growth during each stage, then recalibrate their development efforts and start the process over again.

25

GPS•R: A Tool for Assessing Learning Readiness

Paul Yost, Hilary Roche, and Jillian McLellan
Seattle Pacific University

IT'S SAID THAT some people have twenty years of experience and some people have one year of experience twenty times. Not everyone who goes through an experience necessarily comes out a better leader (or person). The lessons of experience need to be captured along the way. The GPS•R Profile and Interview are two simple tools that leaders can use to assess whether they are ready to fully leverage on-the-job learning in their careers. The letters in GPS•R stand for goals, people, stretch, and reflection—four dimensions that are particularly important for maximizing experience-based development.

We concentrate on these four dimensions for two reasons. First, these dimensions focus on strategies and skills that any leader can learn and develop. Second, they represent strategies that are proactive—leaders can put these practices in place before they enter an experience. The latter is particularly important given how dynamic and frenetic a leader's life can be. If put into place early, learning becomes a natural *part of the job.* — training w/ GPS•R . The GPS•R Profile (see Exhibit 25.1) is a ten-minute assessment that can be easily integrated into a variety of talent management processes. The GPS•R Interview can be used by coaches and HR professionals to help leaders explore each of the four dimensions more deeply. The interview is a good follow-up to the survey, challenging leaders to identify the specifics behind their answers, identify gaps, and be more intentional about their development.

Point 2

Exhibit 25.1. The GPS•R Profile

Directions: Think about your career and the directions that you want it to go in the coming years. As you answer the questions, consider not only your current work, but also any experiences, education, and people outside of the workplace who are relevant. Rate the extent to which each of the following statements describes you. Skip any questions that are not applicable.

1 = Not at All
3 = To a Moderate Extent
5 = To a Very Great Extent

Direction (Goals)

In my career, I have identified:

1. My future career goals (3 to 5 years out).   1 2 3 4 5
2. Specific goals that I want to accomplish in the coming year.   1 2 3 4 5
3. Specific ways that I want to develop in the coming year.   1 2 3 4 5
4. Measures and milestones that I can watch to ensure that I am on track.   1 2 3 4 5
5. Ways I can develop myself outside of work.   1 2 3 4 5

Connection (People)

I have identified:

6. People who will provide candid and honest feedback.   1 2 3 4 5
7. People who will mentor me.   1 2 3 4 5
8. People who will provide social support.   1 2 3 4 5
9. people who will tell me how I am perceived by others.   1 2 3 4 5
10. People who will stretch me to think in new and different ways.   1 2 3 4 5
11. People who will provide advice and coaching.   1 2 3 4 5

Acceleration (Stretch)

I am taking on projects, tasks, and assignments that will:

12. Push me to the edge of my comfort zone.   1 2 3 4 5
13. Challenge me to develop new skills and capabilities that are important in my development.   1 2 3 4 5
14. Stretch me in the areas I have targeted for development.   1 2 3 4 5

Reflection

I regularly:

15. Set aside time to reflect on how I am doing and how I can improve.   1 2 3 4 5
16. Ask myself what's working, what's not working, and why.   1 2 3 4 5

Your GPS•R Profile

Directions: Add up your scores to see how well you have created a strong developmental environment in your current job and positioned yourself for future development.

16 to 50   You have not created a very rich learning environment around you. In fact, you are in danger of finishing the year less employable than you started. Look back over your scores and

Exhibit 25.1. The GPS•R Profile (*continued*)

identify the areas that you would like to improve and look for one action you can take this week that will move you toward your goal.

51 to 70   You have created a rich learning environment that will help you stretch and grow. Find the areas where you are strong and look for ways you might make them even stronger. Find one area where you rated yourself low. What is one step you can take in the coming two weeks to improve in this area?

71 to 80   You have created a very rich learning environment. You might even be feeling too stretched right now. If this is true, look for the people in your life who provide support and energy that you can draw on. Think about when you have faced challenges like this before in your life. What allowed you to get through these times?

The GPS•R Profile

Here is how we introduce the GPS•R Profile to leaders: In today's turbulent work environment, careers are dynamic. Careers are less like a ladder and more like an oceangoing vessel. You may proceed with a general direction, but you will have to make course corrections and navigate as you go. The leaders who are most likely to thrive in this kind of environment are the ones who prepare themselves to learn. No one should leave leader development to chance. There are too many pressures in the moment, too many variables. Leaders who trust that their development will just happen are less likely to capture the lessons of experience, to take on the right kinds of stretch assignments, to adapt to change, to get back on track, or to end up where they eventually want to be. The following four strategies can maximize professional development in dynamic environments:

- Goals—charting a direction about where you want to go in work and life
- People—surrounding yourself with people who challenge, support, and develop you
- Stretch—taking on assignments that will stretch you to develop in the areas you have targeted for development
- Reflection—building moments in your work when you can assess what is working, what isn't working, and applying the lessons to future challenges.

The GPS•R Profile is a way for you to assess the extent to which you have built these dimensions into your work and life. In debriefing the profile, we challenge the leaders to look back over their ratings and dig down to identify the specifics behind the ratings. The discussion should include the following elements.

Goals

Look back over your goal ratings. Where did you score high? Where did you score low? Take a couple of minutes and write out two goals for each of the following areas: Your career goals (three to five years), your performance goals (one year), your development goals (one year), and your non-work goals (one to two years). How specific are your goals? How will you know when they have been achieved? Share one of the goals that is most important to you with the person sitting next to you.

People

Which areas of your network are strong and which areas are weak? If you placed two names next to each area, who would you write down? Did you use the same names? Did they vary? Find an area where you would like to improve your network. Who is someone you could add? Who can you add who would challenge you?

Stretch

In what ways does your current job challenge you most? Given your career goals in three to five years, what are some ways you would like to stretch and develop yourself in the next year? What challenges can you take on that would stretch you to learn in the areas you have targeted for your development?

Reflection

Some of the most powerful reflection happens in real time, in the moment. This might include building your to-do list in the morning, reflecting on your day in the car ride home, or meeting with your team to discuss lessons learned and next steps. When are some opportunities in your daily and weekly activities where you can naturally reflect on your work, either on your own or with others?

GPS•R Interview

In coaching situations, you might not want to start with an assessment, but instead discuss the GPS•R dimensions in a conversation. Below we describe how to begin a GPS•R Interview, how we frame and ask questions during the interview, and how we conclude the interview.

Introduction

Learning is a process or journey, which takes time and determination. The purpose of our conversation today is to think about where you are in your career right now and the strategies that you can employ to move in the directions that are important to you, leverage the relationships in your life, and capture the lessons that experience has to offer—a sort of career GPS. The job you currently have represents an important way in which you can develop, and as you've probably experienced, most learning occurs on the job not in a classroom. Let's take a closer look at some of the opportunities for development you have right now. During the interview, we will discuss four topics:

- Goals: The goals you have for yourself in your career and in the coming year (fifteen minutes)

- People: Your network and the people you rely on in your life (fifteen minutes)

- Stretch: The challenges and stretch in your work (ten minutes)

- Reflection: The ways that you have built reflection into your work and life (ten minutes)

Goals

Let's assume tonight when you fall asleep you don't wake up for several years. During your Rip Van Winkle nap, a phenomenon occurred and you became the kind of person you always wanted to be. Many positive changes have happened, and you feel great. As you envision that future self, it's important to consider the specific steps you need to take to get there.

- Picture yourself waking up five years from now: Where are you? What are you doing in your career? What is happening with your family? How have you grown and developed as a leader? What challenge have you finally overcome?

- Now, move backward in time to one year from now. What were your goals for this year at work? In your personal life? What are you proud that you accomplished this year? How did you improve as a leader?

- How did you track the progress you were making to reach these goals?

People

It's important to surround yourself with people who can help you develop along the way. These are the people who push us to close the gap between our real selves and our ideal selves, providing different sources of information and support. Who are those people for you? Of course, it is okay to list the same people for more than one role.

- Who are the people who provide you with advice, coaching, and feedback?

- If you had to name a mentor(s), who would it be? Who are the people who stretch you to think in new and different ways?

- Who are the people you go to for social support?

- Who are the people you are mentoring?

Stretch

Leaders often learn the most when they are right at the edge of their comfort zones. If are stretched too far, the lessons are haphazard. If people are too comfortable, they tend to relax and not learn as much as they could because they aren't in a rich enough learning environment. Think about the ways that you want to develop as a leader.

- How are you are being stretched and challenged in your current job?

- In the coming year, what are some of the tasks, projects, and assignments that you can take to stretch you in the areas that you have targeted for development?

Reflection

The learning process also includes reflecting on your experiences. There are many different ways that people can engage in reflection. You might read, talk with the people around you, journal, identify your top priorities for the day, reflect at the end of the day on what you learned, meditate, pray, exercise, or play music to clear your mind.

- Think about a typical week for you. How do you reflect? What does it look like for you?

- What was the biggest thing that happened for you this week?

- What did you learn? How do you capture that learning?

Conclusion

As you reflect back on our conversation, what new skills or behaviors can you experiment with and start practicing today? What are some opportunities that you could start taking advantage of right now to help you develop? If we talked again in a week, what would be the evidence that you have moved forward on the topics that we discussed today?

Lessons Learned

- Leaders do not typically think about these topics on their own, but they enjoy the process and become invigorated when given the chance to think more deeply about their development. You might want to highlight this in your introduction to the topic, noting that the GPS•R Profile (or Interview) offers a chance for leaders to step outside of the daily grind of work and spend some time thinking about their careers.

- The tools are especially valuable when people are brought together to discuss them as a group, coaching and developing each other through rich conversations. The tools work across all ages—younger leaders just entering the workforce, people in the middle of their careers, or leaders close to retirement.

- We recommend embedding the GPS•R Profile and Interview within talent management and HR processes that already are in place such as leadership development programs, performance management processes, and executive coaching. Offering these tools as part of a leadership development program, for instance, not only allows leaders to see areas for improvement but also provides them with the opportunities to take action.

- Our work suggests that the four dimensions assessed in the GPS•R are related to several important outcomes, including on-the-job learning and development, career efficacy, career satisfaction, employability, and psychological well-being.

- The GPS•R Profile is designed for development and should not be used for selection or assessment. The items are easy to fake and the dimensions were chosen because they can be developed and can change over time.

26

Asking Questions to Foster Learning from Experience

Sally Beddor Nowak

Agilent Technologies

THE CORPORATE EXECUTIVE Board's (2009) strategic research study on unlocking the value of on-the-job learning found that active intention from the employee before, during, and after a developmental experience led to a 25 percent increase in retention and application of the new skills on the job.

Cal Wick (2003) also described the importance of beginning learning experiences prior to the course with preparation and including a strong follow up after the course to increase the impact of learning. Wick, along with Roy Pollock, Anderson Jefferson, and Richard Flanagan, fleshed out the ideas in *The Six Disciplines of Breakthrough Learning*, published in 2006.

The Agilent learning community holds a shared view that meaningful development occurs as a part of work rather than apart from work and this development is enhanced when employees' attention to learning is activated. Agilent uses a three-phase approach to all learning activities: preparation, learning, and follow-up. Using Robert Brinkerhoff's Success Case Method (2006), Agilent has seen that the impact of learning activities increases when facilitators secure intentionality from the employee and the manager through all three phases. This is important for planned training, a stretch assignment, or any other developmental experience.

Phase 1: Before the Experience

People indicate that they feel both nervous and excited by the opportunity to take on a developmental experience. Individuals can begin by assessing what they can apply from past experiences. This helps to identify which skills and abilities a person can build on. Second, identifying where they have skill or ability gaps helps individuals become intentional and creates a stronger focus on what is important for success. Identifying people one can turn to for help, support, coaching, and mentoring—in addition to the manager—ensures strong support. Each of these preparatory steps serves to lower stress and increase the ability of individuals to focus on development.

Phase 2: During the Experience

People rarely pause when they are in the midst of a challenging developmental experience, like a large project assignment. However, most experiences that provide the greatest learning are neither linear nor easy. Often, as the individual gains new expertise, his or her situation changes and he or she needs new skills to be successful. That is why it is important that managers help employees pause during challenging experiences and identify what has changed since the experience began, what they have learned so far, and who can help coach, mentor, and support them going forward.

Phase 3: After the Experience

Once individuals have gone through a challenging experience, they might breathe a sigh of relief that the experience is now history. However, if they simply move on without considering what they learned from that experience, they are losing out on a significant developmental opportunity. When people look back and explicitly state what they learned from an experience, that lesson stays with them and provides a sense of accomplishment. Comparing the planned outcomes to the actual outcomes helps to identify which solutions worked and which ones did not. The saying "lessons hard taught are well learned" is apt. Individuals learn much from their mistakes, the only failure is repeating them. The post-experience discussion between a manager and employee ensures the lesson will stick.

Figure 26.1. The 3x3 Tool

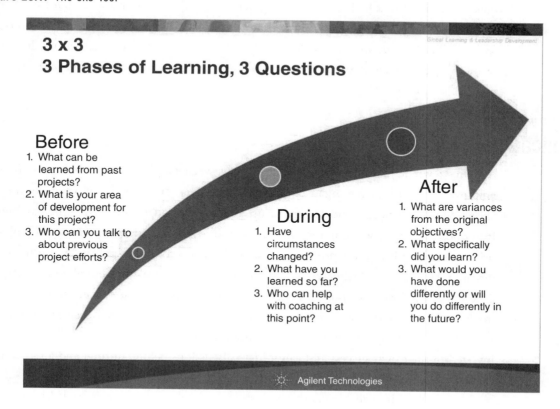

The Tool Development Process

The Agilent Global Learning and Leadership Development Team developed a one-hour webinar to help managers understand their roles in each phase of learning. Using the three-phase approach, we developed the 3x3 Tool (see Figure 26.1), introduced it in the webinar, and then provided it as a follow-up tool. The webinar was recorded and remains available for all managers and employees.

We used the metaphor of teaching a child to ride a bike to introduce managers to the value of being involved before, during, and after a learning experience. This metaphor seemed to resonate for the global audience and provided a useful anchor for the discussion. The managers were asked to think of a time when something they learned had really stuck for them and to recount what had made that happen. Managers responded with comments that supported the questions in the 3x3 Tool. This reinforced the belief that the questions were solid and would drive conversations and activity to increase the impact of learning.

Upon hearing the concept of the three phases, one manager described a debriefing with an employee who had just completed a challenging project. The employee commented, "It is has been a great project, I just wish that I had time for some development last year." The manager realized that he had not been explicit during their conversations about what skills and abilities she was developing throughout the experience. Fortunately, it wasn't too late to apply Phase 3 questions. After she had described what she had learned during the course of the project, the employee remarked, "Wow, I just realized that I have been in development this entire year!"

Application of the Tool

Agilent views development as a partnership between employees and managers. In new employee orientation, the organization encourages employees to "know what you know," "know what you need," and to "speak up and ask for what you need." The 3x3 Tool is introduced during new employee orientation and is also provided as a follow-up tool after orientation. In this way, the program prepares employees to take responsibility for their own development and to partner with their managers to ensure the desired results. Agilent encourages employees to "pull" for their development and request conversations with their managers to ensure they are receiving the support they need. This encouragement has been very effective throughout the world as employees realize that they are the people most invested in their own success and can initiate discussions before, during, and after learning experiences.

The 3x3 Tool is available via the manager and employee resource portal. Managers are provided the 3x3 Tool on the development plan site when the plans are created. Managers then discuss development plans every quarter (or more often) with their employees, using questions for the three phases of development, which are provided on the plan template.

Agilent's 3x3 Tool provides a reminder for managers to engage in questions through three phases of the learning experience. This engagement, properly executed, will increase employees' intentionality and ultimately increase the impact, retention, and application of the lessons that are a part of work.

References

Brinkerhoff, R.O. (2006). *Telling training's story: Evaluation made simple, credible, and effective*. San Francisco, CA: Berrett-Koehler.

Corporate Executive Board. (2009). *Unlocking the value of on-the-job learning (Report of the Learning and Development Roundtable)*. Washington, DC: Authors.

Wick, C.W. (2003). The course isn't the finish line. *Training & Development, 57*(11), 17–19.

Wick, C.W., Pollock, R.V.H., & Jefferson, A. (2006). *The six disciplines of breakthrough learning*. San Francisco, CA: Pfeiffer.

27

Using the Classroom to Create a Learning Orientation

Lori Homer
Microsoft

Anita Bhasin
Sage Ways, Inc.

EVEN LEARNING PROFESSIONALS familiar with the "Lessons of Experience" research can overlook the findings that time spent "in the classroom" contributes to development in unique ways, including giving participants exposure to new ideas, new behaviors to practice, time to reflect, and opportunities to connect with other leaders (McCall, Lombardo, & Morrison, 1988). Further, DeRue and Wellman (2009) and Dragoni, Tesluk, Russell, and Oh (2009) found that individuals with a learning orientation are more likely to reap the developmental benefits from very challenging roles. This chapter illustrates recent efforts at Microsoft to leverage the investment of time in the classroom (one tool for increasing the return on leader development from challenging roles) to increase leaders' learning orientation.

The Idea

Microsoft's culture prizes intelligence and rewards expertise. Growing leaders' learning orientation within that context is an ambitious goal. It's clear, after years of trying, that we will not drive organization level impact on learning orientation via individual level capability building (such as 1:1 coaching) alone. In this chapter, we describe an experiment, using a classroom type setting, to reward curiosity and frame "not knowing" as a leadership act. Further pushing the boundaries of discomfort, we centered our approach on "strategy formulation," a content area in which expertise is highly valued. We outline our experiment, lessons learned, and anecdotal evidence of impact, in the hope that others will be encouraged to experiment with classroom time to optimize the unique value it can provide.

The Approach
Partnership

Traditional classroom approaches to strategy often rely on experts and instruction in analytical methods to understand market trends, internal capabilities, and to arrive at a "best" strategy solution. Even innovative methods often rely on a step-by-step approach or, where an iterative approach is recommended, the phases are prescriptive and logically ordered. At Microsoft, we partnered with Adrian Slywotzky and Oliver Wyman consultants because their approach to great strategy "is *not* about having the best frameworks, templates, or even ideas. It is about asking a few deceptively simple questions over and over."

We used the following "deceptively simple-to-ask and hard-to-answer questions" as our classroom roadmap:

- Who is the customer?
- Where are the highest value opportunities?
- What are the business model options?
- Which possibilities will allow us to succeed?
- How does this opportunity connect to the organization's vision?
- Who are the various stakeholders? What interaction is required with each?
- What competing priorities might derail this strategy?
- What role does the customer play in the implementation?

Further, understanding what we were trying to achieve, Adrian Slywotzky personally adopted our objectives. Adrian emphasized curiosity throughout, encouraging participants to take a learning approach when seeking customer understanding. He also provided powerful role modeling for participants—when they asked him questions, rather than giving advice, Adrian would tell them what questions he'd ask if he were in their shoes. Further, when covering content, he ended each segment with a number of questions the participants could consider asking others, such as customers, direct reports, or more senior leaders, in order to solicit input, share the strategy formation and adoption process, and to help others learn and grow.

Preparation
Live Cases

A valid criticism of "classroom type" learning is the clinical nature of the examples—cases illustrate a specific concept or set of concepts, but their applicability to "real life" problems is limited. In order to increase relevance, we recruited executives and leaders of strategy who were willing to engage with a high potential audience "in a different way" than they may have done in the past (one that has relied heavily on an expert "tell and critique" model). Beyond willingness to engage differently, the leaders also needed to identify a challenge that met five criteria:

1. The challenge is of significant scale, affecting one (or more) of the businesses or suite of products.

2. The market boundaries are being redefined by emerging or converging technology and consumer patterns.

3. A re-evaluation of target customer/markets, the business model, and monetization approach is likely required.

4. The strategy questions are product and customer oriented versus functional or sales strategy.

5. The challenge is both real and urgent for the sponsor, decisions on the challenge are not yet closed, and the sponsor is interested in, and open to the input of, a cross-division high potential team.

While engaging executives and their "real life" challenges was essential to increase both the relevance and the stakes of the classroom experience, preparing the executives to both model learning and encourage curiosity over expertise in their case teams was the real differentiator from standard classroom type learning.

Executives spent a total of four hours with their case team(s); two at the kick-off/beginning of the week, and two more, three days later. In preparing executives for this time with the case teams, we were clear that, while we hoped that one or two fresh perspectives or insights on their challenge(s) might be an outcome, the *most* important objective was that the participants got curious and asked good questions. Executives were invited to treat their project teams more like a board inquiring into the opportunities and risks, and less like a team of strategy consultants or direct reports.

It was surprising to us, given our pervasive expert based culture and even our history with other "strategy focused" events, that none of the executives questioned our approach. In fact, once they understood that we were working with a senior audience of high potentials, and that we were specifically focusing on helping them scale their leadership through asking good questions, their enthusiasm for the engagement actually increased. We expect our objectives and focus resonated with the executives because they had made the transition from "expert" to "creator of experts" themselves.

The Experience
Case Teams

The cohort of thirty was divided into five case teams. The case teams were cross-functional and cross-divisional, with varying levels of familiarity with the problem proposed. Each case team had a team captain who had the responsibility to facilitate being on track and to drive the group toward the deliverable (a presentation of the groups' analyses and, more importantly, additional questions). Throughout the event, the teams and their captains were repeatedly invited to think of the exercise differently from past events (in which the premium was on being smart and knowledgeable). They were told to play the role of board member or stakeholder in, and not expert contributor to, the strategy formulation process.

At the launch, the visiting executives, aligned with our intent, communicated that it was the participants' role to inquire into assumptions, challenge, and ask questions about the information and framing provided. We provided each team with a "subject matter expert" whom they could reference. We invited participants *not* to hold the expectation for themselves (or each other) that they become experts in three days, but rather that they continue to keep top-of-mind the unique value they were positioned to provide: namely, a fresh perspective.

The case team work was about 45 percent of the total program time. It was interspersed with segments of context, framing, and external case examples presented by Adrian Slywotzky and the Oliver Wyman team. The case teams had separate breakout spaces to allow for concentrated focus and to contrast between the "classroom" and case team time.

Asking Questions

Teams were required to use the World Institute for Action Learning (WIAL)'s method of action learning as their group process. Each team had an action learning coach to help the group with reflection and self-monitoring. Within WIAL's method, statements may only be made in response to questions, making questions the catalyst for all conversation, and a natural balance against over-reliance on expertise. The coach's role in action learning is to promote group learning (not the group's progress on the task). As such, he or she may intervene to help the group reflect (e.g., What is the group doing well? What would help the group do better?). After the first round, coaches reported they felt more like "process police" than coaches; thereafter, we slightly modified the process so that coaches would consciously acknowledge and reward higher quality questions over perfunctory, "I'm following the rules" questions. After our second round check-in, the coaches reported stronger results.

Real-Time Feedback for Skill Practice

Another reason we used WIAL's methodology is because the opportunity to consciously develop and obtain real-time feedback on leadership skills is built in to the process. At the beginning of the group work, each leader identifies a skill that he or she will focus on. Through questions from the coach such as "What would that look like to members of your group?" and "How will we know X when we see it?" leaders are coached on making the skill behavioral and observable. Each group member's name and the skill he or she is working on is listed on a flipchart and posted in the breakout room where the group and coach can reference the list. Participants are invited to make note of when they observe a group member practicing his or her skill. Group sessions end with a round of feedback for individuals on where they did exhibit the skill they were working on, as well as opportunities they may have missed to practice the skill. This opportunity to practice a skill, obtain feedback, and almost immediately have another chance to practice and receive feedback leads to increased intentionality and observable skill improvements.

Results

Four of the case teams engaged their case sponsors in paired report-outs. That is, challenges that were similar were paired, and the sponsoring executives attended a two-hour report-out, so they could hear each others' case discussions. This was another intentional (and potentially risky) strategy, given the premium placed on executive bandwidth and time. However, all the sponsoring executives commented on the value and usefulness of having the report-outs in the paired format—both so the groups could stay small and so the case teams and executives could learn from more than one case. The fifth case team reported out at a different time to accommodate the executive sponsor's schedule.

One executive sponsor wrote to his case team following the event:

I really appreciated the level of thinking and the overall dialogue we had this afternoon. . . . The fact that we did the read-out with [the other organization] was especially helpful. Your contributions will certainly lead to [our organization] and [other organization] connecting in a different way moving forward and that alone is worth the time you invested.

In after-program evaluations, all participants said it was a valuable use of their time (75 percent strongly agreed, 25 percent agreed), and that they would recommend the experience to their peers (65 percent strongly agreed, 35 percent agreed). Comments included:

- I was intrigued by Adrian's idea that leaders' best approach to strategy formulation is through asking hard questions. I will definitely use this.

- The focus on meaningful discussions makes a difference.

- Tackling cross-company challenges and learning from them was a great use of time.

- More time spent on asking difficult questions [would result in] more time helping the cohort understand customer-centric thinking.

Even better, episodic and informal follow-up conversations six months after the program indicate that the learning continues. Program participants said they are

- More curious about the customer experience—less insistent on sharing what they know,

- Using the methodology to formulate strategy with their own groups, and

- Doing a better job of growing their directs through asking more and better questions.

Lessons Learned

As the Lessons of Experience research indicates, our classroom type program contributed unique value to our high potential leaders' learning, giving them space to try out new ideas and practice new behaviors, time away to reflect, and opportunities to connect with other leaders. Participants responded well to our intentional focus on these differentiators.

Also, we learned several things that are worth passing along:

- Achieving true alignment with delivery partners on the "asking hard questions" as an organizing principle was both time-consuming and worthwhile.

- Gaining agreement from sponsoring executives on the approach was also powerful and important reinforcement.

- It was helpful, in preparing the sponsoring executives, to tie our requests to their own experiences, both in making the comparison to their transition to executive and in contrasting our requests with other events in which their roles had been to judge and critique.

- If you are asking people to experiment with a counter-cultural behavior, call it out and be explicit about making the classroom a space in which to practice the behavior. In setting our participants up to be consultants, we ran the risk of setting them up to keep behaving as "the expert" or "the smartest guy in the room." Reminding participants they could make a choice to contribute differently (and perhaps, even differentiate themselves that way) was helpful.

- So that the classroom is not an entirely isolated experience, also help participants make the connection of "how and where you might experiment with this skill" on the job.

- Prepare the coaches with both the method (action learning) and the rationale, so they can make adjustments in real time, where necessary.

- Follow up. Had we not talked to participants three and six months after the event, we may not have learned how impactful the framing of asking good questions had been. Also, it was an opportunity for us to learn where and why leaders were not asking more questions—usually, it was because they were very conscious of which environments questions would and would not work in. While not surprising, this demonstrated ability to diagnose and respond appropriately, and such flexibility is, for us, its own victory.

Conclusion

Without question, challenging roles contribute to leader development. Here, we focused on the opportunity to use a classroom program (and all that a program uniquely offers, including new frameworks, time to reflect, and connections with others) as a platform for building leaders' learning orientation. Leaders reported that their learning orientation increased, helping to support their ability to learn from challenging roles. As one leader said, "It has helped me scale, since I have more good questions than I have perfect answers." Additionally, a small (but important) shift has happened in the culture, where "not knowing" and "being curious" can also be interpreted as legitimate acts of leadership.

References

DeRue, D.S., & Wellman, N. (2009). Developing leaders via experience: The role of developmental challenge, learning orientation, and feedback availability. *Journal of Applied Psychology, 94,* 859–875.

Dragoni, L., Tesluk, P. E., Russell, J. E., & Oh, I.-S. (2009). Understanding managerial development: Integrating developmental assignments, learning orientation, and access to developmental opportunities in predicting managerial competencies. *Academy of Management Journal, 52,* 731–743.

McCall, M.W., Jr., Lombardo, M.M., & Morrison, A.M. (1988). *Lessons of experience: How successful executives develop on the job.* Lexington, MA: Lexington Books.

28

Establishing a Learning Mindset

Kerry A. Bunker
Making Experience Matter

E ACH NEW OPPORTUNITY, crisis, or expansion in people's work and non-work lives provides a test of their underlying assumptions and an opportunity to examine and rethink their mental models for successful behavior. Old approaches and habits are often ill-suited for addressing the evolving complexity that accompanies the challenges and changes in people's lives. Yet the prospect of going against the grain of one's preferred responses can trigger fears of loss and failure, which may in turn lead to either denying the existence of the new circumstance entirely or acknowledging it even as the individual clings more tightly to entrenched behaviors and approaches that are no longer appropriate. There are stages in each new wave of the learning cycle in which it simply feels easier and safer to deny or reject the emerging demands of change than to accept the risks inherent in testing out new and unfamiliar strategies and tactics.

One way to help individuals approach challenging experiences with a learning orientation is to equip them with an understanding of some of the basics of adult learning. Most important is the knowledge that learning and change do initially generate stress, discomfort, and performance decrements; however, persistence and practice with new behaviors typically leads to even higher levels of performance.

I use the illustrations in Figures 28.1 and 28.2 to provide a straightforward model of the learning process. Here is how I communicate the key messages embedded in these figures:

Figure 28.1. Anatomy of a Learning Experience

- Let's look at the anatomy of a learning experience (Figure 28.1). They are easily understood because we have all gone through them many times. As we learn more and become more competent at a given task, we also become more confident and more masterful. But there inevitably comes a point at which improvement can only come through changing how we respond to the same tasks or challenges. Often an external force changes the circumstances and we no longer have the option of responding as we have in the past. At this point we must go about it in a new way, which typically causes a period of awkwardness and doubt. Even if the new way is promising, the fact that it is not familiar is enough to make us uncomfortable. We often are less effective applying the new way than we were with the old way. We call this segment of the learning journey *going against the grain.*

- Going against the grain is vividly illustrated by a tale one of my colleagues tells about his trials and tribulations as a promising high school tennis player. It seems the grip he was using for his backhand was reasonably effective, but limiting. Despite his coach's prompting to learn a new grip, he would retreat to the tried-and-true approach whenever he was in the heat of competition. The sensation of not being good during the transition phase of learning was more than he could bear. Failure to integrate the learning proved to be an obstacle to his long-term improvement and success in the sport.

- The learning journey of my colleague is illustrated in Figure 28.2. The most common reason adults balk at trying a new approach or a new set of behaviors is that they are afraid to look bad in front of others. The need to be perceived as competent is so strong it can literally override common sense. Our unwillingness or discomfort with the risk of humiliation or vulnerability gets in our way. In

Figure 28.2. Avoiding a Learning Experience

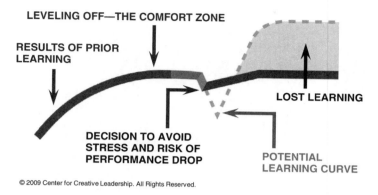

most cases the risk of losing face is much more imagined than real. If we can catch ourselves in the moment of discomfort (staring into the valley of chaos) and do a quick self-reflection, we will often be able to choose not to avoid the learning opportunity. Doing so requires us to examine a mental model that, while still in place, is no longer serving us well. Leveraging this self-awareness puts us in a position to make a conscious choice. It is just such a process that allows us to purposefully update our mental models, leading to new approaches and behaviors.

You can have participants connect the learning experience model to their own experiences in a variety of ways:

- Before presenting the model, ask participants to think about a time when they developed new practices or behaviors that they initially felt were unnatural or against their grain. How did they feel when they were initially trying out a new approach? What impact did the change have on their performance both short-term and long-term? Use their stories to illustrate the learning process depicted in Figure 28.1.

- After describing the dynamics that create an avoided learning experience, ask participants to remember a time when they were learning something new and experienced this process. Does the model help them better understand what was happening?

- After presenting the model, ask participants to contrast a time that they successfully made it through a going-against-the-grain experience and a time when they did not. What had they done differently in these two instances?

29

Tactics for Learning from Experience*

Maxine Dalton

LEARNING FROM CHALLENGING job experiences is essential for leadership development. Individuals can maximize their learning when facing challenges if they employ a variety of *learning tactics*. Some employees, although perfectly willing to take on challenging experiences, use only comfortable, tried-and-true tactics, thus limiting their ability to learn from experience.

Individuals can use four sets of learning tactics when facing a challenging experience: feeling, action, thinking, and accessing others. (See the Background and Resources section at the end of this piece for more information on the origins of this framework.)

- *Feeling tactics:* Individuals who use feeling tactics enhance their learning because they are able to manage the anxiety and uncertainty that is associated with undertaking new challenges. They can acknowledge the impact of their feelings on what they do, trust what their gut is telling them, and confront themselves when they recognize that their worry is causing them to avoid challenge.

- *Action tactics:* Individuals who use action tactics learn by doing. They confront a challenge—hands on, in real time—and figure it out as they go along. They see what works and what doesn't, and use these results to inform their next move.

---

*Note: This contribution is adapted from the author's guidebook *Becoming a More Versatile Learner*, published in 1998 by the Center for Creative Leadership.

- *Thinking tactics:* Individuals who learn by means of thinking tactics work things out by themselves. They recall the past for similar or contrasting situations. They imagine the future and play out the "what if . . ." in their minds. They gather information from books and other sources so that they know the facts.

- *Accessing others tactics:* Individuals who learn by accessing others like to seek advice, examples, support, or instruction from people who have met a challenge similar to the one they face. Or they learn how to do something by watching someone else do it. They may take a formal course or program that is relevant to their situation.

Most people employ only one or two of these learning tactics. A first step in helping individuals expand the learning tactics they use is to have them examine their own preferences for particular tactics. A quick self-assessment can be found in Exhibit 29.1.

Exhibit 29.1. What Are Your Preferred Learning Tactics?

Below is a list of statements representing behaviors in the four sets of learning tactics. Read them over carefully and check the behaviors that you engage in most often when facing a challenging experience.

Feeling Tactics

When I am faced with a challenging experience:

- ☐   I carefully consider how I feel.
- ☐   I confront myself if I am avoiding the work challenge.
- ☐   I carefully consider how others might feel.
- ☐   I trust my feelings about what to do.
- ☐   I acknowledge the impact of my feelings on what I decide to do.

Action Tactics

When I am faced with a challenging experience:

- ☐   I figure it out by trial and error.
- ☐   I use my own experience as my guide.
- ☐   I immerse myself in the situation to figure it out quickly.
- ☐   I don't allow lack of information or input from others to keep me from making my move.
- ☐   I commit myself to making something happen.

Thinking Tactics

When I am faced with a challenging experience:

- ☐   I access magazine articles, books, or websites to gain knowledge and information.
- ☐   I ask myself, "How is this similar to other things I know?"

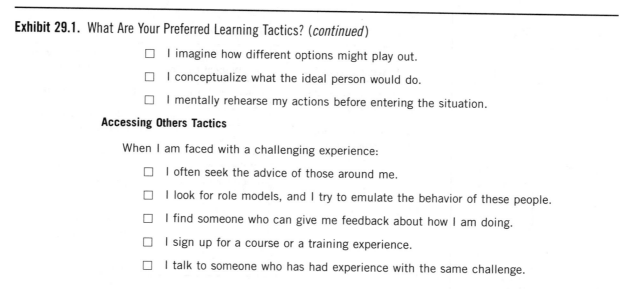

Exhibit 29.1. What Are Your Preferred Learning Tactics? (*continued*)

☐   I imagine how different options might play out.

☐   I conceptualize what the ideal person would do.

☐   I mentally rehearse my actions before entering the situation.

Accessing Others Tactics

When I am faced with a challenging experience:

☐   I often seek the advice of those around me.

☐   I look for role models, and I try to emulate the behavior of these people.

☐   I find someone who can give me feedback about how I am doing.

☐   I sign up for a course or a training experience.

☐   I talk to someone who has had experience with the same challenge.

This is not an exhaustive list of all the possible tactics in a set, but it should be enough to give you an idea of how you like to learn. The set with the highest number of checks is your primary set of learning tactics. You might also have a secondary set with a high number of checks. Rank the sets from 1 to 4 in terms of your preferences, with 1 being the highest.

A second step is for individuals to consider how over-reliance on their preferred tactics can limit their effectiveness as learners. Ask individuals to reflect on how their preferred learning tactics have served them well and the potential results of overusing their preferred tactics to the exclusion of other tactics. The information in Table 29.1 can be used to stimulate (or sum up) a discussion about the overuse of particular tactics.

Finally, individuals need a plan for expanding the tactics they use. The goal is not to immediately begin using the whole range of learning tactics, but rather to target a few behaviors to add to one's repertoire. A plan should articulate the behaviors one wants to begin doing more regularly, when and where these behaviors will be practiced, what support is needed from others, and how one will track progress. Additional strategies for developing competence in each tactic area are shown in Exhibit 29.2.

Background

The learning tactics framework is based on research by Mike Lombardo, Kerry Bunker, and Amy Webb (see Bunker & Webb, 1992) and is grounded in the work of a number of learning theorists, including Reg Revans (action learning), Donald Meichenbaum (cognitive rehearsal), Albert Bandura (social learning), David Kolb (learning from direct experience), and the neoanalytical work of Karen Horney. The self-assessment in Exhibit 29.1 has been further developed into the Learning Tactics Inventory (Dalton, 1999a, 1999b). More on the learning tactics framework can be found in Dalton (1998).

Table 29.1. Illustration of Tactics Overused

	Without Action	**Without Thinking**	**Without Feeling**	**Without Accessing Others**
ACTION		May not have all the vital information. Repeat actions not successful in the past.	Ignore or deny feelings and slip into habitual response.	Reinvent the wheel. Lack support from others; may offend.
THINKING	Procrastinate on dealing with the challenge.		Intellectualize or rationalize to avoid the task.	Miss the insights and support of others. Lack the benefits of others pushing and challenging your thinking.
FEELING	Become paralyzed in the face of the challenge.	Over-respond to the emotional aspects without the calming influence of reason or past success.		Isolate self because of concerns about how others see you.
ACCESSING OTHERS	Talk the issues to death.	Lose the information that resides within formal sources or within yourself.	Over-rely on others, which may lead to others feeling used or perceiving you as incompetent.	

Exhibit 29.2. Strategies for Expanding Your Learning Tactics

Feeling Tactics

- Recall the times that you have been successful in learning something new, even though you were uneasy. What did you do?

- Pay attention when you feel frustrated or anxious in a particular situation. Step back and see whether you can better identify the source of these emotions. What does this tell you about how you are understanding the situation or what your assumptions about it are?

- Keep a journal when you are embarking on a challenging task and note whether your feelings are interfering with your learning.

Action Tactics

- Commit yourself to making something happen this week—something you consider worthwhile but have been procrastinating about.

- Take on a project with a tight deadline.

- Teach someone else a skill.

Exhibit 29.2. Strategies for Expanding Your Learning Tactics (*continued*)

Thinking Tactics

- Ask yourself, "What lessons have I learned this week?" Write them down.

- Look for patterns in similar situations. Ask yourself: "Where have I encountered this before?"

- Keep a journal to track your progress on learning a new skill.

Accessing Others' Tactics

- Find someone who will give you insights and feedback on a problem area in your life.

- Don't assume that your idea is the best one—obtain input from others.

- Pick a role model for a particular skill that you value and observe and interview that person.

References

Bandura, A. (1977). *Social learning theory*. Englewood Cliffs, NJ: Prentice Hall.

Bunker, K.A., & Webb, A.D. (1992). *Learning how to learn from experience: Impact of stress and coping*. Greensboro, NC: Center for Creative Leadership.

Dalton, M. (1998). *Becoming a more versatile learner*. Greensboro, NC: Center for Creative Leadership.

Dalton, M. (1999a). *Learning tactics inventory: Participant workbook*. San Francisco, CA: Pfeiffer.

Dalton, M. (1999b). *Learning tactics inventory: Facilitator's guide*. San Francisco, CA: Pfeiffer.

Horney, K. (1970). *Neurosis and human growth*. New York, NY: Norton.

Meichenbaum, D. (1977). *Cognitive behavior modification*. New York, NY: Plenum.

Revans, R.W. (1980). *Action learning*. London, UK: Blond and Briggs.

30

Narrating Emotions to Enhance Learning

Shirli Kopelman
University of Michigan
Ilan Gewurz
Proment Corporation

LEADERS CONTINUOUSLY FACE situations that are infused with emotions. There is a tendency to view negative emotions as counterproductive because the anxiety, fear, and anger created by power struggles, uncertainty, and frustration can cloud the learning. It is true that negative emotions can be uncomfortable and challenging. Counter-intuitively, such negative emotions may at times be appropriate and even constructive if managed effectively. Ironically, although people may experience positive emotions as pleasant, they can be counterproductive, as well as productive, to learning goals.

Building on our research of NEEM (negotiator expertise in emotion management) and on our experience with business executives developing their leadership skills, we will outline how leaders can strategically manage emotions to enhance learning from experience and apply these lessons in the moment.

The Who and What of Managing Emotions

Learning to strategically manage emotions is critical to personal and professional development. Even if people strive to keep their emotions in check in their professional lives, the emotions will inevitably surface. Emotions are an organic element of social interactions.

Table 30.1. Emotional Landscape

Own and Others	Everyone's emotions must be addressed and constructively channeled.
Conscious and Subconscious	Leaders can help others learn how to manage emotions they weren't even aware they were experiencing and displaying.
Negative and Positive	*Negative* emotions(for example, anger, sadness, frustration, anxiety) and *positive* emotions (for example, joy, happiness) can be productive or counterproductive.
Integral and Incidental	Emotions *integral* to a task arise in response to the focal activity (for example, "I am angry that you excluded me from the team"), whereas *incidental* emotions carry over from unrelated activities or relationships (for example, "I am anxious about driving home in traffic and express that anxiety during the team debriefing").
Authentic and Feigned	People may strategically display emotions they do not actually feel. Ironically, they may begin to authentically experience these emotions.

Thus, rather than minimizing them, leaders must develop a heightened awareness of their dynamics and learn to manage them strategically, which involves knowing how to channel emotions and when to turn their volume up or down. Table 30.1 maps the spectrum of emotions that have to be considered.

There are many theories of emotions, but in general there are three critical phases in how people go from experiencing social stimuli to embodying an emotional response with all its psychological and physiological dimensions: (1) basic perception or attention to the stimuli that generated the emotion; (2) cognitive appraisal or interpretation of this data; and (3) an onset of physiological experiences. To effectively manage emotions as they naturally arise, it is possible to strategically intervene at each or any of these phases.

Self-Narration

Learning to strategically manage emotions is as essential as pausing to think before speaking or acting. A self-narration tool can help you learn to do this (see Figure 30.1). It involves three iterative steps: Leaders can modify their focus and thereby alter what they perceive; they can flexibly reinterpret the event that is taking place; or they can purposefully change the physiological cues to improve their learning potential, especially when pursuing stretch goals that may include emotional side-effects, such as apprehension, anxiety, or overexcitement. Leaders must intervene in at least one step of this process to strategically manage their emotions.

Leaders can use the self-narration template shown in Exhibit 30.1 to prepare for anticipated emotions, narrate emotions as they emerge, and debrief how emotions intervened in a learning opportunity.

Figure 30.1. Self-Narration Process

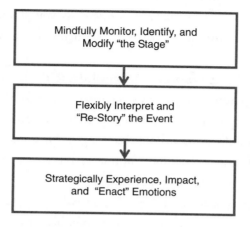

Exhibit 30.1. Self-Narration Template

Step 1: Mindfully Monitor

Mindfully monitor the context and the social environment and identify what it is you were focusing on that triggered an emotional response. What else might you notice—where can you shift your attention—that would impact your emotions in a desirable way (for example, noticing it would help turn up or down the volume on your experienced emotion to facilitate learning)?

Step 2: Flexibly Interpret

What is your instinctive interpretation? What would be an alternative and more productive interpretation? How would this interpretation influence your emotions and turn up or down the volume, or generate a different emotion that is more conducive to learning from this experience?

Step 3: Strategically Enact

In the moment, how might you modify the emotion you are physiologically experiencing? Can you detect early warning signs, label, and successfully shift your emotional experience (for example, take a deep breath and relax your hands)?

To use this tool effectively leaders must develop a heightened awareness and be mindful of their internal emotional landscapes. To illustrate what this kind of mindfulness entails, we often ask leaders to imagine they are writing a play about the scene they are experiencing. Although they are actors immersed in the play, we encourage them to imagine that they are also on the balcony in the director's chair and simultaneously viewing the experience as it takes its course on the stage of a theater. This ability to metaphorically watch the emotional experience from a psychological distance is key to implementing change in real time. We call this process *emotion narration*.

To successfully narrate emotions and facilitate learning in real time using the tool, leaders have to adopt a mindset that will assist in shifting the impact of destructive emotions or heightening the effect of constructive dynamics. The following guidelines for leaders will facilitate effective emotion narration.

Engage mindfully as an emotion narrator. As you simultaneously engage in the social interaction (as an actor) and observe it (as a narrator) be aware of your thoughts, feelings, and behavior.

Recognize and accept emotions. Acknowledging the presence of an experienced emotion undermines its power over you and enables you to take the reins. Just as saying, "Do not think of pink elephants" will provoke thoughts of pink elephants, trying to ignore an emotion may paradoxically make it last longer and strengthen it. Rather than ignoring it, an emotion narrator accepts the emotion as the current dynamic on the stage and then thinks of how to plot the next moment.

Employ nonjudgmental awareness. The overwhelming tendency, especially when negative emotions arise, is to fall into a blaming frame, blaming yourself or others: "He makes me so angry." "She is super annoying." "I'm really disappointed in myself." Being angry with yourself or others for the emotions experienced only spirals you deeper into an emotional dynamic. Awareness without judgment is a key step to transformation.

Seek dynamic flexibility. To implement change you need to believe that change is possible. Emotions are fluid. But as people enter adulthood they lose the ability to let go of an emotion as quickly and fully as they did as children. An emotion narrator's mindset must embrace the ephemeral nature of emotions: They are fluid and their energy can quickly shift.

Engaging this mindset equips the emotion narrator with the ability to mindfully manage emotions and facilitate learning.

An Example of Self-Narration

We recently consulted with a vice president of HR (let's call her Louise) who faced a crisis in her customer service department. One afternoon, all five service agents entered her office to issue a complaint about their manager, Stephan, the head of the department: "He is intolerable and is destroying the department. His default position is to say 'No' to anything we ask, without even considering our requests. He takes credit for our ideas and generally makes people feel small. People are generally unhappy here and we think he has to go."

Louise later described to us that, at that moment, while they spoke, she felt her entire body tense and her head pulse. She had long been aware that the customer service department was not as well run as it could be, but it continually produced happy customers. She felt overcome by anxiety as the possibility of the whole department falling apart came crashing down on her. She was angry with herself at having let it get to this point and was furious at Stephan for not coming to her earlier to let her know things were deteriorating.

As soon as the customer service team left her office, Louise picked up the phone and asked Stephan to come see her. She was upset and could feel the anger building within her, while she thought about the pending collapse of this department, just before the launch of a new product. As soon as Stephan sat down, she heard herself say, "Do you know that everyone in your department is extremely unhappy?" As she unleashed her wrath, she knew it was not the most effective response, but she could barely help herself. Stephan left her office at the point of tears, shaken, hurt, and unsure about his future.

Louise asked us how she could have handled the situation differently and where she should go from there. We re-capped each stage as we coached her through the self-narration tool.

Step 1: Mindfully Monitor, Identify, and Modify the Stage

Leaders mindfully survey the surrounding environment for elements that trigger, intensify, or suppress emotions. Mindfully monitoring the social context—the space and the people—in a nonjudgmental manner creates a distance between you and the emotional dynamics at play and enables you to observe and re-observe the environment and then intentionally modify it, or modify what you pay attention to and what you chose to ignore.

We invited Louise to think about what she was focusing on while the customer service agents were in her office? "At first I just sat there and listened," she said, "and at one point, when the top agent said she was considering leaving, I stopped hearing them and just focused on the impending crisis. I imagined the entire department falling apart, leaving us with no customer service department for the upcoming project, which would be disastrous for the organization. I also spent a lot of time focusing on how badly I messed up. I was very angry with myself for having let things get to this place without intervening earlier. In my head, I started wondering whether, like Stephan, I, too, was a bad manager for not detecting the situation."

We asked Louise, "What could you have focused on that would have enabled you to respond more effectively?" After some reflection, she said, "We have a talented department and the fact that the agents felt it important enough and also felt enough trust to come to me for help was a sign of the culture of communication we had created in the organization and a strong reflection of the team that existed within the department. I suppose I had an opportunity—and an obligation to them—to help improve things." Thus, focusing on these aspects of the interaction led to a different interpretation. We further asked her how she would have felt if she noticed this during the initial interaction. She replied that noticing these facts would have reduced her anxiety, possibly prevented an angry response, and would have enabled her to pleasantly focus on the goals she had set around the culture of open communication and try to learn as much as she could from the team and later from Stephan.

Step 2: Flexibly Interpret and Re-Story the Event

Sometimes you cannot change the point of focus, but the way you interpret the current event will influence your emotions. Acknowledging that your thoughts and feelings are not literal reflections of this team context but rather your personal, subjective interpretation means that other interpretations exist. You have the freedom to interpret and reinterpret the current encounter. Each interpretation may lead to a very different emotional response. If you can flexibly and creatively interpret it, you can selectively choose the interpretation that best serves your strategic goals.

We asked Louise, "After hearing the stories and complaints of the department members, what was the story you were telling yourself?" She said, "I felt immediate anger toward Stephan. I was thinking about all of his shortcomings as a manager and was infuriated with myself for allowing such an incompetent manager to run the department for so long." After a long pause, she added, "I suppose I also interpreted the department's complaint as a form of blame. They knew that I was ultimately responsible for overseeing Stephan and I felt accused for allowing the situation to persist."

We continued to explore her interpretation: "Before you even heard Stephan's perspective, could you think of other ways of interpreting the report?" Louise answered, "Now that I think about it, I realize I never gave Stephan a chance to explain what may have led to this dissatisfaction. Stephan has been in the role for over ten years and, although I always knew he was not the best manager, he was doing something right given the spectacular level of customer satisfaction the firm enjoyed. I suppose rather than interpreting this as a total failure on Stephan's part, I could have recognized that something in the dynamic between Stephan and the team was not working and the challenge was to discover the drivers behind that friction. With this interpretation, perhaps I would have felt more curious and inquisitive, rather than anxious and angry, and possibly excited about a learning challenge that could produce positive outcomes."

Step 3: Strategically Experience, Impact, and Enact Emotions

Ideally, you will have productively managed your emotions by mindfully monitoring and flexibly interpreting your experiences such that the emotion that arises is aligned with your strategy. Thus, all that is left to do at this stage is express the emotion you feel. But sometimes this may not happen quickly enough, or you may not be able to intervene at the monitoring or interpreting stage. Naming emotions at their onset can help. Emotional responses come with early-warning mechanisms reflected in the body. For some people their mouths go dry when they are nervous or their hands sweat when they are uncomfortable. Others might have a tingling sensation in the back of their necks when they are angry or the pace of their breathing might pick up when they are frustrated. The key is identifying these early signs and either going back and re-narrating by modifying the stage, flexibly interpreting the event, or working on enacting a different emotion.

Finally, we asked Louise, "Given that you were not able to refocus or pause and reframe in real time, was there a moment when you felt you were headed down the wrong track in your emotional response?" She was quick to respond, "Yes, when the team told me stories and complaints about Stephan, I felt my head fill with blood and for a second I thought to myself, 'You are too angry to respond. You should thank them for the information and tell them you will get back to them later.' But I guess I did not have the discipline or the willpower to hold back. As soon as I began to talk I knew, deep down, that this was not the best path. I had a similar feeling when I picked up the phone to call Stephan into my office. My whole body was constricted with anger and obviously it would have been wiser to wait before speaking with him. But I was driven by my emotion, and I suppose I had a need to unleash it or get it off my chest, if you will. In retrospect I wish I had listened to my body and my first instinct to wait. At the very minimum, I should have taken a walk to the corner shop to get a sandwich and coffee, or possibly, invited Stephan to come with me on a brisk walk, during which I could cool down. Maybe a breath of fresh air would have been sufficient to enable me to start the conversation with an alternative question, like simply first asking for his perspective as we jointly took strides down the path."

We agreed and noted that not only would this moderate her emotions in the moment, but it would also take her back to Step 1 of the self-narration process, because as Stephan provided his perspective she would have focused her attention on novel facts that would then lead to different interpretations and different emotions.

Louise learned not only how she could have dealt with this situation better but also how emotions could facilitate or derail her from accomplishing her recent personal communication goals—stretch goals she set for herself, as well as the company. Such action-based learning from experience definitely benefits from strategic emotion management.

Final Insights

Self-narration is critical for good leadership. As leaders gain expertise in it, they will learn to mindfully manage counterproductive emotions and facilitate emotions that are aligned with their strategic learning goals. Furthermore, strategic display and response to emotions promote interpersonal resilience and positive relationships, enabling leaders and their teams to continuously learn and enhance organizational processes and outcomes.

Resources

Kopelman, S., Avi-Yonah, O., & Varghese, A.K. (2012). The mindful negotiator: Strategic emotion management and wellbeing. In K. Cameron & G. Spreitzer (Eds.), *The Oxford handbook of positive organizational scholarship* (pp. 591–600). New York, NY: Oxford University Press.

Kopelman, S., Gewurz, I., & Sacharin, V. (2008). The power of presence: Strategic responses to displayed emotions in negotiation. In N.M. Ashkanasy & C.L. Cooper (Eds.), *Research companion to emotions in organizations* (pp. 405–417). Northampton, MA: Edward Elgar.

Kopelman, S., Shoshana, J., & Chen, L. (2009). Re-narrating positive relational identities in organizations: Self-narration as a mechanism for strategic emotion management in interpersonal interactions. In L.M. Roberts & J. Dutton (Eds.), *Exploring positive identities and organizations: Building a theoretical and research foundation* (pp. 265–287). New York, NY: Routledge.

Potworowski, G., & Kopelman, S. (2008). Developing evidence-based expertise in emotion management: Strategically displaying and responding to emotions in negotiations. Special issue on next generation negotiation skills (beyond the deal) in *Negotiation and Conflict Management Research* (NCMR), *1*(4), 333–352.

31

Proactive Feedback Seeking: The Power of Seeing Yourself as Others See You

Susan J. Ashford
University of Michigan

LEADERSHIP IS A complex skill—one that is not learned by simple directives. Indeed, many people consider it an art form. When individuals lead, they are the instrument—leadership is done through their behaviors, physical presence, and talents and in the context of their doubts and fears, their biases and preconceptions. To increase their effectiveness as an instrument, individuals hoping to develop leadership need to know themselves well and understand their impact on others.

Leadership development is never complete. As conditions and people change, learning continues. In fact, the more leadership someone does and the higher level the role from which he or she leads, the more active development needs to be. That's where seeking feedback comes in. If leadership is about setting direction for others and motivating them to follow in that direction, leaders need to understand how they come across to others, what they do that increases others' excitement and motivation versus detracting from it, and how they might improve. To obtain that information in work settings, they often have to seek it.

The Problem of Feedback Flow in Organizations

One thing that can be counted on in all but the rarest of organizations is that leaders do not know as well as they should how others see and are affected by them. This is true because people don't like to share feedback—whether it's the boss dreading the annual performance review process or peers reluctant to share their perceptions of their teammates. People especially don't like to share feedback if their feedback message is negative. Studies show that people avoid giving feedback to poor performers, delay giving them feedback, and distort the feedback to make it seem less negative (Fisher, 1979; Larson, 1986; & Lee, 1993). This problem is only made worse when feedback is being given upwards, across status lines—subordinates are particularly reluctant to give feedback to their bosses. The problem is so prominent that leadership scholars have named it the "CEO disease" and argue that CEOs rarely hear good, accurate information on their own performance within the organization (Goleman, Boyatzis, & McKee; 2002). Jack Welch, the renowned CEO of GE, noted that layers within an organization are like sweaters: If you have enough of them, pretty soon you have no idea of the temperature. Given this reluctance to tell "higher ups" how they are affecting others, any leader who waits for feedback stunts his or her learning and growth.

The Value of Feedback Seeking

To address the interpersonal discomfort that blocks information flow across hierarchical levels, leaders need to seek feedback actively from their subordinates. Ed Koch, the mayor of New York from 1978 to 1989, was famous for engaging his constituents with the question, "How am I doing?" Andy Grove, CEO of Intel, referenced Greek mythology when he spoke of cultivating "necessary Cassandras," people who would tell him the truth about his ideas and behavior. The tool that will help leaders learn the most from experience is within their control, simple to do, and absolutely cost free—developing a routine of seeking feedback.

Feedback seeking may be just as critical in small organizations and even start-ups. For example, a recent _Inc._ magazine issue profiled Jason Freedman, who is credited with developing a business idea that may revolutionize commercial real estate. In developing his idea, Jason engaged in extensive feedback seeking and learning. He notes, "If you're worried about protecting your great business idea from potential competitors, you're not getting the feedback you need to have a chance of making it work." He clearly lives by the adage of "there is no such thing as failure, only feedback" (Freedman, 2012). Freedman sought feedback over a period of years while developing what is widely seen as a winning idea. What if leaders in other organizations were to do the same?

Upon hearing about some of the research on feedback and feedback seeking, one West Coast business owner decided to try it out. She began opening her senior staff meetings with a simple question: "What can I do to support the team in your efforts to achieve the goals and results we identified in our meeting last week?" She notes that the result early on was astonishment: "They were used to me directing the meeting and telling them what I expected; so to have the meeting open with me asking them—in a very sincere and interested manner—put them at ease. Several opened up with some ideas to help to move the whole team in the direction we were seeking." She continues to use this question as an opening to her meetings and to see positive results from it.

Research studies of practicing managers across many companies consistently say that leaders who seek feedback and seek it broadly from the various people they work with (not just from the boss) are seen as more effective by others in the organization (Ashford & Tsui, 1991). This was especially true if the leaders emphasized that they were seeking negative feedback (for example, "What can I do to improve?"). A separate study showed that people who seek feedback are rated as more creative in their performance—something of importance to most leaders today (De Stobbeleir, Ashford, & Buyens, 2011). A third study showed that CEOs of small- to mid-size firms who seek feedback from their top management teams tend to have more committed top management teams, and that this commitment translated into better performance by the firm (Ashford, Sully de Luque, Wellman, De Stobbeleir, & Wollan, 2012). Clearly, seeking feedback from others in the organization pays off, both for the leader who seeks it out and for the organizational unit that he or she leads.

Why Don't Leaders Seek More Feedback More Often?

If seeking feedback is simple, free, and so beneficial, why don't people do it more frequently? The problem is that for most people the learning and development benefits of receiving feedback are weighed against two competing concerns. First, it hurts for leaders to hear that their behavior is not perfect, their direction is not clear, or that their attempts at inspiration fall flat. Like most of us, leaders shy away from disquieting news that might bruise their egos. The best leaders put their hearts and souls into the direction they are trying to create, and it's hard for them to hear feedback (especially negative feedback) about their sincere efforts. That is, leaders often don't seek feedback because they really don't want to know. Many leaders are further hobbled by a more insidious concern—they believe it will look bad to seek feedback, that it will make them look insecure or incompetent.

The irony is that research suggests that people think more *highly* of leaders who seek feedback. They perceive them as more open and caring (Ashford & Northcraft, 1992). Many managers have risen through the organizational ranks having rarely observed their bosses seeking feedback or having seen senior executives opening themselves up to feedback from those beneath them in the organization. As such, a leader's willingness to be vulnerable to others' views makes him or her seem more approachable. Any attempt to promote the seeking of feedback or to build a culture that promotes the seeking of feedback in organizations needs to take into account these two countervailing pressures.

Promoting the Seeking of Feedback Among Leaders

To promote the practice of seeking feedback, it helps to give managers some strategies for doing it. There are three different tactics for seeking feedback from others. The first is direct inquiry, where leaders ask their peers, subordinates, and so forth, (in the style of Ed Koch) "How am I doing?" Leaders can also use a strategy of indirect inquiry by surreptitiously stimulating subordinates to provide feedback (Sully de Luque, Sommers, & Wollan, 2003). For example, leaders can engage subordinates in discussions about work in general and hope to hear comments on the work that have a direct bearing on leadership performance. Finally, leaders can monitor their subordinates and the organizational situation to infer a feedback message. Leaders who are curious about how approachable they are, for example, can answer that question by paying close attention to whether people seem comfortable approaching them. By mindfully watching others' reactions in different situations (for example, do people seem to approach other leaders more than they do you?), leaders gain information about their own behavior (Ashford, Blatt, & VandeWalle, 2003).

These tactics differ in terms of both how much they reveal about a leader's desire for feedback information (direct inquiry reveals a clear desire for feedback) and in terms of the potential accuracy of the information. All strategies for gathering feedback are prone to bias; for example, using a monitoring strategy, if people think they are good at something, they tend to notice events and behaviors that reinforce that perception, thereby giving them more confidence in their self-view. Also, using a monitoring strategy for obtaining feedback does not as a rule give the leader a benefit in terms of the impression he or she makes on others (because others are unaware that the manager is attending to their behavior and using it as feedback).

While directly asking others for feedback doesn't always yield honest answers, it usually brings more accurate appraisals than observing and interpreting a situation. So if direct inquiry communicates to others that the leader is concerned, open, and caring (and thereby encouraging subordinate teams to commit more fully to the organization's goals) and also provides potentially more accurate data, why would a manager rely on monitoring the situation or hinting around via a process of indirect inquiry? Leaders clearly have more to gain by directly seeking feedback from others.

Tools to Promote the Seeking of Feedback

Ongoing feedback is inherently tied to the goals that a leader is trying to attain. For example, if a leader has identified an element of his or her behavior as problematic (for example, listening behavior), that goal serves as the focus of the feedback he or she seeks. A leader may also seek feedback on the state of the team (for example, the level of trust or accountability on the team). This, too, can be the focus of a leader's seeking feedback. Feedback seeking tailored to a specific topic is likely to yield better information than a general "How am I doing?" (Ed Koch notwithstanding). Thus, the first step in seeking feedback is clarifying the focus of the feedback desired. What exactly are you trying to improve?

The next step is to routinize and institutionalize a feedback seeking practice related to that goal. If seeking feedback via direct inquiry, a leader might open weekly staff meetings asking for feedback on some attribute or another, for example about his or her personal behavior or about the functioning of the team. Alternatively, he or she might make seeking feedback the routine end to every one-on-one meeting with subordinates or peers. Executive coach Marshall Goldsmith suggests that leaders should routinely let their peers and subordinates know what they are working on in terms of their development and should ask for input and advice on how to improve.

Seeking feedback becomes both more routine and more noticeable if a leader works out a characteristic prompt that he or she can use. A cue like Ed Koch's "How am I doing?" can work. Better yet, a leader can use a more tailored question, such as, "What advice might you have for me to help improve my effectiveness in [area of improvement]?" or "For me to be the most effective boss for you, what should I do more of, less of, and continue?" Any practice that becomes part of a leader's routine repertoire enhances feedback seeking's impact—both in terms of the information a leader obtains from seeking and with respect to the symbolic impact of their seeking on their subordinates' perceptions of their caring and openness.

If a leader prefers to seek feedback using more indirect methods such as monitoring or indirect inquiry, the process also starts with being clear on the goal or focus of that seeking. Indiscriminate attention to others' reactions to a leader are not recommended—such attention can derail a leader from his or her intentions and lead to too much focus on image and others' views. But with a focus in mind (for example, a leader running a high-level task force might be interested in working on his or her inspirational abilities), the leader can remind himself or herself of that goal prior to task force meetings. That makes it easier to be mindful about observing others' reactions to his or her behavior in the meeting, and how the behavior contributes to or detracts from the group's effectiveness. Then, the leader can make changes in his or her behavior accordingly. Given the difficulty in interpreting monitored feedback cues, however, a leader might want to check any conclusions drawn from such cues with trusted others before acting on them.

Thus, the approach to seeking feedback is simple—get clear on what you want to improve and create a routine practice of seeking feedback with respect to that attribute using either direct or indirect inquiry or monitoring. See the "Feedback Seeking Checklist" in Exhibit 31.1 for reminders relevant to seeking feedback effectively.

There is a collective benefit to feedback seeking as well. In fact, leaders may also be interested in creating a culture of ongoing feedback as part of creating a learning organization. While it is valuable to send messages highlighting the benefits of seeking feedback throughout the organization, the most important step leaders can take to promote such behavior is to do it themselves and hold their top managers accountable for doing it as well. People often mimic the behaviors of those above them in the organization. When top managers seek feedback, their subordinates tend to as well. As that mimicry cascades down the organization, people become more knowledgeable about how they are viewed, where they fall short, and where they excel. As a result, they are able to make the adjustments that

Exhibit 31.1. Feedback Seeking Checklist

About What?

❑ Decide on the goal or focus of interest

❑ But be open to feedback on matters not currently on your radar

How?

❑ For feedback seeking via inquiry, create a routine question or prompt:

- "How am I doing?"

- "I'd love to hear your view of how things are going in the team"

- "What input can you give me for how to improve things around here?"

❑ For feedback seeking via monitoring:

- Pay attention to patterns and consistency in others' behavior before reading a feedback message.

- Beware of over-interpreting or misinterpreting another person's behavior as a feedback message. Check the accuracy of interpretation.

❑ For feedback seeking via indirect inquiry:

- Look for opportunities to stimulate others to talk about your focus of interest.

- Ask others' impressions about your focus of interest.

- Recognize that this tactic yields less accurate information than direct inquiry and carries none of the symbolic benefits.

When?

❑ Close to events where your behaviors of interest are most on display; perhaps directly after

- Speeches you have given

- Retreats you have run

- Difficult conversations you have held

❑ As part of your routine, such as during

- The opening to weekly staff meeting or monthly strategy meetings

  - One-on-one meetings with key staff members

❑ When your seeking is most visible to others

- So you can gain symbolic benefit (showing that you care, are open)

- So that you serve as a role model to others.

From Whom?

❑ Think beyond the boss. Seek feedback from

- Your subordinates—the people you most hope will see leadership qualities in you

- Your peers working with you on projects. They might contribute to your formal performance review and any one of them might become your boss.

Exhibit 31.1. Feedback Seeking Checklist (*continued*)

- ❏ Seek broadly—it leads to new ideas and approaches and higher ratings for creativity
  - Could you seek feedback:

    In customer interactions?

    From peers or mentors in your network who might not interact with you on a day-to-day basis?

    From managers at your level in other organizations?

allow better coordination within the organization and higher performance in the organization as a whole.

For leaders who are able to face their ego and image concerns and risk receiving feedback, the payoff both in terms of image (as caring and open) and follower commitment, as well as in terms of personal learning and development are substantial. If the goal is to develop leaders in organizations (and to improve organizations in the process), one important aspect of achieving that goal is helping leaders to more frequently seek feedback proactively. It is a managerial practice that is simple, free, and beneficial. Leaders just have to keep their egos in check and develop a habit of proactively seeking feedback to enjoy its benefits.

References

Ashford, S.J., & Northcraft, G.B. (1992). Conveying more (or less) than we realize: The role of impression-management in feedback-seeking. *Organizational Behavior and Human Decision Processes, 53,* 310–334.

Ashford, S.J., & Tsui, A.S. (1991). Self-regulation for managerial rffectiveness: The role of active feedback-seeking. *Academy of Management Journal, 34*(2), 251–280.

Ashford, S.J., Blatt, R., & VandeWalle, D. (2003). Reflections on the looking glass: A review of research on feedback-seeking behavior in organizations. *Journal of Management, 29*(6), 773–799.

Ashford, S.J., Sully de Luque, M.D., Wellman, N., DeStobblier, K.M., & Wollan, M. (2012). Proactive behavior and collective outcomes: CEO feedback seeking, TMT dynamics, and performance. Working paper, University of Michigan.

De Stobbeleir, K.M., Ashford, S.J., & Buyens, D. (2011). Self-regulation of creativity at work: The role of feedback seeking behavior in creative performance. *Academy of Management Journal, 54*(4), 811–832.

Fisher, C.D. (1979). Transmission of positive and negative feedback to subordinates: A laboratory investigation. *Journal of Applied Psychology, 64*(5), 533–540.

Freedman, D.H. (no relation). (2012, May). How Jason Freedman cooked up a killer business idea one tweak at a time. *Inc.,* pp. 75–82.

Goleman, D., Boyatzis, R., & McKee, A. (2002). *Primal leadership: Realizing the power of emotional intelligence.* Boston, MA: Harvard Business School Press.

Larson, J.R. (1986). Supervisors' performance feedback to subordinates: The impact of subordinate performance valence and outcome dependence. *Organizational Behavior and Human Decision Process, 37,* 391–408.

Lee, F. (1993). Being polite and keeping MUM: How bad news is communicated in organizational hierarchies. *Journal of Applied Social Psychology, 23,* 1124–1149.

Sully de Luque, M.F., Sommers, S.M., & Wollan, M.L. (2003, August). The question of seeking: Assessing multiple feedback seeking strategies. Presented at the Academy of Management Conference, Seattle, Washington.

32

Feedback: Who, When, and How to Ask

Sylvester Taylor
Center for Creative Leadership

Getting Regular, Constructive feedback, versus waiting for someone to give it, is an important key for people who want to manage their careers and their professional development effectively. Unfortunately, both giving and receiving feedback are difficult for people to master. They know that they need feedback for development but are often unsure about how to get it. At the Center for Creative Leadership (CCL) we teach a simple framework for how to obtain effective feedback. It is both powerful and easy to use. The essential elements are that a person needs to learn: (1) who to ask for it, (2) when to ask for it, and (3) how to ask for it. If people master these three steps, they can greatly enhance their development on the job.

Who to Ask

The best feedback-givers may not be the obvious ones. A boss or colleague may provide valuable input, but learners should take into consideration other factors as well.

1. *Respect and credibility.* They should find someone they trust to be honest, whose opinions they respect, and who will encourage them to improve their effectiveness.

2. *Different perspectives.* Someone who has a different work style will provide opinions and points of view that are new. Learners should seek out someone with

whom they've had a disagreement in the past or someone who consistently seems to see things different way.

3. *Interdependence.* If a learner seeks feedback from someone that he or she must interact with in order for both to be successful, then each will have a vested interest in the other's effectiveness.

4. *Time.* The best feedback comes from those who have had a sufficient opportunity (usually three to six months) to observe a person's behavior in various contexts. With too little time or context, the feedback-giver may provide only first, or surface, impressions.

When to Ask

Before asking for feedback, learners should think about their challenges, expectations, and goals (both immediate and long-term). Rather than asking for general feedback (for example, "How can I be more effective?"), they should be clear about asking for feedback as it pertains to specific goals (for example, "How can I demonstrate that I am a good listener?"). Without that clarity, they will find it much more difficult to ask for—and make use of—feedback. Once they've established goals and received initial feedback (at CCL we generally advise that they pick just one or two goals at first), they should make it a habit by asking for feedback on a regular basis (daily or weekly, for an example). Some leaders I know enlist the help of a partner, and they meet regularly to share feedback. The more often they receive feedback, the easier it is for them to be aware of what they are doing well and what they need to continue to work on.

How to Ask

Much of the quality and quantity of the information that learners receive is dependent on how they ask for it. They are much more likely to receive vague comments and generalizations unless they ask for specific details and objective information. A simple and effective technique for asking for feedback focuses on situation, behavior, and impact (SBI). Developed by CCL and taught to managers and executives for more than thirty years, the SBI method is a way to deliver and receive direct and objective comments on a person's actions without personal attack, incorrect judgments, vague statements, or third-party slights.

Here's how the SBI method works:

Ask about the situation. Ask the feedback-giver to describe and clarify the specific situation in which a behavior occurred. For example, "Can you tell me again the specifics of when and where this occurred? Was it during the meeting with the new vice president yesterday?"

Describe the behavior. This is the most crucial step and the one that takes the most practice. The goal is to get the person providing the feedback to use verbs to describe the actual behavior, not a judgment about what the behavior might mean. When seeking feedback, a person should ask not only what was done but also how it was done. Particular attention should be paid to body language, tone of voice, speaking manner, and word choice. For example, "How was my tone of voice? Was it even? What about when she questioned our numbers?"

Name the impact. The idea here is to get the person providing the feedback to specify the direct, observable impact that the behavior had—not how the behavior might possibly affect the organization, co-workers, a program, clients, a product, or any other third party. For example, "What was the impact of my delivery? How did it make you feel or what did you think as a result?"

The SBI format may also be used to briefly reinforce feedback behavior in a casual way. For example, "This morning in the hallway you asked for my opinion about the decision to launch our new product. You also often ask me to join the group at lunch. That makes me feel included, part of the team."

Or it may be the introduction when further discussion is sought. For example, "You have not commented about the field reports I completed. I am wondering if they are what you were expecting."

Some Final Observations

At first, following the SBI method may take effort or seem artificial. But eventually, paying attention to specific behaviors and giving and receiving feedback using this approach will become a natural part of a person's management style.

The method is direct and effective. By breaking down the perception of performance into the three areas of identifying a situation, describing a behavior, and naming the impact that the behavior has had on other people, it simplifies feedback and makes it easier for people to give and receive it regularly.

When seeking feedback (or when it is being given unsolicited), the learner should encourage feedback providers to state specifically what behaviors (verbal and nonverbal) need to be changed or improved. And they should be asked to describe the consequences of the behavior.

By focusing on situation, behavior, and impact, learners will receive information that is specific and helpful. They are also providing a safe way for others to give information that may be difficult to give.

Finally, learners should remember to say thank you to the feedback provider. Even if they don't agree with the feedback, they can learn from it. Thanking someone for giving feedback demonstrates that the feedback process is valued and it increases the likelihood of receiving more feedback in the future. A form to evaluate the feedback you receive is provided in Exhibit 32.1.

Exhibit 32.1. Evaluating Feedback

When receiving feedback, a person should consider:

Accuracy. Who is giving the feedback? What are their intentions? How much do you respect their opinions?

Value. Is this feedback that you like or something that was hard to hear? Is this something that can be helpful to you? Do you want to know more?

Importance. What are the consequences for ignoring this feedback? What are the rewards? Not all feedback can or should be acted upon. On the other hand, some feedback cannot be ignored.

Representativeness. If you are unsure about whether you should take feedback to heart and make a change, you might want to check it out with a trusted colleague or friend. Do other people share the feedback?

33

Micro-Feedback: A Tool for Real-Time Learning

Tanya Boyd

Payless Holdings, Inc.

AT PAYLESS, PERFORMANCE reviews are held annually, with perhaps a midyear review, and, of course, more frequent coaching and feedback discussions between associates and their managers are encouraged, but engagement surveys and focus groups indicate that these conversations often don't take place. It would be gratifying to be able to claim a culture of feedback, where everybody seeks, gives, and receives feedback on a regular basis, regardless of level or relationship; but the organization is not there yet. Year after year, some of the lowest scores on the engagement survey have been related to coaching and development conversations. The evidence is clear that feedback is a critical element in on-the-job development. Feedback encourages reflection on the experience that a person is having, and it is this process of thinking through the experience and the choices being made as a part of that experience that results in the learning and development. Without feedback, a person can go through a new experience and yet not learn or develop in any significant way. As important as feedback is to development, it is an area of opportunity for many individuals and companies.

Recently, Payless piloted a new approach to tackle this ubiquitous problem. Working with a small start-up company, the organization implemented a type of micro-feedback (see Table 33.1 for benefits and challenges of micro-feedback). There are many similar companies

Table 33.1.   Benefits and Challenges of Micro-Feedback

Benefits	Challenges
• Real-time feedback • Team members as raters are usually close to the associate and experience • Flexibility in questions and format • Lots of data without overtaxing associates • Encourages face-to-face follow-up • Spurs development conversations with managers • Easy interface allows for viewing results weekly, monthly, quarterly—see changes over time	• Potential to become bored or annoyed with frequent surveys • (Specific to tool chosen) Feedback limited to team; some associates would have benefited from broader reach • Questions intended to be set up on a role basis; setting up on individual basis means larger workload for administrator • (Specific to tool chosen) All team members must be included

Exhibit 33.1. Sample Questions

1. With regard to the frequency of your updates to team members on project status:

    a. Keep up the good work!

    b. Do much more

    c. Do more

    d. Do less

    e. Do much less

2. Considering the balance between positive feedback and constructive criticism:

    a. Keep up the good work!

    b. Provide more positive comments

    c. Provide more constructive criticism

    d. Provide more of both positive comments and constructive criticism

    e. Other (please explain)

and products available, as well as the option to design and administer it yourself. The version used at Payless was similar to a 360-degree instrument in format but more flexible in several ways than the organization's traditional 360 approach—which is done on a three-year rotation with content drawn from its leadership competencies. The reports from these 360s do provide valuable feedback, but it is often somewhat general since the competencies apply across the organization and, because they are done infrequently, the feedback tends to reflect overall impressions rather than specific instances.

The micro-feedback approach that was piloted provided feedback on a daily, weekly, or monthly basis, with reports available for these timeframes as well as quarterly and annually (see the sample questions in Exhibit 33.1). The content was based on an associate's role, and there were no restrictions on the number of roles you could set up, which means you could potentially have set up a different survey for each associate (although there are, of course, workload issues with that). This allowed associates to receive frequent feedback about behaviors specific to their roles from the people who worked most closely with them. The survey still maintained anonymity, as feedback scores were rolled up and presented in aggregate. Each question included an option to expand on the rating given with a comment. Comments were provided in the report verbatim, so respondents who wanted to identify themselves or describe a specific incident could do so in that section.

This process is particularly useful for enhancing experience-based development because of the flexibility with the questions themselves. Depending on the tool that was used, each person could write the questions he or she wanted feedback on, or a list of questions could be pre-populated into the tool and people could choose from the list. An associate who was in a leadership role for the first time, for example, could identify five or six key behaviors important for success in the role and craft questions about them. A leader who was going through a turnaround could work with a mentor or his or her manager to identify the critical actions that would enable success and set these up in the tool as questions. Also, since it was likely that the people on the associate's team were either going through a similar experience or were aware of the experience that the individual was going through at any given time, their feedback could be in real time and specific.

Surveys can be sent out at whatever interval the organization decides fits with its culture. Both daily and weekly were tried, and the feedback received from our testers indicated that weekly was preferable. The surveys were not typically very long, but people tended to feel annoyed if they had a new one in their inboxes every day. The surveys themselves rotated questions so you might have been asked one question about your manager, one each about two different peers, and one about a direct report. The actual number of questions on the survey that you received depended on the number of people on the team and the number of total items in the pool. The tool used at Payless ensured that at least two people were asked each question for each associate each week. Respondents did not have to log in to complete the survey; a link was provided and when they clicked on the link people were taken right into the survey, which saved time and meant people didn't have to remember passwords. Completion time was about five to ten minutes, depending on how much time a respondent chose to spend on open-ended comments.

Associates could access their rolling reports at any time. Data became available once the minimum number of responses had been reached, and associates could monitor changes across weeks and then months as data added up. Line graphs showing trends were included so it was easy to see changes over time. Associates being rated felt that having results on a weekly basis allowed them time to absorb the results, make any changes needed, and see whether the changes had an effect. The open-ended comments were included in each version of the report, dated by week. As with most feedback tools, people really liked these open-ended comments because they typically provided the most specific feedback. In this case, that feedback was also usually timely and relevant, and so easier to act upon.

The reports were useful conversation starters for staff meetings with a manager, or could be shown to team members to solicit additional information. Rather than a direct, "How do you think I'm doing in this area?" it is somehow easier for people to respond to, "My report suggests that most of my team feels I could work on this. Even if you weren't one who responded that way, can you think of some ways that I could improve here?"

One question some people in our organization asked was whether this tool would actually *dis*courage coaching and feedback conversations since people could just quickly click a numeric response to a question rather than taking the time to go talk with the person face to face. While this is a legitimate concern, we found that the process actually worked the other way. First of all, spontaneous face-to-face conversations were not taking place prior to implementing the tool so there wasn't much to lose! For associates receiving feedback, the reports gave them an initial "peek" at how people on their teams thought they were doing, and they used these reports in weekly staff meetings with their managers to discuss both areas that appeared as strengths as well as those with room for improvement.

They and their managers would plan how to improve in the areas with lower scores, which often included face-to-face conversations with other team members to gather more detail. For the respondents, because they had seen the questions a particular team member was asking and had to think about and decide on a score to give that person, they often found that they had more thoughts and ideas to provide to their team members, which they at least sometimes decided to go share in face-to-face conversations (often in lieu of writing an open-ended comment). So while the concern was that the tool might discourage feedback conversations, we found anecdotally that it actually increased the number and quality of conversations happening within the teams who piloted the tool.

Keys to Success

Whether this process can be successful depends on a few key areas. First, it is essential to spend time carefully setting up teams, roles, and questions. If the questions do not target critical behaviors, or are not asked in a way that returns actionable data, the survey is a waste of time. Second, make sure that you spend time clearly explaining the purpose of the process and the expected benefits for all who will be involved. You are asking people to invest some of their valuable time and energy in developing their team members, so it is important that they recognize both the value for the other person as well as the benefits that they will receive with stronger team members to work with. Third, it is worthwhile to train managers on how to use the reports during their meetings with the people being rated. The reports contain a host of valuable data and many relevant conversations can result, but if managers are not sure how to incorporate this into a development conversation, maximum benefit may not be reached. A brief training session can help to jump-start these conversations. Last, it is very important that managers buy into the process and keep up on completing their surveys. If team members observe that their managers never take the time to complete their surveys, they will quickly assume that the process is not very important and will tend to opt out themselves.

34

Leadership Journeys: Intentional Reflection Experiences

Nicole L. Dubbs, Andrew K. Mandel, Kristin Ohnstad, and Scott Taylor
Teach For America

TEACH FOR AMERICA, a national nonprofit founded in 1989, aims to build a force of lifelong leaders committed to ending the educational inequity that exists in this country between children who grow up in poverty and their more affluent peers. The organization recruits, selects, trains, and supports ten thousand classroom teachers through a two-year commitment in urban and rural low-income communities across the country, and it aims to catalyze the leadership of the organization's more than thirty thousand alumni. In order to support this growing social enterprise, our eighteen-hundred-plus full-time staff members must live out the organization's core values of transformational change, leadership, diversity, team, and respect and humility. But what does it look like to promote values-based development in these arenas? One promising method to prompt reflection about the extent to which staff members are indeed operating in alignment with these core values is a program called Leadership Journeys.

These journeys are multiday experiences, held outside of offices and in the communities where our teachers work. They help participants explore many different aspects of themselves as leaders by having them do such things as: looking closely at how they operate and at the beliefs that underlie their decisions through reflection on their life stories, exploring their personal identities, receiving feedback from others, gaining inspiration and insight about who they wish to be through an understanding of how others perceive them, interacting with community leaders, and actively considering new models of leadership as they hear first-hand stories from different types of inspirational role models. All these experiences, along with much discussion with others throughout the journey, help bridge the gap between participants' clarified intentions and their current reality. And then they return to their daily work with new perspectives and renewed energy.

Initial Impact

The initial feedback from our Leadership Journeys is promising and makes us curious to continue to learn about how well these experiences have a lasting impact on the way our staff members operate and feel as a part of our organization and movement. In post-journey surveys, participants have comments such as:

> This was one of the most powerful experiences of my life. Diving into my own thoughts and being able to verbalize things that I wouldn't be able to in another setting was empowering and really showed me some of the strengths that I've always had but may have lost over the past few years. I really believe that this was life-altering for me and the experiences I took away from that trip will be a driving force in how I operate within my role and within my own life.

Table 34.1 presents summary results about how participants perceive the impact of the program.

Three Key Factors

We have identified three key elements that are critical for enabling these journeys to have the impact we're seeing: building a supportive, challenging community; provocative experiences; and deep sense-making.

Table 34.1.   Participant Feelings Before and After the Leadership Journey Program

	Before (strongly agree/agree)	After (strongly agree/agree)
I feel connected to our organization.	45%	88%
I feel empowered to be myself in my role.	39%	88%
I feel empowered to exercise leadership in my role.	29%	86%
I would recommend this experience to my colleagues.	n/a	96%

1. Building a Supportive, Challenging Community

We've found that an important starting point for enabling deep, meaningful reflection is building a community in which individuals feel safe to be vulnerable and honest with themselves and each other and where they can be productively challenged. This is particularly important because doing values-based work requires deeply personal exploration.

Building such a community requires that attention be paid to structuring groups, setting expectations and communicating effectively, storytelling, and modeling.

Structuring groups. Structurally, we bring together participants from different teams across the country so they can cross-fertilize ideas and reflections, but we group them so they are at the same approximate level, scope of responsibility, and points in their careers as others to infuse naturally meaningful connections among the peer group. We are also careful not to group participants with people they manage or are managed by; this ensures that there is a safe space in which the members of the cohort become true accountability partners to one another.

Setting expectations and communication. Through initial communication and pre-work, we explicitly name that these journeys are positioned to help each participant find his or her own way, rather than as means to a specific end or outcome that we have for them. We state and reinforce throughout the week that this is *their* experience, and we establish group norms that reinforce risk taking, openness, support, challenge, and lack of judgment so individuals are set up to get the most out of the week. Additionally, we ask participants to share initial reflections about their own leadership stories thus far in their lives, including major challenges and success, in order to build a frame of mind that will help them dig in during the week.

Storytelling. From the very beginning, we focus on people and their personal stories and experiences, rather than roles and skills. For example, during our opening as a group we ask participants to answer three questions: Where is home and what makes it home to you? Who is someone you love and why do you love him or her? What is something you love and why do you love it (thing or experience)? Additionally, we ask participants to send us a song to play for the group, and each day we listen to a few songs together and hear the meaning and significance of the song from the person who chose it. Both of these activities help us connect at a human level and share our stories, producing trust through vulnerability.

Modeling. Facilitators share their own stories, fears, and vulnerabilities with the group throughout the week, which is a critical component of the experience, as it quickly helps to create a safe and open space and tone. Facilitators frame and guide conversations and experiences, while also participating and sharing in those conversations and experiences authentically as learners themselves.

Impact of community on participants' ability to reflect. Participants had this to say about building a community:

This trip, the physical settings, my fellow participants, and the structures for reflection were set up in a way that made it okay to be honest, made it okay to be wrong, not have the answer, be incomplete, and be genuinely confused. I felt supported by the people on the trip in my personal journey, even though it was supposed to be individual Leadership Journeys. Likewise, I realized that my leadership is best enacted when I am surrounded by others, so it was incredibly meaningful to be able to push others in their own journeys as well.

2. Provocative Experiences

As research on adult learning and development would suggest, we have found that deep, meaningful reflection often happens when people are immersed in provocative experiences that disorient, challenge, or provoke them to consider held assumptions, habits, or beliefs. In the context of a supportive, challenging community, provocative experiences are critical fuel for reflection.

Several elements help create provocative experiences: operating in a real setting, learning from others, facing disorienting or unexpected activities, looking in a mirror, and taking part in consultancies and protocols.

Operating in a real setting. Place matters. The Leadership Journeys are not held in conference rooms or classrooms but in the field. Walking across Edmund Pettus Bridge in Selma, Alabama, in the footsteps of John Lewis and others who marched on Bloody Sunday in 1965, leads to a different depth of discussion about courage of conviction than sitting around a table in a conference room. Joining community members to cook a meal alongside residents on a Native American reservation provides valuable fodder for examining one's relationship to community and service. Walking through a New Orleans neighborhood that has undergone massive revitalization and rehabilitation in the wake of Hurricane Katrina enables one to more deeply consider how to rally people around a shared vision for change. Place is a powerful way to spur reflection, foster new insights, and create a shared experience that participants can discuss and learn from together.

Learning from others. We intentionally seek to learn from a diversity of people and from organizations in the communities in which we work. In guided discussions with local leaders, we focus on the nature of their work, the nature of their leadership, what they are learning about what it takes to make change happen, and where they personally thrive or struggle in leading that change. These conversations help participants challenge, expand, or enrich some of the archetypes they may hold about what leadership is or is not and how personal and varied leadership can be in different contexts; the conversations also deepen their understanding of the unique assets and challenges faced by local communities. In addition, learning from others prompts participants to arrive at, or more clearly articulate, their own points of view about leadership and how they can continue to grow to be the best leaders they can be.

Facing disorienting or unexpected activities. We often withhold the itinerary and agenda from our participants to help them stay in the moment and to maintain an element of productive tension and uncertainty. For example, we lead an activity called "100 Minutes," where we drive to an unfamiliar town or neighborhood and, after being greeted by a local leader, tell participants to "get to know the community" in the next one hundred minutes in whatever ways they can. This activity helps people examine how they go about learning about a place, what is easy or natural, and what is hard or uncomfortable; thus, they examine how their choices in this safe, limited exercise may illuminate their broader tendencies, both productive and problematic, for getting to know the communities in which they work.

Looking in a mirror. Provocative experiences can also come from examining oneself. We generate the potential for self-examination in a variety of ways: for example, by having participants take assessments such as StrengthsFinder or Myers-Briggs to gain a better understanding of their styles and strengths; by having them "interview" some of their key personal and professional influencers to develop a better sense of where their beliefs, habits, and values come from; or by having them receive 360-degree feedback from colleagues, direct reports, and peers and then examine the themes and inconsistencies in that feedback with an executive coach. Additionally, we use selected readings such as essays, poetry, and lyrics to help participants examine who they really are and what lies at their core. All of these personal provocations contribute to participants more fully seeing and appreciating themselves, valuing their strengths, and considering the discrepancies that arise between their own self-views and how they are viewed by others.

Taking part in consultancies. We use protocols or consultancies at certain points in the week to help participants dive into their own dilemmas at work and use some of the lessons of the week and the valuable perspective of their colleagues to reexamine how they are approaching those challenges and what new possibilities they might imagine. Similarly, we utilize the four-column, or "competing commitments," protocol developed by Robert Kegan and Lisa Lahey (2001) to help participants uncover the potential assumptions or fears holding them back from changing their behaviors to align with their beliefs.

3. Deep Sense-Making

Provocative experiences only prove useful as learning levers if participants have the opportunity to process these inputs. The Leadership Journey program creates ample space and time for reflection that allows people to make sense of their experiences and come to new insights about themselves and their actions.

In order to promote sense-making, we believe it's necessary to use varied methods, scaffolding, facilitators not teachers, and to recognize that time and space matter.

Varied methods. Though perhaps obvious, it's important to note that we use multiple methods to enable meaningful reflection. For example, we will have whole group discussions, partner discussions, quiet journaling or independent time, or a mix of various methods depending on the time of day, locale, and activity. Furthermore, we encourage lots of informal dialogue and sense-making over meals and during our travel times.

Scaffolding. Although it is possible to do each of the activities discussed independently, we've found that productive momentum is most effectively built by intentionally scaffolding activities of increased challenge and vulnerability over the course of the experience. The arc of layering increasingly challenging provocative experiences and sense-making dialogue together over the week is essential to get to a very deep place with learners. As a culminating activity for the week, we have participants write value statements about their personal beliefs and then share them with others to help build accountability and commitment to living out their beliefs.

Facilitators, not teachers. Given how personal the sense-making from these experiences can be, we've found it's important that the facilitators be able to strike a delicate balance between tolerating discomfort or silence or dissatisfaction when participants may feel stuck or confused and interjecting a question, comment, or personal reflection to refocus or move the group forward. We don't use teaching scripts or any talking points; instead we ask our facilitators to use intentional questions to help participants extract their own lessons and meaning from these provocative experiences.

Time and space matter. The Leadership Journey program recognizes the importance of having time to process, question, sit with feelings of confusion or uncertainty, and engage in dialogue or contemplation. Time is critical for sense-making. Where you are and what surrounds you affect your mood and orientation. We've found that the spaces where we choose to gather can help us create an atmosphere much more conducive to sense-making, and so we seek out stimulating spaces removed from everyday distractions. Whether it be a grove of trees on a college campus, a museum or city garden, a historical site or monument, the journeys draw on the power of place to push sense-making to even deeper levels. We want to ensure that sense-making occurs in environments that are meaningful, relevant, and, ultimately, richly inspiring.

Participants had this to say about the opportunity for sense-making:

> This has been a really powerful experience, even though I consider myself to typically be a pretty reflective and self-aware person. A couple things that made it different: having long blocks of time to reflect or discuss when I couldn't pro-crastinate or avoid difficult questions, and feeling the momentum build towards openness, vulnerability, and deep thinking.

Applying These Principles to Your Organization

Here are a few of the lessons we've learned and some questions we are still pondering as we continue to evolve our approach. They may help you apply these principles to your unique organizational context.

Start Small and Build the Political Will

Our experiential approach to leadership development emerged organically over time through piloting smaller-scale innovations. The Leadership Journey work began as an extracurricular project, with one trip with a small subset of participants. Those "early adopters" became champions for our work by singing its praises to their teams and managers, and the momentum began. More senior leaders heard about our work, engaged with participants, or joined the experiences themselves, and the political will and resources for expansion grew. It would be valuable for you to consider how to foster a culture of innovation for leadership development in order to allow people on your staff to try out new approaches.

Think of What Could Be, Not What Is

Maintain a sense of possibility for what your leadership development programming could look like in your organization. Our journeys—which have involved listening to music, visiting nature, becoming vulnerable and personal with one another, and meeting external leaders—started out as very countercultural experiences for our staff. Rather than reflecting the prevailing ways of being or operating as staff, our experiences helped to introduce or uncover new or alternative ways that our staff could think, feel, and operate, and which we hope are ultimately more aligned to our true intentions. As you consider developing programming, be open to methods and ideas that could be seen as countercultural at first.

Avoid the Cookie Cutter

Finally, make it yours by being attuned to your unique context. We have different journey experiences for staff members at different stages of their development. Our managers are facing different challenges (for example, how to empower others) than our individual contributors are (for example, how to use their voices). The methods we've used to bring our leadership ideas to life are rooted in a deep empathy and understanding of our audience: the staff at Teach For America. Though our methods are somewhat unconventional, they are very connected to the spirit of our work and to our distinct mission, context, and purpose. Tailor your methods to the distinctiveness of your particular situation and the continuum of your staff experience.

Questions We're Still Trying to Answer

What kind of post-journey support should we provide? These experiences are meant to be important developmental catalysts, but they are not the be-all and end-all of what's needed for our staff to lead more effectively. We are in the midst of exploring additional strategies and structures that will ensure our staff members translate the insights, ideas, and commitments from their journey experiences into new ways of orienting and acting in their daily work.

How can we improve evaluation? Our participant and manager surveys, as well as many anecdotes, are providing a lot of useful feedback about the perceived impact of the journey experience. Yet these measures are limited in their rigor, and we aspire to understand the contribution that these experiences are having across different dimensions over time, including staff retention, satisfaction, overall effectiveness, and productivity.

How does this program fit into development as a whole? These experiences are smaller parts of a larger developmental puzzle that we are piecing together. As we build out a more comprehensive, holistic approach to staff development, how do we strike the balance between providing a formal continuum of development appropriate to staff members at various stages of their careers and learning, while simultaneously maintaining room for innovation and new ideas and approaches to emerge?

Reference

Kegan, R., & Lahey, L. (2001). *How the way we talk can change the way we work.* San Francisco, CA: Jossey-Bass.

35

After-Event Reviews: How to Structure Reflection Conversations

D. Scott DeRue
University of Michigan

"We had the experience but missed the meaning."

T.S. Eliot

REFLECTION IS QUITE possibly a manager's least favorite activity. With an orientation toward achievement and performance, many managers aspire to move forward, onward, and upward! As Bruch and Ghoshal (2002) describe in their description of life as an executive, "They rush from meeting to meeting, check their e-mail constantly, extinguish fire after fire, and make countless phone calls." Yet, to learn from experience, people need to digest their experience by asking themselves, "What just happened?", reflect on it by asking themselves, "Why did it go that way?", and relate it to general patterns of cause and effect (by asking themselves, "Has this happened before?"

Developed by the U.S. Army, an after-event review (AER; also referred to as an after-action review) is a structured and systematic process for reflecting on experience and generating lessons that improve future performance (DOA-CALL, 1993). The practice is now used by businesses, not-for-profit organizations, and governmental agencies around the world (Baird, Henderson, & Watts, 1997; Darling, Parry, & Moore, 2005; Garvin, Edmondson, & Gino, 2008; Raelin, 2001).

Individuals can work through the steps below on their own, working with a coach or boss, or as part of a facilitated workshop.

AERs: A Four-Step Process of Structured Reflection

Step 1: Conduct the AER as soon after the experience as possible. Do not wait until the end of the project or an annual performance review process.

Step 2: Describe the experience. Individuals are encouraged to create an accurate picture of the experience they just completed. Capturing what really occurred, as a video camera would record, helps people identify and separate out the biases that preclude an accurate reconstruction of experience.

Step 3: Develop counterfactuals. Individuals are encouraged to engage in counterfactual thinking, which involves imagining "what-if" scenarios about the actions not taken in the situation and some speculation on what the results might have been had those actions been taken.

Step 4: Identify new insights, feedback, and how the lessons of this experience can be applied to improve performance in future experiences.

Instructions for Conducting an AER
Instructions for Facilitators

The purpose of an after-event review is to examine and explore the lessons of experience. The reflection process is designed to break down the barriers that get in the way of smart, talented people learning from their experiences.

As the facilitator, you should:

- Make a concerted effort to draw in people who seem reluctant to participate in the process

- Encourage people to examine the experience with honesty and openness

- Enter the discussion only when necessary

- Help those participating in the review to focus on learning from the experience

- Use open-ended questions to guide the discussion (do not make evaluative statements)

Prior to meeting, have each person complete Form A in Exhibit 35.1. After conducting the critical reflection process, please summarize your discussion with each participant using Form B in Exhibit 35.2.

Discussion Outline

- Introduction and rules
    - Explain the purpose of the critical reflection process and encourage participation

- Describe the experience
  - Ask the person to describe the experience—what his or her own role was in the experience, who else was involved, what happened prior to, during, and after the experience
- Awareness
  - Inquire about the person's reaction to the experience, the challenges he or she faced in the experience, and the impact on his or her confidence as a leader
- Critical analysis
  - Encourage the person to critically analyze the experience, focusing on the leadership approach in the experience
  - Inquire about how the person contributed to the performance outcome
  - Ask the person to think of at least one alternative explanation for his or her performance, and compare/contrast with his or her initial explanation. Encourage the person to consider "what if" scenarios.
- New perspective
  - Ask the person what lessons can be learned from the experience, and what feedback can be derived from this experience. The person should apply insights from the discussion to the experience and focus on future development opportunities
- Action steps
  - Ask the person to derive at least two action steps that he or she can take based on the lessons of this experience to improve his or her performance going forward
  - Ask the person to commit to specific milestones and a timeline for completing these action steps
- Closing comments
  - Ensure agreement from the person on next steps

References

Baird, L., Henderson, J.C., & Watts, S. (1997). Learning from action: An analysis of the Center for Army Lessons Learned (CALL). *Human Resource Management, 36*(4), 385–395.

Bruch, H., & Ghoshal, S. (2002). Beware the busy manager. *Harvard Business Review, 80*(2), 62–69.

Darling, M., Parry, C., & Moore, J. (2005). Learning in the thick of it. *Harvard Business Review, 83*(7), 84–93.

DOA-CALL. (1993). *A leader's guide to after-action reviews.* Washington, DC: U.S. Department of the Army.

Garvin, D.A., Edmondson, A.C., & Gino, F. (2008). Is yours a learning organization? *Harvard Business Review, 86*(3), 109–116.

Raelin, J.A. (2001). Public reflection as the basis of learning. *Management Learning, 32*(1), 11–30.

Exhibit 35.1. Form A: Reflecting on the Experience

Name:_____

Leadership Experience:_____

Date: _____

Location:_____

Describe the Experience

- Who was involved in this experience?

- What was your role in this experience? (Did you have to coordinate or did other people depend on you? Did you depend on other people?)

- What did you do prior to, during, and after this experience?

Awareness

- How did you react to the experience?

- How challenging was this experience? What about the experience made it challenging or not challenging?

Critical Analysis

- How did you contribute to the performance observed in this experience? (Was there an assessment of performance? What did it reveal?)

- How effective were you as a leader in this experience?

- Have you taken the same leadership approach to experiences before? How successful was it in previous situations? How effective was it in this situation? What was similar/ different about these situations?

- Do other people in your team or in other teams have approaches to leadership similar to yours? How do these approaches work for them?

Exhibit 35.1. Form A: Reflecting on the Experience (*continued*)

- What is a different leadership approach you could have taken in this experience? What might have happened if you had taken this alternative approach?

- Did you have the competencies (e.g., technical, thinking, and interpersonal skills) needed to be effective in this experience?

New Perspective

- What did you learn from this experience about your leadership capabilities?

- Given what happened in this experience, how will you lead differently in the future?

- In what ways could you develop your leadership skills in the future? What opportunities do you have to develop further as a leader?

- In what ways do you need to change your attitudes, expectations, values, leadership approach to be a more effective leader?

Action Steps

- List at least two actions steps you plan on taking based on your learning from this experience.

Exhibit 35.2. Form B: Documenting the Critical Reflection Process

Name:_____

Facilitator:_____

Date of critical reflection:_____

Leadership Experience:_____

Awareness

- How challenging was this experience for the participant? Explain.

- Did the participant come to an awareness of his or her leadership capabilities through the experience? Why or why not?

Critical Analysis

- List the key issues that the participant identified when critically analyzing the experience.

New Perspective

- What new perspective(s) regarding his or her leadership capability did the participant take away from this experience?

Action Steps

- List the action steps the participant plans on taking after this experience.

36

Scaffolding Reflection: What, So What, Now What?

Claudia Hill

Korn/Ferry International

EVERY EXPERIENCE IS a transaction that takes place between an individual and his or her environment. Dewey (1938) notes that learning from experience means that you make backward and forward connections between action and consequence. Kolb (1976) adds that learning occurs when knowledge is created through the transformation of experience. However, experience alone provides no guarantee of learning. Most educators agree that the transformation of experience comes about through an active and recursive process of reflection.

"What? So What? Now What?" Model ✳ Point 1

In guided-reflection discussions, a facilitator or coach helps individuals engaged in a learning experience recall what has just happened, analyze the implications of their actions, and assimilate what they have learned. There are many models of reflection; one process that can be used to elicit individuals' thoughts and feelings is the "What? So what? Now what?" scaffold of questions proposed by John Driscoll (1994). The simple queries represent an accessible way of sequencing questions to help individuals make the transition from understanding what happened to what it means to them. The nested nature of these questions creates an easily repeatable process that can become natural and integrated into group process. The sequence is explained below.

What?

The first phase of this sequence asks individuals to return to the experience and access their sensory memories. Sensory memories are made up of information from the environment that is stored in temporary memory (Clark & Wittrock, 2001). This series of questions is critically important, particularly when facilitating learning with a group. Short-term memories of an event that are shared create a common set of perceptions and set the stage for the next phase of the discussion. Typical questions asked in this stage include: What did you just do? What happened first, next, or last? What did you intend to do? What did you observe?

While asking these "What?" questions it is important to surface differences in perception; the goal is to create as clear a description as possible of the shared experiences. With this clear picture, the facilitator can move the discussion on to the next phase.

So What?

With a clear description of the event, the facilitator can begin to ask "So what?" questions. These engage individuals in critical thinking about the impact and consequences of their own actions. Here is where individuals begin the critical process of accommodation and assimilation that transforms experience into knowledge. Explicit comparison of the outcomes of actions just taken with existing mental models (assimilation) can lead to the acceptance of new models (accommodation). Some examples of "So what?" questions are: What was good about what happened? What could have been better? How does this apply to you specifically? How was that significant? What struck you about that? What do you understand better about yourself or your group?

Discussions driven by "So what?" questions can provoke insights and new or transformed knowledge.

Now What?

If the "What?" phase of the process engages individuals' memory, and the "So what?" phase engages them in critical thinking, the final phase requires the individuals to employ their imaginations. Questions in this phase take the lessons from the experience and engage participants in reapplying them to other situations. The questions are directed toward helping individuals apply the general knowledge they have gained during the experience specifically to their own situations. Some examples of "Now what?" questions are: What will you do again or do differently next time? When, where, or how will you take different action? What would you like to do with that information? How could you repeat that experience?

In a group reflection discussion there are bound to be differing perspectives and lessons realized. The facilitator's role during this process is to elicit and respect the legitimacy of all perspectives and intentions.

Action Learning Case Story

The power of this framework is its simplicity and versatility. You can use it to structure formal debriefing sessions for a group of people engaged in a learning experience, or in one-on-one coaching discussions between a manager and employee. The following is a brief story that illustrates the model as it might be used in practice.

Setting

An action learning team was debriefing after a long and very challenging initial meeting. The team was made up of senior leaders from a hospital system in a major city. Participants were both clinical and functional leaders. The team was chartered to explore options for productivity improvements in the emergency services department of the hospital.

What?

In debriefing the experience, the coach asked, "What were your goals at the outset of the meeting?" Participants responded that they had intended to explore the problem and to develop a problem statement. The coach went on to ask, "What happened?" Participants related that the meeting started out okay but that as soon as the problem was shared communication started to break down. A team member then asked, "What caused the breakdown?" They noticed that the clinical members of the team were concerned that "productivity improvements" would be defined as staff reductions, which they could not approve. Functional members of the team included leaders from HR, IT, and finance. They expressed their belief that no real productivity improvement could come about without putting the question of staff headcount on the table. As a result of this impasse, no progress was made by the team and many felt that the project itself was an impossible exercise—at least with the staff on hand.

So What?

One team member, who recognized the predictable nature of this conflict, leaned back in his chair and said, "So what could we do differently to get a different result?" Team members noted that this type of breakdown in communication occurs when leaders represent their functional roles as they try to deal with longstanding dilemmas involving people and staffing. One member realized that they could have surfaced the conversational impasse as a problem to be solved rather than allowing it to derail the work of the group. Another suggested that they focus on what they could agree on in order to get some momentum and potential solutions to the problem. The group agreed that these were good suggestions.

Now What?

Having diagnosed the problem and developed reasonable action steps, the coach began to encourage the team to ask "Now what?" questions. A team member asked, "When and where might we get a chance to try out a different approach?" Another member suggested that for the next few meetings the team deliberately put aside productivity opportunities that involved headcount reduction and concentrate on all the other alternatives that might be developed. The team agreed to try this approach.

Conclusion

The team went on to form a powerful team dynamic of partnership that allowed members to evaluate a number of options and develop recommendations that eventually saved the hospital more than $100,000 in the first year after implementation, and not one job was lost or clinical principle compromised.

Individual Coaching Case Story

The "What? So what? Now what?" framework is also very useful in one-on-one coaching conversations, as illustrated by the following interaction.

A mentor and her protégé were talking after a long working day at a client site, when the mentor asked the protégé to "pick a story that you would particularly like to share."

(As an aside, storytelling is a wonderful way to get at "What?" information. When a person tells a true story, he or she is in effect playing the experience backward, as you would with a movie. This type of reflection carried out in a relaxed approach elicits both memory and emotion.)

The protégé remembered a wonderful evening she had spent with a friend at the Opéra Comique in Paris the previous week. She recalled listening to Joyce Di Donato, whom she felt was a wonderful lyrical soprano. The mentor asked the protégé, "So what was most memorable for you about the evening?" The protégé went on to try to explain what she particularly enjoyed about the experience; she recalled the singer's voice quality and the ease with which Ms. Di Donato varied tones and tunes with the apparent lack of effort characteristic of a real master, and she also remembered how much she enjoyed the singer's simplicity as a person and the joy with which she seemed to spend the evening. The program was set up in such a way that the singer had been able to pick songs she particularly liked, and all could see how much she was entertaining not only her audience but herself as well. The protégé summed up memories by saying the evening was an experience of mastership, quality, simplicity, joy, and shared pleasure.

The mentor then asked the protégé "Now what?" questions. She asked her protégé to "think further and tell me what this woman could specifically mean to you?" In response the protégé shared that she understood that she had reached that moment in her career when she wished to experience exactly this combination in her work. She felt that she was no longer a newcomer, that she knew her job more than well, and that she wanted exactly this: to keep practicing in such a way that her work would turn into an art and she could combine mastery with playfulness and pleasure.

The mentor then asked, "What can you do to get there?" From that point the conversation began to focus on the practical action steps the protégé could take to create the conditions that would allow her to practice artistry in her work (Tailleur, 2011).

Final Words

In each case, the facilitator encouraged the others to recall events, explore those events from multiple perspectives, and finally to speculate on how they could learn from the experience and develop a future action plan. The "What? So what? Now what?" model is a useful and simple tool that facilitators and coaches can use to help any team transform experience into useful and practical learning.

References

Clark, R., & Wittrock, M. (2001). *Psychological principles of training*. New York, NY: Macmillan.

Dewey, J. (1938). *Experiences and education*. Toronto, Canada: Macmillan Canada.

Driscoll, J. (1994). Reflective practice for practice—a framework of structure reflection for clinical areas. *Senior Nurse, 14*(1), 47–50.

Kolb, D.A. (1976). *The learning style inventory: Technical manual*. Boston, MA: McBer.

Tailleur, F. (2011, February 21). Consultant. (C. Hill, interviewer).

37

Life Journeys: Developing for the Future by Looking at the Past*

Kerry A. Bunker
Making Experience Matter

MANY OF THE strengths, values, and behaviors that people express in their day-to-day lives have roots in the lessons they have learned from a lifetime of experiences. An exercise called the Life Journey Activity provides individuals with an opportunity to examine some of these life lessons by creating a visual representation of their personal life journey. The Life Journey Activity serves multiple purposes in encouraging individuals to more actively engage in learning from their experiences.

The activity invites examination of one's experiences through the lens of learning, growth, and change. Busy people, engaged in their work, with pressures to deliver results, may focus on their performance and what they have accomplished rather than on how they have developed as leaders over time. The activity can challenge them to be more aware of and to better articulate what they have learned from key experiences. And seeing oneself as having the ability to learn and change increases the person's confidence as a learner.

The activity encourages reflection on the kinds of experiences that stimulate learning and the role of self and others in capitalizing on those experiences. By looking at their past history, individuals can identify what drives and supports their learning—and thus can craft their future experiences in ways that enhance learning.

---

*Note: This contribution is adapted from the author's publication (with Michael Wakefield) *Leading Through Transitions: Facilitator's Guidebook*, published in 2010 by Pfeiffer.

The activity offers the opportunity to share one's own experiences and to hear about those of others. Telling stories to others often prompts new realizations. Hearing others' stories allows one to see a more diverse range of experiences, opening one's eyes to other possible avenues for learning. And the bonding that occurs between members of small groups who share their life journeys can launch peer learning partnerships that extend over time.

The Life Journey Activity is typically used in a workshop setting. I have used it in general assessment-for-development leadership programs and in more focused workshops on developing learning agility and on leading organizations through transitions. The activity includes two phases separated by a break.

Phase One: Introduction, Preparation, and Getting Started (45 to 60 Minutes)

Introduce participants to the Life Journey Activity by briefly describing *what* they will be doing (for example, drawing a map of the journey they have created in life thus far and sharing it with others) and *why* you are asking them to do it (to better understand how their life journeys have shaped them so they can use those insights in their continued journey). Then hand out and read through the instruction sheet for the Life Journey Activity (see Exhibit 37.1) with the participants and ask them to begin.

Guidance for the Facilitator

Sharing some personal examples of pivotal learning points in your own life journey helps to bring comfort and clarity as individuals begin this activity. Reflect out loud about one or two key moments in your life when you faced adversity or challenge, or made a tough decision at a fork in the road. How did you feel in that moment? What do you value in the experience as you look back on it today? Sharing your personal reflections will relax the participants and give them comfort in joining in the activity. I suggest that at least one of your stories come from outside work. People need support and encouragement to capture as many key events from their entire lives as they can remember.

Some participants may need additional time to reflect and draw. Therefore, Phase One is best positioned before a meal break or other major pause.

Make the rounds during the map-preparation session to offer guidance, answer questions, and provide support to the participants as they are creating their life journeys. Although they may need to leave the room to spread out, it is often helpful if they remain in sight of one another. Seeing how others are approaching their maps often helps those who are struggling to better frame the task. People often feed off the collective group energy to sharpen their ability to address their own life histories. Remind them that they are not expected to become artistes in creating their life journeys. They are simply preparing a graphical capture of their lives that they can share in conversation with a few of the other participants.

Exhibit 37.1. Participant Instructions for the Life Journey Activity

Your Life Journey

One of the keys to guiding yourself and others through the challenges of change and transition involves exploring who you are as a person and how you came to be that way. Many of the strengths, values, and behaviors we express in our day-to-day response to the demands of our environment have their roots in the lessons we learned from experiences faced throughout our lifetimes. This activity will provide you with an opportunity to examine some of these life lessons by creating a visual representation of your personal life journey.

Use a sheet of flipchart paper as a canvas to create a map of the journey that you have followed through life thus far. Allow yourself to be expressive. Like your life, the map will probably be filled with twists and turns rather than neatness and linearity. Feel free to use color to convey the emotion and impact of different experiences. Let your memory be your guide.

This exercise should be fun—it's not an art test! Just use the opportunity to communicate visually, to discover and represent some things about your life that might not come across otherwise.

Below are some examples of ways that the picture of your life journey might communicate important messages both to you and others:

- Peak experiences that punctuated your life and caused you to grow

- Forks in the road where you had to choose what to pursue and what to let go of

- Hardships and obstacles that tested your mettle and your resiliency

- Significant people who impacted you (for well or ill) at various stages in your journey

- Bumpy spots and unpaved roads where the going was slow and uncertain

- Sudden shifts that took you by surprise and tested your ability to navigate

- False starts and dead ends—places where you had to back out or make a U-turn

- Situations in which you opted to accelerate or to apply the brakes

- Close relationships—important people who entered your life or left you along the way

- Roadblocks and detours—stressors placed in your path by others

- Communities you joined—places where you felt connected and committed

- Situations in which you derailed, ran out of gas, or collided with someone

- Significant milestones and achievements—key destinations reached

- Roads not taken—appealing avenues that you avoided or failed to explore

- Times when hindsight left you wishing you could have a do-over

List inspired by William Bridges, *The Way of Transition*, 2001.

Phase Two: Sharing (45 to 60 Minutes)

Divide the participants into groups of three to five to share their life journeys. Ask the groups to manage their time so that everyone's story is shared in the allotted time.

Ask participants to share their drawings and walk their groups along the paths they have followed in life: What were they wrestling with along the way? What were key experiences? What were they learning and how? Who joined or left them along the way? What lessons did they learn that they would pass along to others?

When not sharing their own stories, the participants' role is to listen in order to understand: they should try to put themselves in the storyteller's shoes, ask questions to clarify what they don't understand, and practice being empathetic.

Guidance for the Facilitator

The life journey group discussions are generally a powerful bonding and learning experience. Participants talk about facing challenges, overcoming adversity, making difficult choices, and the emotion of change and transition. Your task is simply to open the door to let the participants share the power of the experience.

After the group sharing, facilitate a ten-minute debriefing of the experience with the entire group. Tell the participants that you do not want them to share any personal details of their group's discussion, but rather to share their thoughts about the experience of having the discussion: Was this a good activity? Why? What did they learn from the life journeys of their partners? What will they take away from the experience?

Encourage participants to record their experiences. If participants are keeping journals as part of the workshop experience, for example, it is useful to end the session by asking them to take a few moments to write down their thoughts, reflections, and lessons learned from the dialogue.

References

Bridges, W. (2001). *The way of transition: Embracing life's most difficult moments.* Cambridge, MA: Perseus.

Bunker, K.A., & Wakefield, M. (2010). *Leading through transitions: Facilitator's guide.* San Francisco, CA: Pfeiffer.

38

Strategies for Facilitating Learning from Experience

Claudia Hill
Korn/Ferry International

A S A MANAGER, coach, or talent professional, you are in a unique and privileged position. You can create and structure learning events for employees, and then help those employees identify the lessons of experience by role modeling your own learning and facilitating the learning process. Your actions directly impact how employees engage in developmental experiences, and the level and quality of learning that occurs from those experiences. You are essential to the growth and development of employees in your organization, and in this article, I want to identify several specific strategies and facilitation techniques that you can use to help employees learn from experience.

The ability to facilitate learning from experience is not developed overnight and requires its own learning journey and much practice. The very best facilitators are said to be "learner centered." Learner-centered facilitation requires that you relentlessly focus on and adjust to meet the needs of the employee. You will have to observe physical cues, assess energy levels, contrast what is and what is not said, build in regular feedback, and integrate input gathered from a variety of sources. Learner-centered facilitators put the individual's needs at the center of any development effort, not the needs of the facilitator or even the organization. Effective facilitators ensure that the learning content and approach is aligned with the employee's learning goals and needs. Below are several strategies—each with advantages and disadvantages—that you can use to help employees learn from experience.

Strategy 1: Transactional Facilitation

Transactional facilitation is ideal for delivering a consistent message to participants on a limited range of subjects. Safety training is a common example. In most organizations, the content of safety training is mandated and consistency of message across a large number of participants is essential. Questions are encouraged as a way of checking knowledge, and an expert transactional facilitator will align the discussion to participants' questions. The transactional facilitator uses accelerated learning techniques, including application and practice, to encourage interaction and engagement. In addition, success at the transactional level of facilitation requires the capacity to listen intently and to ask good questions that promote further inquiry. In most cases, this strategy involves presenting learners with prior experiences related to the topic and then facilitating a discussion about lessons to learn from those experiences, similar experiences that the learners were involved in, and general principles that can be applied across experiences.

Strategy 2: Socratic Facilitation

Socratic facilitators choose not to present or deliver information in a controlled, transactional manner. Instead, Socratic facilitators continuously acknowledge and encourage the sharing of learners' embedded or tacit knowledge. These facilitators often de-emphasize their own expertise or experience while emphasizing their role as a catalyst of learning and encouraging interaction between and among the learners. The facilitator models intellectual humility and an intensely dialectical approach while inductively seeking to discover the meaning and lessons learned from employees' own experiences. This facilitator will structure group reflection activities, turn questions back to the group, ask provocative questions, encourage individuals to ask provocative questions of each other, and foster critical reflection. The Socratic facilitator does not allow a planned agenda to dominate the learning process; for them, an agenda is simply a loose set of guidelines.

This approach is best suited for situations in which the learners have some background knowledge and the behaviors that must be learned are complex or the environment within which performance occurs is variable and unpredictable. Some examples for which this approach may be optimal include developing coaching skills or improving change leadership capabilities.

Strategy 3: Dialogic Facilitation

The dialogic facilitator is primarily interested in fostering shared meaning and understanding, rather than identifying specific lessons from experience or bringing things to a planned conclusion. The dialogic facilitator appears to be employing very few "techniques" at all. In fact, if you were watching this facilitator carefully, you might reasonably come to the conclusion that this facilitator is not doing anything, and you even might conclude that he is very lazy. The purpose and focus is to challenge learners to think with a well-timed question or comment. Once he asks a question, a dialogic facilitator will quickly step out of the discussion and allow the employee(s) to direct the discussion and identify key lessons learned. In this sense, control of the discussion and, ultimately, the responsibility for learning, process, and pace is shared among a learning community that includes the facilitator. Action learning coaching is a perfect example of this type of facilitation.

The challenge that most professionals have in adopting this strategy is the need to control the discussion or the direction of learning. Expert dialogic facilitators understand that adults have complex mental models that shape their understanding of the world, and the facilitators create conditions and very broad guidelines that allow them to share those models with others in service of going beyond what is already known and accepted. These facilitators operate with the knowledge that learning from experience is different from acquiring information or coming to an answer. These facilitators acknowledge that learning starts with each individual from where he or she is at in the moment. Finally, dialogic facilitators embody the principle that learner-centered development is not a passive process, but rather involves active and conscious engagement from employees.

Key Differences Among Facilitation Strategies

The strategies differ from one another in three important ways: (1) the locus of control of the learning, (2) the direction of interaction, and (3) the expected outcome of each approach. In transactional facilitation, for example, the facilitator controls the discussion, interactions, and learning agenda and goals. In Socratic and dialogic strategies, the learner, not the facilitator, drives the locus of control, interaction, and learning objectives. Table 38.1 provides a synthesis of the three facilitation strategies and their differences.

Table 38.1. Synthesis of Levels of Facilitation

Locus of Control	Direction of Interaction	Best Uses
Strategy 1: Transactional facilitation		
Presenter directed	Two-way flow of information	Learning specific skills when the individuals lack basic background knowledge and confidence.
Strategy 2: Socratic facilitation		
Shared control	From participant to facilitator	Developing conceptual knowledge and skills. Individuals should have some knowledge or experience with the concept and some degree of self-confidence.
Strategy 3: Dialogic facilitation		
Participant controlled	From participant to group	Developing conceptual knowledge and skills within a group of learners. Individuals may be experienced and have a great deal of self-confidence.

39

Teachable Point of View: Learning to Lead by Teaching Others

Scott McGhee
U.S. Cellular

THE ACTIONS OF our associates and our leaders at U.S. Cellular are guided by a strong commitment to our organizational business model—what we call the Dynamic Organization (see Exhibit 39.1). We believe that this model and the resulting actions derived from it differentiate us from our competition. The values and behaviors at the core of the model in Exhibit 39.1 enable the four surrounding components (also in Figure 39.1), leading to outcomes that create winning business results in a way we can be proud of.

Although the Dynamic Organization model is taught to associates from the first day they join the organization by weaving it into new hire orientation and all our training programs, the real teaching of the model is carried out by leaders, both by modeling the values and behaviors of the Dynamic Organization and through intentional teaching.

To be an effective leader of the Dynamic Organization, we ask leaders to develop a *leadership teachable point of view* (LTPOV), based on the work of Noel Tichy (2009) in his book, *The Leadership Engine*. As a new first-level leader attending a foundational "Coaching for Performance" workshop, U.S. Cellular leaders begin developing their teachable points of view. Developing and delivering this point of view requires reflection on one's life journey and values, the ability to use inspirational storytelling to connect with and motivate others, and a willingness to improve through practice and feedback.

Exhibit 39.1. Leadership Journey Line Exercise

What Is Your Life Story?

The process of developing your Teachable Point of View starts by understanding your unique life story. Your personal story will help you remain grounded in who you are and what you stand for. In this first exercise, you are going to draw your Leadership Journey Line. On the space provided below, plot the emotional events of your leadership journey. Label the critical events and the emotional peaks and valleys along the way. Think about how your ideas, values, and lessons learned about leadership were shaped over the course of your life.

Leadership Journey Line

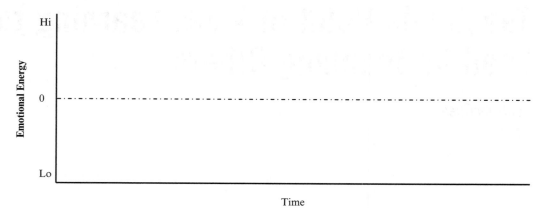

My Major Life Events and Lessons Learned

Significant Events/Experiences	Lessons Learned	Why Important
1. _____	_____	_____
2. _____	_____	_____
3. _____	_____	_____

Reflection Questions

1. Looking back over your entire life's experience, what is the moment that you are most proud of as a leader? Describe the moment. How did you feel? What about you as a leader were you most proud of?

2. Looking back over your entire life's experience, what was your most disappointing moment as a leader?

3. What leadership lessons did you learn from these experiences?

Figure 39.1. Dynamic Organization Model

Elements of the Leadership Teachable Point of View

In Tichy's view (2009), effective leaders are teachers, and the LTPOV is a teaching tool. To lead and thus teach effectively, one must develop a point of view about ideas, values, emotional energy, and edge. Leaders have *ideas* about how to deliver business results. They have *values* that guide how they act and make judgments. They display *positive emotional energy* and stimulate the same in others. And they display *edge*, the willingness and ability to face reality and make tough choices.

An effective LTPOV engages the listener and has impact. To be engaging and impactful, the LTPOV is delivered as a story. In his article, The Four Truths of the Storyteller, Peter Guber (2007) best describes how to go about delivering a teachable point of view (p. 56):

> Here is the challenge for the business storyteller: He must enter the hearts of his listeners, where their emotions live, even as the information he seeks to convey rents space in their brains. Our minds are relatively open, but we guard our hearts with zeal, knowing their power to move us. So although the mind may be part of your target, the heart is the bull's eye. *To reach it, the visionary manager crafting his story must first display his own open heart.*

Making the LTPOV engaging and impactful also requires the leader to display authenticity and vulnerability.

We ask the leaders to spend significant time in self-reflection and introspection and to examine their own leadership journeys to find a memorable story that will reach the audience and pull them along.

Developing the Leadership Teachable Point of View

The first-level leaders attending the workshop are asked to develop the first draft of their LTPOV as part of their pre-work. Four weeks prior to the workshop, these leaders receive a nine-page instructional guide to help them in their LTPOV development. We expect that working through the guide will take several hours. Elements of the guide include:

- A leadership journey line exercise to help leaders find a life story to build their LTPOV around (see Exhibit 39.1)

- Reflective questions about business strategy to help leaders formulate ideas about how they and their team drive winning business results

- A values exercise to help leaders identify a list of important values that guide their work as a leader (see Exhibit 39.2)

- Reflective questions to guide leaders in understanding how they create a climate of positive emotional energy

- Information about the concept of leadership edge

- Storytelling tips to help the leader craft an engaging narrative

The pre-work package also includes a link to a video example of a U.S. Cellular leader delivering a leadership teachable point of view.

Delivering the Leadership Teachable Point of View

Late in the morning of the first day of class, facilitators share their own LTPOVs in front of the class as a model. Class participants are divided into groups of three. Each group finds a quiet place in the facility for group members to deliver their LTPOVs to each other. Each participant has a maximum time of twenty minutes to deliver his or her LTPOV (including any feedback from their classmates). The groups return to the classroom to debrief the activity. The participants' evening assignment is to tweak their LTPOVs based on feedback and on their observing other LTPOVs. We encourage them to steal shamelessly! Participants deliver their LTPOVs again the first thing the next morning (in a different group of three people). After the workshop, participants deliver their LTPOVs to both their leaders and their direct-report teams.

We emphasize that leaders need to continue to refine and improve their teachable point of view throughout their leadership careers. As they put their LTPOVs into action in their own work and as they teach others, they will continue to learn how to effectively lead in ways consistent with the Dynamic Organization model.

Challenges in Implementing the LTPOV Process

We frequently find that these new (usually young) leaders have little experience in crafting an engaging story, and often they do not immediately grasp the lessons given in the initial

Exhibit 39.2. Values Exercise

Values

"Leaders consistently display the values and behaviors of the Dynamic Organization through words and actions."

Clear ideas empower associates by providing direction, expectations, and *common purpose.* Values inform *how* the ideas will be achieved. Values are the basis of leadership in the Dynamic Organization. Leaders are defined by their values and their character (George, McLean, & Craig, 2008).

Reflecting on your Leadership Journey Line, come up with your list of important values that guide you and your work as a leader. Work through the following list quickly, putting check marks next to any values that should be on your list of core leadership values. As you do this, watch out for picking up values that are desirable and noble, but are not values you express in your leadership or by your example. Feel free to add values not on the list that better depict a core value of yours.

❑ Self-Sufficiency	❑ Compassion	❑ Learning	❑ Teamwork
❑ Fun	❑ Inclusiveness	❑ Humility	❑ Authority
❑ Fulfillment	❑ Individuality	❑ Wealth	❑ Creativity
❑ Honor	❑ Fair play	❑ Happiness	❑ Achievement
❑ Faithfulness	❑ Freedom	❑ Edge	❑ Security
❑ Duty	❑ Ambition	❑ Change	❑ Openness
❑ Practicality	❑ Influence	❑ Responsibility	❑ Objectivity

Values come to life in your leadership. Narrow the list and identify only the critical few values that are *most* important to your life and your leadership and must be on your list at all times. In the table below, write your own definition of what each value means for you. After you have listed and defined them, go back and rank-order them by their importance to you.

Value Name	Value Definition	Rank

Reflection Questions

1. Which of your values are the most essential to you as a leader in the Dynamic Organization?

2. Which ones are desirable but not essential? Put an asterisk next to the values that are uncompromising. Make sure there are strong linkages between your ideas and values.

instructions and video examples. Often their LTPOV amounts to a list of experiences or values, and does nothing to captivate or intrigue the listener. The raw material for a compelling story is often there, and the participant needs some coaching to see how to develop the story and how to make connections for the listener. We often see dramatic improvement in the LTPOV by the second round.

The best LTPOVs are often stories of failures or struggles to be overcome. It is this display of vulnerability that creates the connection with the audience and makes the leader real and approachable to the people he or she leads. New leaders often enter their leadership journeys with the exact opposite frame of mind. They feel they must know everything, be perfect, and show no weakness. This "ah-ha" moment is often a significant event for the participant in this workshop.

Finally, although the development of the LTPOV is done in a safe environment, some participants are still reluctant to deliver their LTPOVs to their leaders and teams after the workshop. The workshop has an eight-week follow-on period to drive transfer of learning to the work environment. This includes a social media site for the participants to stay connected and share experiences. We continue to explore ways to drive post-workshop accountability.

References

George, B., McLean, A., & Craig, N. (2008). Why leaders lose their way: They forget or ignore their true north. *Executive Excellence, 25*(8), 3.

Guber, P. (2007). The four truths of the storyteller. *Harvard Business Review, 85*(12), 53–59.

Tichy, N. (2009). *The cycle of leadership*. New York, NY: HarperCollins.

40

Implementation Intention: A Refinement to Leadership Development Goal Setting

Luke Novelli, Jr.
Leadership Development Resources Global

AT THE CONCLUSION of leadership development programs, it is not unusual for participants to have gained significant insights into how they can be more effective leaders back in the workplace. Most of the participants also have a high level of intentionality to make changes when they get back to work. However, converting those intentions into sustained actions has been a pervasive problem for leadership development initiatives. A refined goal-setting process at the conclusion of such programs—one that specifically draws attention to implementation intentions—can be helpful in addressing this problem. Such a process should enhance the likelihood that participants will take full advantage of on-the-job experiences to learn effectiveness-related leadership behaviors, skills, and perspectives they identified.

Every program I have been involved in as a facilitator has had some sort of goal-planning form for participants to complete at the end of the program. The leadership development literature is replete with best-practice examples of the forms used in a large number of organizations. These forms typically have in common a number of sections: the goal statement; identification of behaviors that are linked to the goal; benefits to accrue to the individual, the team, and the organizations; resources needed; obstacles to overcome; support needed from specific individuals; and a timeline for intermediate milestones. I have started adding an implementation intention section to goal planning forms and have tested this approach with mid-level and upper-level central bankers in Asia.

Implementation Intentions

New York University psychology professor Peter Gollwitzer's research on implementation intentions provides guidance for converting intention to change into actual changes in behavior (Gollwitzer, 1999; Gollwitzer & Schaal, 1998; Gollwitzer & Sheeran, 2006). Essentially, the notion is to identify specific situations that will serve as a trigger or cue to perform goal-related behaviors whenever the situation is encountered. This lessens the burden on internal processes and shifts to an automatic cue by the external situations. The theory is that individuals can delegate the initiation of goal-directed behavior to external stimuli by forming so-called implementation intentions or if-then plans with the following format: *If* situation x is encountered, *then* I will perform behavior y. In fact, I have observed that forming implementation intentions facilitates detecting, attending to, and recalling the previously identified specific situation. In the presence of these cues the initiation of the specified goal-directed behavior can be made more immediate and does not require conscious intent. This concept can be applied to leadership development goal setting to identify, on the action plan, where and when people will engage which specific behaviors related to their development. This approach helps people identify opportunities to practice and use behaviors and skills within their current work environments.

Here are two examples of development goals with implementation intentions specified:

- *The goal:* Develop weekly schedules showing all my important meetings for the coming week throughout the rest of the year. *The implementation intention*: If it's 9 p.m. on Sunday, then I will make my schedule for the coming week.

- *The goal:* Demonstrate patience by not reacting angrily when I strongly disagree with someone's comments. *The implementation intention*: If I feel myself getting angry during a conversation, then I will take three deep breaths.

Leadership Development Implementation Intentions

I have used an *if-then* section on leadership development goal-planning forms so that participants can capture their implementation intentions. These implementation intentions must be tightly connected to both their goal statements and the behaviors they have identified that will enable them to accomplish the goals. Such connections are illustrated in Exhibit 40.1.

The typical description of implementation intentions comes when the action planning form is introduced. I spend only a few more minutes on the implementation intentions section. It is here that I strive to build credibility for the technique to enhance the likelihood that participants will follow through on it.

Exhibit 40.1. Examples of General Goals, Behaviors, and *If-Then* Intentions

General Goal	Behavior	If-Then
Build better relationships with the marketing team to improve planning coordination.	Commit one hour per week for lunch with a marketing team member to get to know the person and understand the issues the team is dealing with.	*If* I am reviewing my weekly schedule on Monday morning, *then* I will call a marketing team member to schedule a lunch meeting.
Become more personally connected to my subordinates.	Participate with subordinates one time per week in informal activities to learn more about their personal lives	*If* I am invited to join the team for lunch, a birthday celebration, or a walk around the manufacturing floor, *then* I will look for a way to say yes.
Demonstrate strategic thinking	Offer my support or critique of a proposed strategy and the reasoning behind my position	*If* a discussion about strategy occurs during an executive team meeting, *then* I will offer my opinion concerning the proposed strategy's soundness, along with my rationale.

I acknowledge that the concept of using *if-then* statements does not, on the surface, seem likely to have much of an impact on goal attainment. I then very briefly describe the research in a few sentences (for example, fifteen plus years of scientific research, rigorous examination comparing *if-then* statements with other formats, and the contexts in which implementation intentions have been found to enhance goal accomplishment).

I then admit that when I first came across the concept, I was a bit skeptical; however, I decided to experiment. The first experiment involved a goal of reducing my consumption of Diet Coke. I formulated the intention as, "*If* I am thirsty, *then* I will drink water." The result is that I have not had a Diet Coke since I stated the intention. The second personal experiment involved flossing. I had developed a pattern of daily flossing immediately after a dentist visit, but then a steady tapering off as time passed since the visit. My implementation intention was, "*If* I am brushing my teeth in the morning, *then* I will floss." The result has been a significant increase in my flossing between dentist visits.

I want to communicate the message to program participants that implementation intentions have worked for me on things that I wanted to change. I want to do everything that I can to build credibility for using implementation intentions as part of their goal-setting process. I strongly suggest that you conduct your own experiments regarding implementation intentions prior to introducing the concept to program participants or coaching clients. You should form these experiments around things that you would be willing to share with others. Again, the purpose is to build credibility for a technique that is likely to be seen as quirky by many participants.

A note of caution: implementation intentions should not be presented as a panacea. It is clear from the research that a highly motivated goal is required. It should be a goal that the individual really wants to accomplish and that involves a change that the participant clearly sees as beneficial. Participants should also be advised not to list too many implementation intentions, perhaps two or at the most three. These should be for the behaviors or activities that are most fundamental to the developments they seek to achieve. Implementation intention is a tool that can be used to aid people in making changes they sincerely want to make; they are not a magical incantation.

Implementation Intentions Research

I have found it helpful to provide some implementation intentions research evidence to support the efficacy of implementation intentions. Gollwitzer and several colleagues have spearheaded the implementation intentions research for more than fifteen years. There is a substantial body of research results (see Resources) that support implementation intentions efficacy for promoting goal accomplishment. The studies have been primarily conducted in health-related and personal improvement areas (for example, vaccinations, exercise, and dieting). However, I see a clear connection to leadership development goal setting. The key research finding is that people who identify specific situations and specific actions they will take in these situations make more progress on goals they have set and are more successful reaching their goals than those who do not identify these specifics.

Research findings that help explain why implementation intentions work is also useful to share:

1. They reduce the choices available during real-time situations that call for the implementation intention action and call forth pre-specified actions triggered by a situational cue.

2. They make salient the obstacles to and opportunities for practice by identifying them ahead of time.

3. They generate more automatic behavior when the situation arises, reducing forgetfulness or not recognizing the opportunity.

4. They reduce the self-regulatory load of real-time decisions by making behavior enactment automatic through situational cuing.

Conclusion

Implementation intention has potential to help leadership development program participants turn their lofty intentions into a back-at-work reality. Consequently, it is more likely that those who follow through on their implementation intentions can benefit from the vast of amount of learning that is available in the workplace but is often overlooked. The concept is not difficult to grasp, and the formulation of effective implementation intentions is not difficult. Empirical research has demonstrated their efficacy in a broad range of contexts. However, their application in the leadership development arena appears to be relatively new. I encourage leadership development practitioners and coaches to begin to experiment with implementation intentions as part of their goal-setting process.

References

Gollwitzer, P.M. (1999). Implementation intentions: Strong effects of simple plans. *American Psychologist, 54*, 493–503.

Gollwitzer P.M., & Schaal B. (1998). Metacognition in action: The importance of implementation intentions. *Personality and Social Psychology Review, 2*, 124–136.

Gollwitzer P.M., & Sheeran, P. (2006). Implementation intentions and goal achievement: A meta-analysis of effects and processes. In M. Zanna (Ed.), *Advances in experimental social psychology* (Vol. 38, pp. 69–119). Amsterdam, Netherlands: Elsevier.

41

Twelve Questions for More Strategic Work and Learning

Kelly McGill

Expedia, Inc.

EXPERIENCE-BASED DEVELOPMENT makes use of a wide range of on-the-job learning opportunities, from special projects to short-term assignments to action learning teams. Regardless of the type of activity, the leader taking on a developmental assignment has two aims: to achieve positive business results and to learn from the experience. Given that these assignments are typically complex and challenging, involving multiple stakeholders and time pressure, it is important for the leader to approach the task with a comprehensive plan created in dialogue with others. Drawing from best practices in project management and business process engineering, I created a set of straightforward questions, called Strategies 12 Questions (see Table 41.1), to provide leaders with a common roadmap for attaining business results and successful development.

Leaders readily see how the twelve questions apply to the work they are charged with accomplishing—many of them have been exposed to formal planning processes at some level. Generating answers to these questions in conversation with team members and stakeholders not only increases the probability of successful project and business outcomes, but helps develop leaders' analytical skills and strategic thinking capabilities. What might be less natural for leaders is to apply the same set of questions to the work of learning from the experience. Yet, just as a comprehensive and well-vetted plan is needed to achieve successful business outcomes, leaders need a comprehensive and well-vetted plan to ensure

✳ Point 2

Table 41.1.   Strategies 12 Questions

Work	Learning
1. What is the goal?	
What do your team members, clients, and partners in the organization see as the goal of the work? Is everyone looking at the same target and outcomes?	What do you intend to learn from the experience? Why have you been given this opportunity? How do others expect you to grow from it?
2. How do you measure success?	
What metrics matter to everyone involved? What are you trying to accomplish for your client? What if you don't accomplish what you set out to accomplish? How would the client group suffer?	How will you know whether you have achieved your learning goals? How will others assess your improvement? What are the consequences if you don't accomplish your learning goals?
3. Where are you now?	
What is the common picture of where things are today? What needs to change? How difficult will that be?	Where are you currently on the learning curve for what you aim to improve? In what ways do you need to change? How difficult will that be?
4. What is the timeline?	
When are project deliverables due? What are the target dates for completing each phase of work?	When do you and others expect to see progress?
5. Who are the key influencers and stakeholders?	
Have you had a conversation with everyone who has a vested interested in the work or can influence what you are trying to accomplish?	Have you had a conversation with everyone who has a vested interest in your learning goals or can influence your ability to reach them?
6. What and who are the necessary resources?	
Do you have the tools to implement your plan smoothly? Will you need additional resources in terms of people, money, or even facts and data?	Do you have the tools and resources to maximize your learning from this experience, for example, time and tactics to reflect or access to a coach?
7. What are the key steps or milestones?	
What are the four or five major milestones that will indicate whether the work is heading in the direction of your goal? What would have to happen to make you pause and change direction? Who would make that decision?	What are the four or five milestones that will indicate that you are making progress on your learning goals? What would indicate that you need to rethink your direction?
8. What are the obstacles or objections?	
What might get in the way of success? Is the organization ready for the goal you are trying to accomplish?	What might get in the way of your learning? How can you anticipate and limit these obstacles?
9. Who are the key supporters and challengers?	
Who might object and why? Who is really supportive of the work and why? How will you get to know both groups better?	Who might not want you to change your behaviors or approach to leadership? Who can you count on to support your development?
10. What are the options?	
Are there other options you should be considering to achieve the goal? Are challengers offering a better approach?	What other opportunities for learning does this experience hold? How can you be focused on your learning goals but also take advantage of other opportunities that may arise?

Table 41.1. Strategies 12 Questions (*continued*)

Work	Learning
11. How and when should you communicate?	
Are you prepared to communicate early, often, and consistently?	Who should you update regularly on your progress toward learning goals?
12. What and when is the ROI?	
What is the business case for the work? What is the cost in terms of human capital and dollars? What will be the return on this investment?	What is the business case for your development? What is the cost to the organization? In what ways will your growth benefit the organization?

successful developmental outcomes. The table illustrates how the same set of questions can be applied to the task and to learning.

The Strategies 12 Questions can be used for a wide range of activities across functions and business needs. With practice, the set of questions becomes less of a tool and more of a way of thinking about any task or challenge the leader faces—a way of thinking that will continue to prompt learning and development.

42

Building a Board of Learning Advisors

Marisa Bossen and Paul Yost
Seattle Pacific University

LEADERS RECOGNIZE HOW important it is to expand and leverage their networks to be effective in their roles, propel their careers forward, and help others overcome organizational hurdles. Managing one's network often falls to the bottom of a leaders' to-do list. The temptation instead is to focus so much attention on executing the business strategy that leaders forget the critical role that relationships play in their success. Sometimes, leaders simply do not take the time to think strategically about the people who are (or should be) in their networks. Here are two simple, quick, and easy activities to help leaders in all stages of their tenure think through developing their network and building a personal board of advisors.

Activity 1: Designing a Developmental Network

First, introduce leaders to the concept of a developmental network: A developmental network is a collection of people who aid in a person's personal and professional development. Developmental networks help leaders to meet strategic goals, accomplish their daily work, and achieve their personal development goals. These interactions can take a number of forms: mentoring, feedback, emotional support, advice, coaching, challenging a person to think in new and different ways, and giving insight into how one is perceived by others.

Ask the leaders to review the information in Table 42.1 to learn more about the various roles people in one's developmental network can serve, the benefits of each, and questions they can ask to learn the most from someone serving in each role.

Table 42.1. Developmental Network Roles

Role	Definition	Ask someone in this role	Benefits
Mentor	Someone who takes an active interest in your career and provides career development and social benefits.	"How did you get to where you are today?" "What's the best path for me to take to get to where I want to go in my career?"	May vouch for you to get a promotion/avoid a layoff Can connect you to their networks Provides role modeling
Feedback	Someone who provides feedback about your current and past performance.	"How am I doing?" "What went well?" "What could I do better next time?"	Points out potential improvements in behavior Highlights the positive behaviors that should be repeated in the future
Emotional Support	People from all areas of your life you trust and with whom you discuss the career and personal challenges that you face.	"I'm worried about ___" "I'm excited about ___" "Guess what happened to me today."	Relieves stress and anxiety Provides encouragement Helps provide outside perspectives on situations Bolsters confidence in decisions
Advice and Coaching	Someone who provides present- and future-oriented help and insight about how to proceed with a particular task, obstacle, interaction, or event.	"What worked for you in a similar situation?" "How can I get unstuck?"	Gain insight on how to solve problems Boost motivation to press forward Learn tips for accomplishing tasks leading up to goals
New and Different Ways of Thinking	Someone who stretches and challenges you to consider new and different options or viewpoints and who pushes you out of your comfort zone.	"How would an engineer look at this?" "What would our Hong Kong office say?" "Should I accept this offer to lead another organization even though it's in an entirely different industry than what I've known for the past decade?"	Helps the leader consider multiple perspectives Helps solve workplace and personal conundrums Leads to creative and expanded solutions Promotes learning
How Others Perceive You	Someone who constructively tells you what others think of how you are performing or how you come across so that you can use this information to shape your behavior, performance, and social interactions.	"What do our clients want from me?" "What's my reputation around here?" "How did people react to my presentation this afternoon?"	Provides a competitive edge that accelerates personal development Aids in establishing better relationships with other people and ultimately improves performance

Explain that it is possible for these roles to overlap and be embodied in the same person. For example, a mentor can also provide emotional support, which can turn into new and different ways of thinking about a problem. However, wise leaders also keep their developmental networks varied in order to maximize the benefits they gain from them and by cultivating relationships with a myriad of people they can rely on and to whom they can turn for help. An additional benefit to establishing a large developmental network is that if an important person in one's network relocates, retires, or is otherwise unavailable, there are other people who can fulfill the same role. This makes a network more resilient and less affected when one person leaves.

Next instruct leaders to take a few minutes to reflect upon which people in their lives fulfill each role, using the worksheet shown in Figure 42.1. Ask them to list as many names as apply on the indicated lines. Some roles might have one name. Other roles might have many. Afterward, ask them to note what roles, if any, are under-represented. These areas are where intentional focus should be used when engaging in future networking. Suggesting that leaders reflect on *why* these roles are lacking in their network can be helpful in determining how to best bolster those categories. Challenge the leaders to think about the people they would like to recruit to round out their network.

Figure 42.1. Developmental Network Worksheet

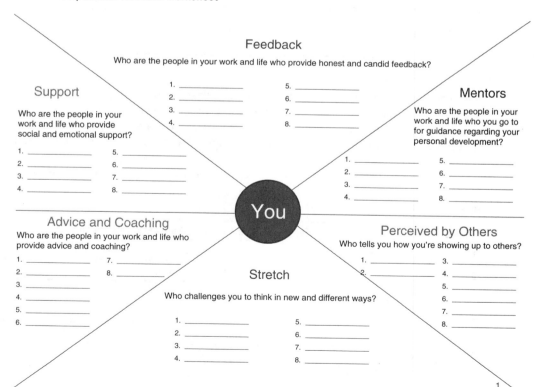

Activity 2: Creating a Board of Advisors

When leaders have identified their broader developmental networks, they can move on to think about their personal advisory board. The concept of a personal board of advisors is simple. It is made up of five to seven key strategic contacts in the developmental network whose knowledge and experience best aligns with aiding the leader's future goals and aspirations. What sets board members apart from other people in a developmental network is that board of advisor members are generally in positions where the leader hopes to be in the future. At work, they might be in jobs the leader hopes to move into someday. Outside of work, the advisor might be a trusted advisor (for example, a wise friend or family member). The potential advisor might have already experienced a similar transition that the developing leader is currently facing at work or in other roles in the leader's life, such as parenthood, a midlife crisis, or retirement. Advisors do not necessarily have to be more senior than the leader. It is the advisor's expertise that is important, not age or position. An advantage of having a board of advisors is that, rather than adopting strategies based on the modeling of one person (a single mentor, perhaps), one can create a unique leadership style based on blending styles from many different people on the advisory board.

Next, ask leaders to use the worksheet shown in Exhibit 42.1 to generate a list of potential board members. When helping leaders create a board of advisors, have them refer back to their developmental network. Several members in the network should be people they already frequently turn to for emotional support and feedback. These people might include a trusted friend, a current or past mentor, a peer at work, a spouse or parent, a senior executive, a respected expert in one's field, or a religious leader from one's faith.

Exhibit 42.1. Your Board of Advisors

Directions: Imagine for a moment that you are a business of one. Take a few moments and think of the seven people you would like to have on your personal board of advisors. These should be people who can provide advice and insights across all of the areas of your life. Include at least two people who would be a significant stretch for you (that is, people whom you think would never say "yes").

Once you have identified the names, write two questions you would like to ask each of them.

My Advisory Board

Names	Two Questions I Would Like to Ask This Person
1	
2	
3	
4	
5	

Two people who would really stretch me

1	
2	

Encourage leaders to not limit themselves to their developmental networks. Advise them to stretch themselves to include at least one person who could potentially help them get where they want to be in the future.

Once the leaders have lists of names for their personal advisory boards, instruct them to generate two questions that they would like to ask the individuals they have listed. Have them consider a list of the problems they are up against and the burning questions that they want answered. Such questions might include:

- I have been struggling with _____. What advice do you have for me?
- What path did you take to get to where you are today?
- What advice do you have for someone like me at this stage of my life and career?
- What are your secrets for juggling all of the different roles in your life?
- What are three wishes you have for *your* future development?
- How do you personally measure success?

The simple act of devising a list of questions can be developmental because it compels leaders to think outside the limits that they have created for themselves. At any time, a leader taking on this developmental exercise might have a chance encounter with that person he or she has identified as "stretch." It is wise to be ready for any chance to obtain developmental support.

Invite leaders to identify at least one person on their advisory board list to ask for a little bit of his or her time. For instance, a leader might extend an invitation for coffee or lunch. Leaders may be hesitant to ask a busy person to set aside time to meet with them. To address this concern, challenge leaders to think about people who have approached them as mentors. When was that an okay experience? Why then should it be hard to ask others for wisdom and insight in the same way? At the worst, the advisory board member says No.

If the conversation with the advisory person goes well, the leader can ask for a follow-up meeting. If the board member is a friend, scheduling regular meeting times to catch up can be useful. Challenge leaders to put one of these conversations on their calendars this week.

Lessons Learned

Some insights have emerged as we have conducted this exercise with a variety of leaders. First, leaders should not limit their developmental networks or boards of advisors to their jobs. Developmental networks should encompass work and personal time, given that they are intertwined. For example, we have seen some people list their children in their "stretch" networks! Including both realms can help people manage all of their roles (boss, parent, sports coach, PTA president) so they can do all of them better.

It is critical that a leader using this activity not stop at listing names on the template. The act of generating questions for each advisory board member is a developmental activity. In other words, this developmental exercise can complement other developmental activities and processes. It can be added to management training classes, to performance development discussions, or to develop his or her own team members by helping them build their boards of advisors.

43

Building a Learning Community Through Reflection and Experimentation

Jennifer Jaramillo
Accenture
Kristen Schultz
University of Michigan

IN FAST-PACED, high-stakes environments, people face leadership challenges constantly—and they don't always know it when these challenges are happening. Learning through experience is critical and is often the most valuable way for individuals to grow. But without *reflecting* on these experiences, these lessons are not fully captured.

Business school is a whirlwind, for some people more so than the previous five to ten years they spent in the working world. But the challenges faced are similar: working in teams, managing others, prioritizing multiple projects simultaneously, maintaining presence among high achievers, and determining our next professional moves. We attended the Stephen M. Ross School of Business at the University of Michigan. As students, we knew that we were in school to learn and grow, and especially at Michigan Ross, we knew we were there to become leaders.

During our second year in business school, the almost five hundred students in our class and the approximately two thousand total graduate and undergraduate students at Michigan Ross knew we were gaining leadership through experience. But something was missing. It was clear that students would discuss challenges with one another—about recruiting for a job or managing the board of a program—but what would result was advice or simply an understanding nod; growth through experience was not a primary focus. We had a group of business school students at a top school—high achievers with high potential. But were we, as a school and as a group of peers, tapping into the potential of each individual as much as we could? Were we taking advantage of the potential of our community as much as we could? We did not think so. We knew we could aspire higher.

Our solution to this challenge was the Ross Leadership Initiative Project X, more fondly referred to as RLIx, a leadership program based on the idea that self-aware leaders, and communication and connections between these leaders, can transform individuals and elevate an entire community. The mission of RLIx is to provide Michigan Ross students with opportunities to explore, experiment with, and enhance their own leadership development through ongoing, peer-facilitated activities centered on self-reflection and strong interpersonal relationships.

In many ways, RLIx provides a structure for something students are already looking for—an everyday channel for personal reflection and meaningful relationship development. Because the each year's program committee is comprised of students who participate in the program and are part of the target audience, the program reflects the needs of the students. Since RLIx is created for and by the participants, buy-in from the community is more readily attained and maintained.

Designing RLIx: Building a Foundation for Reflection

The program's multidimensional mission requires RLIx to have multiple levels of interaction: personal, interpersonal, and communal. At the personal level, the participant is given a different self-reflection exercise every week throughout the program duration, about fourteen weeks. Over the course of the term, the exercises evolve from self-centric and eventually broaden into leadership within the larger community structure. The activities challenge participants to define who they are (both at their best and worst), what they value, and what kind of leaders they are. They also challenge participants to be purpose-centered and focused. Examples of activities are included in Table 43.1.

At the interpersonal level, each participant is assigned a small group of four to five peers they meet with regularly throughout the term. The role of the group is to support, challenge, encourage growth, and hold one another accountable. In these small groups, participants share their reflections with one another every week in two-hour sessions. The small size of the groups allow for intimacy and trust to build among the members, as noted by this participant:

> The most powerful part of RLIx for me was the opportunity to have open, thoughtful, insightful conversations with people I would not have otherwise interacted with

Table 43.1. Sample Reflection Activities

Activity	Description
Five Best and Worst Selves	Reflect on and write down five times when you were at your very best and five times when you were at your very worst. Think about how these ten experiences uniquely prepare you to be a leader.
Value Box	Bring an item representative of a critical experience that has shaped a value that is fundamental to who you are. Share your experience with your group.
Reflected Best Self™	Request positive feedback from significant people in your life. Synthesize it into a cumulative portrait of your "best self." Optional: Have another group member review your feedback and share the themes that emerged from a third-party perspective.

at Ross. I spend a lot of time talking with my friends and thinking personally about the types of issues we discussed in RLIx, but the experience of talking with and getting to know people from different social groups, different sections, and different career backgrounds was invaluable. It was actually a fulfillment of something I had always thought I would get out of business school, and RLIx was really the only forum for it that I experienced this year.

The small group size is also optimal for minimizing coordination costs, critical for our busy participants. Early on, each group is encouraged to develop a statement of values so that members themselves can determine the level of commitment to the program and the rules by which they will abide.

The small group sessions are led by a peer facilitator who is also a participant in the group. The peer facilitator is responsible for selecting the reflection exercises from week to week, using the facilitator's guide—which includes a listing of reflection techniques, tools, and activities to use in the small groups—as a resource. The facilitator is also responsible for scheduling the reflection sessions and facilitating the discussions. In addition to the time spent with their groups, the facilitators also meet to share lessons learned and to support one another. However, they are encouraged to remain peers within their group with regard to sharing their own reflections and obtaining input from the group on the most appropriate way for their group to advance through the program.

At the broader level, social media captures the essence of the personal transformations and inspires the greater community to engage in similarly impactful interactions. As part of the program, participants are invited to write a blog entry on what leadership means to them. These inspirational stories are posted on a website to share with the entire school and beyond. For the participants, it challenges them to synthesize what they learned through RLIx, and through their business school experience, into a concise story about their unique leadership experience. More importantly, it establishes a legacy to encourage future RLIx classes and to multiply the impact of the RLIx program beyond the direct participants. Figure 43.1 illustrates the RLIx program activities and the frequency of each activity.

Figure 43.1. RLIx Program Activities

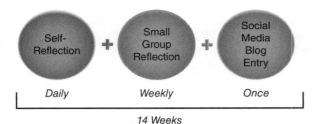

Identifying the Participants and Groups

Co-creation is an essential design principle in order to ensure the lasting legacy of the program and the relevance of RLIx. Identifying the "right" participants is crucial to the success of the program. The program committee consists of five individuals who represent each business school class and are also leaders within the Ross community. Each year, students who graduate are replaced by current RLIx participants who excel and show interest in the committee. This group continues to implement and improve upon the program.

The next step is to identify the participants. For the inaugural class, the program committee opted to specifically select students and nominate them for the program. In order for the program to gain traction, it was imperative that the initial participants demonstrate leadership, be open to the idea of self- and group-reflection, maintain the spirit of co-creation as RLIx evolved, and be champions for the program. Because the first cohort established the program's credibility and popularity, the second year of the program saw more interest than program capacity. To handle the increasing numbers, the program committee now uses an application process and students are asked a series of short questions in order to gauge fit for and commitment to the RLIx program. Applicants are also asked to indicate desire and capacity to act as a peer facilitator.

After participants are identified, they are organized into diverse groups that share a common experience. Diversity of race and gender, professional background, and country of origin, among other characteristics, are critical to creating meaningful dialogue among participants. The diversity is balanced by organizing the individuals into groups that have a shared set of experiences in the Michigan Ross microcosm of a "workplace." For RLIx, the common experience is the current year in school. For example, first-year graduate students are able to relate to one another with their current fears and frustrations, while second-year graduate students can reflect on how they were each able to overcome those trying experiences.

As mentioned earlier, the program committee members served as the peer facilitators during the initial pilot. For subsequent classes of small groups, one participant per group is invited by the program committee to be a peer facilitator. Characteristics of a successful

Figure 43.2. RLIx Program Structure

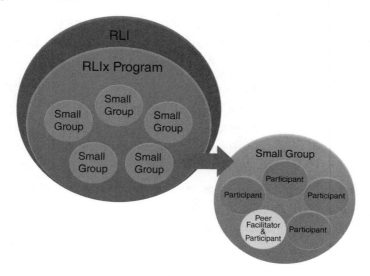

peer facilitator include reliability and organization, a demonstrated sense of self-awareness, strong leadership skills, and high potential to be a champion for RLIx. Peer facilitators are trained prior to meeting with their small groups and are encouraged to meet regularly throughout the program term as a support group. Moreover, those who had served as peer facilitators for the previous classes are able to act as coaches for the new group of facilitators. The RLIx organization structure is included in Figure 43.2.

Implementing RLIx

The program is intentionally designed to provide minimal structure to allow for the organic development of the participants and the small groups. This is particularly important for the target audience of high performing individuals who are already leaders in some capacity. This approach also provides the flexibility required for diverse groups at varying levels of progress. In addition, it helps to maintain buy-in since each group can determine its own level of commitment and focus. During the first two years, the program committee tracked the activities each group decided to undertake, the pace at which they moved through these, and the way in which each group chose to use the reflection activities. The same patterns emerged.

Some groups take a more structured approach, with high expectations for the activity-based work each group member will bring to the session each week. Others allow for a more relaxed environment, in which the group meeting is the only time team members commit to doing activity-based work. For other groups, the meeting time exists less for activities and more as a support group. This distinction is somewhat due to the facilitator and the management of the group. But in large part, this is based on the current experiences of the participants themselves.

Dynamic and proactive feedback throughout the program is key to the co-creation process. For example, peer facilitator meetings allow all participants to benefit from the varying structure of each group. During these meetings, the status of each group is shared: activities, progress, challenges, and group dynamics. Tracking and testing the differences between groups provides insight into how future groups should be run. Moreover, at the end of each cohort, the program committee uses an online survey to ask participants for structured feedback on the program and its outcomes for each individual. The results identify significant information on how to shape the program moving forward. For example, based on feedback from the pilot, we determined that the optimal program duration is fourteen weeks. This allows time for the participants to get into the rhythm of reflection and to develop trusting, deep interpersonal relationships.

Although the focus of RLIx is the process of reflection, its multidimensional mission also requires engaging the broader community. Social media is used to capture the participant outcomes and the impact of the program. As noted earlier, the content outputs of RLIx are displayed in blog form, also serving as a channel to multiply the impact of the program beyond the direct participants. This display helps to develop the community as a whole by institutionalizing the importance of reflection and awareness of self and of others. An additional goal of the blog is to encourage readers to comment on the stories that move them, participate in the dialogue about leadership, and even share their own stories.

In addition, the RLIx program committee plans to highlight the most popular or interesting stories in an annual event where the authors of the stories would be invited to talk about their experience in front of the entire community. The event is intended to be a capstone to the program for the year. It would also serve as a marketing event to raise awareness about RLIx for potential future participants.

Lessons Learned

Not everyone is ready for the openness or intensity of the experience that is required for participation in RLIx. We determined that it is better to allow for a graceful exit for those individuals that do not fit with the program, rather than force participants to stay in the program. It is a disservice to the individual as well as the small group to which he or she is assigned because the individual's lack of engagement impacts the dynamic of the entire group in ways that will detract from the other participants' growth.

One filter for fit is through the application or nomination process. If someone who is not right for the program has made it through the entry process, it will become apparent within the first couple of weeks. In the third week, it is suggested that the peer facilitators check in with each of the participants, using a survey if necessary, to identify any individuals who may want to exit the program. For participants who indicate that they might not be satisfied, facilitators should follow up with them to identify whether it is a program quality issue or an individual issue, and determine the appropriate action. The program committee should consistently check in with the peer facilitators to support changes to the program and/or the exit of participants as necessary.

The first two cohorts of RLIx participants (about sixty total) who completed the program reported very positive results in their reviews. Students who had not participated in RLIx asked how they could do so, and feedback was overwhelmingly positive from students, faculty, and even those outside the business school. Participants in the program rated it highly in the close-out survey. Nearly every participant found his or her small group to be one of, if not the top, highlight of the experience with RLIx. Moving forward, the program intends to take advantage of those beneficial group dynamics and relationships by starting groups even earlier in participants' business school careers, and possibly maintaining those same groups year over year.

A less positive theme was that the program's facilitation was, in some groups, too organic. To mitigate this challenge in future groups, the facilitator's guide has evolved into an activity catalog in which techniques and activities are organized by intended goals such as "Personal Reflection" and "Learning from Others," and "Experiment and Test." This will provide both the necessary structure and flexibility that individuals and groups require, while focusing on the specific goals over time.

Building Your Own RLIx

RLIx transformed how our community experiences leadership development and practices leadership reflection. A similar program can be reconstructed to suit the needs of any organization. As a manager intending to build an "RLIx" of your own, here are some critical dos and don'ts to consider:

Do . . .

- Establish a program committee that includes representatives from your target audience.

- Build enough structure to provide appropriate support (for example, a facilitator's guide) but enough flexibility to allow groups to progress at their own pace.

- Develop a selection process that will identify participants and peer facilitators who exhibit leadership, are open to the idea of self- and group-reflection, can maintain a spirit of co-creation as the program evolves, and can be champions for the program.

- Ensure that peer facilitators meet regularly to support one another and share lessons learned.

- Build intentionally diverse groups, but ensure that they have common ground (for example, all managers, entry-level workers, or line workers).

- Conduct a pilot to test your program plan.

- Kick off the program with an event including all participants.

Don't . . .

- Force the activities or timing onto groups. Let them find their own purpose and focus.

- Forget to consistently solicit feedback from facilitators and participants. Then institute those changes.

- Underestimate the effect—either positively or negatively—of one participant on the whole group; have a one-on-one conversation with such individuals to make them aware of their impact and to share suggestions on how they can better support the group.

- Forget to celebrate the individual growth and deep relationships that developed during the program. Hold an event at the end of the program to acknowledge all of the participants and perhaps allow some to share their stories.

Resources

To read personal accounts and stories related to RLIx, visit http://rossblogs.typepad.com/rli/.

Many of the reflection activities used in RLIx were inspired by the Center for Positive Organizational Scholarship at the University of Michigan. More information can be found at www.centerforpos .org.

44

Using Communities of Practice to Cultivate Leaders of Integrity

John R. Terrill

Seattle Pacific University

GIVEN THE COMPETING demands placed on business and the growing complexity of organizational life in general, the need for highly capable, ethical leadership is more critical than ever. Without such leaders, peril looms, as demonstrated by the devastating impact of ethical breaches in financial services and other sectors of the global economy in the latter part of 2008. According to the Edelman Trust Barometer, 2012 CEO credibility in mature markets experienced its largest decline in the survey's history. Business must repair its reputation, reestablishing trust with the public in ways that are authentic and enduring. Unless a critical mass of leaders act in ways that fortify public confidence, the long-term prospect for business to thrive will be greatly diminished.

One of the most important—yet elusive—contributions that human resources professionals can make in this regard is to help leaders develop a more holistic understanding of ethical leadership. At the Center for Integrity in Business (CIB) at Seattle Pacific University, we understand integrity as a nested concept that incorporates personal, corporate, and systemic dimensions. At a personal level, integrity is about consistency—speaking the truth and walking the talk. At the corporate level, integrity is about aligning values throughout an organization. And at a systematic level, integrity is about working in partnership with other institutions to enable more people around the world to flourish. Effective, ethical leaders function consistently and with integrity in all of these settings. They know *who* they are and *what* they believe, and they can navigate the moral nuances and conflicting beliefs that often characterize broader organizational and societal relationships and responsibilities.

Cultivating Leaders of Integrity Through Communities of Practice

The capacity to traverse all three overlapping levels of integrity is indicative of higher-order moral reasoning. Unfortunately, most leaders may have limited awareness to operate at such a level. The good news is that ethical decision making can be cultivated. On-the-job development can be an important context for building deeper moral awareness through real-time experiences and assignments and through networks of people at work who encourage personal growth and development. However, as important as these real-time work experiences and relationships are, there is no guarantee that moral mentoring will occur, thereby prompting the need for greater intentionality. Communities of Practice (CoPs) can be a powerful, experiential way to foster integrity-oriented commitments by disrupting the status quo and moving people out of a narrower understanding of how values apply in different decision-making contexts. The idea is simple, yet profound. CoPs—composed of people who share common problems, concerns, and/or deep interests about an ethical issue—come together to expand their knowledge and skills and to learn how to address moral dilemmas.

At the CIB, we've structured short-term and ongoing CoPs with leaders *within* and *across* various industries, targeting personal, corporate, and systemic ethics-related issues. Examples include the following:

- A short-duration CoP to explore issues related to business and government in creative partnership. This topic area was targeted because of the high degree of mistrust that often exists between members of these two communities—business often resists increased regulation, and government often questions the motives and citizenship of corporations. This inherent tension serves as an effective disorienting experience that heightens sensitivity to the different moral responsibilities and roles that leaders face in different types of institutions.

- A monthly breakfast CoP, where a diverse set of businesspeople gather to connect on broad topics related to leading with integrity in the marketplace. Monthly discussions include topics such as ethics in marketing, financial services, technology development, entrepreneurship, and hospitality management. Speakers and roundtable discussion questions are chosen to probe multiple perspectives and a wide variety of ethical issues across industries.

- A CoP to explore the role of business in helping alleviate economic need at home and around the world entitled: Bottom Billions/Bottom Line: The Role of Business in Ending Global Poverty. This topic was targeted because of its moral demands and the varied stakeholders (for-profit, nonprofit, and governmental) that must work together to shape sustainable and scalable solutions. Big, complex problems are often good soil for CoPs.

When building integrity-oriented CoPs, we've built on principles by Wenger, McDermott, and Snyder (2002), and we have found certain operating disciplines to be important, including:

- Ask guiding questions to clarify purpose. If you're not sure what the greatest needs are, invite deeper reflection by posing questions. Where are members struggling? What are the "presenting" ethical issues? What concerns are behind these issues? What are important ethical goals and aspirations that community members agree on and seek to fulfill? Questions like these tap into existing energy and establish common ground.

- Create a rhythm that allows the community to evolve naturally. For example, the monthly breakfast CoP creates a stable setting for relationships to develop by meeting regularly once a month on Thursday mornings from 7:30 to 9 a.m.. The breakfasts are occasionally supplemented with informal discussions and off-site gatherings.

- Build natural on-ramps and exits for participants. Both stability and fluidity are needed for the long-term health and viability of CoPs. They are not intended to be static. At our monthly breakfast CoP, about one-quarter of the participants are first-time visitors. Invite people to come and go as they desire, and resist the temptation to institutionalize your communities.

- Welcome different levels of participation but ensure that a core community is in place. At our monthly breakfast CoP, we're seeking ways to equip and encourage a group of "knowledge leaders" who attend regularly. When others are unsure about the CoP or do not yet have in-community relationships, the consistent presence of respected leaders signals to others that the CoP is a dynamic learning opportunity.

- Invite participants to extend conversations in ways that feel natural to them. After sponsoring a national conference on the role of business in alleviating global poverty (and at the urging of participants), we held a series of follow-up "idea labs," where members could continue to build connections and sustain conversations in a smaller, peer-oriented setting.

- Provide enough structure. Although CoPs can self-organize, communities often require some degree of oversight and structure, which may include physical and virtual space to help members interact and share ideas. In our CoPs, we're leveraging social media to share resources and provide connection opportunities outside of regular gathering times. For example, after hosting an interdisciplinary conference on technology, culture, and Christian spirituality, we created intentional online space to keep the conversations and collaborations moving forward.

- Establish rules for discourse and engagement, if necessary. Ethics-oriented CoPs exchange sensitive information. It is essential to establish ground rules to guide personal interactions and knowledge-sharing.

Within the context of CoPs, participants are challenged to re-conceptualize their mental models for making moral sense of the world. Leveraging such opportunities takes planning and should influence how you build your CoPs. For example, research suggests that people move through predictable, sequential stages of moral growth. The case presented in Exhibit 44.1 provides a conceptual map for how a well-designed CoP might help a leader build deeper ethical understanding.

Given the long-term timeline that we believe is often necessary for moral change, it might be tempting to dismiss shorter-term CoPs as ineffective interventions. However, well-designed week-long programs have been shown to support longer-term developmental growth. The key is designing experiential communities that create disequilibrium in people's meaning-making systems and can lead to deeper level learning. People's responses to such disorienting experiences can create windows of opportunity for change and maturation.

Any efforts to develop ethics-oriented CoPs should take into account that moral development may not always be linear. A leader may develop a growing awareness of a corporate and/or systemic dimension of integrity, and then circle back to engage in deeper work on personal ethics-related issues. CoPs are effective tools to prompt and facilitate long-term ethical development, and that can actively counter the compartmentalization strategy that often separates business life from private life.

In a classic 1968 *Harvard Business Review* article that still resonates in some circles today, Albert Carr advocates on behalf of a bifurcated view of integrity, suggesting that bluffing in business should be viewed as game strategy—like bluffing in poker. He suggests that when people enter their business lives, they're no longer private citizens, but players who are held to different standards of morality. Accordingly, in Carr's view, "the business strategist's decisions must be as impersonal as those of a surgeon performing an operation—concentrating on objective and technique, and subordinating personal feelings."(Carr, 1968, p. 149) The issues raised by Carr are a good example of the kinds of tensions that can be examined in an integrity-oriented CoP. The future of business and, more broadly, our global

Exhibit 44.1. Nancy's Ethical Challenges: Prompting Change Through a CoP

Through blurry eyes, Nancy blinked at the LCD alarm clock at her side. It was 2:18 a.m., and she couldn't sleep. Her mind was spinning. She enjoyed her job as the CEO of a rapidly expanding mobile application development company, but the pressures were piling up. With increasing numbers of smart phone and tablet computer users worldwide, her company had enjoyed meteoric growth. In just eighteen months, revenues had increased tenfold, and the number of employees had quadrupled. Business was good, but. . . .

One prospective client had approached her about designing application software for an online gambling product that, although legal and in high demand, she found morally objectionable. Should she take the business? Her gut said "no," but she wondered how some of her board members might react. Another customer sought her assistance on a project she believed wasn't ready for market. Not seeing value for her client's customers, Nancy tried to counsel the company to wait until it further refined its concept. Her client seemed agitated by her reservations. Should she continue to raise objections and risk losing the business?

Her restless thoughts now drifted to pricing issues. Recently, she had designed a new product that her competitors had not yet been able to replicate. Nancy could charge a hefty premium for this feature, but should she? How much profit was enough? By charging the higher fees, did she run the risk of alienating customers? It was now 2:44 a.m.; she was wide awake.

* * *

The ethics-oriented CoPs hosted by the CIB prompt disorienting questions, such as Nancy's "How much profit is enough?" late-night query. CoPs grappling deeply with these kinds of questions create dislodging experiences for members, so that they can establish different, higher-order meaning-making frameworks. For example, Nancy seems to be relying on her board's approval to guide some of her ethical decisions. A trusted CoP could both challenge this default setting and empower her to make decisions based on her internal compass of right and wrong. In addition, CoPs can be effective in inviting different perspectives for ethical decision making. An effective CoP could prompt Nancy to view her divergent stakeholders as being less *in opposition*, and more a part of a dynamic, ongoing process that is continually allowing her to develop her own and her company's moral identity. A community that might be helpful to Nancy at this juncture of her personal development could involve leaders from business, government, and nonprofits, which would force her to think across different types of institutions, at a larger scale, and at a greater depth of moral complexity, which together require Nancy to think and act in new ways.

society, hinges on high-integrity leadership. Through CoPs, companies can play a crucial role in developing moral leaders who are ready for the challenges ahead.

References

Carr, A.Z. (1968, January/February). Is business bluffing ethical? *Harvard Business Review*. Retrieved from http://web.ebscohost.com/ehost/pdfviewer/pdfviewer?vid=4&sid=e9ee939f-0375-4f00-891e-a41e49d8c323%40sessionmgr113&hid=124

Wenger, E., McDermott, R., & Snyder, W.M. (2002). *Cultivating communities of practice: A guide to managing knowledge*. Boston, MA: Harvard Business School Press.

45

CompanyCommand: A Peer-to-Peer Learning Forum

Nate Allen

U.S. Army, National Defense University

PICTURE FOR A moment that you are a front-line Army leader in combat and you've just taken your first casualty. The emotions are overwhelming and your soldiers are looking to you for guidance and leadership. Where do you turn for the insights you need to lead your organization through this crucible?

With this scenario in mind, consider Stephanie in Iraq, whose unit took its first casualty. The Army has policy, regulations, and doctrine on how to appropriately honor soldiers killed in action. However, what Stephanie really needed was the voice of experience from those who had walked in her shoes.

CompanyCommand is an online peer-to-peer collaborative community of practice for Army company commanders (see Exhibit 45.1). In this forum, junior officers throughout the organization can connect laterally across unit boundaries to share what they are learning, provide advice, and create new knowledge for novel challenges (Dixon, Allen, Burgess, Kilner, & Schweitzer, 2005). The forum was profiled in *Harvard Business Review* as a breakthrough idea in 2006 and continues to offer a powerful approach to building learning communities.

By connecting through the *CompanyCommand* team, Stephanie was rapidly in contact with leaders who themselves had experienced casualties in Iraq and could give her relevant

Exhibit 45.1. Who Are Company Commanders?

Company commanders are Army officers responsible for a unit of approximately 150 soldiers. They are distributed in more than 120 countries globally and are at the level in the organization that strategy is operationalized—in this sense, the Army might have a well-developed strategy that, if not implemented effectively at the company level, will go awry. On the other hand, such strategy could be flawed or incomplete, and yet if these front-line leaders are able to collaborate and adapt on the ground, the organization will be effective. In a civilian context, company commanders would be similar to a construction project manager or manufacturing plant manager.

and sound advice—including how to conduct a meaningful memorial service and sample condolence letters for family members.

Or consider Stan, who deployed to combat expecting to be a staff officer the entire deployment. But when a company commander from his unit was killed in action, Stan's superior directed that he prepare to take charge of the company within days. Through the *CompanyCommand* team, Stan was able to connect with three other leaders who had experienced the same thing—taking command in combat of a unit whose commander had been killed in action. The three officers were able to provide Stan with highly refined and relevant advice based on their practical experience with this situation—including insights on how to help his new unit grieve the loss of its past commander while also getting back in the saddle to conduct its demanding mission.

Rob Cross and Lee Sproull (2004), in their article "More Than an Answer: Information Relationships for Actionable Knowledge," describe why leaders like Stephanie and Stan often prefer to turn to fellow practitioners first when encountering a challenge, rather than using a knowledge management database or asking a superior officer. The authors found that leaders often need meta-problem solving. In other words, a safe conversation with fellow practitioners can help draw out and unearth the underlying issues. Furthermore, Cross and Sproull found that practitioners often need encouragement and support to take action. Words such as, "Hey, it sounds like you are on the right track. Go for it!" can be empowering for a young leader who already knows the courageous decision she needs to make. In environments that are highly dynamic, like combat, the voices of peers are especially meaningful. In this milieu, learning and adaptation are essential to effectiveness, and traditional hierarchical approaches to learning struggle to keep up with the pace of change. As a result, much expertise and understanding reside at the edges of the enterprise, where practitioners interface with the environment, and not necessarily at the core or top of the organization.

While it would seem ideal for peer-to-peer conversations to be hosted in a face-to-face setting, the reality for a large distributed organization is that one's peers with relevant experience are often miles away. Using online collaborative forums to connect front-line leaders enables them to suspend many of the limitations of location and time, allowing them to rapidly collaborate and learn from each other in meaningful and relevant ways regardless of their location. See Figure 45.1 for a screen shot of the *CompanyCommand* professional forum.

Figure 45.1. *CompanyCommand* Professional Forum

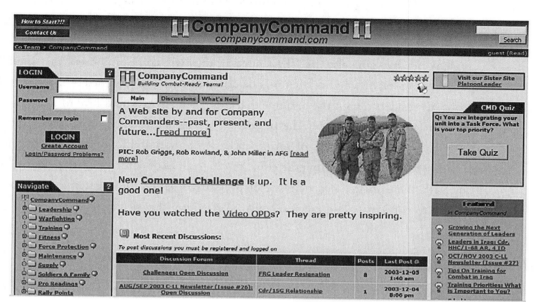

So you might be thinking: "I'm sold. I want this for my organization! But, how do I do this and where do I start?" Following are eight essential insights to get you started on your journey—insights that are drawn from the hard-earned lessons of the *CompanyCommand* experience.

If *They* Build It, They Will Come

One of the critical factors to *CompanyCommand*'s success is that it was developed *by and for* experienced company commanders—not *by* the Army's information technology department *for* commanders. Furthermore, membership is restricted to past, present, and future commanders.

To make something like this happen in your organization, first identify the specific group to focus on—such as project managers or plant managers. It's recommended that you select a practice that is distributed across the enterprise and is critical to organization-wide performance. Then, pull a team of experienced and respected current leaders in that practice into a three-day workshop in which *they* design and populate the collaborative space that *they* would love to use, ensuring that it will add value to their work. As a part of this process, these leaders identify essential areas that members of their practice need to be effective at. For example, within the *CompanyCommand* forum these functions include topics such as war fighting, training, caring for soldiers, and physical fitness. If a company does these things well, that unit will be effective. These topic areas inform the taxonomy and help to structure the forum's organizing framework. Volunteers then step up to be *topic leads*, who help facilitate and guide content development for specific areas based on their expertise and passion.

Many organizations use the "If *we* build it, they will come" mindset. They establish an IT-supported tool, only to find that no one uses it and it's not sustained over time. However, if front-line leaders design the resource that they themselves would love to use—now that's a different conversation! Apply the principle "If *they* build it, they will come" and you've already increased the chances of forum success a hundredfold. Current practitioners not only bring relevance, grounding the effort in the realities of contemporary practice, but also bring with them their social network of peers from across the organization, who can be recruited to participate and take on active roles within the forum.

Create a Core Team

Another essential success factor for the *CompanyCommand* forum is the core team. Among numerous forum development activities, this team provides facilitation, recruits new members, guides technology decisions, and develops learning initiatives for the forum. The core team is comprised of a small full-time staff and a larger network of volunteers. It follows the Red Cross model, in which the full-time staff serves in such a way as to free up the volunteers to add value to the greater community in their area of passion and expertise. For example, managing the budget and operational issues would be more a full-time staff concern, while a volunteer might develop and facilitate a conversation around a topic of personal interest or experience. Additionally, the full-time staff recruits new volunteers on an ongoing basis, enabling the social network, forum conversations and content to stay fresh and alive. Furthermore, the core team conducts an annual face-to-face huddle—called the On Fire Rendezvous—in which new team members are developed and strategic initiatives are identified and resourced for the upcoming year. The *CompanyCommand* experience would advise that at least one member of the full-time team be a rotating member who is pulled in directly out of the field and focuses on recruiting colleagues and keeping the content relevant.

Forum Core Purpose = Practitioner Effectiveness

A forum's core purpose must be centered on effectiveness within the specific practice it is focused on. At the end of the day, if a forum is adding exceptional value to members' on-the-job effectiveness, they will participate (see Figure 45.2).

Everything about the forum experience is looked at through this lens. To illustrate this focus on effectiveness, the *CompanyCommand* team envisions members' learning curves shifting up and to the left as a result of each interaction they have within the forum. For

Figure 45.2. Targeting the Learning Curve

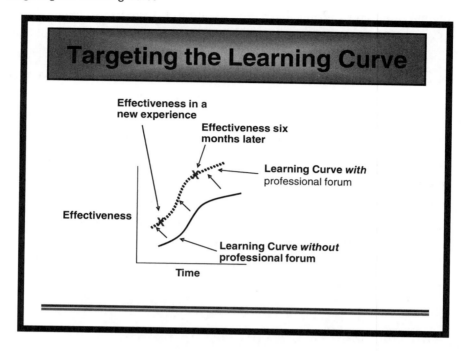

example, a new company commander is at a greater level of effectiveness than he otherwise would be had he not been engaged in the forum. This enables the core team to determine which conversations and content to facilitate in the forum and which opportunities to decline because they hold no relevance for company commander's effectiveness.

Practice the Three Cs of Forum Facilitation: Connection, Conversations, and Content

The user experience within the *CompanyCommand* forum is centered around *connection, conversation,* and *content*. Each time members log into the forum they *connect* with like-hearted practitioners who have relevant experiences that relate to their point of concern or interest. They initiate or join meaningful *conversations* that add value to their practice, while also connecting with quality *content* that enables them to do their jobs more effectively.

Let's take Stephanie's situation to illustrate this point. When a leader's unit takes a first-time casualty, she should easily connect in conversation with experienced leaders who themselves have lost a soldier, while at the same time connecting with relevant content that adds value to her point of learning need—in this case, examples or letters of condolence to family members, memorial service ideas, and video interviews with commanders sharing their experiences of dealing with casualties and losing a soldier.

Focus on Continuously Developing the Three Architectures

Online professional forums have three architectures—*technical, social, and learning*—each of which is necessary but not sufficient on its own. For example, an online forum could leverage the latest eye-watering technology, but without grassroots ownership and a vibrant social movement it won't succeed. Likewise, a non-intuitive, overly complex, or poorly designed user experience will lead to forum failure, no matter how strong the social ties are or how relevant the learning is. Keeping an eye on continuous development of these three architectures will increase the likelihood of long-term forum success. Furthermore, with the technical architecture in mind, the *CompanyCommand* experience would advise use of leading-edge commercial, off-the-shelf forum software rather than an in-house developed solution. This approach will ensure a technology partner who is constantly updating the resource with cutting-edge collaborative technology, while allowing the core team to focus more of its efforts toward the hard work of developing contemporary learning and social architectures—and at the same time keeping an eye on pushing the technology in unique and experimental ways.

Identity Is the Pathway to Vibrant Participation

To engender participation within a forum, foster a sense of professional identity. For instance, let's take medical professionals. People expect their doctors to stay current on the cutting edge of medicine. As doctors come across new learning in their practices, their professional identity demands that they share what they have discovered with the greater medical community at large. This is a powerful construct to have working within any social system—that of taking on the identity of a *professional*—in which members are continually learning and advancing the state of practice. Furthermore, intentionally developing a sense of generalized reciprocity within a community of practice fosters greater participation. In other words, developing a culture in which members express a professional obligation to give back in the same way that they've received—not to the individual who helped them, but to the greater community. With this idea in mind, as new members gain substantial value from the more experienced members of the forum, they are inspired with a vision to *pay it forward generationally* to each successive cohort of leaders coming into the practice. Over time, this is an extraordinary force to have woven through the fabric of any learning community—far more powerful than any type of approach that tries to artificially incentivize people to share their knowledge.

Blend Virtual and Face to Face

A mistake that is sometimes made by efforts like *CompanyCommand* is to think solely in terms of the online space. Experience advises that localized face-to-face gatherings of practitioners will result in greater participation in their online forum. At the same time, the online experience enriches and broadens the localized venue. With this in mind, the *CompanyCommand* team facilitates huddles called Leader 2 Leader (L2L). These opportunities take various forms and often feature content that has been developed or is emerging from within the forum. Trust and a deeper sense of involvement are developed through L2Ls, thickening the connecting tissue within the community and fostering greater participation and ownership.

Establish a Rhythm

Last but certainly not least, establish a rhythm within a forum; develop a cadence for implementing a portfolio of learning interventions that are conducted on a monthly basis. For a forum to flourish it needs a rhythm of fresh and highly relevant learning injections that members can count on and accommodate in a routine manner. A few examples from the *CompanyCommand* forum include: (1) sending out a monthly forum newsletter that highlights new content and conversations that members are engaged in; (2) facilitating a priority conversation each month that has relevance to all company commanders around a current organizational challenge or opportunity; (3) conducting a video interview with a current company commander that is then featured on the main page of the forum; and (4) sponsoring a reading program in which commanders who desire to read a book with their junior leaders receive the books for free and then participate in a forum conversation about the book.

References

Cross, R., & Sproull, L. (2004). More than an answer: Information relationships for actionable knowledge. *Organization Science, 15,* 446–462.

Dixon, N., Allen, N., Burgess, T., Kilner, P., & Schweitzer, S. (2005). *CompanyCommand: Unleashing the power of the Army profession.* West Point, NY: CALDOL.

46

Virtual Roundtables: Using Technology to Build Learning Communities

Jonathan Winter
The Career Innovation Group

B Y THE EARLY 2000s, bringing together busy executives from around the world for face-to-face innovation events was proving more and more difficult. But such events were important to us as a research and development organization (and membership organization) with a strong ethos of collaboration and knowledge sharing. Thus, alongside a decreasing number of face-to-face events, we introduced "Hot Topic" teleconferences, which came to be called Virtual Roundtables. Their purpose is to share and distil the wisdom of diverse large organizations on management-related topics, especially people management, without the participants having to leave their desks.

The advantages of going virtual were obvious: no costly and environmentally damaging airfares; minimum time away from the office; greater geographic reach. But which of the features of our face-to-face events could be achieved on a call? Knowledge sharing requires a high degree of trust and openness, aided by slow conversations over a meal. Deep innovation requires time to reflect, aided by getting away from the office. What is possible via telephone and Internet?

Over the subsequent years we discovered the answers to these questions. The Virtual Roundtables have proved to have enduring appeal. Here are some of the things we've learned, for anyone wanting to enable similar conversations that capture and distil the wisdom and latest practices of experts and practitioners.

How the Process Works

After identifying a topic that will resonate and a provocateur to stimulate thinking, the main components of a successful Virtual Roundtable are

- *The Invitation.* Invitations are sent out four to five weeks ahead of the Virtual Roundtable. This notice period fits the profile of our target group; it could be different for other types of people. On receiving an acceptance, we send an Outlook appointment with full details, including two or three questions to consider in advance, so participants are prepared to share a "knowledge gift" on the call. A maximum of fifteen participants are allowed to join, and the ideal number is eight to ten, normally from non-competing organizations.

- *Timing and Duration.* Ninety minutes is the ideal time to enable a substantive discussion on a complex topic, without participants becoming exhausted! We have tried sixty minutes, but find that the final thirty minutes is the most productive time of all.

- *Facilitation.* Each call has a chairman appointed in advance. They have a script so that ground rules are covered, permission is gained for e-mail address sharing, and the conversation is steered through three broad phases of dialogue. The chairman has a preparation call with the provocateur to agree the questions for participants, so they all come prepared to share.

- *Ground Rules.* It is helpful to share some ground rules. The most important of these is confidentiality. We ask people not to share what they hear in a way that can be identified with a particular company or individual. Other practical ground rules include not using hands-free or mobile phones, and taking part in the whole call (those who are unable to make at least the first sixty minutes are asked not to attend, because it disrupts the conversation).

- *Documentation and Follow-Up.* Each Roundtable is carefully written up by a scribe (edited and approved by the chair and provocateur). This provides a valuable aid to remembering the details of the roundtable conversations. A record of the event also distils and disseminates the group wisdom. The record is distributed by e-mail, and the e-mail addresses are made visible to all recipients.

Three Phases of the Virtual Roundtable Conversation

The conversation is divided into three phases, each of which is allocated approximately thirty minutes:

1. *Insight.* In this phase, after a few minutes of introduction by the chairman, participants introduce themselves in under sixty seconds. They share their name, role, and something about the importance (or difficulty) of the topic for their organization. This builds a picture of who is round the table, the issues they face, and their organizational context.

2. *Innovation.* The middle phase is an open discussion among participants, who share current practices and ideas for the future. This is usually kicked off with a five-minute introduction from the provocateur.

3. *Impact.* Finally, the group spends some time looking at the practical barriers to change as well as those things that enable change (see Exhibit 46.1 for the facilitator's script for launching the impact phase of the conversation). Often this is a discussion about how to influence others in one's organization or how to create demand. During this phase the chairman checks with participants to see whether or not there are burning issues not yet discussed, which can then be included before the end of the call.

Exhibit 46.1. Sample Facilitator Script

Impact

"In the final Impact part of these Roundtables we usually spend some time talking in very practical terms about how to bring about change and improvement, and how to achieve the things you believe to be important from our conversation today.

"So I suggest we start with the first very broad question. We've heard about good practice. What are the real barriers to introducing some of these, in your own experience?"

Check in with people at around 70 minutes to determine reaction to where we are with the call. Which issues would they most like to discuss in the remaining minutes? Re-set the concluding agenda if needed, but don't miss the final 10 minute round of "takeaways."

For reference, here are some possible prompt questions:

- Have we understood the root causes of the issues we've talked about?

- What actual actions could be taken that will have impact?

- What help and support do you or your colleagues need (internally or externally) to achieve some of these things?

- What are the risks if nothing is done? How can those risks be made more apparent?

- What is the first step?

- How does the conversation in organizations need to change for this to happen?

- If the time is not right for this, but the problem is looming, how can we do the groundwork now so that we'll be ready when the time is right?

- What's already on the senior leadership agenda? How can we influence that agenda?

- Who are the real influencers in this, and how can they be reached?

- What other smart or creative strategies might help to bring about change?

Successes

We regularly convene key functional leaders with global roles in some of the world's best-known organizations. The cumulative effect of these events is a network of people who are top practitioners in their fields. And despite not being part of their "day jobs," people are surprisingly committed to take part and see the experience as a quick and easy way to invest in their own learning and to grow their networks. Unlike large-scale webinars, these events enable everyone to take part, and—given that most people have never met—the degree of candor and contribution is remarkable.

Many different components go into a designing a successful Virtual Roundtable, but three are of key importance:

1. Using a roundtable diagram on which people can see their names around the representation of an oval table is a simple feature that pays big dividends (see Figure 46.1). People gain a sense of being there with others, and the diagram makes it easier to keep track of who goes next when everyone is invited to participate. Video and other kinds of visuals, including real-time graphic facilitation, tend to distract from the conversation. If slides are used during the conversation, we make it a point to return to the roundtable diagram at regular intervals.

Figure 46.1. Roundtable Diagram

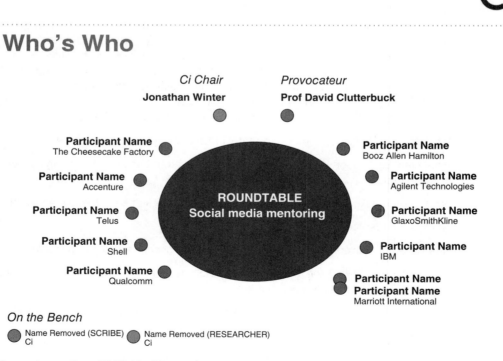

2. Beginning and ending the call by going round the table so everyone has a chance to speak. The final round question is crucial: "What have you learned or what are you taking away?" This question leads to a very positive round of comments, consolidating key learning from the event.

3. The roundtable chair requires one vital skill: the ability to cut people off without offending. In a room full of important strangers, this encourages concise introductions and it keeps the event on time. A positive interruptions such as "That point you just made about X is a really important one. Has anyone else experienced that?" or "Thank you very much, Michael, for that introduction. That brings us to Deepana, who is next round the table."

Lessons Learned

Originally, we hoped that these events would be a catalyst for more substantial collaborative action to address the issues identified, since this is what we had experienced through face-to-face forums. Now we realize that Virtual Roundtables are best seen as a quick knowledge sharing opportunity. These transient virtual relationships are not the best context for practical collaboration.

We make no promise of "magic bullets," yet a few people—usually those who are less experienced—go away disappointed that nobody around the table has the solution. Participants leave the call with one or two ideas and a reassuring sense that they are not alone in facing the challenges that accompany change. To help avoid lowest common denominator discussions, we have added a provocateur to each call, who speaks for just five minutes to stimulate thinking or to showcase an innovative solution and then participates in the discussion.

We suspect that only a few people act on our encouragement to connect one-to-one after the event and share further. Most people are not proactive in growing their networks (a key skill for executives now and which will become even more important in the future). Harnessing social media, such as LinkedIn, helps participants stay connected.

Some of the best roundtables have been the smallest and least formal. This suggests that these virtual conversations could be done with much less work. The right blend of social technology and calendar integration will perhaps at some point reduce the amount of preparation needed to organize and facilitate a conversation between ten and fifteen people.

Section 3

Human Resource Systems: Designed for Experience-Driven Development

293

Section Introduction

The first two sections of this book focus on the leader—how leaders can identify developmental experiences and how they can accelerate their growth in the experiences. The contributions in this section discuss how organizations can build experience-driven development into their HR systems. Stand-alone initiatives tend to be short-lived. Experience-driven development initiatives that are built into an organization's HR and business processes tend to last longer.

The contributions in this section start with an overview of integrated talent management, and then highlight key intervention points at which experience-based development can be introduced in the talent management lifecycle: selecting and on-boarding leaders, equipping managers to develop the people who report to them, building experience-driven development into the performance management system, leveraging on-the-job development in training and action learning, and making leadership experiences a central element in the succession management planning process. The authors provide a wide variety of practical, concrete ideas.

Four themes emerge across the contributions (here and also in the other sections of the book), words of wisdom that can be lost when the contributions are read individually. They are worth thinking about and considering as you do your work in this area.

Move the business forward and develop aspiring leaders at the same time. In organizations today, performance and development are often framed in competition with one another. Sometimes they are. For example, when trying to decide who to place in a critical senior leadership role, the debate often centers on the tension between placing a seasoned leader who can perform well on day one or placing a less experienced leader into the position that will be stretched and developed in the role. But performance and development are not always in conflict. Several contributions in this section propose ways that performance and development can complement each other. Several HR practices in this section are crafted in a way that leaders are developing themselves as they are running the business. Most directly, look at the contributions that directly address this tension (*Performance and Development Through Conversations, Performance Management and Leadership Development,* and *Performance Management Catalysts for Experience-Driven Development*). See also the sections on developing managers (*Leaders Coaching Leaders,* and *An Exercise for Managers*). Likewise, the action learning programs (For example, *Business-Driven Action Learning, Action Learning with Community-Based Nonprofits,* and *Better Together*) are designed to tackle current business challenges and develop leaders in the process.

Consider the HR practices and processes that you own: How can you move the business forward and develop aspiring leaders at the same time?

Make it valuable for the leader. Building HR practices that move the business forward is necessary but not sufficient. HR systems and processes also need to be valuable to the leaders themselves if they are going to survive. The HR practices in this section are designed not only for the company, they also clearly help leaders increase their leadership capabilities. They answer the question, "What's in it for me?" For example, the on-boarding interventions (see _New Leader Assimilation, Virtual On-Boarding,_ and _On-the-Job Development That Starts on Day One_) accelerate a leaders' ability to get up to speed in a new role and simultaneously develop a set a meta-skills that will increase leaders' ability to learn from future experiences. In the same way, training programs that focus on experience are significantly more likely to be seen as valuable by their participants (see _Training and Experience-Driven Development, Bringing the Real World into the Classroom, Cultivating Learning Agility,_ and _HoTspots_).

As you think about the HR practices that you lead, ask yourself, "Is this a practice that leaders will feel like they _have_ to do or something they _want_ to do?"

Keep it simple. The HR processes described in this section are simple, but they are not simplistic. Elegant is probably the right word. They represent sophisticated initiatives that are built on a deep understanding of how leaders learn. However, they land lightly on the managers. They are the smart phone applications of leadership development: sophisticated concepts with a simple user interface. The _Profiles for Success_ contribution is a good example. Behind the scenes, significant work was done to identify the key developmental experiences for HR professionals and then build these into a process that encourages lateral moves within the company that will be truly developmental. Yet, to users the process is extremely simple— a list of rich lateral experiences to choose from. The _Succession Planning_ and _Building for Breadth and Depth Through Experience_ contributions provide two other great examples of this principle. In the same way, the contribution on _Building Experience into Simulations_ and the _Mentoring_ contribution emphasize the importance of simplicity and ease of use for the system users.

As you think about your HR practices, ask yourself, "Do leaders think this is simple?" If the program requires an instruction manual, you have probably already lost the battle.

Change is the rule, not the exception. Throughout the contributions, the dynamic nature of organizations is a common theme. For most of us, change feels like the only thing that remains constant. The authors consistently describe the many ways that they were required to modify and adapt the HR practices to address new challenges that emerged _while_ the programs were being developed and _after_ the programs were launched. What is particularly interesting is the way that the initiatives were designed. They were almost all built in a way that could naturally adapt to the emerging challenges. For example, the chapter on _Integrated Talent Management_ is not about building a pretty model with all of the right boxes and arrows, but about the _process_ over a three year period to put an integrated talent management system that met the changing needs of one organization. _Identifying and Assessing for Learning Ability_ draws attention to the need for leaders that can adapt to change. _Hot People-Hot Jobs_ describes a dynamic process to identify and develop high potential leaders and _Multicultural Women in the Pipeline_ describes how changing demographics will impact organizations in the future. The chapter on _Communities of Practice_ identifies how to build a global consortium where people develop each other and share best practices across organizations.

As you consider the HR practices that you are leading, ask yourself, "Am I building systems that will be able to self-adapt to future challenges when I am gone?"

The contributions in this section offer a plethora of ideas that can be integrated into most organizations. Don't forget to consider the ideas presented in the other sections of the book that complement and enhance the HR practices that are offered here.

47

Integrated Talent Management and Experience-Based Development

Norm Tonina
Grameen Foundation

ALMOST THREE YEARS ago a colleague and I were asked to conduct a human capital management assessment for the Grameen Foundation USA (GF), a $20 million nonprofit that operates in eight countries to help the poor, especially the poorest, create a world without poverty. Quickly expanding our work into more of a culture and organization effectiveness assessment, we spent a month interviewing employees across the organization and the globe in order to gain a clear understanding of the state of GF, its culture, and its organizational practices. (See the Resources at the end of this article for a list of sources that I consulted to guide our work.)

Our assessment culminated in a presentation to GF's Executive Leadership Team (ELT) with a current-state assessment and a set of four recommendations, many that top-notch HR organizations would partner with the CEO to lead:

1. Refine organizational practices that clarify decision making, drive accountability, and foster greater agility.

2. Evolve performance management to ensure the new system delivers greater focus and consistency, improves goal-setting rigor and organizational alignment, and improves differentiation in ratings and rewards.

3. Define and articulate a GF talent strategy based on differentiation, developing the next level of leaders, and driving toward business results.

4. Reset the role of human resources at GF beyond focusing on executing transactions and adding value to GF's business and talent systems.

At that point, having satisfied our assessment deliverable and thinking that it was time for us to move on, we were asked to stay and begin implementation of the recommendations as consultants. (Eventually, I became GF's first chief human resources officer.)

Understanding that this was not only an organization effectiveness project but also a mini-culture transformation, we huddled on how to start our work and identify the cultural paradigms we wanted to challenge as we proceeded. This led us to believe that engaging the entire organization in a transparent, direct dialogue was imperative. Through a series of e-mail communications and, eventually, all-staff meetings and listening sessions, we laid out an integrated approach to implementing our recommendations (see Figure 47.1).

We found it important to lay out our work in an integrated, systemic way, in a way that the pieces fit together and reinforced each other, rather than laying out a set of activities. This was most obvious to us as we thought about talent management and development-

Figure 47.1. Model for Talent Development

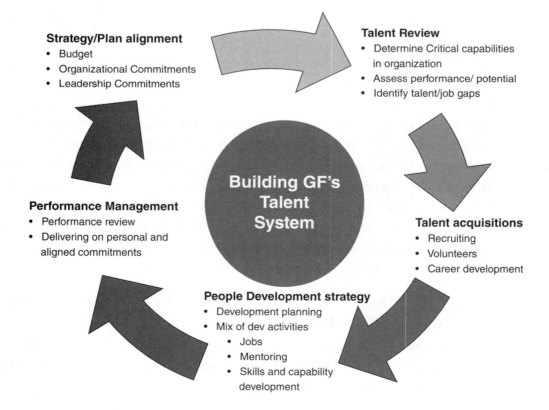

based experiences. Working with a $20 million nonprofit, we didn't have exorbitant resources to dedicate to talent management and development; thus, we quickly concluded that tightly coupling talent management and development with everything going on across GF, and developing talent through the day-to-day work as it was pursued, was the single most credible and expedient approach to making progress. We also found it necessary to be transparent with how long the process would take, the changes the organization would face, and the fact that the organization would learn as it went along and evaluate and adjust along the way. Just recently, as the latest piece of the work was launched, I used this same slide (Figure 47.1), now two years old, in GF's monthly all-staff meeting that catalogued the ground that has been covered while underscoring the importance of the next phase of the journey.

Where to Start

Any organization approaching this kind of work needs to start with the strategy it is pursuing and the results the organization is working to deliver. GF implemented a strategic plan to have more "sandals on the ground" in the countries it operated in during the coming year, rather than driving programs centrally from the United States. With the new organizational strategy implemented, the base for the organization was defined, and work went ahead. Each member of the ELT set his or her "commitments," the bold, multi-year goals with more specific milestones and measurements for the specific deliverables that would be achieved over the course of the current fiscal year. Once set, the leaders cascaded their commitments down through their organizations in an attempt to create better alignment and to clarify for each employee how his or her deliverables fit into the bigger picture of both their leader's organization and GF. This addressed the problem that many nonprofit organizations face—having so many needs that the scope expands and the organization loses focus.

Talent Management at the Grameen Foundation

With clear goals set and employees better understanding how their efforts fit into the larger GF picture, the organization moved on to design and execute a GF-wide talent review as part of a larger executive retreat. To facilitate more sophisticated GF talent discussions, my consulting partner and I designed a set of capabilities that we believed were distinguishing for where GF was at that point, taking into account some of the cultural shifts we were trying to embed. We were careful to not refer to capabilities as competencies; having been involved in competency development in the past, we knew there was not the budget or the time to build a validated competency model.

The capabilities, which have been now been through talent-review cycles and over a dozen more rigorous leadership assessments, have stood the test of time with no more than a handful of tweaks. One of my fondest memories to date of my time at GF is about being at a retreat and completing the first talent review literally in a dark cabin because the leaders would not allocate any more time to the process when designing the agenda but yet wouldn't end the talent review until every employee was discussed. The talent review not only underscored the depth of talent GF had within the organization but also the various roles each employee could play and his or her areas for development, along with gaps in talent that the organization had to address through either recruiting or development.

With the organization's development needs identified as part of the talent review, it was decided to begin by launching a mentoring pilot program. Mentoring was chosen as a starting point because of the short time to launch a program demonstrating a commitment to employee development while also leveraging the broad expertise that existed within GF's leadership team. Mentoring was a prime example of how the organization could pursue talent development within the context of day-to-day work. The mentoring pilot resulted in fifteen mentoring matches. Also, a handful of stretch assignments was identified that would provide employees the opportunity to get exposure to a new experience or a different leader. With the mentoring pilot launched and stretch assignments executed, the organization built out a development framework for a more comprehensive approach to growing our employees (see Table 47.1).

As outlined in this table, the approach to capability building tilted toward leveraging experience-based development rather than overly investing in training. GF did eventually choose to partner with Learning in NGOs (LINGOS) to deliver skill-based learning opportunities based on its platform's ability to deliver consistent learning opportunities globally, although the entire early focus was leveraging experience-based development. During the first year of leveraging this approach, the organization played with many different on-the-job-development opportunities, including partnering an employee with a leader to write a white paper, appointing a chief of staff to the CEO as a development opportunity, providing project-based stretch assignments, and sending employees abroad to work on projects in the field or fixed-term assignments. As GF learned from each of these development opportunities, some more successful than others, the organization refined its thinking and approach.

In terms of learning from others, GF has been able to parlay its learning from the mentoring pilot into an organization-wide mentoring program that employees opt into, with HR facilitating mentor matches based on an employee's expressed development interest. The organization has also grown to leverage more coaching, especially in the leadership space. To clarify the difference between mentoring and coaching, a former colleague of mine probably offered the crispest definitions I have ever heard: Mentoring is about learning that occurs based on the mentor's experience, whereas coaching is about a coach helping an employee learn through his or own experience. Having observed coaching relationships that have gone on endlessly in the past, GF has tried to use coaching more surgically. The organization leverages coaches (myself, other HR employees, or sometimes, pro-bono external coaches) to partner with its leaders in specific development situations to help them learn

Table 47.1. People Development Strategy-Building Capability

Components of Development	Strategy	Focus Area	Activities
	In-depth capability assessment	Assessment	Talent review Leadership assessment based on 360s
	Individual development plans for identified key talent	Commitments	Performance commitments dedicated to capability-based development plans after talent review Feedback
Learning on the job (70 percent)	Develop capabilities through challenging assignments Development occurs primarily on the job or in stretch assignments.	Job experiences Special assignments	Identify key assignments and stretch experiences Executive exposure Greater control or decision making Field assignments
Learning from others (20 percent)	Mentoring/coaching Support for on-the-job development or in stretch assignments	Mentoring Coaching	One-on-one ELT mentor or board assignments Coaching from direct "manager as coach" Exposure to ELT meetings and board Candid feedback, 360 assessments, in-training forums, and so on
Learning through training (10 percent)	Create targeted training appropriate to developing critical capabilities missing in the organization Create tools to assist with self development	Training	In-house training led by managers with select skills/capabilities Creates better understanding of the business of the Grameen Foundation Develops "training" managers Online training through a learning-management system

from their experiences. My dream is to build a set of leaders who can then turn around and leverage more of a coaching style, in appropriate situations, with their employees to ultimately create a "culture of coaching" across the Grameen Foundation.

Lessons Learned

After working in the software industry for twenty-one years and then taking a brief respite from the working world, I found the opportunity to work in a nonprofit on a six-week assessment project to be a great way to start thinking about how I wanted to spend the next phase of my career. Two and a half years later, I realize just how rich the experience is that I have gained from GF. I believe I have built a "playbook" for entering an organization, assessing its current state, and driving change. I also take away from this experience a number of critical lessons:

Think Systemically

Practitioners usually find it attractive to jump in and fix something. They often receive feedback such as, "Performance management is broken" or "Our leaders just don't get it" or "We need better managers" or "I just don't know who gets to make this decision." Most people are tempted to fix the problem at hand without stepping back and taking a more systemic look at what is happening in the broader organization.

Starting your work with a deeper organizational assessment will give you the strongest possible foundation for building and implementing a talent system (or whatever name will resonate within your organization). And the best part about the assessment process will be the opportunity you have to engage the entire organization, create a dialogue with employees, and build trusted relationships. Once you have taken the time to do that deeper assessment, you will find solutions that reinforce the bigger changes you are trying to drive and that are much more tailored to your organization's specific challenge, and which therefore have a greater chance at success. Completing an organization-wide assessment takes commitment and time but will result in far better solutions and, ultimately, success. (See the Resources at the end of this article for organizational assessment resources.)

Engage the Employee Base

Many organizations will claim that talent is their greatest asset, yet go about their work without regularly engaging their employees. Many of the larger programs I have driven have been the result of direct conversations with employees. You can't always touch every employee in every project, but through a combination of one-on-one interviews, smaller employee feedback sessions, focus groups, and an employee experience survey conducted every eighteen months, GF has a good sense of its employee satisfaction and concerns (of course, as with most organizations, GF does still have its share of concerns).

One thing I try to do when I visit GF offices is to hold listening sessions (an approach that has been emulated by many of our leaders). A listening session is a one-hour meeting with any employee in that office that is interested in attending. I usually start with a five- to ten-minute introduction on topics on my mind, but then turn the floor over to the attendees for them to share their thoughts and ask me questions. Through this process, we are breaking down barriers and creating a culture where more transparent dialogue is increasing and valued, where employees feel safer to challenge the status quo, and where, I hope, greater trust is being built.

Transparently Communicate

Since the very beginning of my tenure, I have worked hard to model transparent communication (because the assessment my colleague and I completed said employees did not think GF's leadership was very transparent). In reality this wasn't always easy to do. For instance, I had to ask the CEO to stand up in front of employees very early in my tenure and tell them there were going to be layoffs without knowing how many or who would be impacted. But at the end of the session, one employee who was recently let go by a competitor said that his prior employer had let people in the organization go when they showed up to work one Monday morning without any prior notice. He went on the praise the transparency of GF's leaders by entering into a discussion with employees about the financial challenges and he ended with how impressed he was by the leadership's conviction to stand up there and have a dialogue with staff. Shortly thereafter, when we reduced our U.S. benefit offering, I was transparent about the need, for those still with the organization, to participate in cost savings to ensure a more sustainable future; there was very little pushback. In my listening sessions, I often receive questions that I don't feel comfortable answering in their entirety, although I am clear with employees about what I can answer and the reason why I cannot answer the full question. As a result of improving trust within GF, I feel as if employees are much more direct with leadership and confront tricky issues without letting them fester.

Respond to Employee Feedback, Try New Approaches, and Be Open to Evaluating and Adjusting

I spent a lot of time with my first-generation Italian grandparents as a child and I remember them encouraging me with simple adages. "If at first you don't succeed, try, try again" is the adage most apropos to this learning. I have found employees will not fault an organization for trying new things if the underlying intent is to improve a situation or respond to their feedback. A simple example: Recently, GF modified the way it held monthly all-employee staff meetings, based on feedback it received. At the end of the meeting one employee commended the organization for listening and making a change so quickly. Let's face it, very few changes hit the bulls-eye the first time. People need to have a mindset of making a change and then evaluating and adjusting accordingly. This enables leaders to continuously move closer to the result they were intending while also modeling for employees that moving closer to a goal is something to strive for.

Understand the "Art" of the Work

Practitioners regularly have "a-ha" moments in the work they do. I have come to believe, most significantly over the last ten years, that to do the work I do I need to be grounded in theory and principle and the "science" of our field. But to be successful at the work I do, I need to be more nuanced, to know when to pull instead of push, to know when to sit back rather than interject, to help a leader extract a learning rather than tell the leader what he or she just learned, to know how to influence an outcome rather than lead to the outcome. This is the art of the work and, I believe, what often separates a successful project or set of outcomes from those not so successful. To make this transition requires practitioners to shy away from content and focus on process and to relinquish the need to receive credit for an outcome.

Final Thoughts

In reflecting on my two and a half years at Grameen Foundation, I think it is very important to close by acknowledging that, even with the notable progress that the organization has made, there is so much more to do. Perfection is not attainable in our roles or the organizations we serve. GF has lots of things that go well today but some things that don't go as well. In the most recent employee-experience survey, I am pleased to report that some focus areas discussed in this chapter have resulted in significant improvement from our last survey in several areas that were targeted for improvement. Commitments have resulted in employees seeing a greater link between their work and GF's mission (79 percent favorable, up 17 points) along with greater clarity for their work (75 percent, up 13 points), while continuing to extract meaning from their work (90 percent, up 10 points). GF employees also feel as if they are learning and growing by delivering work that challenges them to use their knowledge and skills (82 percent, up 9 points) along with having a manager that is increasingly invested in their development (68 percent, up 10 points). In the areas of collaboration, work group collaboration across teams (75 percent, up 14 points) and cooperation within work group to achieve strategic goals (83 percent, up 6 points) also showed strong improvement. Innovation, the lifeblood of GF's work to improve the lives of the poor, also showed strength, with employees feeling encouraged to seek out new ideas and solutions (84 percent, up 16 points). Finally, employees also say that GF culture remains strong, with a 74 percent favorable rating. In terms of areas of focus moving forward, GF still has work to do for its employees to understand what a progressive career could look like in the organization, along with improving the functioning of GF's governance bodies. I look forward to the work on a career architecture and leadership coaching to deliver similar improvements in the future.

Organizations are ever-changing, responding to shifts in the external environment, adjusting strategy, pursuing a new business or closing an old one down, losing a key leader, and so on. If perfection is your goal, you will end up being nothing more than tired and dejected. For example, I am frustrated that some survey scores continue to remain flat and will require a new approach or initiatives to tackle. Practitioners must be clear that their role is to put leaders, and ultimately their organizations, on a different path, a path closer to achieving sustainability for the long term. HR has an incredibly important role in making this happen.

Acknowledgments

Obviously, every artist needs a canvas and the canvases for HR practitioners are the organizations they serve. I would like to thank the Grameen Foundation for sharing its organization with me these last two and a half years. I especially want to thank the leaders I have had the pleasure to work most closely with—Alex Counts, Jennifer Meehan, David Edelstein, Joshua Tripp, Camilla Nestor, Julia Soyars, and Peter Bladin—for entrusting their organization and themselves to me and for working to endure my endless feedback, whims, coaching, ideas, and irreverence. I am humbled by the mission focus, tenacity, thought leadership, and patience you demonstrate as you work towards creating a world without poverty.

I also need to acknowledge the work of my HR comrades. Natalie Yount was a tireless partner in the consulting portion of this work and was a helpful mirror when I most needed it. We shared lots of insights and laughs and, quite frankly, we probably kept each other from getting to the point of insanity in those more frustrating moments that change-influencers experience.

Finally, to my HR team—Astha Parmar, Beverly Jackson, and Sherita Coates—I would have been lost and felt very alone these last two years, since joining GF full-time, without you. Your efforts have been tireless in trying to practice a different type of HR. Thanks for tolerating my mind shifts, dealing with my rants, and helping me to see the impact we were really having in the organization.

Resources

To conduct organizational analyses, I have found it most useful to pull pieces of models and tools from various sources and build a hybrid approach that leverages multiple frameworks. The following is a list of sources I recommend any practitioner reference as he or she thinks about how to help improve the performance and functioning of an organization:

Galbraith, J. (2002). *Designing organizations: An executive guide to strategy, structure, and process*. San Francisco, CA: Jossey-Bass.

Hill, C., & Jones, G. (2008). *Strategic management: theory*. Boston, MA: Houghton Mifflin Company. (See especially Chapter 1: "Strategic Leadership: Managing the Strategy-Making Process for Competitive Advantage.")

Waterman, R.H., Peters, T.J., & Phillips, J.R. (1980). Structure is not organization. *Business Horizons, 23*(3), 14–26. (McKinsey's 7s model.)

Weisbord, M.R. (1978). *Organizational diagnosis: A workbook of theory and practice*. Reading, MA: Addison-Wesley.

48

Identifying and Assessing for Learning Ability

Paul Yost and Jillian McLellan
Seattle Pacific University

ASSESSING THE ABILITY of leaders to successfully navigate challenging assignments and key leadership transitions in their careers has become increasingly popular. What is assessed is broad, and what "it" is called varies widely—*learning ability, learning agility, learning capacity, leadership agility,* and *adaptive leadership,* to name only a few. Organizations are increasingly using learning ability as an indicator of leadership potential. The ability to successfully navigate a novel leadership role and learn as you go is especially valued in today's dynamic organizations. Rather than a single attribute, the capacity of a leader to learn and navigate through novel situations is best understood as a cluster of diverse attributes (such as intelligence, divergent thinking, tolerance for ambiguity), cognitive framing (such as adopting a learning orientation, self-awareness), and learned behaviors (such as feedback seeking, reflection).

Many people assume that if a person is high on one leadership capability he or she will be high on other capabilities, but this thinking is problematic. It is important to remember that one capability (for instance, intelligence) might be completely unrelated to other dimensions such as openness to feedback, self-awareness, or the ability to work with others. All of the dimensions will impact a leader's ability to adapt and learn from experience. Thus, it is important to identify the full range of characteristics and behaviors that are critical for leaders in your organization.

Learning ability has a stable, trait component, but it also can be learned and developed. It is important to distinguish between learning ability characteristics that are relatively hard to develop (for example, tolerance for ambiguity) versus habits and behaviors that are relatively easier to develop (for example, building a development plan). This distinction is important in deciding which characteristics you focus on. In selection and promotion decisions, you will want to focus on stable traits. If the focus is development, you will want to focus on behaviors that can be learned. This distinction is important. Identifying someone as having "low learning ability" when talking about practices that can be developed (for example, feedback seeking, reflection) is unfair to the person and likely will eliminate promising future leaders from the pipeline because bad assumptions are being made about their ability to grow and develop over time.

Assessing Leaders' Learning Ability

Organizations tend to use three methods to assess the learning abilities of leaders: (1) learning ability questions, (2) behavioral interviews, and (3) formal assessments. We'll discuss each of these in turn and provide some examples. Following that, we'll discuss some lessons learned and offer some tips for you to consider as you are assessing learning ability in your leaders.

Learning Ability Questions

In preparing to write about this topic, we asked our leadership development colleagues and the other contributors to this book to send us any questions that they use to assess people's learning ability. Here are some of the questions that they sent:

- Can you tell me about a key event in your development as a leader—something that led to a lasting change in your approach to leadership? What happened, what did you learn, and what you did do to capture the learning?

- Can you tell me about a time when you made a big mistake, were in a high-visibility assignment, or had to fix a critical problem? What did you find most challenging and what did you learn from that experience? (You might not directly ask about learning to see whether the person offers what he or she learned from the experience.)

- How do you see yourself spending your time in the first ninety days on this job?

- Can you tell me about something that you feel you have mastered? What was it and what did you do to master it?

- Was there a leadership challenge that you faced where you didn't know the answer but had to figure it out as you went? What happened? What are three actions that you took to navigate through the challenge?

- Given that a high degree of business acumen is important to many roles in our organization, how have you developed your business knowledge and how have you applied that knowledge to solve a specific work related problem or challenge?

- Can you tell me about a specific time when you were given new information that affected a decision you had already made? What was the outcome?

- Can you give me an example of a time when the impact of your message was contrary to what was intended? How did you rectify the situation?

- Everybody fails. What is one of your biggest failures? What did you learn?

- In which specific areas of the organization are you really interested in expanding your knowledge? How do you intend to achieve this?

Behavioral Interviews

Behavioral interviews (and formal assessments) offer a more structured and systematic way than questions to assess learning ability. The basic premise of behavioral interviewing is that past performance is the best predictor of future performance. Behavioral interviews are better than simple questions for two reasons: first, they focus on behavior—on what the person did, which is harder to fake; and second, they include standardized scoring to identify what is a good versus bad answer and to ensure everyone is assessed fairly, because everyone is graded on the same scale. For example, one way to predict how a candidate might transition into a new role is to find out and assess how he or she has approached new roles in the past and navigated through them. Prompts to elicit these experiences might include any of the questions suggested above or more specifically directed inquiries like the following:

- Tell me about a time when you led a team that had to start something from scratch. What happened? What did you do? What was the result? What did you learn?

- Tell me about a time when you took over a team or project that you needed to fix. What happened? What did you do? What was the result? What did you learn?

- Tell me about a time when you had a failure or mistake. What happened? What did you do? What was the result? What did you learn?

- Tell me about a time when you were on a team and it didn't go well. What was your role?

- Describe a time when you had to implement a significant organizational change. What was your strategy for gaining buy-in? What challenges did you encounter? How did you overcome those challenges?

- Give a specific example of a time when you failed to handle a problem or situation effectively. Why do you think your solution was ineffective? What, if anything, did you do after you recognized the problem was not handled appropriately?

- Describe a time when you were able to overcome a failure by starting over and accomplishing something that led to better results and execution.

As noted above, behavioral interview questions should have standardized scoring. The evaluation of the answers might include the extent to which leaders:

- Identify lessons that they learned in the experience (unprompted)
- Discuss how they applied the lessons that they learned to future problems (unprompted)
- Identify strategies that allowed them to learn as they go and navigate through the challenges (for example, the extent to which they were willing to take on stretch assignments; discuss seeking feedback and coaching in the assignment; experiment and assess the results; leverage the talents of other people and their teams to compensate for weaknesses, blind spots, or areas in which they are not the expert; and are able to change and adapt their strategies to new situations)

The original research on the lessons of experience also identified several lessons that commonly emerge in each type of experience. For example, in a person's first supervisory role, most leaders learn that being a manager is more than being the technical expert: The manager's job is to learn how to get things done through other people. One thing you might want to look for in the behavioral interviews is the extent to which interviewees talk about capturing these kinds of lessons.

Formal Assessments

Several off-the-shelf assessments exist that might also be used for selection or development (see the sample list in Table 48.1). The strength of using an assessment is that it doesn't need to be created from scratch. Assessments have often have been tested and validated with a variety of leaders at a number of organizations. Assessments also usually provide feedback reports to participants that allow leaders to benchmark themselves against other leaders, and most feedback reports also include developmental actions that leaders can pursue in areas where they are weak. Of course, all assessments are not created equally. Some are well tested and researched. Some are not. If you decide you want to use a formal assessment, there are some important issues to consider as you are evaluating your options.

First, will you be using it for selection, promotion, or development? If you are using the learning measures for selection or promotion, you will need to make sure the assessments are validated and how a candidate's score on an assessment is related to the job requirements. Work with a selection expert (for instance, a qualified I/O psychologist) and your legal department to ensure that the measures are valid, fair, and nondiscriminatory. If you are using assessments for development, you will likewise want be confident that they assess and

Table 48.1. A Sample of Learning Ability Assessments

Assessment	Purpose	Description
Formal Assessments		
General Mental Ability Tests	Selection	Research suggests that general reasoning ability is especially important in complex roles. A number of measures are available but often require certification to administer and often show adverse impact for protected groups. Abilities commonly measured include reading, comprehension, verbal ability, math, reasoning, and classification.
Prospector	Development	A multi-rater measure to assess the leadership skills most often found in successful executives and the learning behaviors needed to acquire those skills. Items measure two general dimensions: learning to learn (seeks opportunities to learn, seeks and uses feedback, learns from mistakes, open to criticism) and learning to lead (committed to making a difference, Insightful—sees things from new angles, has the courage to take risks, brings out the best in people, acts with integrity, seeks broad business knowledge, adapts to cultural differences).
Choices Architect	Selection or Development	A multi-rater assessment used to identify leadership potential. This assessment measures four general factors: Mental Agility, People Agility, Change Agility, and Results Agility.
viaEDGE	Development	A self-assessment to provide insight into learning agility and assist in determining leadership potential. The four general factors listed in Choices Architect are measured in addition to self-awareness.
Hogan Business Reasoning Inventory	Selection or Development	A self-assessment to assess a person's ability to solve problems and make business-related decisions, and the ability to reflect on one's past actions, determine where the problems have occurred, and then devise methods to avoid repeating those problems in the future. The assessment measures two different kinds of problem-solving: Tactical Reasoning and Strategic Reasoning.
Hogan Development Survey	Development	A self-assessment of personality based performance risks and derailers. Dimensions that are measured include: Excitable, Skeptical, Cautious, Reserved, Leisurely, Bold, Mischievous, Colorful, Imaginative, Diligent, and Dutiful.
Learning Tactics Inventory	Development	A self-assessment to help leaders Identify their preferred learning profile and behaviors, develop tactics to improve learning effectiveness, and create learning goals that improve performance. This measure includes four scales, each representing a different tactic for learning: Action, Thinking, Feeling, and Accessing Others.
Informal Assessments		
GPS•R (See page 157 in this book.)	Development	A short, sixteen-item self-assessment to help leaders determine whether they have created conditions that will help them take on challenging assignment, navigate them successfully, and capture the lessons of experience. Dimensions that are measured include Goals, People, Stretch, and Reflection.

(continued)

Table 48.1. A Sample of Learning Ability Assessments (*continued*)

Informal Assessments

Learning Orientation	Development	Two self-assessments are regularly used in research to assess whether people have adopted a learning or a performance orientation to their work. Don Vandewalle has a thirteen-item measure that assesses if a person focuses on learning, proving his or her capabilities or avoiding situations where competence is questioned. Scott Button, John Mathieu, and Dennis Zajac have a twenty-item scale to assess a person's learning and performance orientations.

Note: See the 1997 article by D. Vandewalle, "Development and Validation of a Work Domain Goal Orientation Instrument," in *Educational and Psychological Measurement, 57*, 995–1015, and the 1996 article by S.B. Button, J.E. Mathieu, and D.M. Zajac, "Goal Orientation in Organizational Research: A Conceptual and Empirical Foundation," in *Organizational Behavior and Human Decision Processes, 67*, 26–48.

develop skills that will make leaders more effective in their roles; however, the legal stakes are lower.

Second, how good is the assessment? Assessments can be judged on a variety of dimensions. Some of the basic elements include:

How well does the assessment measure what it claims to be measuring? The easiest way to assess the psychometric properties of a measure (its reliability and validity) is to find someone in the organization who is an expert in assessments and ask him or her or to find an expert at a local university (look in the organizational behavior department in a business school, in the industrial/organizational department in a school of psychology, or for an educational testing expert in a school of education). If you choose to use a formal assessment, then publishers of these assessments should make reliability and validity information available to you as a potential user. If you don't see a technical manual for the measure available on the publisher's website, or if the psychometric information isn't in the facilitator's manual, then ask for that information. You or the expert that you employ will be assessing the instrument to assess such issues as reliability, construct validity, predictive validity, and external validity.

- Reliability is an indication of the extent to which scale items correlate with each other, indicating that they measure the same underlying factor. Reliability can also be a measure of whether scores are stable over time. This will be important if the assessment is used for selection to predict a candidate's future success. Do the questions and items designed to measure a dimension correlate with each other?

- Construct validity tells you whether the measure correlates with other measures that are designed to measure the same thing (for example, if self-ratings of feedback-seeking correlate with other people's ratings of feedback seeking).

- Predictive validity indicates whether the measure correlates with the outcomes you would like it to (for example, future job performance and advancement rates).

- External validity indicates whether the measure can be used with leaders like the ones in your organization (for example, if the assessment has been used in the past with leaders in similar jobs, industries, and cultures).

Are the measure and the feedback report written in a way that leaders will accept? In practice, accurate measurement is only one goal; the other goal is to promote positive change. Leaders hate measures that feel too "researchy" and don't use the language of "real" people. If you want to drive change, make sure users can easily see the importance and usefulness of the measures you choose to use.

How will you use the feedback? Finally, if assessments are used in selection, you need to decide how much feedback you want to provide participants. External candidates are often not given specific feedback, although this is becoming somewhat more common, but feedback can be very beneficial for internal candidates to highlight areas for future development. After all, internal candidates might be future leaders.

If the assessments are used for development, it is often useful to embed them within a development program where participants can review their results with a coach, or in groups with their peers, and develop strategies to leverage their strengths and improve on their weaknesses. The quality of the feedback report is particularly important in promoting follow-up actions. Is the feedback report easy to understand? Does it suggest actions that the leaders can take based on their results? Is the advice something that leaders will actually do? A good way to test the quality of a feedback report is to take it yourself and see how much your behavior changes the next week!

Lessons Learned

It is crucial to discover what matters in your organization. Some of the learning-ability dimensions will be particularly important in your organization; others won't. The list of possible dimensions is immense (see Table 48.1). One way to identify the ones that are most important in your organization is to identify the characteristics and behaviors of leaders who navigate key leadership transitions particularly well. For example, what are the traits and behaviors of the leaders who make the transition into senior leader roles particularly well? What are the characteristics and actions of leaders who succeed in a global assignment?

Another strategy is to identify the factors that tend to derail leaders. Do derailing leaders lack a network? Are they not open to feedback? Do they fail to attract talented people? Are they not perceived as trustworthy and honest? Do they move so quickly that they are seen as abrasive and brash? Do they move too cautiously? If you can figure out what causes leaders to fail, the opposite will point toward the attributes and habits that allow leaders to navigate challenging roles successfully.

Remember that learning ability can be learned. We all have some things that come to us more easily than others because of personality traits or because of the earlier experiences in our lives. But people are adaptable. They can change. When leaders think about learning ability, they tend to assume that it is a trait—that some leaders have it and others don't. (They also tend to assume that they do have it.) Thinking of learning ability as simply a trait can be problematic and a bit ironic because it suggests that people are either born great learners or not. In other words, the assumption is that learning ability cannot be learned.

It is important to make clear that research suggests that leaders are likely to have strengths and weaknesses in their abilities to learn from experience. Leaders differ in their abilities to manage ambiguity, seek feedback, reflect, and to handle complex thinking. However, research also suggests that leaders can learn how to do all of these things better. They can adopt habits to overcome weaknesses or find ways to build a team around them to help compensate for weaknesses (for example, building a team with people who are willing to challenge their ideas). As you assess people on learning ability, make sure you emphasize to leaders in the organization that these factors can be improved and provide ways they can improve in areas where they are weak. After all, we all are likely to struggle in some areas!

49

On-the-Job Development That Starts on Day One

Brad Borland
Kelly Services, Inc.

EFFECTIVE LEADER SELECTION is essential for ensuring organization and individual performance while also building leadership bench strength and successor talent. Although the leader selection process at Kelly Services was good, the post-selection development process nearly always lagged behind the real need (for both the organization and the leader) to immediately begin development of the person selected. The Talent Management and Leadership Development Team realized that the organization was missing a key opportunity to re-use selection data to immediately launch development. A collaborative process with HR generalists, senior hiring managers, and employees was established to launch development planning *before* the candidate even began the job. By launching experience-based development earlier, the transitioning leader can more quickly gain new role confidence and competence, hit a performance stride right away, and feel that the organization is investing in his or her success.

In more specific terms, the selection data is used to ask and answer simple, yet targeted, development questions:

- What does the leader (new to Kelly or new to role) need developmentally to become even better?

- What does the leader need to acquire (knowledge, skills, or abilities) or improve in order to accelerate performance?

- What are the leader's strengths (which are likely why he or she was selected)?

- What are the leader's gaps (which could impede his or her selection)?

- What are the development priorities?

- Given the development priorities (usually thoughtfully limited to one or two), what are the means and methods that should and could be used to drive real development (beyond the new organization information typically covered in orientation)?

- What experiences are most necessary to drive high-impact, near-term development? This is perhaps the most important question.

It is repeatedly emphasized to leaders that it is important to consider both strength-based development (building a strength) and gap-based development (shoring up a gap), and that development is often best executed using experience. Neither of these points seems to be well or instinctively known.

Partnering to Craft a Development Plan

Once these questions are answered, the assigned HR generalist and the hiring manager are guided to create a *draft* development plan. I emphasize *draft* because Kelly is intentional about development being a *with* versus *for* interactive process. It is believed that the plan should not to be imposed on the hiring manager, generalist, or leader. The *with* partnership creates greater and more authentic conviction and regard for the development targets and tactics. The draft is used to help engage the transitioning leaders earlier in their tenures in guiding and owning their development than had previously been possible. It is now planned to occur within the first few weeks of a leader starting his or her role. The draft also gives hiring managers an advantage, as typically they had struggled to meaningfully identify targeted and relevant early-term development, including the best methods to drive true growth.

The development plan identifies key underdeveloped, role-relevant competencies discovered during selection. With guidance, the group selects up to two competencies that could make the biggest performance impact once well honed—for example, embrace and practice collaboration, execute the organization's strategy, make decisions with results in mind, or create competitive advantage. To assist development, a fairly typical development-plan framework is used (see Exhibit 49.1). The most attention is paid to Questions 2, 3, and 4.

Using the competencies identified, a list of experiences that could drive development is brainstormed—and the list continues to grow. See Exhibit 49.2 for examples of experiences

Exhibit 49.1. Development Plan Framework

1. Leadership competency for development:

2. Specific development objective:

3. Once this development objective is achieved, what will be different and/or better? How will you be behaving differently?

4. Behavioral action steps, for example, experience, education, and training (see attached development examples) to achieve your development objective:

5. Timing:

6. Support required:

7. Actions completed: (completed later)

8. Results achieved, including any feedback received: (completed later)

Exhibit 49.2. Example of Experiences Generated to Support a Competency

Competency

Embrace and practice collaboration: Drives One Kelly philosophy by managing across functions and ensuring leaders operate effectively within a matrix structure.

Associated Behaviors

- Drives collaboration among individuals and teams and across businesses.

- Creates synergies by aligning his or her team members to common goals and challenges.

- Involves others in decisions and plans that impact them.

- Addresses and resolves conflict directly and constructively.

Sample Experiences

Cross-boundary focus: Attend key stakeholder(s) operational meeting(s) to understand their most important results; meet with stakeholders to discuss/contrast results between groups; participate in each other's strategy and business planning processes to ensure plans align and render no unintended consequences; review each other's quarterly results together with an eye toward mutual and ongoing improvement; volunteer to assist a fellow leader to tackle a tough issue.

Vertical focus: Invite/engage a diverse range of employees to help you guide annual goal setting; participate in skip-level meetings to understand varying points of view; expand your list of "go-to" people, to whom important work is delegated, to be intentionally diverse.

generated for the competency "embrace and practice collaboration." The hiring manager uses the list of sample experiences to guide a development-planning discussion with the new leader. Initial points of emphasis include: (1) sharing selection-based strengths and gaps; (2) identifying the most important competencies for development; (3) providing the rationale for Kelly's early-term focus on development and especially experience-based development; (4) sharing the draft development plan and inviting the new leader to adapt it as needed for his or her learning style and ideas; and (5) setting another meeting to review the draft and agree on a final plan. The HR generalist also helps the leader refine the draft plan. Once the plan is agreed upon, the new leader and hiring manager set a date to review progress.

Post-Experience Learning Transfer

It is also emphasized that execution of an experience is still only developmental if the leader takes the time to reflect and review what was learned. Kelly recommends that all leaders slow down to synthesize: what they learned; how they will use it on the job, including what they commit to doing or doing differently; and what they would do differently next time when setting out on a development experience. Leaders should also review their plans of applied learning with their managers and share the most important points with others whom they also are trying to similarly develop.

Although Kelly still needs to use this method more broadly and over a longer period of time, the initial results have been exceedingly positive. It jump-starts a leader's transition, creating positive feelings of meaningful engagement (and hopefully retention), and it is a time-saver that produces real development for the hiring managers. From literally every vantage point, the approach has been touted throughout HR as a means to both accelerate performance and build the leadership bench.

50

New Leader Assimilation

Tanya Boyd
Payless Holdings, Inc.

A KEY EXPERIENCE for a leader is taking on a new role, whether it is becoming a leader for the first time or moving to a new area or team. For all new leaders, one of the keys to success is a rapid start.

The New Leader Assimilation process, which originated at General Electric, is a frequently used approach to increase the speed with which a new leader and his or her team are able to function effectively together. Common estimates suggest it can take six to eight months for trust and understanding to be built between a leader and his or her team members. New leader assimilation is intended to jump-start that process within the first two months of a new leader's role. The assimilation process achieves accelerated results by providing a safe forum for basic information about a leader and team members to be shared and by surfacing issues, concerns, expectations, and questions early on, thus laying a foundation for open candid discussions in the future. While most leaders are already proactive in getting to know their teams, the presence of a facilitator without the leader removes any concern that team members may have in speaking frankly and openly about their needs and concerns.

The basic steps of a typical New Leader Assimilation are as follows (see Figure 50.1, New Leader Assimilation Process):

Figure 50.1. New Leader Assimilation Process

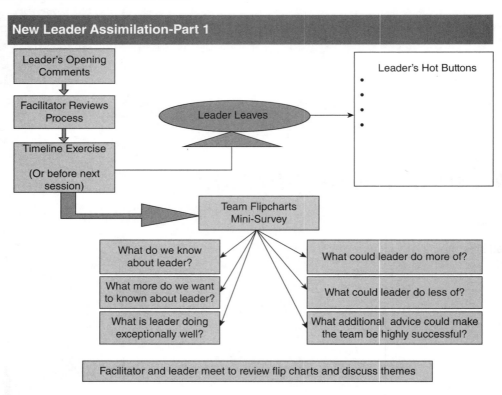

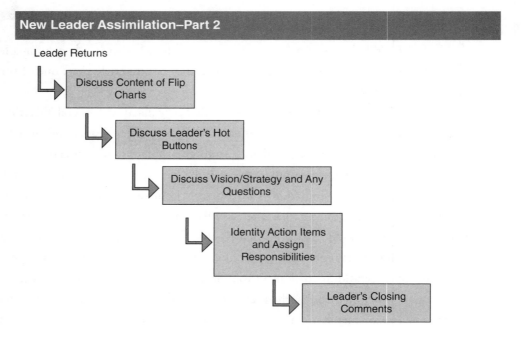

1. The facilitator and the leader meet to review the process and finalize the questions. The leader sends out an information letter to the team members to let them know about the process (see Exhibit 50.1 for an example).

2. The facilitator, the leader, and the team members meet together briefly. The facilitator explains the purpose of the exercise and the agenda for the rest of the day. The leader voices his or her support for the process and encourages team members to be open and honest in the feedback they share.

Exhibit 50.1. Sample Letter to Participants

Dear Team Members,

I look forward to our time together as a team [date] [time]. The location will be [place]. Remember that we will have a team dinner immediately following [location]. Please plan to join if you can. On [date] for the leader assimilation session, we will spend time with [name] as facilitator.

The purpose of this session is to accelerate the development of an effective working relationship among our team through getting to know each other as people, not just bosses and co-workers. The process will allow us to more clearly understand each other's needs and to begin working through them. You will have an opportunity to share some information about yourself personally and professionally and to give me some "live" 360 feedback by generating responses to a series of questions.

Thanks in advance for your thoughtfulness and preparation for this session. I encourage you to be both specific and candid in your feedback to ensure that the team maximizes the opportunity to provide me feedback and dialogue on how we can work together effectively.

The pre-work for the session is described below.

1. Prepare a timeline of your life, both personally and professionally (this can be handwritten; no copies needed).

    a. Include the important milestones that you believe make you who you are.

    b. Be prepared to share two of these milestones with the group; you can discuss the remainder of your timeline at a future session with your supervisor.

2. Think of your responses to the following questions. The team will generate responses to these questions when I am out of the room, and we will go over these responses at the second session (anonymously).

    a. What do we know about [leader]?

    b. What do we want to know about [leader]?

    c. What is [leader] doing exceptionally well?

    d. What could [leader] do more of?

    e. What could [leader] do less of?

    f. What additional advice could make the team be highly successful?

Have a *great* weekend and I'll see you next week!

Thanks,

[Leader]

Exhibit 50.2. Tips for Facilitators

As a facilitator you will be effective to the extent that you:
- Are able to communicate the value and import of the process to the team you are facilitating and energize them to participate fully.

- Already have or are able to earn the team's trust so that they will speak freely about any concerns without fear of identification/retribution.

- Record accurately using the words/phrases of the team, their questions, observations, etc.
- Control the process to ensure that the key areas are covered in a timely fashion with quality inputs.

Privacy Issues

- Explain to the leader that you told the group they could ask any questions . . . but that the leader wouldn't necessarily answer every question if they seem too personal or the leader simply doesn't have an answer. It is the job of the facilitator to avoid this whenever possible.

  - For example: "Who did you vote for in the last election?" Leader response: "I am not going to say . . . but I'll tell you I was very tempted to vote for someone not on the ballot."

  - For example: "What are your religious beliefs?" Leader response: "I believe some areas of our personal lives should remain private." Any of these types of questions could be answered or gracefully deflected.

- During a review session between facilitator and leader, the facilitator should basically be present but quiet while the leader reviews all the charts; available to clarify questions, translate scribing, and give a general description of tenor of meeting. The facilitator should also flavor any strong points: "There was a lot of emotion around this item."

3. The leader departs. The facilitator and the team members spend two to three hours answering a series of questions about the leader, usually with the aid of flipcharts (see Exhibit 50.2 for facilitation tips). Names are not associated with comments. Common questions include (see Exhibit 50.3 for additional questions):

   - What do we know about [leader]?

   - What do we want to know about [leader]?

   - What concerns do we have about [leader] coming?

   - What should [leader] know about us?

   - What main problems/challenges will [leader] be facing?

   - What additional advice could make the team highly successful?

4. The facilitator meets with the leader to share the responses to the six questions, being careful to share only what was said and not who said it.

Exhibit 50.3. Optional Questions

- What are our concerns about the new leader in this role?

- What specific suggestions do we have for overcoming these concerns? How can we help ensure our team's success?

- What are the major problems/issues the team will be facing in the next twelve months?

- What are the opportunities for us with this new leadership?

- What are the key elements of our vision?

- What is currently working well for our organization?

- What is getting in our way?

- If you could change one thing about the way we work together, what would it be?

- Is there anything else we should discuss to improve our effectiveness?

5. The whole team meets together, and the leader provides thoughts and responses to what the team came up with during their session. This step often involves prioritizing and creating plans to address potential or current problem areas.

Optional Modifications and Additions

Some options to consider include:

- Involving the team members in determining the questions to discuss.

- Follow-up sessions four to six months later to determine what has changed between the leader and the team members or within the team itself, and to focus on a new set of actions.

- Where trust is already established, the new leader may lead the discussion.

At Payless, we have taken this basic process and made a few changes that we have found to enhance the results. The New Leader Assimilation process has been one of our most successful interventions in terms of leader satisfaction; sometimes new leaders are skeptical or hesitant before going through the process, but all become strong proponents of the process after going through it with their teams.

We have found that when leaders and team members get to know each other on a personal level early in the process, and not just as bosses or co-workers, it benefits communication and teamwork. Because of this, we have added a component to the new leader assimilation process that we call Timeline. Both the leader and the team members write out a basic timeline of their lives, including key events in their personal and professional lives that they believe helped to shape them into who they are now. The facilitator draws a long timeline on the wall, and team members write or draw three to five of their key events. Following that, team members and the new leader talk through these events. Leaders have commented that knowing these personal aspects of their team members' lives helps them to identify with them and gives some indication about what motivates them. Team members have said that hearing about key events in the leader's life helps them to see him or her as approachable. We have used this technique as an icebreaker and to kick off the follow-up session where the leader and the team meet together to discuss what came up during the initial session. Because there are usually many more than five key events on a person's time-line, leaders often take time during individual conversations with their team members to go over the remaining key events.

Another addition we made to the new leader assimilation process is to have the leader identify his or her "hot buttons," which we define as ways of working or communicating that bother them. We ask the leader to write a list of hot buttons, and we discuss them after going through the content of the flipcharts gathered in the initial meeting with the team members. By putting those issues in front of the team, members can reduce their fear and uncertainty about what the new leader will expect or how the expectations will differ from the team's previous leader. For example, if I know that my leader does not like to be bothered during the lunch hour, I can avoid the awkwardness of stopping in during that time and being rebuffed. If I know that a leader prefers receiving an email rather than a phone call, I can make sure to contact him or her that way and avoid creating an annoyance. This meeting's discussion usually provokes some laughter and a sense of relief.

We have also found it useful to include a follow-up session about six months after the initial session, at which time team members look at the action plans they committed to during the initial session and update their progress as well as reaffirm or redefine their current direction. This is also a good time for a brief follow-up on what the leader is doing exceptionally well, what the leader could do more of, and what the leader could do less of.

The New Leader Assimilation process helps to ensure that the experience of being a new leader is successful, whether it's a first-time leadership position or a move into a new role. The process is also useful when a leader and his or her team are going through a challenging experience, such as a turnaround. We have had great results applying this tool to help leaders in such circumstances reconnect with their teams and make positive progress toward goals. The tool's power arises from its immediate effect. The relationships between the leader and team members are completely different when they walk out of the room from when they walk into the room. Those benefits also last over the long term.

51

Virtual On-Boarding

Ritesh Daryani
Expedia, Inc.

EMPLOYEES ARE THE most precious assets of any technology company. They are the life blood of the organization. The pain is immense if the company starts to bleed its human capital. Successfully on-boarding leaders is critical to their success. Transitions also offer one of the greatest opportunities for leaders to develop and build the skills that will help them learn from experience. They are ready to learn and open to feedback. Transitions also represent a critical period when leaders are more likely to derail.

Recently, a colleague and I were reviewing the attrition data of new hires at an organization where I previously worked. It was very high in the employee population that has been with the company for less than a year. We decided to further focus in on the reasons why new hires were leaving the organization within this short span. Focus groups, surveys, and interviews were conducted to understand the issues better. Based on the analysis, a cross-functional team was formed to favorably decrease the attrition of employees who were leaving within a year of joining the organization. The team was made up of representatives from various business groups—for instance, IT infrastructure members, people managers, business leaders, learning-and-development professionals, compensation specialists, and HR business partners. These people had a role to play to make the on-boarding experience memorable. Also, a project plan was proposed to reduce bench time and make employees billable within thirty days and hence drive faster and more effective assimilation of the employees into the culture of the organization.

The project taskforce used an extremely structured approach to run the project. The team started the project with a needs assessment. Feedback was collected from the hiring managers, recent new hires, and leaders to understand the current on-boarding experience. Focus-group discussions were conducted during the needs-assessment phase to collect immediate feedback to improve the existing on-boarding program. Employee survey data, exit interviews, and direct feedback from employees were some of other sources to understand the needs. Themes were identified and became the basis for the recommendations and the action items in the project plan.

Some of the key findings during the diagnosis phase were: a lack of connection between new hires and their managers during initial days in the organization (because the workforce is virtual, this literally meant that people were beginning work without meeting their managers); a lack of support from managers; no face-to-face interaction on the first day; a lack of education for various stakeholders, such as manager education on how to engage new hires effectively; little understanding of organizational culture; and little ongoing infrastructure support, such as help in organizing one's laptop and access to various applications, during the first sixty days.

The program team chose more than twenty action items to be a part of the project plan to transform the on-boarding experience for new hires. The goal was to revamp the on-boarding program in order to facilitate the employee-manager connection for all new hires. Conscientious efforts were made to ensure that new hires understand the culture of the organization early in their careers with the teams. The key deliverable was to create a brand-new on-boarding program that would include components such as cultural-sensitivity training, a new-hire checklist (see Exhibit 51.1), a buddy program for new hires, fifteen- and sixty-day surveys to collect the feedback from the new hires, a one-stop portal of resources for new hires for the first sixty days, education modules for hiring managers and buddies to emphasize the importance of assimilation, and a checklist for the managers to provide the structured steps to assimilate new hires effectively.

An agenda for the first week was created. It spreads over four days. Day 1 starts with induction, conducted by HR Partners at thirteen on-boarding locations across United States. The induction module for Day 1 facilitates face-to-face connection with new hires to provide some hand-holding comfort during the first day. The module covers introductions, an overview of the organization, strategy, and questions related to new hires joining. The HR partners provide an overview of what the first week will look like. A detailed e-mail is sent to new hires on various resources and on tasks that must be completed during first week after joining the company. The next three sessions during the first week are virtual, via Microsoft Live Meeting, and provide details on various tools and resources for new hires, a session with the internal IT department on how to set up the IT infrastructure, and a session on cultural sensitivity.

The cultural-sensitivity session comprises aspects such as jargon and terms that are used within the company, underlying assumptions, and cultural differences expected in a diverse organization. The sessions also include discussions about varied management styles,

Exhibit 51.1. New Hire Checklist

Pre-Joining Activities

❏ Complete the list of nineteen formal job requirements at hire

❏ E-mail your passport-size photo and scanned signature to on-boarding team (ID Badge purposes)

❏ Print and sign a copy of your offer letter and supporting documents—Bring with you to joining location on Day 1

Day 1—Start Date

❏ Arrive at joining location at specified time

❏ Meet with the HR representative to complete the on-boarding. Be sure to bring original work authorization documents

❏ Contact your hiring manager for project details

❏ Receive Live Meeting calendar invite for new hire orientation

❏ Receive Live Meeting calendar invite for IT orientation

❏ Receive Live Meeting calendar invite for cultural-sensitivity training

❏ Receive e-mail with log-in details from U.S. on-boarding team

❏ Receive Business Code of Conduct and Personal Data Forms

Day 2

❏ Attend the cultural-sensitivity training via Microsoft Live Meeting

❏ Pick up/receive allocated assets

❏ Log into the network

Day 3

❏ Attend the IT session via Microsoft Live Meeting

❏ Enroll for medical benefits

Day 4

❏ Attend the new hire orientation via Microsoft Live Meeting

❏ Update bank and legal details for payroll processing (demonstrated in orientation)

Additional Activities After Day 4

❏ Order business cards (optional)

❏ Order additional assets (laptop, cell phone, and so on) if needed

❏ Submit W4 form

❏ Register for pay statements (after first payday)

specifically differences in managing teams and coaching team members. For examples, managers may not schedule one-on-ones on a weekly basis but that doesn't mean managers don't care about team members and are not invested in developing and coaching their teams.

We know from recent research that transitions represent one of the most powerful times when leaders are challenged in ways that can increase their capabilities. They also represent times when derailment is most likely to occur. Since the first on-boarding program was rolled out in the organization, the feedback has been positive. New hires have especially appreciated the content of the cultural-sensitivity module because it has helped them assimilate faster. The program has provided the new hires with an overview on what they could expect as they work with managers and employees during various client engagements. It has also helped the new hires in building relationships quickly and effectively.

Another important milestone in the transformed program was to create an education module for hiring managers and buddies. The manager's module on new hire engagement incorporates a problem statement that emphasizes why it is important to engage new hires early in the process, discusses the ROI of reducing the attrition, and takes managers through a checklist to provide an overview on important tasks of hiring managers (see Exhibit 51.2). The manager's checklist has provided a clear direction to hiring managers on the tasks they have to perform during first sixty days of new hires joining in order to assimilate them effectively.

Exhibit 51.2. On-Boarding Manager Checklist

Pre On-Boarding

❑ Contact the new hire at least two days before the joining to check whether he or she has any questions.

Day 1

❑ Welcome the new hire and spend an appropriate amount of time answering questions and giving a high-level overview on the unit/project structure.

❑ Organize workspace and provide the new hire with information on tools and equipment such as laptop, phone, business cards, and so on.

❑ Connect the new hire to his/her buddy from the team.

❑ Organize lunch with colleagues/direct reports.

Week 1

❑ Provide information to the new hire on Week 1 meetings with internal and external stakeholders.

❑ Schedule daily calls with the new hire for Week 1 to ease the transition process.

❑ Discuss organization/unit structure, goals, responsibilities of the job, key services, and contacts. Share the URL to unit-specific information.

❑ Provide information on technical trainings, certifications, and so on.

❑ Send out announcement, both internally and externally, stating what the new hire's role is and how the individual can be reached.

Week 2

❑ Have weekly meetings or twice a week meetings during which the hiring manager seeks the feedback and addresses the concerns or challenges.

❑ Help the new hire gain exposure and establish credibility by inviting the individual to the right meetings.

❑ Work with the new hire to set up his or her performance goals, if eligible.

The buddy education module was created for both buddies and hiring managers to provide them with an overview of the importance of the buddy program, to discuss the profile that is required to be an effective buddy, and to describe the role of a buddy and expectations about it. It also presents tips on how to build effective buddy relationships with the new hires. Buddy education facilitates awareness among both the managers and the buddies and provides a platform for them to ask questions related to challenges they face while working with new hires. In addition, the buddy program is a great resource for new hires to navigate within the company during early days.

In addition, a new hire portal was created that can work as a one-stop shop for all the new hires. It is organized in such a way that it can work as a repository for all the new hires for first sixty days. It includes information on various policies, presentations, FAQs, links to videos, and tools that can be used by the new hires. Once all these changes were implemented, it was important to craft surveys to gauge the satisfaction of new hires with the on-boarding program. Two surveys were built to capture the feedback on the new-hire experience during the first fifteen to sixty days of joining the company. These surveys were used to bring enhancements to the existing program. For example, people were asked to elaborate on how the buddy program assisted their integration into the organization.

As most of these sessions were virtual, there have been extra precautions taken to enhance the learning of the new hires. The first day is face-to-face to build the rapport and familiarize the new hires with the company. The rest of the sessions are conducted via a Microsoft Live Meeting because it is a simple and easy-to-use tool that can be run by multiple computer platforms—as compared to other technologies like videoconferencing or Second Life. Apart from the tool, there has been additional emphasis on making sessions more interactive, encouraging participants to ask questions, and conducting the session with a moderate pace. Additionally, these sessions are supplemented by other resources such as a user-friendly new-hire portal, checklists for managers (see Exhibit 51.2), and educational modules for managers and buddies.

After the implementation of the transformed program, it was noticed that early attrition went down and the quality of the feedback on the on-boarding process improved dramatically. The program positively impacts the assimilation of new hires. The biggest success has been a reduction in bench time and an enhancement in productivity, which led to better productivity revenue. The managers and the buddies have become more aware of effectively assimilating the new hires during their first sixty days in the company.

There has been tremendous learning while working on transforming the on-boarding experience for new hires. Finding an extremely resourceful sponsor early in the process and creating a cross-functional team helped the team to stay on track during the design phase and later during the implementation of the new program. One of the more important lessons learned was to appoint the right people to the taskforce with complementary skills and abilities. It was also important to organize the weekly cadence to track the progress over three months. In addition, conducting a needs analysis using various sources was the basis of findings and action items and assured that critical new hire needs were addressed. If data had not been collected prior to designing the program, the taskforce's efforts may have been futile. The most valuable sources of information in the process were the new hires that joined the organization within the last six months who provided candid feedback about how to improve the on-boarding experience.

Finally, another important learning was the value of benchmarking the practices of outside organizations that are in similar lines of business and have similar business realities. The benchmark data helped in comparing ideas that could be adopted in the current context. Overall, it was a fun program that brought incredible value to the business with a clear-cut dollar impact on the bottom line.

Leaders Coaching Leaders: Cascading Leadership Development Through the Organization

Robert J. Thomas, Claudy Jules, and Joshua Bellin
Accenture

52

Managers as Developers

W. EDWARDS DEMING once said that "learning is not compulsory . . . but neither is survival." The fact is, learning *is* compulsory for leaders. Leaders need to learn, adapt, and change, particularly if they want their organizations to follow suit. But leaders rarely learn alone, and the experiences that teach the deepest lessons rarely announce their arrival. Coaches—professionals who help leaders squeeze insight from experience by asking clarifying questions—are rarely available in sufficient numbers to meet the demand for learning in the moment.

In this article, we describe how two very different businesses—India's Tata Group and UK-based utility National Grid—train leaders as coaches as a core part of a process of experience-based leader development. These companies expect leaders to be teachers—to have, for example, a teachable point of view—but they also expect more (see also *Teachable Point of View: Learning to Lead by Teaching Others* on page 243 of this book). They expect leaders to be coaches who listen, clarify, encourage, and embolden other aspiring leaders so that when learning opportunities emerge they can be put to use immediately.

Underlying Concepts

Three concepts—crucibles, coaches, and community—are central to the approach to experience-based leader development deployed in Tata Group and National Grid.

Crucibles refers to the fact that people learn their most enduring lessons about leadership through experiences that test them in fundamental ways—what Bennis and Thomas (2001) called *crucible experiences*. Crucibles draw attention to the need for behavioral change. They also provide valuable insights into the conditions under which people will practice long enough to see improvements in their performance (Thomas, 2008).

Coaches refers to the fact that people rarely learn alone. Coaches help people learn from experience by asking productive questions, assisting them in clarifying their situations and their aspirations, and sometimes just by providing a breathing space to pause and reflect. Executive coaches are valuable, but managers are more likely to see crucibles and other learning opportunities as they occur. Their ability to ask the right questions at the right moment and their contextual knowledge—when combined with real coaching skill—can have a powerful impact on the growth of an aspiring leader each and every day.

Community refers to the fact that it takes a network of people with shared goals, training, and vocabulary to build staying power into a process of leader development. Leaders need a community because they need to learn continuously—otherwise, adaptive change for the organization is impossible. Likewise, coaches need a community because they need to learn technique from one another. Without a community of learners, it's impossible to accomplish sustained behavioral change.

From "Captains to Coaches" in the Tata Group

With more than one hundred operating companies in seven business sectors across eighty countries, the Tata Group is India's leading multinational corporation. It generated revenues of US$83.3 billion in 2010–2011, approximately 58 percent of which was outside India. More than 425,000 people worldwide work for the Tata Group, considered India's oldest and most respected brand name. The Tata Group has grown exponentially over the past decade, making forays into new geographies and businesses.

Tata Group was one of the original collaborators with the Center for Creative Leadership (CCL) in extending the lessons-of-experience framework to non-Western companies. The framework was later incorporated into the Tata career model and woven into the curriculum of the Tata Management Training Centre (TMTC). In recent years a strong need has been felt by senior leaders of the group to embed a culture of coaching across organizational levels that could enable creation of a robust leadership pipeline. The favored approach was to engage current leaders more in growing next-generation leaders.

The tough question was how to engage current leaders. Senior executives in the Tata Group, like their counterparts worldwide, had their hands full running their businesses. Yet group leadership, particularly executive director R. Gopalakrishnan, envisioned TMTC to be "an unbeatable think tank and knowledge base that keeps Tata Group leaders at the cutting edge of their profession." As such, TMTC was challenged to create and offer to C-level executives in the hundred-plus group companies an opportunity to acquire the skills and the mindset necessary to be active participants in the cultivation of next-generation leaders. The TMTC was further challenged to create an approach that was tailored to time-starved senior executives, involved measurable results, and would lead to the creation of a community of coaches who would support each other in learning through practice.

A program called Captain to Coach: A Practicum for Senior Tata Leaders was the response to that challenge. Beginning with a two-and-a-half-day workshop, C2C (as it has come to be known) features hands-on learning through practice and intense role-play sessions. Participants are videotaped in action as they enact role plays based on day-to-day business situations. These sessions are followed by group and individual debriefings and creation of individual development plans. The intent of the role plays and exercises is to give experienced senior executives both competence and confidence so that they can incorporate coaching methods and tools into situations as routine as business and operations reviews, one-on-one conversations (for example, performance reviews), town-hall gatherings, and skip-level meetings.

The C2C workshop (detailed in Figure 52.1) encourages senior leaders to reflect on the crucible events that most powerfully shaped their self-concepts as leaders and how they

Figure 52.1. The C2C Workshop Framework

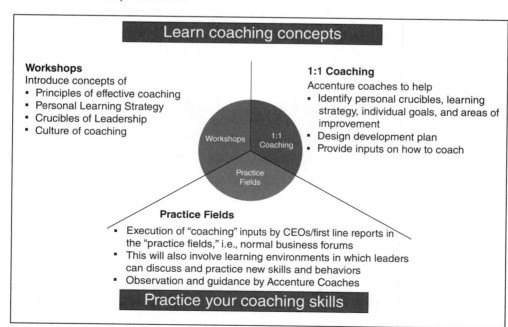

behaved. In particular, participants are encouraged to identify the role that coaches—formal or informal—have played in their development and to actively describe the environments those men and women created that enabled learning to occur. They are then introduced to basic coaching principles—with care given to distinguish coaching from mentoring, so that the coaching skills of active listening, clarification, and joint sense-making are added to the mentoring skills of direction, storytelling, and articulating a teachable point of view. The importance of practice is emphasized continuously so that executives feel that it's acceptable to not be an expert right away and so that they can become accustomed to seeking out feedback and advice from peers who are also coaches.

The notion of a community of coaches—parallel to that of a community of leaders (and learners)—is repeated throughout the workshop and beyond. During the workshop, participants are asked to identify the myriad people they influence and who influence them in the process of getting their work done. They explore how organizational culture is created and reproduced over time and how important culture is to sustaining the status quo. And, finally, they are asked to develop a plan of action for creating a "culture of coaching" in the Tata Group. One outcome of this last effort has been the creation of a C2C program for mid-level managers with five to twelve years of experience.

More than one hundred executives, along with the TMTC faculty, have been trained in coaching skills. Evidence of the effectiveness of the program has included detailed written and verbal feedback from the participants and nominations for an additional two hundred participants from six of the largest group companies. Three categories of insights were reported by participants immediately following the program (average score of 3.7 out of a possible 4.0 in evaluative rating) and in later assessments: (1) greater comfort and facility in using "everyday occasions" for having coaching conversations; (2) more productive annual and semi-annual performance reviews; and (3) a better experience talking with one's superiors and peers in search of coaching advice. Each participant has incorporated development and practice as a coach into his or her individual development plan.

Institutionalizing Coaching at National Grid

National Grid, one of the largest investor-owned global energy companies and second largest utility in the United States, initiated a journey in 2008 to dramatically improve performance safety, customer service, reliability, and efficiency. Its UK parent had acquired its way into the U.S. in the mid-2000s, and its new Electricity Distribution Operations (EDO) business was struggling with an array of divergent operating models, technologies, performance metrics, organizational cultures, and union agreements. For years, it had been paying penalties to regulators because of service outages and its dismal record of recovery from those outages.

Top management was convinced that a sustainable organizational transformation could not be accomplished without significant behavioral change on the part of its extended leadership team (ELT), a cadre of approximately eighty utility veterans who had been with National Grid and its forebears for twenty years. They knew that whatever approach they took would confront skepticism, suspicion, and territorial behavior. Dr. Eden Alvarez-Backus—vice president of global leadership, learning, and development—made it clear at the kickoff: "The experiences that these eighty-plus people have will set the tone for how everyone thinks and feels about learning and development."

EDO management wanted an approach to leader development that would match in ambition the overall effort to transform the company. In other words, this was to be no ordinary classroom-based leadership "training" program. The approach would be steeped in both reflection and action. Indeed, the first wave of transformation would be aimed at helping incumbent leaders become coaches who would, in turn, help executives and managers change the rest of the company *and* change themselves in the process.

The process for the ELT began with a self-awareness phase consisting of individual assessments. Reviews included 360-degree assessments complemented by personality and leadership profiles (PLPs) and inventories of learning styles. Each ELT manager then went through personal coaching with an Accenture consultant, complete with an in-depth debrief on the results of his or her individual assessments. This phase quickly confirmed that the ELT participants were eager to know more about what it took to be a high-performance leader *and* how to be an effective coach to peers and direct reports (see Exhibit 52.1). It reaffirmed the role of coaches as part of the learning process.

Exhibit 52.1. How Ready Are You to Coach?

This checklist will help you assess whether you have the skills that are essential to become more effective as a coach.

- ❑ The people I coach don't hesitate to share their problems with me.
- ❑ It is easy for me to be positive, encouraging, and optimistic in coaching others.
- ❑ I am quite comfortable asking people about what's personally important to them.
- ❑ I am quite patient and am not easily frustrated when those I coach have difficulty formulating their goals or plans.
- ❑ It is easy for me to understand and relate to the feelings of the person I am coaching.
- ❑ I am sure that the person I am coaching can see how important it is to make and keep one's commitments.
- ❑ I always take time to ensure that the people I coach are clear about what they are trying to accomplish.
- ❑ It is easy for me to set aside my own judgments about my coachee's aspirations.
- ❑ I work to ensure that the people I coach have a clear sense of what they need to do next.
- ❑ I find it easy to clear my mind and focus on the person I am with in a coaching conversation.

Later coaching sessions gave participants an opportunity to reflect on how they could bolster their leadership skills and what was needed to do so. Here, Accenture coaches spent more time with the ELT leader-coaches in mining their personal crucibles—and guiding them in how to have similar conversations with their direct reports. The success of this effort depended on having built a space for genuine dialogue, psychological safety, and trust. These allowed for the possibility of shifts in both mindsets and behaviors based on conscious choice. As ELT leader-coaches envisioned new images of themselves, they also became more aware of the things that were in the way of their effectiveness. This prompted many to think through what was needed from their bosses, peers, or subordinates to help them measure up against new leadership demands.

This new cadre of leaders as coaches subsequently played an integral role in EDO's organizational change process. For example, in communication sessions with direct reports and then with employees, each leader-coach was able to promote his or her "use of self" as a tool for heightening awareness of the meaning and consequences of the organization's transformation.

Group meetings and then one-on-one meetings provided practice fields (see Exhibit 52.2 on how leader-coaches can reflect in action) in which leader-coaches could build an even greater range of potential for new, responsible choices of behavior. Doing this required a present-centered orientation and frequently caused the EDO leader-coaches to actively contemplate who they were, what mattered most to them, and what (and how) they could learn from success and failure experiences in here-and-now relationships.

There is ample evidence that the leadership lessons have stuck with the ELT. For example, the number of "lost time" injuries (on-the-job injuries that mean employees must take time off) was halved. Reliability metrics improved significantly. The program also led to a myriad of qualitative adaptations—for example, in the language the ELT used and the

---

Exhibit 52.2. How Leader-Coaches Can Reflect in Action

Ask yourself: "Do I have the insights to be an effective coach?" Reflective questions such as this or "What do I want?" are simple enough, but they push leaders to think about solutions to their own situations. Good coaches are great reflectors. They engage in reflective exercises—that is, they routinely conduct unbiased assessments of themselves so that they can mine their immediate experiences to gain deeper insights. Doing this, however, quite often requires practice. For insight into what types of questions leaders can ask themselves—in the moment—as they practice reflecting-in-action during one-on-one discussions or staff meetings, we offer the following:

- How do I know that there is a problem or opportunity here?
- To what extent does my coachee(s) see this as a problem or opportunity?
- Who benefits from the continuing existence of the problem or opportunity?
- If my coachee(s) could fast-forward one year, what would have taken place?
- If my coachee(s) does not do anything specific about the situation what are the consequences?

development mechanisms they described when interacting with each other. It was not uncommon to hear a manager talk about meeting with his or her coach or to learn about another manager who was assembling his or her "personal learning strategy."

Conclusion

Companies like Tata Group and National Grid demonstrate the value added by coaches to experience-based leader development. Far from being an add-on, coaching can transform the way leaders think about their roles on a daily basis. When equipped with the right skills and the confidence to exercise them, leaders can be coaches in a way that accelerates the growth of more leaders—a vital prerequisite for survival in an era of turbulence and change.

These case studies, although brief, suggest at least five takeaways for professionals in the field of leader development. First, the lessons of experience are likelier to take hold when there is top management commitment to owning the process of leadership development and in the engagement of others as coaches. The sponsorship of a Tata Group executive director and a National Grid group chief executive gave license to their direct reports to take a chance in being coached and, in turn, coaching other managers. It also underscored the importance of coaching as part of the suite of essential leadership attributes.

Second, being able to work with a coach made it possible for leaders to devise a personal learning strategy that helped them challenge their most fundamental assumptions about themselves and the world around them and to mine the most memorable lessons about their leadership as they unfold.

Third, by practicing new skills, talented leaders are far more likely to learn and thus to adapt and survive. With the help of a coach to hold personal mirrors up, leaders are able to discuss successes and failures confidentially and one on one. With the help of peer coaches and then a community of trained coaches, individual executives can exercise their skills with confidence.

Fourth, our research and experience with different clients convince us that leadership will increasingly be a contact sport, requiring leaders to know how to coach and advise each other in real time.

Finally, openness to learning has to precede arrival in a leadership development program or coaching relationship for enduring behavioral changes and long-term effectiveness of individuals in complex organizations.

References

Bennis, W.G., & Thomas, R.J. (2001). *Geeks and geezers: How era, value, and defining moments shape leaders*. Boston, MA: Harvard Business School Press.

Thomas, R.J. (2008). *Crucibles of leadership: How to learn from experience to be a great leader*. Boston, MA: Harvard Business School Press.

53

An Exercise for Managers: Developing Talent Through Assignments

Cynthia McCauley
Center for Creative Leadership

MANY MANAGERS ARE aware of the power of a stretch assignment for developing their direct reports. However, most struggle with how to evaluate which assignments are a good match for which direct reports. I have found that a little education about developmental assignments, plus a chance to discuss a case that highlights the issues that such assignments raise in organizations, can equip these managers with the basic ideas to more proactively use assignments as a strategy for developing their direct reports.

In workshops to educate managers about using assignments to develop their direct reports, I typically start by asking the managers to reflect on their own key developmental experiences and to share those with one another. I then provide a framework that describes the types of job challenges that stimulate on-the-job leadership development and the leadership skills and perspectives that individuals report learning from these types of challenges (see Table 53.1). Before they move on to applying the framework to their own context, I ask them to read and reflect on the brief case shown in Exhibit 53.1.

The case describes a middle manager (Christine) primarily in terms of her strengths and weaknesses as her boss sees them. It then presents three different developmental assignments the boss is considering for Christine and asks the participant which one he or she would choose and why. The participant typically focuses on matching the assignments to the developmental needs of the middle manager. This is indeed a central concern in choosing

Table 53.1. Skills and Perspectives Developed from Various Job Challenges

Job Challenges	Skills and Perspectives
Unfamiliar Responsibilities: Handling responsibilities that are new or very different from previous ones you've handled	Learning agility Self-awareness Business knowledge and skills
New Directions: Starting something new or making strategic changes.	Taking risks and innovating Dealing with ambiguity Strategic thinking
Inherited Problems: Fixing problems created by someone else or existing before you took the assignment	Problem solving/decision making Perseverance Managing change
Problems with Employees: Dealing with employees who lack adequate experience, are not highly competent, or are resistant to change	Confronting people problems Dealing with conflict Balancing toughness and empathy
High Stakes: Managing work with tight deadlines, pressure from above, high visibility, and responsibility for critical decisions	Decisiveness Managing up Handling stress
Scope and Scale: Managing work that is broad in scope (involving multiple functions, groups, locations, products, or services) or large in sheer size (for example, workload, number of responsibilities)	Coordinating and integrating work Delegation Creating work systems
External Pressure: Managing the interface with important groups outside the organization (for example, customers, vendors, partners, regulatory agencies)	Influence and negotiation Building consensus Building external relationships
Influencing Without Authority: Influencing peers, higher management, or other key people over whom you have no authority	Collaborating with others Navigating the organization Systems perspective
Work Across Cultures: Working with people from different cultures or with institutions in other countries	Cultural awareness and sensitivity Adaptability Managing across distances
Work-group Diversity: Being responsible for the work of people of both genders and different racial and ethnic backgrounds	Valuing diversity and difference Managing teams Ethics and integrity

an assignment for development, and it is useful for the workshop participants to start practicing how to think about the ways in which different kinds of assignments can provide different kinds of learning opportunities. However, because each of the three options can provide a reasonable learning opportunity for Christine, the participant has to bring other factors to bear to decide which one of the assignments is best. In doing so, some of the complexities of giving stretch assignments to direct reports are surfaced and can be discussed among the participants.

Exhibit 53.1. Which Assignment for Christine?

Christine is a thirty-eight-year-old, middle-level manager in the marketing department of a large manufacturing company. She has primary responsibility for several products and must coordinate these efforts with marketing managers responsible for other products in the same product line. She has four direct reports and manages a total staff of sixteen. The great deal of coordination she does has taught her how to build and maintain positive relationships with her peers. She is viewed less positively by her subordinates. She is not viewed as a particularly strong leader or as good at identifying and developing talent beneath her. She is, however, extremely bright—quickly learning new technical and business information as she moves into new positions. She also has a strong drive to succeed. Her boss has noticed that she is great at solving fairly structured problems but founders when given more unstructured, ambiguous problems. He is also concerned that she always tackles problems with a marketing orientation, not always taking other perspectives into account.

Her boss knows of three developmental opportunities he might advocate for Christine:

1. Working on a cross-functional team headed by the director of human resources. The team is responsible for revamping the organization's compensation system.

2. Working on a special project with the vice president of public relations. The VP wants the company to in some way have more connections with K–12 education in the communities where it has offices. He is looking for a talented staff member who could study this issue and make recommendations.

3. Heading up a new marketing research group. This position would be responsible for staffing and setting direction for this new group.

Which assignment would you advocate for Christine and why?

Steps in Using the Case
Step 1: Pick the Best Assignment

Ask participants to read the case individually and pick an assignment for Christine. As an added activity, you can break the participants into small groups to discuss the alternatives and arrive at a group decision. The advantage of this approach is that more people typically become involved in the discussion. There's also the between-group competitiveness that often stimulates more energy around the case. The disadvantage is that you might have less variability in which of the three assignments is chosen. When using the individual approach, I always have some people who chose each of the three alternatives. This is helpful in debriefing because the thought process that went into choosing each assignment can be shared. When using the group approach, I haven't always heard all three alternatives represented. However, if this happens you can always ask, "Did any group consider this alternative?" That will make it possible for you to hear some of the thinking behind choosing or not choosing that alternative.

Step 2: Share Assignment and Reason Chosen

Ask for a show of hands on how many picked each assignment. Then go through each assignment, asking those who chose it why they thought it was the best match. In addition to listening for which developmental need they thought the assignment addressed (for example, the cross-functional team would expose Christine to other functional perspectives, the special project would give her the opportunity to work on a fairly unstructured problem, and heading up the new group would require her to lead and develop her staff), listen for mention of three other factors:

- The first is the *risk involved* in putting Christine in each of the assignments. A stretch assignment always contains the risk of poor performance or even failure. The three assignment options are ordered in terms of risk—with risk being assessed primarily in terms of how much the overall success of the endeavor (that is, the taskforce, the special project, and the new group) would depend on the performance of Christine. Ask the participants what they think about this risk, how they have managed this learning-performance tension in their own situations, and how a boss might work to mitigate the risk.

- The second factor is the *strengths* that Christine brings to the assignment. Individuals will likely be more effective in a stretch assignment if they have strengths to readily apply to the assignment. In fact, this mitigates some of the risk. Ask the participants what strengths Christine brings to each of the assignments.

- The third factor is the potential *developmental role other people* in the assignment might play (for example, the director of human resources, the vice president of public relations). The case doesn't provide any information on whether these individuals could or would play an active role in Christine's learning and development. However, it is not unusual for participants to note that they thought about this—for example, might the vice president of public relations be a great role model for developing others? Again, this is another factor that can mitigate risk.

Step 3: Discuss Additional Information Needed

Ask the participants what additional information they wish they had as they were deciding among the assignments. If the developmental role of others hasn't come up yet. It likely will as a response to this question. For example, a participant could say that he wondered whether Christine would continue to report to her current boss if she moved to heading up the new marketing research group because the boss already knows how the assignment will be a stretch for her and what to pay attention to in coaching her. Another factor that might be voiced: "I would want to know which of these assignments is most motivating for Christine." If this doesn't come up, as a facilitator, you can bring it up. This is another key issue to ask the participants about: How do they balance the tension between what is most motivating to the individual and what is most needed by the organization?

Step 4: Review Key Questions

Wrap up by noting the key questions to ask yourself when assessing whether a particular assignment is a "good stretch" for developing a direct report. These questions include the following:

- Would the assignment provide opportunities to develop competencies that he or she needs to continue improving as a leader?

- How much of a risk would the organization be taking by putting him or her in this assignment?

- Would the assignment take advantage of some of his or her strengths as a leader?

- Are there some relationships built into the assignment that would enhance learning?

- What would be most motivating to your direct report?

A Final Note

When working with managers who are all from the same organization or the same type of organization (for example, police departments, higher education), I have customized the case so that it better reflects the realities of those managers' work setting. This requires partnering with someone who knows the setting well and can help you translate the elements of the case into that setting.

54

Performance and Development Through Conversation

Jonathan Winter
The Career Innovation Group

NOT EVERY ASPECT of business is visible or appears in the annual report. Conversation is one example. Conversation is the place where work is done. It is the place where objectives are set, feedback is given, problems are resolved, praise is received, support is offered, and people learn and develop. Through conversation, a company's brand comes to life. Yet, despite its vital role in organizational performance, the quality of conversation is hard to see, unmeasured, and largely unmanaged.

Several global employers, including Deloitte, GlaxoSmithKline, Marriott, and others embarked with us to consider the critical role that conversations play in the workplace. This involved mapping the work-related conversations that employees have with their managers, mentors, peers, HR managers, customers, and friends and family outside work.

The research revealed a surprising picture. Although many positive conversations were taking place, there were some very big "conversation gaps" (Winter & Jackson, 2004). On average, four in every ten people said they have a topic they would like to raise with their managers but were not doing so (Career Innovation, 2004). When the results were analyzed, over half of the missing conversations were about careers and development. Lack of time and lack of trust were given as the key reasons that the conversations were not taking place. Furthermore, these employees were dramatically less engaged in their work and three times more likely to say they intended to leave the organization.

This is a problem for organizations that want sustainable performance. Managers and teams may set brilliantly clear objectives for the coming weeks or months, but, the absence of future-focused conversations about people's development and their long-term career plans threaten long-term organizational performance. The lack of career and development conversations was a key barrier to the long-term adaptable and resilient of an organization's workforce. What is needed is a recipe not only for current performance, but for *performance improvement.*

It is tempting to try to address this by introducing a new or better process for development and career conversations. That may help, but it is only a partial solution. However, as other studies have also discovered (e.g., Kidd, Hirsh, & Jackson, 2004), we found that most development conversations were taking place outside formal settings. The challenge therefore is to embed the right mix of behaviors and practices so that future-focused conversations take place in many different ways.

We set out to help organizations find some practical ways to tackle this challenge. They ranged from online conversation feedback to in-depth coaching. Here are two of the simplest and most powerful solutions that organizations have valued.

Practical Solution 1: Talk About the Conversation Gap

One organization conducted a conversation gap survey internally, to identify the conversation challenges they faced (see Exhibit 54.1 for some of the topics). They shared the data through a cascade briefing process to highlight the importance of future-focused development conversations in improving retention, engagement, and performance. Another division set up half-day Hot Topic sessions for senior leaders to reinforce the strategic importance of improving the quality of conversations. A repeat survey two years later found that the number of people reporting a "conversation gap" with their managers had dropped from 46 to 27 percent. In both divisions, the communication initiative was combined with practical help for managers, such as workshops on coaching skills and senior leader accountability for improving development conversations. Arguably the most powerful intervention was simply to highlight the research data. As a result people everywhere started asking: What's your Conversation Gap?

Practical Solution 2: Provide a Simple Structure for a Conversation

Inexperienced managers may shy away from career and development conversations because they do not know how to go about structuring such a conversation. There are many models for development conversations, but what is most important is to provide managers with a simple model that gives them confidence and helps them do development conversations well.

Exhibit 54.1. What's Your Conversation Gap

Use this table to assess which honest conversations you have had with your most valued team members recently, If there are gaps, consider when and how to fill them. The topics listed here are those that people most often feel unable to raise.

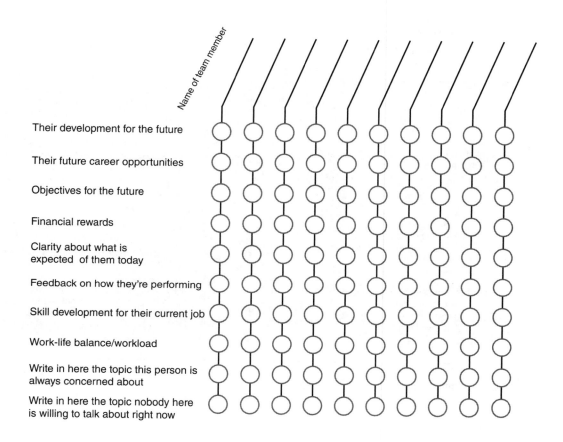

Name of team member

- Their development for the future
- Their future career opportunities
- Objectives for the future
- Financial rewards
- Clarity about what is expected of them today
- Feedback on how they're performing
- Skill development for their current job
- Work-life balance/workload
- Write in here the topic this person is always concerned about
- Write in here the topic nobody here is willing to talk about right now

RATE THE QUALITY OF YOUR CONVERSATIONS

Use the scoring scheme below to rate your development conversation performance and to highlight critical gaps and unsatisfactory outcomes requiring urgent attention:

⑤ Full and frank dialogue, all issues discussed to mutual satisfaction

④ Full and frank dialogue, some issues discussed to mutual satisfaction, but some subjects not brought to conclusion

③ Partial dialogue, some issues discussed but no subjects brought to mutually satisfactory conclusion

② Conversation is one-sided, some key issues tabled but little progress

① Conversation very unsatisfactory, no resolution or meaningful progress

⓪ No conversation

Figure 54.1. Linking Career Conversations to the GROW Model

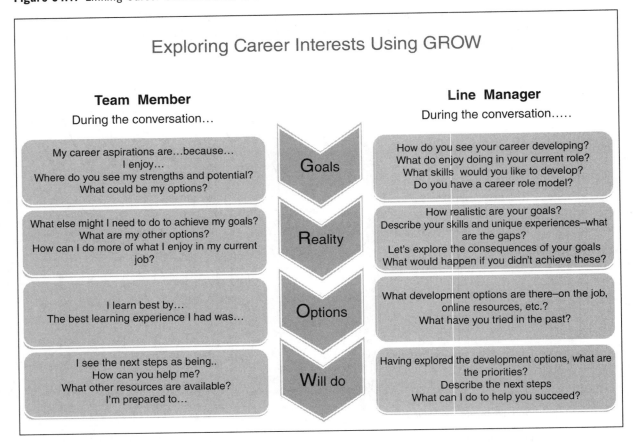

In one organization, a framework for career and development conversations was based on the GROW coaching model, which was already used in the organization for performance conversations (see Figure 54.1).

In another organization, we created a briefing for HR Business Partners that was cascaded in the organization by managers and teams. The short PowerPoint presentation contained an explanation of why career and development conversations are important, what resources are available, and how these conversations fit into the performance cycle. The briefing included a simple conversation structure that managers and employees could use as catalysts for the conversations (see Table 54.1).

The conversation models have also been turned into an online tool. The tool takes managers through the preparation process using a simple model of Explore-Focus-Act. Table 54.2 shows example questions using the Explore-Focus-Act framework.

Table 54.1. Conversation Model as Part of a Cascaded Manager Briefing

Preparation	Employee and Manager should: • Be clear about roles and responsibilities • Be fully focused on the conversation • Be open and honest • Listen as well as talk • Use questions to understand each other • Take a structured approach leading to a development plan
Step 1: Career Aspirations	• What is your experience so far—your "career story"? • What are the high points of your career? • What motivates you? • What is your ideal role? • What career goals do you have?
Step 2: The Current Situation	• What are your strengths, successes and potential? • What roles could you do in the future? • What development needs do you have? What are your "skill gaps"? • What obstacles might you face?
Step 3: Development Options	• What development activities could you do (for example, projects, assignments)? • What actions will you take to develop yourself?
Step 4: Development Planning	• What support do you need? From whom? • What resources are available to help you? • What is your timeline for taking action? • How will you update your development plan?

Table 54.2. Career Conversation Planner

Explore	Focus	Act
Career Journey Career Interests and Values Strengths	Career aspirations Development Opportunities	Goals and Objectives Next Steps Support Networking

Sample Questions

Tell me about your career and how you got to where you are today. What are the things that motivate you at work? How do you think others see you? What are you really known for?	What do you see as your potential career options? What skills/knowledge will be in greatest demand in the future? How could you find out? How could you create opportunities for yourself?	What objectives are you going to set yourself? How will you access the resources and people you need to help you? How can you take a proactive approach to building your professional network?

In all of these approaches, trust is key (Scholefield, 2004). When we asked people who they trust and why, many talked about the long track record of these relationships. Trust is built when a manager is genuinely committed to the employee's success, and compliments and criticism are more effective within a trusting relationship (Tamkin, Pearson, Hirsh, & Constable, 2010). The idea of a relationship "bank account" can be helpful, with positive deposits and negative withdrawals influencing levels of trust.

Bringing It All Together

We use the term "engaging conversations" because when space is created for conversation and when questions are used to uncover people's hopes for the future, the effect can be dramatic. This is the difference between a top-down cascade of business objectives and genuine dialogue toward partnership.

In smaller organizations, senior leaders play a critical role. It is vital that CEOs and other directors show that investing the time is a valued activity, that even in short conversations "being fully there" makes a vital difference, and that the investment of time leads to benefits such as improvement of morale, ease of delegation, and staff retention. In large, complex organizations, the challenge is greater. Large-scale change will require a many-stranded approach and significant time (three to five years) to build a high-trust culture in which honest conversations can take place. Amid busy jobs, finding time to invest in these kinds of conversation with colleagues will always be difficult. The best advice from our experience is to keep it simple. In most organizations we need fewer formal processes and more optional, light touch "semi-formal" activities that simply encourages people to make time and space to sit down, switch off the computer, and talk about what really matters to them. See Exhibit 54.2 for essential tips that managers can use to promote engaging conversations in their team.

Exhibit 54.2. Hints and Tips for Engaging Conversations

- Make time for conversations outside formal processes.

- Take time to ask your employee what he or she is learning currently.

- Schedule time during every team meeting to share "lessons learned."

- Prepare yourself. Make sure you give the other person your undivided attention during the conversation.

- Be aware of the kind of conversation you are having. Is it coaching, career development, or about performance on the job?

- Share with your team what you know about the skills and jobs that will be valued in the future.

- Take time to waste time. Set aside time during the week to informally wander the hallways and connect with people on your team.

- Seek feedback from employees about your conversations with them.

References

Career Innovation. (2011). *Career resilience: Building a change-ready organization.* Oxford, UK: Career Innovation.

Kidd, J.M., Hirsh, W., & Jackson, C. (2004). Straight talking: The nature of effective career discussions at work. *Journal of Career Development, 30,* 231–245.

Scholefield, M. (2004). *A guide to trust.* Oxford, UK: Career Innovation with The Relationships Foundation.

Tamkin, P., Pearson, G., Hirsh, W., & Constable, S. (2010). *Exceeding expectation: The principles of outstanding leadership.* London, UK: The Work Foundation.

Winter, J., & Jackson, C. (2004). *The conversation gap.* Oxford, UK: Career Innovation. See www.theCgap.com

55

Performance Management and Leadership Development: Paradox or Potential?

Robert McKenna and Robleh Kirce
Seattle Pacific University

WHEN YOU THINK about the last road trip you took, which did you enjoy most, arriving at your destination or the voyage you undertook to get there? For many people, it is difficult to choose one over the other. They love the actual arrival and the sense of achievement that comes from getting there, but they also love the drive, stopping along the way to take in some new sights, reflecting on where they've been, and meeting people in the towns and convenience stores. Others just want to get there. Show them the way to get there and let them get there as fast and efficiently as possible. No rest stops or ports of call, just a singular focus on the destination. Regardless of your preference, it is clear that the journey has an impact on your experience of the destination and vice versa.

The tension between performing well in a job and being intentional about learning from experiences is similar to the tension between enjoying the destination and enjoying the ride. Both certainly matter, but figuring out how to hold a person accountable for getting there while also helping him or her learn along the way is a realistic dilemma for many practitioners. The purpose of this contribution is to highlight the tension between employee development and performance management and to provide strategies that HR professionals can use to address this inherent tension.

The Natural Tension

Performance management processes focus on the destination or desired outcomes. They measure and communicate how well an employee is achieving outcomes or exhibiting the behaviors necessary to effectively perform in the job. Performance management processes include everything from performance tracking systems to goal-setting processes. These tools are also used by managers to have conversations with employees about their performance and progress. Although learning and development are obviously relevant and impossible to divorce from performance, performance management focuses primarily on the achievement of organizationally specified outcomes.

Employee development processes, however, are designed to intentionally facilitate individuals' learning and growth, for their sake and for the sake of the organization. This may include the documentation of strengths and areas for development, stretch assignments, strategic networking, and even one's sense of career purpose and direction. Employee development can also include areas outside of work that less directly impact job performance (for example, external networks, community activity, family, volunteer activities). And these processes inform conversations between employees and their managers about employees' learning and development.

Although employee development and performance management processes share certain elements, attending to both introduces a natural tension (see Figure 55.1). Managers and employees contribute to this tension when each asks the question, "What's in it for me?" Systemic dilemmas are created when managers decide that employee development should be carried out only for the sake of meeting the strategic needs of the organization and has little or nothing to do with employees' career goals and aspirations. When managers replace

Figure 55.1. Performance Management and Employee Development

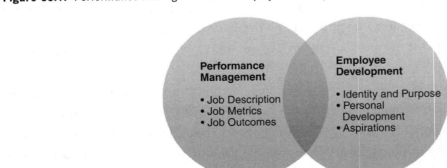

genuine concern about employees' personal identity and experiences with job descriptions, metrics, and organizational outcomes, they leave out half of the equation.

Individual employees think constantly about who they are (identity), why they are in their jobs (purpose), where they are going (direction), and how they are doing (accountability). Although performance management and employee development are focused on different things, they are inseparable. An individual's development contributes continually to job performance and the individual's ability to overcome challenges.

The Impact of Tension on Processes

A natural tension plays out in organizations every day as they seek to create increasingly efficient processes to manage performance and develop employees, for example:

- Should senior leaders be placed into jobs where they can perform optimally or jobs where they are developed?

- Should employee development conversations be separate from employee performance conversations?

- Who should own an employee's development—the employee or the manager? What if they disagree?

- Should managers be given access to employees' development plans without their permission?

- Should 360 survey data be used to assess performance, determine pay increases, or as input into development plans?

Although organizations often see the benefit in providing some development for their employees, they also want to see direct benefits to the organization associated with their development endeavors. Take the last question above as an example. Given the time and resources necessary to complete 360 evaluations for employees, why not get the most out of the investment and use the data for both development and performance evaluation? Unfortunately, when respondents know the data collected will be used for administrative purposes (for example, pay increases or personnel decisions), scores typically become inflated, lenient, and generally less accurate (Jawahar & William, 1997). This inaccuracy creates a problem because employees won't improve unless they believe their feedback indicates that change is necessary (Smither, London, & Reilly, 2005), not something they are likely to perceive from inflated and lenient scores.

Managing Polarities

The performance-learning dilemma is often framed in either/or thinking. Organizations become caught in the polarity, creating a swing over time from one extreme to other. An organization might use its 360 process for development alone until managers are angry that "nobody is being held accountable." The system is then used to assess performance for a couple of years until managers become angry that "employees aren't being honest" and make the decision to use it only for development. This begs the question: When organizations face polarities like this, are they doomed to vacillate between the two extremes? Fortunately, the answer is no. There are three common strategies to deal with polarities, but it requires HR professionals to play a proactive, strategic role rather than simply waiting to take orders from the top.

To manage polarities, practitioners can: (1) look for a higher-level purpose that suggests which side of the polarity is most critical; (2) choose one side and find ways to mitigate the weaknesses on the other side; or (3) look for questions that transcend the polarity. The 360 feedback process can be used to illustrate each of the three strategies.

Strategy 1: Look for a meta-purpose. In the case of the 360 process the meta-question might be: Which use of the 360 process will best support the overall business strategy? An even bigger question might be: What is the purpose of business and what is the role of employees?

Strategy 2: Choose one alternative and mitigate for the other one. When determining how to best roll out a 360 process, managers benefit from intentionally considering the advantages and disadvantages of each alternative and how they can maintain the integrity of a tool while integrating it into both development and performance processes (see Table 55.1). Knowing what research suggests about 360 data, one might decide to use the data for development. Does this mean that the survey results cannot have an impact on performance management? Not necessarily; the 360 data might be used for development, but the activi-

Table 55.1.   Should 360 Feedback Be Used for Performance or Development?

Performance	Development
Advantages	
Increases accountability Provides metrics for how a job is being performed	Increases accuracy Provides holistic understanding of how one is perceived
Disadvantages	
Biased ratings Lack of candor	Lack of incentive to improve Seen as unrelated to job outcomes
Mitigation	
Use data for development in Year 1 and performance in Year 2 Allow employee to select raters Be up-front about confidentiality decisions	Clearly identify relevance to performance Use 360 results for development Be up-front about confidentiality decisions

ties that come out of the data are added to the manager's performance plan. This highlights the fact that a single tool can be leveraged to benefit employee development and performance management by focusing on the intersection of the two.

Strategy 3: Transcend the problem. The real issue might not be about the 360 process at all but considering it in the context of all of the other talent management systems in the organization. For example, perhaps employee survey results are already being used to drive development. Perhaps the quality of manager-employee conversations is more important than the 360 feedback process. Maybe the wrong people are being selected into management. If any of these factors are true, any investment in the 360 feedback process is a wasted effort when considered within this larger context.

The same tensions can be seen during succession planning conversations (see Table 55.2). Here, decision-makers debate whether to give an executive a developmental stretch assignment or an assignment where he or she can perform at high levels because his or her ability to be successful has already been proven.

Development and Performance: Creating a Both/And Culture

Regardless of whether you are a consultant, a manager, or an HR executive, you have to make decisions about performance management that will impact the way you do employee

Table 55.2. Should Succession Management Focus on Performance or Development?

Performance	Development
Advantages	
Organization immediately benefits Supports short-term business strategy Team members benefit from previous experience	More leadership capacity in the long term Communicates that organization values development Demonstrates that the organization values the employee
Disadvantages	
Prioritizes immediate business needs over employee's needs Less leadership capacity in the organization Talent could leave in frustration	Success is likely to be more resource intensive Higher risk to business outcomes Talent could leave because they are now more employable with the new development
Mitigation	
Co-create a performance+development plan Create a developmental component in the assignment Communicate the reasons the individual is being placed in the position	Provide a mentor Support individual's development edge with a network of competent people Communicate the reasons the individual is being placed in the position

development (and vice versa). Often in these situations there is no right decision. Instead, there is only the best decision possible, and the consequences you choose to accept as a result of that decision. That best decision is defined as the one that meets the strategic needs of the organization *and* promotes an environment in which employees can realize their potential. This is easier said than done.

There are no rules that guarantee the best decisions. Use the questions in Exhibit 55.1 as you are creating and implementing employee policies and plans. An honest assessment of the inherent tensions between performance management and employee development is a great place to start in your efforts to better understand and manage these tensions.

Exhibit 55.1. Performance and Development: Creating a Both/And Culture

Directions: Answer the following ten questions to rate the effectiveness of the current employee development and performance management processes in your organization.

☐ Yes ☐ No Do your employees and you have the same definition of performance management and employee development within your organization?

☐ Yes ☐ No Are the intentions behind performance management and employee development tools communicated to everyone?

☐ Yes ☐ No Have you researched how other companies are managing the tension your organization is facing?

☐ Yes ☐ No Do your best and worst performers' performance management and employee development conversations take the same amount of time to plan and to complete?

☐ Yes ☐ No Are there any processes in place that are explicitly focused on the identity, experiences, networks, and personal motivators of employees?

☐ Yes ☐ No Have you considered what the resistance will look like and how you will respond to it?

☐ Yes ☐ No Have you identified the other employee development and performance management processes going on and how this new process integrates?

☐ Yes ☐ No Do your performance management and employee development systems motivate people to perform well *and* learn on the job?

☐ Yes ☐ No Do you find your employee development programs personally useful in thinking about the experiences you have had, the lessons you are learning, the purpose in your work, and your networks of support?

☐ Yes ☐ No Does your performance management process clearly identify the goals that employees are accountable for achieving in their jobs, and the extent to which they are making progress toward those goals?

Scoring: If you answered, "yes" to at least seven of these questions, it is likely that your performance management and employee development programs are well designed and clearly articulated. If you answered "yes" to four to six of these questions, there are things your organization is doing well, but could be improved. A score of one to three would suggest the need for changes. Use these questions to identify areas where your program management and employee development programs and processes could be improved.

References

Jawahar, I.M., & William, C.R. (1997). Where all the children are above average: The performance appraisal purpose effect. *Personnel Psychology, 50,* 905–925.

Smither J.W., London, M., & Reilly, R.R. (2005). Does performance improve following multisource feedback? A theoretical model, meta-analysis, and review of empirical findings. *Personnel Psychology, 58,* 33–66.

56

Performance Management Catalysts for Experience-Driven Development

Paul Yost
Seattle Pacific University

THE PERFORMANCE MANAGEMENT system in an organization is a natural place to challenge leaders to think more strategically about their development and the development of their direct reports. Very few organizations, however, take advantage of the opportunity. Employee development all too often is a box that appears at the end of the yearly performance goal form, even though performance management systems are the natural place for leaders to consider both their performance goals for the coming year and the ways they should develop themselves to meet future challenges.

Performance Management Systems That Drive Development

A number of things can be done to foster development in the context of performance management.

Separate the performance and development conversations. In most organizations, the performance management system includes three conversations in the process: (1) goal setting, (2) development plans, and (3) performance evaluation. Managers will often pressure human resources to combine the first two steps in the process. After all, it is a lot more efficient, and doesn't most of this book argue that development occurs while leaders are performing their jobs? Regrettably, although good in theory, there are serious repercussions when the two conversations do occur at the same time. The development part of the conversation tends to be short-changed. It often turns into a conversation focused on the employee's performance weaknesses because the beginning of the conversation is framed around performance and goals for the coming year. Career aspirations and future assignments seldom come up in this framing. Development can also be short-changed by the employee. In a time-limited conversation, the employee is going to focus the most attention on the performance goals that he or she is going to be held accountable to. Employee development is important, but definitely a secondary concern to pay and job requirements. No wonder performance and development are in conflict in many organizations.

One of the best ways to increase the visibility and saliency of development in an organization is to require that it be discussed in two separate conversations. By separating them, the development conversation is more likely to focus on long-term goals and create the space to talk about future assignments. Some organizations make this a mid-year discussion, which also serves as a check-in on a person's performance goals (but this latter is secondary to focusing on development). If the organization insists that performance and development should be combined at the beginning of the year, organizations should strongly encourage bosses to schedule two meetings to discuss the two topics. This will probably cost managers an extra hour per employee to meet with them. However, it seems like one hour to discuss goals at the beginning of the year and one hour to discuss future development isn't a lot. It is a rather small investment given how important both topics are in the long-term success of the organization.

Make 70/20/10 part of the development plan form. Left on their own, people tend to default to a list of training programs as the development activities they will pursue in the coming year. The solution is to make on-the-job development more salient. One simple strategy is simply to add checkboxes next to the list of developmental items in the development form (see Exhibit 56.1), where people are prompted to self-categorize the development activities that they list. The section can also begin with an introductory paragraph that highlights talks about the importance of on-the-job development and other people in addition to training. Provide web links with suggested ideas. In this way, the form itself points people toward the richest developmental experiences.

Create a list of developmental experiences. More often than not, leaders and employees alike are simply looking for ideas. People list training courses as developmental activities because a list is easily available. To prime the pump for on-the-job development, make a list of on-the-job development activities equally easy to find on the company's intranet with a direct link in the development form. Exhibit 56.2 provides an example list. For more ideas, see *Developmental Assignments: Creating Learning Experiences Without Changing Jobs* by Cynthia McCauley (2006) or *Eighty-Eight Assignments for Development in Place* by Michael Lombardo and Robert Eichinger (1989), both published by the Center for Creative Leadership.

Add a self-check at the end of the performance-management form. Another simple idea is to add a self-assessment at the end of the develop form or an online self-assessment. The

Exhibit 56.1. Developmental Activities Form That Points People Toward On-the-Job Development

Development Activities

Identify the leadership development activities you would like to pursue in the coming year. Remember, most development occurs *on the job* (70 percent); the second most comes from *other people* (20 percent), and the rest comes in *formal training* (10 percent). To ensure you are maximizing your development, your developmental activities should follow this same pattern.

Development Action Plan	
Development Activities	**Type of Learning**
	❑ 70% Learning on the job
	❑ 20% Learning from other people
	❑ 10% Learning through training
	❑ 70% Learning on the job
	❑ 20% Learning from other people
	❑ 10% Learning through training
	❑ 70% Learning on the job
	❑ 20% Learning from other people
	❑ 10% Learning through training

self-assessment should *not* be a heavy-handed rules-based form (for example, "Have you identified specific measures to assess your progress?"). Make it fun and valuable to the person filling it out (for example, "Am I developing skills that will make me more employable three to five years from now?"). A sample self-check is provided in Exhibit 56.3.

Audit the performance management process. Another way to increase the emphasis on experience-based development is at the organizational level. A sample of performance and development plans can be audited to assess their quality. Exhibit 56.4 provides an example of some of the factors that might be evaluated. This information can then be fed back to the senior-leadership team as a way to prompt them to increase their support of good development. The sample can be small (as few as twenty-five forms) or you could audit the development plans in a high-visibility population (for instance, participants in the company's high potential program), where they should be exceptional.

Define career paths in the organization. Career paths create a natural catalyst for development. In fact, the pull is so strong, it can become problematic when employees think the only way to advance is to move into management. People in organizations are quick to condemn the problem but ignore the potential they could be channeling into productive development. A first step organizations can take is to define management and technical

Exhibit 56.2. Developmental Activities

Below are a variety of developmental assignments that leverage on-the-job development. They include large projects that will likely require a job change and smaller experiences that can be easily integrated into a person's current job.

Start-Up Assignments

- Launch a new product or service in an emerging market.

- Develop and launch a new internal organizational process.

- Build a team from scratch to take on an emerging business challenge.

Fix-It Assignments

- Take over a poorly performing business unit that needs to be turned around.

- Volunteer to clean up an internal organizational process that is inefficient.

- Look for processes in your sphere of control that need to be improved.

- Volunteer to lead a poorly performing team.

Managing Multiple Stakeholders

- Manage a high-visibility project that includes stakeholders from multiple geographies, business units, or functions.

- Take over a project with multiple customers with different and often competing needs.

External Experiences

- Find a nonprofit organization where you can volunteer your leadership skills.

- Become part of a nonprofit board of directors.

- Join a professional organization and take on a leadership role.

Learning from Other People

- Ask a senior person in your field to be your mentor.

- Identify a small group of people you will regularly go to for feedback. Consider including your manager, two colleagues, two direct reports, and your internal/external customers.

- Find someone who can act as a peer coach.

- Find a project with a team on which your ideas will regularly be challenged.

Exhibit 56.3. A Development Plan Self-Assessment

How Good Is Your Development Plan?

Directions: Think about the development plan that you just put together. Check all of the items that apply.

☐ I'm developing skills that will make me more employable in three to five years.

☐ Over 70 percent of my development activities are skills that I will be developing on the job (for example, taking on a challenging task that will stretch me in areas I have targeted for development).

☐ At least 20 percent of my development activities are learning from other people (for example, meeting with a mentor, peer coaching, and getting feedback).

☐ I am intentional about my development; I'm not just letting it happen.

☐ I'm excited when I look at my development plan for the coming year.

☐ I am taking on tasks and assignments that will stretch me in the areas I have targeted for development.

☐ My development goals are specific.

☐ I am role modeling the kind of development I expect from my direct reports.

☐ I have identified opportunities that will allow me to drive the business strategy and develop myself at the same time.

Exhibit 56.4. Performance-Management Audit

Criteria	Target	Actual
Completion Rates		
Performance goals completed on time (%)	100%	
Development plans completed on time (%)	100%	
End-of-year performance reviews completed on time (%)	100%	
Performance Goals		
Specific goals (%)	90%	
Aligned with the business strategy (%)	90%	
With metrics (%)	90%	
Development Goals		
Specific Goals (%)	90%	
With metrics (%)	80%	
Types of development activities		
Learning on the job	70%	
Learning from other people	20%	
Learning from training	10%	
Average number of development activities per development plan	3+	

career paths to keep people out of management positions that would be a bad fit. Most stop there. A variety of other possibilities exist. Functional career paths lay out a natural progression that people can follow to develop broadly and deeply. Functional paths don't have to be vertical but can include a number of horizontal moves to broaden a person's expertise. For example, global organizations often require leadership experience in multiple geographies before leaders are qualified to move into general-management positions. See the *Profiles for Success at Collective Brands: Building a Framework for Internal Transitions* contribution on page 459 of this book and Jennifer Kennedy Marchi's contribution on The Monitor Group's career paths on page 451 for examples of how two organizations have encouraged lateral career paths.

Ask people about their career aspirations. Another overlooked and simple way to encourage employee development in the performance management process is to ensure that there is a place for people to document their career aspirations. This does two things: First, it prompts employees to think about them; and second, it can be a catalyst for conversations with their managers. Once aspirations are known, a manager can provide advice, help connect an employee with the right people, look for projects and opportunities to help the employee develop in the desired direction, and provide advice (or provide realistic feedback if the aspirations are unrealistic).

Link experiences to the competencies. Many organizations have a competency model. Unfortunately, they often stop there when people are triggered to start looking for ways to develop the competencies that the organization has said are so valuable. Organizations leave employees and their managers on their own to figure how they should develop the competencies. Without guidance, the default solution is often to sign the employee up for a training class rather than find a way to help the employee develop his or her competencies on the job. Instead, organizations can create simple resources that point the person in a different direction. For any given competency, such as driving results, they can identify the job assignments that might build this skill, such as managing a sales or production team. They can also provide ideas about how the person might develop in place, for example, by leading a team with a clear deliverable and a challenging deadline, or draw on other people, for example, by finding a mentor or role model recognized for his or her ability to drive results. The trick is to capture people's attention with the competencies and then point them toward on-the-job development.

Lessons Learned

All of the above suggestions are relatively simple ideas, but that is not to say that they will not require determined energy and commitment to build them into the organization's larger HR systems. The default position in a lot of organizations is that anything coming from HR is administrative and should be minimized. Historically, HR systems have often deserved this reputation. But performance expectations and employee development are critical to the long-term success of any organization. The performance management system is a natural place to capture people's attention and focus them not only on performance but on how they can develop leaders and employees to meet future business challenges. The return on investment is significant. If done well, people can perform their jobs and develop themselves every day as long as they have placed themselves in positions that will stretch them to grow in the areas they have targeted for development. But there continue to be barriers.

Performance will trump development if nothing is done. To paraphrase a popular Peter Drucker quote, performance will eat development for lunch if no one is fighting to make employee development a priority. In the performance management group, the energy is naturally focused on performance measurement and compensation. Development is added on. In practice, this means that "development goals and activities" is a box that is added at the end of the form. "Development conversations" are what managers do when employees are not meeting their goals. The case needs to be made passionately and often that employee development is critical to the long-term success of the organization.

Build partnerships. If you manage the performance management process, find ways to partner with other people in human resources (for example, the talent management group or the leadership development group). Look for ways that you can help them build experience-driven development into their programs and then use the performance management system to encourage these changes. If you are an HR generalist in the field, look for ways that you can link the HR processes together for your management team. For example, when you talk about performance management, always start with a chart that links it into the bigger talent management process (for instance, selection, performance management, and development planning). Similarly, look for opportunities to talk about performance goals and employee development as complementary processes. Finally, if you manage an HR process outside of performance management (for example, talent management, leadership development), build resources and tools that support your work but that can easily be integrated into the performance management process. Build them so they are stand-alone tools that can be directly linked into the management. For example, create some resources that can easily "bolt onto" the current system. For instance, a list of developmental assignments could be created to support any program. A link could then be provided to the performance management team that they could build into their guidelines and into the performance management form itself.

Keep it simple—make the manager's job easier. As you are building experience-driven development into the performance management system, your goal should be to build tools and resources that make the managers' job easier. The resources should be so helpful, so intuitive, and so easy to follow that it would be crazy for managers to not use them! In the words of one manager I worked with, "As soon as I need to read the directions, you have lost me." Managers are busy doing lots and lots of important work. If you want to impact their behavior, find a way to make their jobs easier. In the midst of e-mails, client meetings, budget reports, and employee meetings, what are the tools and resources that you can provide them that will make experience-based development a natural part of the conversations they have with their employees—with no directions required?

57

Training and Experience-Driven Development

Paul Yost
Seattle Pacific University

A FRAMEWORK THAT starts with the assumption that 90 percent of a leader's development will occur outside of the classroom forces a person to think about training from a whole new perspective. In this outside-in model, the training program isn't the point, but a catalyst to drive leadership development outside the classroom. Formal training becomes an accelerator for on-the-job development. Classroom leadership development still serves a few critical functions:

- To highlight the on-the-job experiences that are most critical in a leader's development (for example, what is the short list of key leadership development experiences?).

- To practice and develop meta-skills that will promote growth in the experiences (for example, seeking feedback, reflection).

- To remember the important role that managers play in developing their direct reports and helping them to learn from experience.

Figure 57.1 illustrates a continuum we might use to think about leadership training and development in this framework. Formal classroom training represents one end of the

Figure 57.1. A Continuum of Training and On-the-Job Development

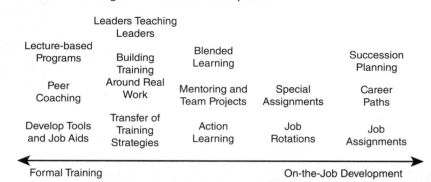

spectrum and on-the-job development represents the other, but the whole spectrum is considered from the experience side. Contrast this with the typical leadership development program that starts with the training and discusses pre-training and post-training conditions that promote transfer. Even the word "transfer" implies that the center of the action is the training program rather than the reality that the training program is one event among many significant events in a leader's development. Starting with experience opens up new ways to turn training into a catalyst for on-the-job development.

Formal Training

Building experience-driven development into formal classroom training might start with a mini-lecture on the lessons of experience, including a reflection activity on the key experiences in the participant's career, a review of the key experiences in the lessons of experience research, followed by identification of the key experiences that the leader would like to pursue in the future. Activities might also include building development plans for one or two direct reports. Senior leaders can share the key experiences they learned in their careers and advice for aspiring leaders in the company. The training class itself might be more of a workshop where leaders are working on real world problems and coaching each other; in essence, bringing the work into the classroom. See Elaine Beich's contribution, *Bringing the Real World into the Classroom* on page 375 of this book for several other great examples about integrating experience development into training. Also look at the ExperiencePoint contribution, *Building Experience into Simulations*, on page 397 of this book.

Transfer of Training

Imagine that more learning and development occurred before or after class than during it. Let's push the idea even further, and imagine that 90 percent of the learning occurs before and after class. If true, what would need to happen before, during, and after class for that

Figure 57.2. Training That Promotes More Learning Outside the Classroom Than Happens Inside It

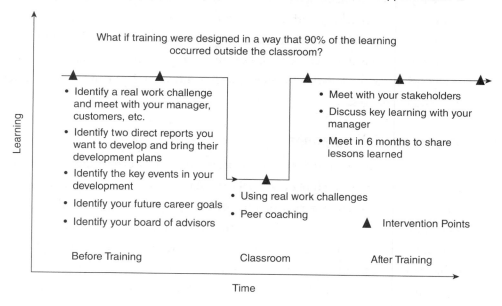

to occur? How can we trigger that kind of learning? Figure 57.2 illustrates several strategies that could serve as catalysts. Leaders could be encouraged before training to meet with their bosses to discuss next steps in their careers. They could meet with clients and employees before the training workshop and bring that information to use during the workshop. Participants could bring the development plans of two direct reports to practice building on-the-job development into the developmental activities. To encourage post-training work, a follow-up class could be organized six months later to discuss what happened and share lessons learned. Peer coaching groups might meet during the class and could be encouraged to continue to connect and coach each other leading up to the follow-up class.

Action Learning

Eventually, leadership development that is focused on a real business problem becomes so applied that it looks like action learning. The balance between development and work tips toward the work side and the projects become the focus with development happening along the way. Projects are short-term with a limited scope, but the stakes can be high since action learning projects are often sponsored by senior leaders in the organization. (See *Business-Driven Action Learning* on page 413 of this book.)

Mentoring and Communities of Practice

People play a critical role in a leader's development. Mentoring programs offer a structured way to promote learning from other people. (See *Mentoring: Building Leaders in Powerful*

Developmental Relationships on page 405 of this book.) Likewise, communities of practice can be organized to encourage the sharing of best practices and lessons learned, with opportunities for peer coaching within and between organizations (See *Better Together: Building Learning Communities Across Organizations* on page 433 of this book.) In these cases, classroom experience is not even needed. Learning comes through others. Development can be embedded in the work with a mentor providing advice and guidance in the context of daily tasks and challenges.

Special Assignments and Job Rotations

Take action learning to its logical conclusion and it will evolve into putting a promising leader into a special assignment that will stretch him or her in an undeveloped area. Take a lot of short-term temporary assignments, put them in a pre-planned sequence, and the result looks a lot like a formal job rotation program. The classroom, if it is used at all, becomes a catalyst to prepare participants before they enter the job rotation program or as a chance to meet with fellow job rotation candidates during the process to share what is happening, provide mutual support, and share lessons learned. At this stage, the majority of planned development truly does happen on the job.

Job Assignments

At the extreme, we find ourselves thinking about longer-term job assignments; the focus of *Lessons of Experience.* Leaders are developed when they are in trial-by-fire, edge-of-your-comfort-zone experiences where learning isn't just an option, but required to survive. Leaders start feeling like classroom training is getting in the way if it doesn't help them meet the challenges that they are facing right now and developing the skills to meet those challenges. Sound familiar? Under the old training model, these trainee complaints are likely to be seen as a leader who isn't very open to learning (aka, learning what the trainer thinks is important). *HoTspots: A Blended Group Learning Solution to Extend Traditional Training* on page 389 of this book highlights how a learning management system can be built to directly support the needs of the participants as they are trying to solve real world challenges.

As you read these contributions, I challenge you to think about the chapters from the perspective of a business leader who is challenged to grow and develop in his or her job every day. Ask yourself: How can the programs be rolled out so they support and accelerate that learning? How can the programs be designed so they are catalysts for greater learning on the job?

58

Bringing the Real World into the Classroom

Elaine Biech

ebb associates inc

LEADERSHIP IS CHALLENGING. It can even be daunting if one enumerates the many complex skills required by leaders. These skills range from the basics needed by everyone in the workplace, such as communication, to those that are leadership specific, such as crafting a vision and providing motivation and direction to reach that vision.

With all there is to learn, how can you ensure the experience you deliver meets the needs of the future leaders in your classroom? One of the most successful approaches is to incorporate events, issues, and actual data from your organization. You may be the world's best role-play designer and game developer, but nothing compares to the real thing. Since so much is happening in your organization, you shouldn't have to make up anything!

The rationale for success is obvious. Adults prefer to devote energy to learning things *[when training do training that applies it directly to the job.]* that they believe will help them do their jobs better, cope with daily life more effectively, or solve a specific problem. Developing content in response to these needs is the most helpful to adult learners. When you relate classroom training to real life, the organization also gains because more people realize what is required for organizational success.

[Point 1] Bringing actual experiences into the classroom is an approach that allows learners to engage in their organization's real world situations. They gain insight, knowledge, and skills that help them understand and appreciate the organization's real world dilemmas and challenges.

Four Steps to Experiential Activity Design

These four steps to selecting experience-driving activities for a classroom help ensure that you focus on the learner as well as provide benefit to the organization.

1. *Prioritize the Objectives.* Review the objectives that have been identified for the classroom experience. Which ones seem to be the highest priority? You could ask yourself, "If there were one or two skills that would be the most beneficial to the learners, which ones would it be?" You may want to ask others for input. Perhaps you could ask someone who is in a leadership position, "If you could select one or two objectives from this class that would have prepared you better for your job, which ones would you choose?" In addition, think about the real-world situations in which they will need to apply the skills. What are their needs in those situations?

2. *Specify Required KSAs.* List the knowledge, skills, and abilities (KSAs) learners must develop in order to achieve the objective. For example, the objective "lead a problem-solving team" suggests a long list of KSAs: leveraging diversity, building a team, gathering data, analyzing problems, and a host of others. In an experiential situation, learners learn by reflecting on their experiences and by developing personal insights and understanding through involvement. This may be done with little facilitator support. Experiential learning involves people working things through for themselves and developing their own understanding. In some instances there may be no facilitator observation. To enable success, you must consider the basic skills learners will require prior to the activity. In the team problem solving example, learners would need basic communication skills, conflict management skills, and goal setting skills to ensure success with an experiential learning activity.

3. *Identify a Need.* Selection is the most critical step. You want participants to address a real-world need or an issue that they will face on the job. On the other hand, you do not want to select something that is so critical to the organization's success that it creates failure anxiety among the participants. If you have worked within the organization for several years, you can probably pinpoint an organizational concern or upcoming dilemma. If you need ideas, interview others in the organization for their thoughts and examples. You might consider a need that is prevalent throughout the organization, such as a lack of knowledge about corporate strategy. You might also consider a one-time need, such as coordinating a social responsibility event. Select something that meets an organizational need and that allows participants to learn and practice new skills.

4. *Design the Activity.* Relying on both the developmental needs of the learners and the identified needs of the organization, you can design an activity that is both

valuable and memorable. Learners need to gain knowledge or skills or improve their attitudes. By designing an activity that initiates the learning process, you create an atmosphere conducive to constructive review, ensure that any conceptual thinking leads to meaningful conclusions, and that organizational improvements meet the objectives. Use the resources available, SMEs can add real-life examples, organizational documents can provide required content, and records from recent databases can provide necessary statistics. As always, you will have constraints that limit the design, including time, money, and support. From these constraints you can develop case studies, problem-solving clinics, hands-on practices, critical incidents, role-playing situations, and other experiential activities that focus on real daily work issues. It is critical to ensure participants assimilate the concepts to ensure transfer of learning to other situations. To facilitate this, you may wish to add a follow-up activity such as journaling, action planning, creating a checklist or job aid, listing discussion points to share with their managers, or other reminders of what participants learned and how they will implement it.

In summary, the ultimate experience will engage, stimulate, and challenge participants in an environment where they become absorbed in the task. Use the questions in the design checklist in Exhibit 58.1 to ensure a successful experiential learning design.

Leadership Experiences in the Classroom

These three examples provide you with my own real-life experiences of bringing the real world into the classroom.

New Leader Orientation

An organization wanted their new leaders and managers to get up to speed faster. Everyone recognized that it took at least a few months for new employees to understand their new jobs and how things operated, but after that managers wanted more from their employees. As a part of the orientation design, we conduct a learning session after new employees have been on board for about three months to help them understand the overall organization and their roles in it. We cover many topics and have several department heads come into the classroom to interact with the new employees. But the activity that receives the most attention is one in which we provide participants with a list of questions in advance and ask them to interview their managers and their managers' managers prior to arriving in class. They are also asked to review the organization's vision, mission, and values statement and come prepared for a discussion about consistencies, inconsistencies, and other current organizational actions. At the end of the two-day class, the new leaders create individual action plans highlighting how they will be more proactive in their roles and how they can

Point 2 (handwritten annotation)

Exhibit 58.1. Design Checklist

1. Prioritize Objectives

    • Which objectives do I believe are the highest priorities?

    • Which objectives would the CEO say are priorities?

    • Which objectives do participants view as priorities?

    • Which objectives are most supportive of the organization's vision?

2. Specify Required KSAs

    • What knowledge, skills, and abilities are required to achieve the objectives?

    • How is attitude related to the objective(s)?

    • What foundational skills will learners require for success?

3. Identify a Corporate Need

    • What organizational need requires attention?

    • What one-time events are on the horizon?

    • Who could I ask for suggestions?

    • How would the need address learners' attitudes?

    • How does this need allow learners to practice new skills?

    • Which need is most closely aligned to the objectives and KSAs?

4. Design an Experiential Activity

    • Is the need real enough to create excitement, and also safe enough to allow learning?

    • How do I create a safe environment that enables learners to experiment with new skills and knowledge?

    • How will participants experience real life in this activity?

    • What is required to ensure learners interpret what happened and why?

    • How do I ensure that conceptual thinking leads to meaningful conclusions?

    • How might a discussion about attitude ensue during the review?

    • What will make certain that what is learned is applied in the workplace?

    • What follow-up activities can I suggest that will help the learners apply what they learned in the future?

be a positive force in achieving the organization's vision. After implementing this design for a year, managers recognized the value of this session and made certain that new employees set aside time for the session.

Mid-Level Leadership Development

One organization is reinventing itself and its culture. In the past, people came to work and did their jobs, but did not become involved in planning or focusing on the future.

It was believed such planning was senior leadership's responsibility. The organization has a very low turnover rate and recognized that changing the culture was going to require developing and engaging current employees. At the same time, the organization restructured its leadership development design, with a belief that "everyone is a leader." The key skill that seems to prevent managers from being more proactive was a lack of "critical thinking" skills and experience. Once this need was recognized, it was built into the organization's development planning. As an example, the mid-level leaders attend a development class bringing four things with them: the organization's vision, mission statement, corporate goals, and department goals. In small groups they address questions. The activity has a different focus each time depending on what is happening in the organization. For example, the organization recently changed its performance and contribution system so the questions surrounded these changes. Questions are aimed at developing critical thinking. Near the end of the session the CEO or one of the vice presidents drops in on the class and leads a discussion about what they are learning about the organization and themselves. The questions encourage critical thinking and do not have easy nor correct answers. Examples have included: What would you change about X? Can you describe what led you to suggest that series of steps? Can you define the principle behind that thought process? How would you solve X? How will that decision affect department X? What would result if X? What choice would you make about X? What evidence exists that X? Can you provide an example of how that might work in this situation? The point of this effort is to prepare employees who will be the future leaders for the changing world. The session usually ends by asking the learners to identify the issues on which they think leadership should focus.

High Potential Leadership Development Project

I designed a leadership development program for one of my government research clients to support their high potential future leaders. The organization opens the application process each year, and about 50 percent of all applicants are selected to create a new "class." The candidates attend an off-site leadership development program as a first step, where they obtain comprehensive feedback on their strengths and needs. Within six months of initiation, each new class must select a project and complete it as a team. The planning and design are done in a classroom setting, but some parts (depending on the project) may be done outside. For example, one class created the organization's first business plan, which was implemented by leadership. Another class chose to create a video that would be shown to high school students and on kiosks provided by the STEM (Science, Technology, Engineering, Math) effort to encourage students to pursue science and technology careers. Throughout the project, facilitated discussions address what participants are learning about themselves, leadership, and teamwork. In addition participants are expected to maintain journals of their experiences and their personal learning goals.

Conclusion

Designing experiential learning activities into the classroom ensures that learners have an opportunity to practice skills. Designing activities that relate to the learners' immediate needs ensures that the skills they are practicing are directly related to the challenges they face. Bringing the real world into the classroom benefits leaders and the organization by giving leaders the skills required to solve today's problems and prevents those of the future. As Malcolm Knowles is widely attributed as saying:

> We will learn no matter what! Learning is as natural as rest or play. With or without books, inspiring trainers, or classrooms, we will manage to learn. Educators can, however make a difference in what people learn and how well they learn it. If we know *why* we are learning and if the reason fits our *needs* as we perceive them, we will learn quickly and deeply.

59

Cultivating Learning Agility: Lessons from the Microfinance Sector

Lyndon Rego
Center for Creative Leadership

Vandana Viswanathan
CoCoon

Peg Ross
PCI

THE CENTER FOR Creative Leadership (CCL), CoCoon Consulting, Grameen Foundation, and Continuum partnered to address a looming leadership development gap in the microfinance sector. Microfinance is a relatively new field that has emerged as a solution to address the challenge of global poverty. Microfinance institutions primarily make small loans to women borrowers in urban, semi-urban, and rural areas. The loans are intended to help the women generate income that enhances the lives of their families. Grameen Bank, a pioneering microfinance institution, was the recipient of the Nobel Peace Prize in 2006, along with its founder, Dr. Muhammad Yunus.

The Need

India is a nation where microfinance has seen explosive growth in the past. Annual growth rates for many microfinance institutions approach 100 percent, and these institutions are experiencing yet greater borrower demand and capital inflows from philanthropic and financial markets. These forces have stretched the talent capacity of microfinance institutions, particularly at the middle manager ranks. Mid-level managers typically lead field units and are accountable for managing the business, the customers, and their teams in the field. In many ways, they are the face of the microfinance entity in the field. For a microfinance institution to scale, grow, and sustain itself, skillful middle managers are critical.

The middle managers are often young, from modest educational backgrounds, and have only a few years of experience under their belt. Charged with managing fast-growing and geographically dispersed operations that must balance both social and financial goals, these middle managers are often described as "crisis leaders" and "mini-CEOs."

CCL and CoCoon were tasked with creating an approach that would address the development needs of these middle managers. The solution, informed by research conducted with microfinance institutions across India, had to be affordable and scalable. It had to prepare managers to deal with crises and to lead their growing teams as the organization scaled. For the microfinance organization, the investment in development had to have a tangible payoff.

While microfinance institutions sorely needed capacity building, it was challenging for them to pull middle managers away from the field and into a classroom for more than a day or two. We asked ourselves: "Can these field leaders learn in the field?" We also heard some skeptical beliefs about leadership development programs that characterized them as events where people lounged in air-conditioned classrooms while instructors lectured on topics that had little staying power in the minds of learners.

We drew on the Lessons of Experience research findings, especially data gathered in India (Wilson, 2010). The data we gathered in our field research echoed these findings: managers learned on the job and accelerated their learning when they had bosses who took the time to mentor them.

The Approach

We formulated a three-month leadership development approach and framed it as the Field Learning System (see Figure 59.1). This system was based on a Learn-Apply-Teach methodology that CoCoon had successfully used in other projects. This methodology challenged the microfinance managers to quickly apply their learning via developmental assignments and share those lessons with their direct reports, creating demonstrated results and cascading learning within the organization.

Because of the need to reduce training costs and place the responsibility for learning squarely in the middle managers' hands, we used self-paced workbooks as a primary delivery methodology. The workbooks introduced different leadership concepts and tools to the participants, preparing them to actively engage in applying those concepts before they came into the classroom—in the field and at their own pace. Classroom sessions were brief and

Figure 59.1. The Field Learning System

	LEARN	APPLY	TEACH
FIELD 3 months	Awareness and understanding concepts and tools Through the workbooks and the mobile application	Reflection questions and field assignments and challenges to help apply the concept, and deepen understanding Through the workbooks, mobile application, and peer learning community calls	Teaching assignment –to teach own team and peers Using the workbooks and mobile application as teaching aids; processing learning on the peer learning community calls
	Simulated activities to apply the concepts in field situations in a microfinance entity, and learning capsules to process learning		
CLASSROOM 6 days	Self awareness– where do I stand vis-à-vis these competencies? Multiple applications of the tools and concepts	Understand how to apply concepts and tools in work situations, and the outcomes of the same	Teach and share learning and similar experiences with peers

focused on the application of lessons. The workbooks were coupled with a peer-learning community supported by phone meetings and a customized Android mobile application, enabling the participants to stay in touch with each other and report on learning challenges and outcomes as they moved through the learning process. A Learn-Apply-Teach design grid was used to create the content in the workbooks and the mobile applications (see Figure 59.2). The idea was to help the individual to learn at three levels: self, others, and the system.

Based on the need for learning agility in a fast-paced environment, cultivating greater awareness and mindfulness became a key pillar of the program. In the field research, we heard that there was no "user manual" that could be provided to these managers to deal with the ambiguity and change they tackle in their roles. The program's focus on mindfulness enabled the managers to be more introspective in addressing new challenges, encouraging them to pause and question their own assumptions and to seek fresh perspectives garnered by consulting others. Given the dynamic nature of the microfinance industry, we also wanted the managers to hone their ability to learn on an ongoing basis in order to sustain and enhance their effectiveness. We wanted to help them build "learning to learn" as a competence so they could see challenges and change as learning opportunities.

For training methods, we focused on creating low-cost, scalable models. CoCoon brought extensive expertise gained by working with microfinance organizations as well as

Figure 59.2. Design Grid

	LEARN *What have I learned?*	APPLY *What and how will I apply it?*	TEACH *What will I teach? How will I teach this to others?*
Self	Identifying my mental models • Why are they important and relevant? • How do I understand my mental models?	Becoming aware of my mental models • What are my mental models in my role and what I do? • How does learning about mental models change things? • What are the challenges of working mental models?	Raising group competence • How do we become aware of our own mental models? Sharing and playback
Others	• How do I understand/work with different/others' mental models?	• How do I use mental models to better communicate and influence, surface and manage conflict?	• How do we get better at sharing our mental models? Sharing and playback
System	• How do mental models shape culture? • How do we challenge and change our mental models?	• How can I apply my knowledge of mental models to lead change, (future, innovation)?	• How do we not become limited by our mental models? Sharing and playback

large companies. We factored in the need to contextualize the development lessons with practical microfinance-based simulations and case studies drawing on CoCoon's work in the sector. In the field research study, we heard managers tell us over and over again that they had learned a lot from adversity and the challenges that came with increased responsibility. Guided by this, we used some of the field-level challenges they faced with stakeholders as scenarios in the simulations. We also linked the simple tools, methods, and approaches associated with each module to these scenarios in order to help managers understand how they could be more effective by using their lessons from the program in these situations.

The initial three-month program prototype was tested with a group of microfinance managers from an organization in India. The managers worked in field and corporate roles and reflected diversity in education and experience. Participants were provided with a smart phone that allowed them to access the mobile application.

The participants reported that the three-month program enabled them to learn and practice new skills. They reported becoming better listeners who engaged with their direct reports in a more consultative fashion. They also reported an increased ability to model what they'd learned with their teams. Importantly for the organization investing in the training, participants noted that the program helped them generate solutions that increased profitability and revenues. For example, two of the participants faced significant loan defaults in their region—the poorer clients were not keeping current on their repayment obligations. The middle managers discussed one of the concepts they learned in the program, a classic SWOT analysis with their teams (looking at strengths, weaknesses, opportunities, and threats), and collectively agreed to apply SWOT analysis to each defaulted household's circumstances. They hoped to identify ways they could work with the clients to get them back on track. Over a three-month period, loan defaults decreased from twelve hundred to six hundred, and the region's chief executive attributed 100 percent of this positive change to the SWOT analysis process. A formal pilot is underway that will yield additional program impact data.

Tools

Two tools used in the program are Life Journey Mapping and the Learn-Apply-Teach Workbooks.

Life Journey Mapping. Drawing a life journey map was one of the initial assignments participants were asked to complete before the program, and they were asked to bring their maps to the program kick-off (see Exhibit 59.1 for the instructions for this activity).

The assignment was designed to help the participants reflect on their personal journeys and recognize what they had been able to learn from adversity and challenges and to help them see critical inflection points in their journeys, repeated patterns in their actions, and the shifts and course corrections that may have taken place. In the classroom, participants shared the maps with small groups of peers at the front end of the session with the purpose of building shared empathy and trust. As is often the case with these maps, they reverberated with the loss and triumph that constitute their lives. Participants invariably felt a deeper sense of appreciation for their colleagues, building trust and relationships. The candor expressed by the participants in these activities also began to infuse the program with a sense of openness and trust that characterized subsequent interactions.

Exhibit 59.1. Life Journey Mapping

Instructions for creating a life journey map:

- Obtain a sheet of poster paper and some colored pens or pencils.

- Using the paper, draw your life journey starting from the time you were born to the present.

- Chart all the key moments in your life—big changes, achievements, and setbacks.

- Try to draw these visually. For example, you might draw a school to indicate your time in school, or stick figures of your family, or a thunderbolt to indicate a shock you experienced.

- Write in text some key indicators of what took place or how the incidents affected you.

You will be sharing this map later with your program classmates, so don't include anything you want to keep confidential. Keep in mind, however, that the more you can share, the greater the potential for establishing a closer relationship with your colleagues.

Learn-Apply-Teach Workbooks. We developed workbooks as a tool for self-paced learning in the field. Many middle managers did not have regular Internet access during the day, or even consistent network access on their mobile phones. Our initial field research indicated the managers would be open to learning through bite-sized modules during their travels in the field. This led to the creation of workbooks and mobile applications for the three major program modules to help them learn and review at their own pace during pockets of time they found for themselves in the field.

The workbooks were divided into sections and organized by key concepts:

- *Section 1: WHAT is the concept? WHY is it useful?* The concept is explained using a model or a visual. Then, a story or an anecdote, typically set in the microfinance context, brings the concept alive. For instance, we explain the SWOT analysis concept by sharing how a vegetable vendor in an Indian village used such an analysis to examine whether he should open a larger grocery store.

- *Section 2: HOW does it work? HOW can I use it?* Participants are given simple guidelines and tips on a specific concept, and then how they can apply it. For example, in the workbook on mindsets, participants are given a set of questions to help them identify whether they have a growth mindset or a fixed mindset. This is followed by a simple exercise to reinforce their learning and deepen their understanding.

- *Section 3: A practical assignment for the participants.* The assignments challenge participants to try new things in the workplace, teaching their teams new skills or changing processes. Reflective questions help participants process their learning once they complete the assignment.

We learned that participants appreciated the workbooks because of the familiar stories and examples that simplified the concepts. Some participants told us they carried the workbooks with them and read some of the sections over and over until they understood them. They even asked whether they could obtain or make copies of the workbooks to share with their teams!

Lessons Learned

We found that the managers embraced the program and were eager to learn. They were willing to complete the demanding pre-work and self-paced learning assignments. The pre-work and the assignments were positioned as prerequisites to attending a classroom event. Completion and adherence to the schedule were tracked through the peer-learning community calls. They relished opportunities to connect with each other and to share learning.

The practical capstone simulation was among the best-received aspects of the program. It enabled the participants to apply the lessons they had learned in an integrated way that connected the dots between different concepts, as well as between theory and practice.

The mobile application, which faced technological hurdles, has been a lesser success. The peer learning functionality of the app has been the most successful element, rather than the content delivery and reporting mechanisms. Further experimentation is needed to refine this solution in order to achieve its promise.

Reference

Wilson, M.S. (2010). *Developing tomorrow's leaders today: Insights from corporate India.* Singapore: John Wiley & Sons (Asia).

60

HoTspots (HubsOfTraining): A Blended Group Learning Solution to Extend Traditional Training

Eric Berg
LINGOs

INTERNATIONAL HUMANITARIAN RELIEF, development, and conservation organizations face enormous challenges building the core skills of their staff in the developing world. Severely constrained financial resources coupled with geographic dispersion, multiple language demands, and a mixed skill level audience make these program design and delivery challenges unique. In 2005, a group of organizations created LINGOs (Learning in NGOs) a nonprofit consortium of international NGOs (non-governmental organizations) designed to facilitate the sharing of learning resources and experiences within the sector. In 2010, the Project Management in Development–Professional (PMD Pro) certification framework was created by a subset of LINGOs members to improve the project management capacity of managers responsible for delivering programs in the developing world. Created over several years and field-tested by more than two hundred managers from fifteen international organizations, the PMD Pro framework became the first internationally recognized, non-organization-specific standard certification maintained by a third party (PM4NGOs) in the field. The first PMD Pro1 preparatory classes were conducted in South Africa and Zambia in 2010 and to date more than four thousand people from over fifty-five countries have taken the examination required for certification.

However, as outlined above, the challenge remained to find a way to reach the tens of thousands of development workers who needed to learn how to apply professional project management techniques and methods despite the resource constraints and geographic dispersion challenges faced by all humanitarian relief and development organizations. Initial pilots were conducted using online technologies to bring the training to a wider audience—eliminating the need for both participant and instructor travel costs. However, intermittent Internet connectivity resulted in limited success of those efforts. (Where connectivity was strong, the results matched the face-to-face training results. However, in very weak connectivity locations, learners became frustrated and gradually dropped out of the courses.)

In addition to Internet connectivity challenges, post-course follow-up had revealed uneven application of tools and techniques among the learners who had completed a face-to-face course at their national office. Further exploration revealed a lack of support for the application of new tools among the other project managers in the local office as well as a need to support course graduates with coaching on the tools with their specific projects.

So beginning in 2011, a new approach was taken to the initial instruction on PMD Pro1. The approach has become known as HoTspots or Hubs Of Training. What follows is a description of the program, results of implementation, and lessons learned.

A keystone to the HoTspot concept was the focus on practical application of learning in real-life situations and group learning by having project teams that were working together in the field participate in the training together. The "examples" chosen by the teams were their actual projects. They were able to use the learning environment as a place where they actually did some of the designing and planning for the work they were doing when not in class. And, the participants in those HoTspots became familiar with each other's project elements and were able to support each other with ideas and suggestions that had worked on similar projects in the areas. That way, the learning was taken out of the theoretical arena and into application from the very beginning. It also avoided the trap that we had seen in earlier classes where a single participant might go back to his or her field assignment and try to apply new techniques only to be told "we don't do things that way" by colleagues who hadn't experienced the training.

The focal points of these HoTspots were the Area Development Programs—or ADPs—which are the geographic regions that are the center of development programming for children and communities. The ADPs selected for the program were in South Africa (Bloemfontein, Johannesburg, and Okhahlamba), Lesotho (Maseru), Zambia (Lusaka and Choma) and Mozambique (Maputo). In addition, Malawi (Lilongwe and Blantyre) and Swaziland (Maphalaleni and Lubulini) were the first to pilot in February 2012.

Each HoTspot was outfitted with a computer equipped with a 3G Internet connection, an LCD projector, and a group USB VoIP speakerphone. With this equipment the participants in the room were able to watch presentations by the instructors and other offices, ask questions, and make presentations of assignments given to each HoTSpot. Each ADP participated as a "node" in all online sessions conducted as part of the course and quickly became known by their ADP names, as in "Maseru here" or "Choma here." Instructors and others would address questions to the HoTspot nodes rather than to individual class members, creating a sense of team within the HoTspots.

The HoTspot approach had four major objectives:

1. Reach more field-based project managers and support staff without incurring participant travel costs

2. Provide a mechanism for groups of project managers and/or project teams to work on their own projects while learning new tools and methods

3. Enable instructors from throughout the world to participate in the training without travel costs, making more efficient use of human resources

4. Avoid removing project managers from the field for training

Equally important were the two overall learning objectives for the training:

1. ADP managers would understand the foundation concepts of professional project management, including Project Identification and Design, Start-Up, Planning, Implementation, Monitoring, and Evaluation and Transition.

2. ADP managers and their teams would be able to apply the basic tools of project management, including charters, Work Breakdown Structures, Network Diagrams, Risk Registers, Issue Logs, Monitoring Plans, and RACI diagrams to their projects.

From the outset it was agreed that the course would be as rigorous as the face-to-face course and would include the PMD Pro1 online examination for certification followed by sessions on post-certification action planning. It was also decided that the course could not drag on over many weeks and should be completed within a two-week time period. The face-to-face course took five full days to complete and experience had showed that two to three hours per day was the limit for the amount of time learners could reasonably be expected to remain focused and uninterrupted in their field offices.

As a result of these limitations, participants would be required to do a significant amount of pre-work prior to the start of the HoTspot course and that there would be "homework" each class day that focused on the core content. Class time would be reserved for application work as group and online time would focus on a global tutorial and coaching on content studied independently the prior day. This also promoted the transfer of learning beyond the classroom.

Because instructors were only going to be online with the HoTspots for one and a half hours each day, it was decided to run two courses concurrently—one in the morning and one in the afternoon. The morning class would meet from 9 a.m. to noon and the afternoon class would meet from 2 p.m. to 5 p.m.. Of that three-hour time period, the group would be online together with the global instructor for one and one half hours. The remainder of the time was focused on working as a group on specific assignments related to their own projects. Each node was free to work on projects that related only to their ADPs and national office without needing to "compromise" on a generic example. This enabled participants to begin the learning transfer process immediately as content was being presented because participants were required to "test" the concepts they were learning against the realities of their own projects.

The theoretical concepts in project management tend to be quite easy to understand. However, the complexities are often only revealed in the application of those concepts to working projects. The PMD Pro1 certification preparation course is based on content found in the 125-page PMD Pro Guide and Syllabus. All class participants were expected to have read the guide for the first time prior to the first day of class and they were also expected to have taken the sample PMD Pro 1 examination online at the PMD Pro exam site. In addition to the Guide, Syllabus, and Sample Exam, a series of screen casts were created that covered major points in the PMD Pro Guide. Each day, participants were given reading assignments in the Guide to reinforce key concepts, assigned screencasts to view, and given group assignments to be completed by their HoTspot after the online class for the day was over. These assignments focused on the application of the tools and techniques covered that day to projects their ADP and teams were working on. This practical application of tools allowed the participants to practice with real-world conditions and gave them the opportunity to obtain feedback and coaching assistance from the global instructor when they encountered difficulties.

In addition to the virtual classroom sessions and the local node meetings, the course provided us a social network environment that allowed asynchronous activities to occur between class sessions (see Figure 60.1). Posting of assignment results by each node allowed the other HoTspots to observe and learn from the work of their colleagues in other countries. It also promoted dialogue between the HoTspots on similar projects. (Most ADPs run projects for child well-being, HIV/Aids caregiving, and livelihoods development). In addition, the social networking site was used to post photos and profiles of participants, which enhanced the "social learning" component that is often absent in online programs. The Forum section of the platform was used for commenting on others' assignments. The same platform was also used as a class document repository and to provide links to self-study materials, assignments, and recordings of the classes for those that might have missed attending the "live" session.

By the second Friday of the course, all HoTspots were ready to take the online certification examination. This was the only time that a persistent, uninterrupted Internet connection was actually required. To make certain of this, certain HoTspots had solicited the support of their IT departments to either supplement the 3G connection or provide con-

Figure 60.1. Sample Social Networking Learning Site

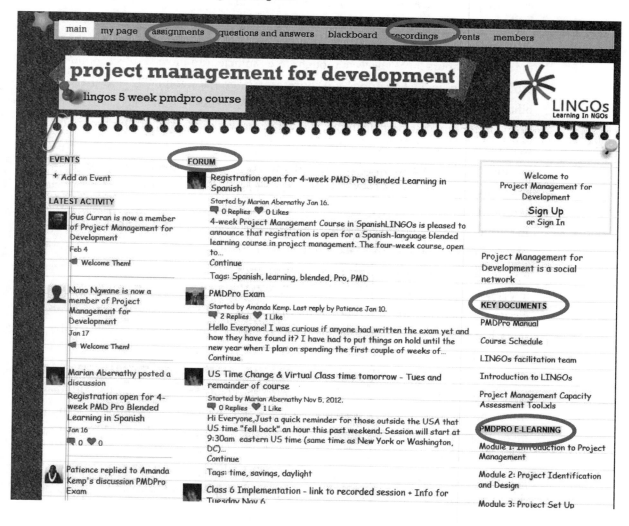

tingency plans in the event of a power outage. All HoTspots were successful in getting their participants through the examination in the allotted time. Pass results for the blended participants mirrored the pass statistics for previous face-to-face courses and in one case exceeded them. (It is believed that the requirements of pre-work and the discipline required for the self-study components resulted in more study time being invested by the blended learning participants.)

The remainder of time on Friday was devoted to post-certification action planning. Each participant prepared and presented his or her plans for application of tools within the projects. This exercise is done during the afternoon of the final day of the face-to-face course as well. However, because the participants had been working with their own projects throughout the course, the blended participants had already begun applying the tools and the post-course monitoring of results shows that blended participants applied more tools more frequently than the face-to-face participants did.

One of the most important "lessons learned" in reviewing the conduct and results of the blended HoTspot approach was the advantage of having local "facilitators." Initially, the online office hours on Skype were thought to be sufficient to provide direct support to each HoTspot on individual questions and concerns. However, it was quickly clear that the online office hours were not frequently used. Because the classes were not scheduled during those times, it appears that participants scheduled other work activities during those hours and were therefore unable to use the time for coaching. Several of the HoTspots benefited from having a local trainer who had completed a train-the-trainer program for PMD Pro1 available in the office of the HoTspot. These local trainers had been identified by senior managers and peers as individuals who had excelled at the application of project management tools and techniques in their own projects and had an interest and aptitude for sharing their experiences with others. These local trainers were used by the local HoTspots as coordinators, facilitators, and technical assistance providers for the technology. While they were not information presenters in any way, they were available to the group to answer questions and discuss alternatives with the groups as they completed their class assignments. Not all HoTspots had local trainers available and it appears that those that did had a deeper, richer learning experience than those that did not.

As expected, the pre-work was a critical part of the success of this approach. (For Pre-Work Tips see Exhibit 60.1.) While monitoring the completion of the reading or the watching of the screen casts was impossible, it was possible to monitor the completion and results of participants taking the sample exam. Previous experience in face-to-face courses had taught that taking the sample exam was a critical step in motivating the participants. Many participants had been project managers for several years and entered the course with confidence that they already knew professional project management. When they received very low scores on the sample exam, they realized how many professional practices they were completely unfamiliar with, as well as industry standard terminology. One goal of the entire effort was to create a common language for project management in the organization and using industry standard terminology was important to that task. Interviews with previous participants had revealed that a turning point in motivating individuals toward more intense self-study was the sample exam.

One final lesson learned was the value of having a group of people taking the blended course at the same time. Previously, individuals had enrolled in courses and attempted to complete them at their desks using headsets. Unfortunately, their colleagues in the office didn't recognize or respect the fact that they were occupied in a formal learning experience and frequently interrupted them during class sessions. When a small group was collectively working in a small room with a projector and VoIP speakerphone, others in the office were clear that training was underway and avoided interrupting the group.

Exhibit 60.1. Tips for Pre-Work

Most trainers love the idea of using pre-work as a way of enriching the face-to-face experience and thereby shortening the required classroom time. However, experience has shown that getting participants to complete pre-work can be an elusive goal. Here are seven tips that improve your chances of successfully employing pre-work.

1. **Don't Use the Term Pre-Work.** The term pre-work implies that the class hasn't started. If the work is required, then the "pre-work" is as much part of the class as any other instruction. We make it clear that the class starts when the assignment for reading/sample exams are given—not when the class convenes for the first time.

2. **Don't Overwhelm the Learners.** Once trainers decide to use pre-work, they often push as much of the straightforward "factual" content into pre-work elements. This tends to discourage the learners from taking the work seriously or leads to a superficial coverage of the material presented. Limit the amount of pre-work to no more than ten hours.

3. **Provide a Schedule for Completion.** Learners find it helpful to have a pace at which they are expected to complete the work. Humans tend to procrastinate so learners often think they can complete the work the night before the class. This isn't possible, so it is helpful to publish a reasonable schedule for completion along with reminders and, if necessary, consequences of falling too far behind.

4. **Make Testing a Part of the First Meeting.** Make it clear that learners will be given an exam when the class starts meeting. The test not only serves as a motivator but also a "wake-up call" for those learners who may have felt they already knew the material.

5. **Share the Reason for Pre-Work.** Learners find it helpful to know why they are being asked to do the pre-work (see number 6 below). Make sure they understand why it is necessary and the consequences of not doing the work.

6. **Use Pre-Work Outputs in the Class.** Pre-work allows learners to create practical real-world examples that can form the basis of case histories that are developed in class.

7. **Focus on Results, Not on Process.** Even when the pre-work may not have been completed prior to the beginning of class, if testing and use of pre-work products are part of the class, participants who failed to complete the work prior to the start of class will find themselves using evenings after the class starts to catch up. As long as this doesn't detract from the experience of others, it is the result—them completing the work—that counts.

In summary, the HoTspot approach was deemed highly successful in accomplishing all four of its major objectives (see above). Participants scored equally well or better on the certification examination and demonstrated application tools at an equal or more frequent level than previous face-to-face participants. A significant reduction in overall costs was achieved and project managers were able to continue to manage their projects without being removed from the field.

One interesting by-product of a previous HoTspot training with another organization was the increase in the number of female participants in the training. Previous statistics for face-to-face training indicated that approximately 75 to 80 percent of the participants were male. However, for the blended learning/HoTspot approach, slightly more than 50 percent of the participants were female. Women often have primary caregiver responsibilities in these communities (in rural locations in Latin America, Africa, and Asia, for example) making it difficult for them to attend classes that would necessitate them being away from children and families for several nights. Because travel was not required for the blended courses, women were more likely to sign up. NGOs such as World Vision and Oxfam perceive this as a real benefit of using a blended learning approach versus other alternatives.

The success of the HoTspots has led to the plan that all PMD Pro1 courses will be delivered via this approach in the future with face-to-face courses being reserved for the more advanced application requirements of PMD Pro Level 2. All new PMD Pro1 trainers are being taught not only how to deliver the courses in a face-to-face environment but also in a blended environment. This requires significant new skills for the trainers but promises a much broader and deeper penetration of the professional project management capacity building for the organization.

61

Building Experience into Simulations

James Chisholm, Greg Warman, and Andrew Webster
ExperiencePoint

WHAT'S A SIMULATION? That's a fair question! The universe of learning simulations is expanding rapidly. So much so that the word *simulation* has, confusingly, come to suggest vastly different things to different people. To help orient you, we feel it's useful to describe the characteristics of simulations within our corner of this growing universe:

- Simulations focus on critical and complex leadership concepts (for example, leading change, innovating).

- They are event-based, even when online technology has a critical role.

- They are facilitator-led, thus providing additional expertise, guidance, and feedback.

- And, finally, simulations are team-based, enabling both collaboration and competition.

For further clarity, here's what we won't be covering: experiences that teach simple relationships and rote processes; dynamic role play (which is an experiential education topic unto itself); and anything where a computer is a human surrogate (in our opinion, computers don't make very good people).

Leadership Development

Experience is a particularly effective teacher for two types of leadership development: *catalyzing epiphanies* and *building capabilities*.

Experience succeeds at catalyzing epiphanies by challenging and disrupting a person's mental models. Everyone has witnessed that "teachable moment" when results differ from what people were expecting, their default approach is challenged, and suddenly, they become open to seeing and doing things differently.

Experience succeeds at building capabilities because leadership is a practice. Indeed, it isn't something you just know. It's something you do. The know-how critical to succeed as a leader is textured and nuanced and is best acquired and honed by doing.

Yet experience is a teacher with serious flaws. It takes a long time; it's fraught with risks (mistakes can carry a high price); and, because of complexity, it can result in confusion rather than clarity.

The simple beauty of simulations is in their ability to make experience an even better teacher. By removing the superfluous and closing the gap between decisions and results, simulations compress time—the essentials of a multi-month project can be experienced in mere hours. Because they offer a safe space for mistakes, learning occurs without risk to careers or company coffers. And through a combination of select content, well-designed user interfaces, and targeted scoring, simulations can focus users' learning.

Key Design Principles

After nearly two decades in the simulation industry, we're happy to share what we've learned through experience and, in so doing, hopefully spare you some pain. Whenever we create a simulation experience, we're guided by a set of design principles that have consistently proven effective. These principles should not be considered mutually exclusive or collectively exhaustive, but we're optimistic they'll help you have a go at the design and integration of simulations in your leadership development. See Exhibit 61.1 for a checklist of these design principles.

Principle 1: Elevate Engagement

The challenge is to create *flow* by ensuring the exercise is challenging enough to amplify interest but not so difficult that it feels frustratingly impossible or creates feelings of inadequacy. Tactics that can help accomplish this include the following:

Set the stage early by connecting the exercise's purpose with the realities faced by the audience. Additionally, you can pique an appetite for what's to come with a *brief* explanation of why a simulation is a meaningful learning tool for the topic at hand and with an overview of what people will tackle and how they can succeed.

Exhibit 61.1. Simulation Design Checklist

Principle 1: Elevate Engagement

❑ Have I connected the exercise's purpose with my audience's realities?

❑ Do participants make decisions within the first five minutes of the session?

❑ Have I structured activities and facilitation in the exercise in accordance with an "engagement arc"?

❑ Have I built humor into the simulation scenario?

Principle 2: Make It Realistic, Not Real

❑ Does the simulation scenario avoid fantasy themes?

❑ Is the simulation scenario close enough to reality that the situation *feels* familiar?

❑ Can I map the exercise to real business challenges?

❑ Have I encouraged action via tight timelines and imperfect information?

❑ Have I simplified the scenario to promote lesson clarity?

Principle 3: Build in Risk and Competition

❑ Have I found ways to celebrate different types of success?

❑ Have I avoided highlighting those teams that performed poorly?

❑ Does the exercise avoid linking simulation performance to real-world performance evaluations?

❑ Does the exercise prompt intra-team discussion and debriefs?

Principle 4: Chunk the Learning

❑ Does the exercise provide knowledge "just in time"?

❑ Are participants able to immediately practice concepts they've just learned?

❑ Do complex decisions have scaffolding?

Principle 5: Focus on What Matters

❑ Have I nurtured a storytelling environment?

❑ Is the scoring aligned to learning objectives?

❑ Does the simulation interface highlight the metrics and decisions that matter?

Expedite "time to first decision" by keeping the preamble to a minimum. When people hear they will play a game, they're usually anxious to start. Too much discussion or presentation up-front can cause enthusiasm to wane quickly. This might mean challenging the impulse to put theory or scaffolding up-front. Even a simple decision like "What should we name our team?" can build engagement and a sense of ownership over the outcome.

Respect the engagement arc through the exercise's structure and masterful facilitation. In early prototypes, perform a monotony audit to identify and fix unproductive downtime. That said, downtime can be used deliberately to signal the completion of a phase, offer time to rest and reflect, or connect with the burning issues back at the office. Seek also to match simulation activities to the predictable ebb and flow of audience energy. For example, you can combat the post-lunch coma with activities that require group collaboration. Finally, a facilitator can increase engagement by intervening when teams are confused or when teams are dangerously close to major missteps.

Have a few laughs by building humor judiciously into the exercise. Humor engages people at an emotional level, and emotion drives attention. Attention facilitates learning.

Principle 2: Make It Realistic, Not Real

A well-designed simulation takes something very complex (the real world), distills it down to the essence of what needs to be taught, and reconstructs it again to feel realistic. Finding the sweet spot requires you to build enough realism to gain credibility with the user but not so much that users assume the specifics of their world apply. On another dimension, you need to offer sufficient complexity to facilitate learning transfer but not so much that game play becomes muddled. Tactics that can help accomplish this include the following.

Avoid metaphorical scenarios that can be dismissed as irrelevant. Some simulations offer opportunities to explore underwater kingdoms or visit remote planets. Although potentially fun and useful for generating epiphanies, metaphorical simulations can hinder transfer. Moreover, the greater the fantasy, the greater the likelihood it will be called out as exclusively fantasy.

Stay one step away from reality so that the scenario is familiar to people. This helps reduce the time required to explain the world of the simulation and consequently provides greater time for learning. We find simulated challenges that have some universal components at the center of the story (for example, organizations that operate in silos or need to improve specific practices) work well. Also, scenario surface features (like specific terminology) prompt application. Indeed, language is one mechanism for ensuring people recognize opportunities to practice what they've learned back on the job.

Map to real business challenges so that people can more clearly connect the dots between insights and application.

Use tools to help with decisions. In the words of Buckminster Fuller, rather than attempting to teach people a new way of thinking, "give them a tool, the use of which will lead to new ways of thinking." The use of tools within a simulation is an excellent method for on-ramping individuals to application.

Give participants too little time and imperfect information so that they are forced to act rather than overanalyze. Action results in feedback, from which people have the opportunity to learn. This helps cultivate a critical meta-skill—the ability to make decisions quickly even when all the facts are not available.

Simplify the universe to promote lesson clarity. One of the biggest challenges in the simulation design process is managing stakeholder input to keep everyone focused on learning outcomes and not on adding details that dilute this focus. Start with a narrow decision set to reduce complexity. Complexity can always be layered in afterward, but it comes at a cost and these costs must be weighed. For example, a simulation of a packaged goods company may focus on just a handful of products (note that with even two products, users can explore the dynamics of tradeoffs). As another example, simulations of organizations can use a few stakeholders as proxies for the myriad of interests in the system. These abstractions help limit distractions and enable lesson clarity.

Principle 3: Build in Risk and Competition

Risk and competition are related and serve at least two goals. First, they enable bravery. Sufficient risk and competition prevent people from knowingly making poor decisions. However, too much risk and competition scare people away from trying something new. Second, they enable interaction with others. Team-based competition encourages collaboration, promotes learning from one another, and is fun. Although some feel that competition is at odds with collaboration, it is undeniable that competition, in some form, is a part of the reality everyone works in, so it is important to replicate it here. Tactics that can help accomplish this principle include the following.

Celebrate success. By defining success in multiple ways (for example, boldest move, regardless of success; most improved; winner of the round; or most consistent), people can enjoy the benefits of competition without the demoralizing effect of losing. And further to this point, should you choose to rank-order teams, our advice is to celebrate the teams at the top without revealing the order of teams at the bottom.

Avoid tying simulation results to a real performance evaluation. A strange thing happens when the simulation becomes an explicit measure of skill: People stop focusing on the learning content and start trying to game the system. We also find that highly valued incentives/prizes can serve to distract from the learning.

Prompt conversations both within and among teams. Competition allows for intra-team comparison and, properly facilitated, can result in teams learning from one another. Why did one team succeed? Why did another fail? What would an optimal hybrid of these teams' performances look like? How did decision-making processes differ? A well-designed simulation works like an inkblot test from psychology—team members project their own experiences and biases on different pieces of content and then must learn from one another to achieve consensus. In our opinion, human interaction trumps tech interaction and usually results in very powerful learning.

Principle 4: Chunk the Learning

Metering out the learning material in a simulation is useful to ensure participants have enough to practice with but not so much that they fail to digest the critical points. Tactics that can help accomplish this include the following.

Think "just-in-time" by providing learning bursts that naturally precede a specific simulation activity. In our Design Thinker simulation, we carefully explain a single bite-sized concept, ask participants to practice in the group, and then ask teams to apply it in the game.

Beyond chunking "what to do," seek opportunities to layer in best practice around "how to do it." At the start of our Experience Change simulation, we teach the use of gestalt language ("In my experience") as an effective meta-skill for influencing and sharing personal experience. As people work through concepts, they're also practicing good process.

Scaffold complex decisions by providing mini-exercises that help teams build the constituent knowledge to make the decision.

Principle 5: Focus on What Matters

The balance to be achieved is between guiding too much, such that discovery learning is lost, and guiding just enough that people's attention is on what they must learn. Tactics that can help accomplish this include the following.

Nurture a storytelling environment to encourage discovery. Simulations are mechanisms for conversation, and storytelling is how we share our experience. When designing a simulation, it is useful to think of the exercise as a container for users' stories and that the role of technology is to increase the volume of that container.

Align scoring to learning objectives. To do this, there are several items to consider. For instance, how will you weight different factors? If a team can earn just as many points for finishing on time as they can for making the most revenue, the team learns that the two are equally important. Another consideration is: What are the new perspectives or new ways of doing things you want folks to try? If teams are rewarded for decisions that reflect specific behaviors, they are more likely to practice those behaviors. And what are the true drivers of performance? Change leadership research suggests that company change efforts don't succeed when they fail to achieve stakeholder buy-in. As a result, our Experience Change simulation has buy-in as the focal metric.

Design interfaces to direct attention to the things that matter most. A good interface helps users understand where they are in the process, reveals relationships between data, and presents cues for action. Here are a few items to include: a progress bar indicating stage of completion; an information tab to access key documents, videos, and pictures; a single decision-making area; and a metrics area. In user testing, listen carefully for the "How do I . . . ?" questions and other moments of user confusion. Unless explicitly desired by the experience, these represent opportunities for improvement in the design.

The Evolution of Our Thinking

The opportunity to work with some of the best educators in the most prestigious organizations, coupled with our education at the not-so-prestigious school of hard knocks, has shaped our point of view. It's worth understanding a (little) bit about what got us here and the current trajectory of our thinking, so you can interpret and build upon what we've discovered.

The early days: In the formative years our simulations were applied as an alternative to lectures in leadership development programs. This was for senior executives or high potential performers from organizations that had noticed holes in knowledge or were seeking to reward people with exposure to leading-edge thinking.

Pre-financial crisis: The "sexy alternative" demand still existed, but the mandate had changed so that there was nearly always a performance gap identified, and learning interventions were expected—although not necessarily measured—to close those gaps. Some thinking related to actual project work became the norm, often taking the shape of action learning. This was a helpful evolution for simulations, which gave people the opportunity to try things out in a practice field before making any public commitments about how they might apply a given concept. Simulations became commonplace.

Today: The application expectation has grown stronger. Investment in leadership development often comes now with an explicit, and always an implicit, investment in moving the needle on at least one initiative. Learning is no longer enough. Organizations want results if they're sending their executives out of the offices for a day or more.

The development field has transitioned from (1) "providing business education" to (2) "building capability," and is now pushing harder to (3) "solve problems." It needs that outcome of (3) for the inputs of (1) and (2). People need to build solutions and shape a path for further meaningful work while they're having fun with a simulation. And of course, they need to do it all in less time.

See Table 61.1 for an overview of how program design adjusts, depending upon the needs that evolving expectations have created.

Creating effective simulations is an exciting challenge, and we hope some of what we've shared will help guide and inspire you to jump in and create your own learning experiences. If you are excited to dive in and get started, you should start small and with an experimental mindset. Consider gamifying an upcoming meeting. Create an opportunity for your colleagues to come together around a common challenge, provoke sharing of their own experiences, reward effort and outcome, and have all leave with a common (and unforgettable) experience. Have fun and let us know how it goes!

Table 61.1. Typical Program Designs

	Pre-Simulation	Simulation	Post-Simulation
1. Leadership Programming "Play with Purpose"		Up to 250 people 4 hours to 2 days	
2. Leadership Development "Building Capability"	Readings Assessments	20 to 50 people 1 day	Further reading
3. Leadership Initiatives "Solving Problems"	Surveys Challenges	10 to 20 people 1 to 2 days	Application Project planning

62

Mentoring: Building Leaders in Powerful Developmental Relationships

Dana Kendall
Seattle Pacific University

FOSTERING MENTORING RELATIONSHIPS among your employees is one way to invest in their personal and career growth, as well as increase knowledge transfer and social capital in your organization. Mentoring is the dynamic, developmental partnership between a relatively experienced individual (mentor) and a relatively inexperienced individual (protégé). Mentorships involve more than short-term, focused coaching or skills training. By contrast, an effective mentor will intentionally invest in their protégés' long-term career growth by: (1) using their influence in the organization to promote and protect the protégé, (2) providing stretch assignments, coaching, and feedback, and (3) offering personal support and friendship.

Because most employee development occurs on the job, in real time, leaders need to build strong networks to accomplish work, develop themselves, and find social support.

The Problem with Just Hoping It Will Happen

There are several potential reasons for why mentoring is not occurring in an organization. First, mentoring relationships are less likely to spontaneously develop in highly competitive organizations. Second, most mentors tend to select protégés who are already high potentials. Outgoing, high performing protégés are the ones who attract and hold the attention of high-profile mentors, whereas those who do not show immediate signs of natural work ability and/or a comfortable sense of sociability are often overlooked. Additionally, women and minorities often report having difficulty accessing a high-ranking mentor to help them navigate through the unique challenges they face in breaking through the glass ceiling.

Finally, on a broad level, it may simply be more difficult to sustain longer-term social relationships than in years past. Technological complexity, mobility, financial pressures in a tight economy, and challenges associated with balancing work and life all serve to stretch our bandwidth. Many of the same factors that prevent meaningful mentorships from forming (i.e., busyness, competitive job markets, financial strain) are the very same dynamics that make it imperative that individuals have mentors to ensure they are contributing to the organization and enhancing their marketable skill sets.

How to Craft and Implement a Mentoring Program
Tailor the Program to Your Organizational Goals

Decide on one primary purpose for the program. What are the outcomes that you eventually would like to achieve as a result of the program? How does the purpose for the program align with the organization-wide strategy? Look for ongoing programs that you can use as a platform for the mentoring program. Examples include the following:

- Socializing newcomers to the organization or work group

- Encouraging leaders to learn from and develop each other

- Preparing the next generation of organizational leaders

- Advancing women and minorities through the glass ceiling

- Supporting leaders who are exploring their future career directions or are struggling in their current roles

Leading with a clear program mission is essential because the structure of the program (for example, recruiting, training, evaluation) will vary, depending on the purpose.

At this point, you can also decide on the duration of your program. Most mentoring programs formally continue for six months to two years, depending on their purpose. For example, six months may be sufficient for an on-boarding mentoring program, whereas one or two years may be more appropriate for working toward more long-term goals, such as preparing protégés for advancement into leadership.

Finally, plan the level of support you will invest in the process. For instance, some organizations invest heavily in matching mentors and protégés. Other organizations create a structure and process for leaders to create their own mentoring relationships. Organizations also differ in the ongoing support they provide. For example, some organizations plan regular events for mentors and protégés to meet together, either for pure recreation or for mentorship maintenance. Other organizations provide a small budget for mentors to take their protégés out for lunch or coffee.

Building a Structured Mentoring Program

Below is a list of best practices that pertain to some of the most important structural elements in building a mentoring program. Exhibit 62.1 summarizes the key questions that mentoring program managers should ask themselves at each stage of the process.

1. Recruiting Participants

Mentoring programs tend to work best when participation is voluntary, especially for mentors. Additionally, you will need to consider your mentor's skills. Much of the success of a mentoring program rests on the skills and dedication of the mentors. How will you screen your mentors to ensure that they will be providing protégés with mentoring that is aligned with the objectives of the program? For instance, if the goal of your mentoring

Exhibit 62.1. Crucial Questions to Ask

Stage	Crucial Questions to Ask
Recruiting mentors and protégés	What are the qualities the mentors should have?
	What is the time commitment expected for mentors?
Matching	What are the key objectives for the program?
	How can the matching strategy be aligned with the objectives?
	How can technology and sponsoring mixers be used to match participants?
Training	What, if any training, is needed to support the mentoring program?
	What tools and resources can be created to improve mentoring relationships and meet the program goals?
	What behaviors are critical in mentoring relationships (e.g., listening, coaching, skill development, sponsorship)?
	How can participants create the right expectations early-on?
	What boundaries should be established to promote a healthy mentorship?
Monitoring and evaluating	What were the original objectives for the program?
	How can we measure the extent to which these objectives are being met?
	How will we build a case for some benefits that will take months or years to actualize?
	What happened to the people who dropped out or did not participate? Are their outcomes being tracked also?

program is succession planning, your mentors should be established leaders who are familiar with and supportive of the strategic direction of the organization. If the goal is socializing new leaders in the organization, ask yourself whether your mentors (1) possess the knowledge that you would want passed to the protégés and (2) are representative of the type of culture you wish to promote.

Pitfalls to Avoid: Provide mentors with realistic time commitments before they sign on. One of the difficulties protégés often report is that their mentors are too busy to meet with them. As part of training/orientation for mentors, discuss ways to help them free up their time for their protégés or how they can build mentoring into their ongoing tasks (e.g., inviting a protégé to a team meeting and discussing what happened afterwards over lunch).

2. Matching Mentors and Protégés

There are many choices of matching strategies. Some give full control to participants as to pairings. For example, you could host an event like a party or dinner where participants get to know one another and naturally pair up. Other matching methods give participants very little input into who they are matched with. Sometimes mentoring program managers simply match individuals randomly or by convenience (e.g., geographic proximity). Still other methods involve protégés choosing from an online pool of mentor profiles or using computer software to aid in matching, based on similar interests, career goals, etc. Allow participants as much input into the matching process as possible. This is not always doable if the program has very specific goals (i.e., succession planning or advancing minorities), or if ten protégés happen to select the same, popular mentor.

Pitfalls to Avoid. You should provide an "exit strategy" for program participants if a match is not working out. Differing values, work schedules, distance constraints, and even harassment and abuse can all pose hazards that are best anticipated and addressed (not necessarily belabored) beforehand. Because protégés are generally in a position of less power, empower them to end the mentorship through the proper channels if things are not working out.

3. Training

Provide at least minimal training to participants with the following information presented. To begin, present the purpose of the program and the outcomes that the program should accomplish. During the training, create a space for mentors and protégés to communicate one another's expectations. Create guidelines and expectations for the mentors and protégés. The guidelines might include the following.

For mentors, guidelines might include: How often the mentors and protégés should meet; guidelines around confidentiality; ideas for opportunities that they can give protégés to push them on the learning edge while supporting and protecting them in the midst of it; and how to give feedback that is forthright in a caring way.

For protégés, guidelines might include: how to receive feedback, respecting a mentor's time, and how to be proactive in the relationship by asking questions and initiating the scheduling and agendas for meetings.

Pitfalls to Avoid. Providing effective mentoring is not easy. Conversely, it is often a sacrifice of time, resources, and even reputation, in the case of struggling, "risky" protégés. Do all you can to prepare your mentors for their roles. Provide times and spaces for them to meet to support one another as well. Perhaps training would be a good time to help them think through hypothetical situations (e.g., times when mentors put their reputations on the line for a protégé, and he or she does not follow through. How can the organization help mentors manage this risk?)

Finally, encouraging conversations between mentors and protégés regarding places and times where they can meet in the future may be helpful for establishing norms for the mentorship going forward. It is a good idea to solidify these details and expectations before the relationship is well underway. For example, they each can disclose how comfortable/feasible it will be for them to meet outside of work hours as opposed to meeting during work time. Additionally, they can discuss their own schedules and the possible constraints that could hinder meeting on a regular basis. Protégés often report that mentors are too busy to meet with them on a regular basis, so engaging in these kinds of conversations up-front may help ensure that both dyad members are thinking ahead about ways to prioritize the mentorship.

4. Monitoring and Evaluating the Mentoring Program

Decide early on who will be in charge of managing and evaluating the initiative. Then decide how and when data will be collected. Many organizations employ brief, anonymous online surveys throughout the program in order to keep an ear to the ground on how things are progressing and troubleshoot any difficulties. You can also employ voluntary focus groups early in the program and then again at the conclusion of the program to provide more nuanced, richer insights than surveys can capture.

Pitfalls to Avoid. Keep the program objectives in mind. In other words, what did you initially set out to accomplish? If you wished to develop protégés as leaders, how will you assess their skills at the conclusion of the program? If you wished to teach protégés how build their own network of mentors, how and when will you assess their capacities to do so? Sometimes the benefits of an effective mentorship do not accrue for protégés right away. For example, salary raises, promotions, or other opportunities that resulted from skills gained in the mentoring relationship do not occur until some time has passed. How will you account for this lag time in the evaluation process? Is there a way you can compare individuals who participated in the mentoring program versus those on the waiting list, in terms of their outcomes and effectiveness? Each of these questions will help set up your evaluation plan for success.

What If Our Resources Are Insufficient to Build a Structured Mentoring Program?

In the absence of a formal company-wide program, there are a number of simple and low cost strategies you can pursue to begin building a mentoring culture in your organization. First, in the on-boarding process, provide new employees with tip sheets on how they can find their own mentors. The logical place to begin is the supervisory relationship, with the ultimate goal of branching out to build a network of mentors. Because supervisors/mentors often have so many challenges demanding their attention, focus your efforts on teaching employees to be effective protégés. In practice, this will look slightly different in each organization. Work with your HR department to come up with ways to teach individuals to interact with supervisors and other potential mentors in ways that maximize results. Generally speaking, individuals need to practice building connections by capitalizing on mutually beneficial exchanges. For instance, if a supervisor wants a quick tutorial on some unfamiliar aspect of technology, a younger subordinate can offer to lend a hand in teaching those skills in exchange for extra coaching on long-term career goals. Supervisors and mentors appreciate protégés who are not just "takers," but rather look for ways to reciprocate.

Second, provide mentors and protégés with a guide to identify the goals of the mentorship and impose their own structure regarding how objectives will be met and how often they will plan to meet. (For an example of a completed mentoring guide, see Exhibit 62.2.) Tailor the guide to your own organization's culture and objectives. Mentoring tools will help focus the goals of the mentorship as well as encourage employees to be intentional about their growth and development. Finally, providing these kinds of tools is a cost-effective way to send a powerful message about the extent to which the company values developmental relationships, even if a full-scale mentoring initiative is not yet feasible.

Final Thoughts

Mentoring relationships offer a significant opportunity to enhance experience-driven leadership development. Helping people throughout the organization draw on and support each other is too important to leave to chance. Employees will be more likely to engage in and value healthy developmental relationships with a little guidance, help, and support. Mentoring can be learned; it consists of skills that are practiced and improved over time. Organizational structures and programs can go a long way in providing a supportive environment to develop such capabilities, sometimes at a relatively low cost. A number of additional resources exist to build a strong formal mentoring program (see the Resources list). Strong commitment to your employees—your organization's most powerful resource—is essential for fostering a culture in which investing in others' growth is esteemed, appreciated, and prioritized.

Exhibit 62.2. Sample Mentoring Plan

Mentorship Goals

Jennifer (the mentor) will help Lisa (the mentee) to:
- Expand her network in the organization

- Develop her marketing skills

- Develop her long-term career goals

- Improve her ability to do her current job well and "get things done" in this company

Anticipated Challenges	Advance Planning for Challenges
Lisa is new to the company and the department. Neither Lisa nor Jennifer has a lot of extra time so conversations are probably going to need to take place over lunch or other down times. Jennifer is currently managing multiple mentees and subordinates.	Lisa and Jennifer will meet once a month over lunch. Lisa is responsible for scheduling the meetings. For the sake of flexibility, other meetings will have to take place by phone or via the web.
Mentor Responsibilities	**Protégé Responsibilities**
Jennifer will introduce Lisa to key individuals in the company who will be valuable in helping Lisa do her work and in exploring future career opportunities in the organization. Jennifer will provide Lisa an opportunity to review the annual marketing plan and present part of it at the monthly meetings. Jennifer will provide feedback after each presentation. Jennifer will meet with Lisa at least once per month.	Lisa will draft a list of the key stakeholders who can help her get her work done and future career paths she would like to explore. Lisa will create and bring an agenda for each meeting. Lisa will prepare a section of the marketing plan for the organization. Lisa will seek feedback from her mentor and write down specific actions she will take to improve based on the feedback.

Resources

For more information on implementing structured mentoring programs, see:

- Allen, T.D., Finkelstein, L.M., & Poteet, M.L. (2009). *Designing workplace mentoring programs: An evidence-based approach.* London, UK: Wiley-Blackwell.

- Ragins, B.R., & Kram, K.E. (2007). *The handbook of mentoring at work: Theory, research and practice.* Thousand Oaks, CA: Sage.

For more information on helping employees understand how to be a good mentor and a good protégé, see:

- Ensher, E., & Murphy, S.E. (2005). *Power mentoring: How successful mentors and protégés get the most out of their relationships.* San Francisco, CA: Jossey-Bass.

Business-Driven Action Learning

Yury Boshyk
The Global Executive Learning Network

63

BUSINESS-DRIVEN ACTION LEARNING (BDAL) is an approach used by companies and organizations to engage their people in exploring and resolving critical challenges and opportunities, while at the same time enhancing their leadership development and self-awareness. It integrates aspects of project-based action learning, which appeared on the organizational development scene in the late 1980s with traditional action learning as developed in the United Kingdom by Reg Revans and others.

Action learning relies on sets, or groups, of no more than six people working on business problems and leadership dilemmas. It is grounded in principles that stress mutual help and collaboration, empowerment, "questioning" inquiry, learning and reflection. Action learning works at a pace faster than or equal to the rate of change, and teams or task forces tackle real business challenges that face their organizations. Figure 63.1 illustrates the key elements of BDAL.

BDAL started life primarily in global companies in the early-1990s, and over the years many organizations have incorporated the method into their management and executive programs. BDAL can be used to create experience-based learning systems for all enterprises—small, medium, and large. Action learning interventions don't have to be limited to leaders. They can also involve a company's stakeholders (for example, customers, suppliers, government officials, and civic society NGOs). Some aspects of the BDAL method are used in public service education as well. While most BDAL occurs in management and executive

Figure 63.1. What Is Business-Driven Action Learning?

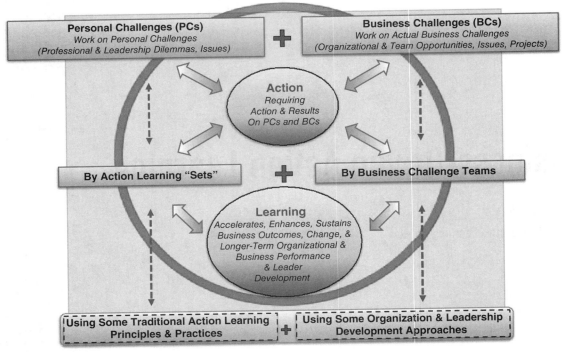

programs, BDAL can also be initiated in almost any context where work takes place. The crucial element with BDAL is its multiple foci on explicit organizational, team, and individual learning.

There are several objectives and components to a BDAL approach and program. In order for BDAL to be successfully optimized, all of its components should be included and aligned with one another. Seven components have emerged as particularly important in building effective BDAL programs (see Figure 63.2):

1. *Top executive ownership:* Sponsorship, support, and active engagement.

2. *Information capture and knowledge sharing:* The use of technology, such as websites and collaborative tools, to cascade learning.

3. *Company-wide sharing and collaboration with business challenge stakeholders:* Engaging those who know, who care, and who can do something about the business challenge.

4. *Individual development (personal and peer coaching and sharing, personal development plans, reflection):* The use of coaches, assessments, 360 feedback, and learning tools to assist and encourage individuals to gain greater self-awareness that leads to behavioral change.

Figure 63.2. BDAL: The Seven Key Components

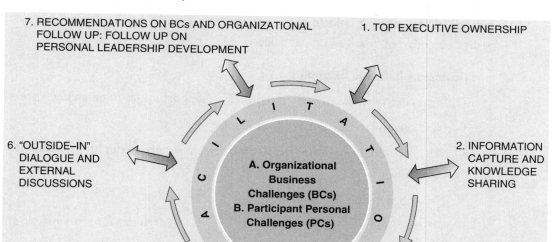

5. *Teamwork on business challenges and action learning sets on personal challenges:* Self-managed sub-teams that address the business challenge and small groups or teams that help clarify thinking and acting on personal challenges.

6. *"Outside-in" dialogue and external discussions:* Conversations that involve stakeholders, thought leaders, customers, and others about the business challenge and other issues relating to the external environment of the organization; also, discussions with external peers on leadership and personal business challenges.

7. *Recommendations on business challenges and follow-up.* Organizational implementation and evaluation and further personal leadership development: A plan for what top executives in the organization will do with the recommendations and what further commitments and actions will be undertaken for leadership development.

Crafting the Business Challenge

At the heart of BDAL is a business challenge (or opportunity) for the organization. A business challenge is an issue without a clear and obvious solution. The top leadership of the company is responsible for providing business challenges for the BDAL program and to participants. These are almost always in the form of dilemmas that demand clarification, exploration, analysis, a decision, and recommendations. Business challenges are usually strategic in nature and bold in scope because they tend to be the nature of issues at the senior executive or board of directors level.

Business Challenge Examples

- What are some exceptional growth-related opportunities in emerging markets?

- How can we accelerate growth in mature markets?

- What are some key future trends and how do we get to the future ahead of our competition?

- How do we stimulate innovation?

- What are some critical elements that we need to consider for our strategic and sustainable growth?

- How do we create a $1 billion service- and solutions-based business?

- If a low-market share competitor disrupts the market, how can we compete?

Each business challenge is accompanied by a detailed background document (a business challenge statement) that outlines the reasons why this is an important issue for the company. The statement contains a detailed listing of what is expected from participants tackling the business challenge(s). Internal and external subject matter specialists provide background on the business challenge, but that background isn't as important as the participants' generating fresh questions about the business challenge in order to stimulate innovative recommendations. In some companies no participant is allowed on such a program if they have expert knowledge about the business challenge in order to ensure a completely fresh look at the issue.

Identifying Personal Challenges

The other major objective of BDAL is to help individuals better understand themselves and do something about their personal leadership and business challenges. These challenges can be daily dilemmas, problems, or seemingly unresolvable matters. Personal leadership challenges often speak to leadership and management situations such as leading without authority, doing more with less, motivating subordinates and fellow team members in difficult times, or engaging with clients and their work.

Personal challenge discussions are addressed in action learning sets—small teams of leaders who coach each other using a systematic and inclusive process developed by Revans and by others. Through a structured yet largely self-facilitated process using open-ended questions, sets help clarify issues for individual leaders and assist them throughout the process associated with individual behavioral change. Facilitation is carried out throughout

Exhibit 63.1. Sharing Personal Challenges with Set Members

- Describe your personal leadership and/or leadership challenge (PC) through a narrative account
- Each presenter gets equal time (from 30–60 minutes)
- Others in the set (usually no more than six) ask **open-ended** questions
- Decide on action points to take forward and commit to, and share this with the group
- Report on ensuing events at a subsequent meeting of the group

a BDAL program and in the action learning sets, but only when requested by participants and only as required to initiate the process.

Action learning sets meet regularly throughout the program to discuss their personal challenges. Exhibit 63.1 describes the process that leaders use to share their personal challenges within their sets.

"Outside-ins" connected to work on the business challenge and personal challenge are a very critical component of the BDAL method. Outside-in interviews can be with clients, suppliers, thought leaders, government and regulatory officials, and even competitors. BDAL participants are encouraged to interview these people by asking open-ended questions and not to prepare questions or checklists that are designed to confirm or refute their opinions.

Working in small teams of two to three people, each team takes the time and makes the effort to learn as much as possible about the leader and about the business. This is not tourism but a serious and thorough process of capturing, analyzing, and sharing new perspectives from the "outside," as can be seen in Figure 63.3.

Each meeting is written up thoroughly and then shared with other members of the larger team of participants. Each write-up also has a section on what they learned from the experience, using what is referred to as "The Seven Dimensions of Learning" (see Figure 63.4).

The preparation for these meetings involves an effort to ensure proper alignment and relevance for participants, the company, and for the external dialogue partners. This element of BDAL works best when there is good collaboration and alignment established well before and after a program between executive sponsors, participants, internal subject-matter experts, and external specialist organizers.

Eventually, the completed write-up finds its way to the program website for sharing within the entire company after the program. It becomes the repository and the center of information, knowledge, and collaboration before, during, and after a management or executive program. The lessons gleaned from dealing with business challenges and personal challenges remains on the website for both private and general use and for post-program alumni networking.

Figure 63.3. Preparation and Implementation of the "Outside-In" Conversations

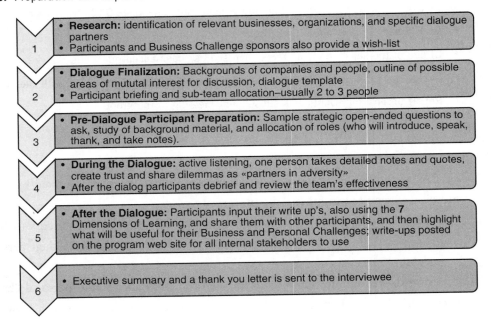

1
- **Research:** identification of relevant businesses, organizations, and specific dialogue partners
- Participants and Business Challenge sponsors also provide a wish-list

2
- **Dialogue Finalization:** Backgrounds of companies and people, outline of possible areas of mututal interest for discussion, dialogue template
- Participant briefing and sub-team allocation—usually 2 to 3 people

3
- **Pre-Dialogue Participant Preparation:** Sample strategic open-ended questions to ask, study of background material, and allocation of roles (who will introduce, speak, thank, and take notes).

4
- **During the Dialogue:** active listening, one person takes detailed notes and quotes, create trust and share dilemmas as «partners in adversity»
- After the dialog participants debrief and review the team's effectiveness

5
- **After the Dialogue:** Participants input their write up's, also using the **7** Dimensions of Learning, and share them with other participants, and then highlight what will be useful for their Business and Personal Challenges; write-ups posted on the program web site for all internal stakeholders to use

6
- Executive summary and a thank you letter is sent to the interviewee

Figure 63.4. The Seven Dimensions of Learning

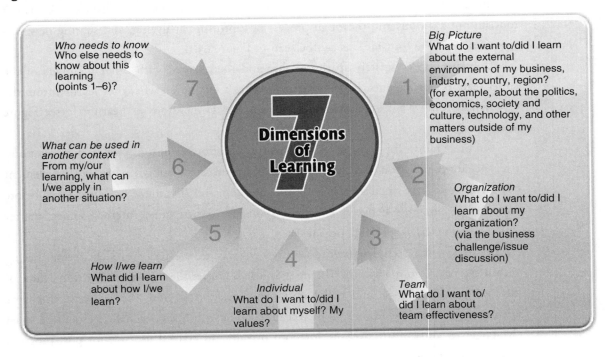

Who needs to know Who else needs to know about this learning (points 1–6)?

What can be used in another context From my/our learning, what can I/we apply in another situation?

How I/we learn What did I learn about how I/we learn?

Individual What do I want to/did I learn about myself? My values?

Team What do I want to/did I learn about team effectiveness?

Organization What do I want to/did I learn about my organization? (via the business challenge/issue discussion)

Big Picture What do I want to/did I learn about the external environment of my business, industry, country, region? (for example, about the politics, economics, society and culture, technology, and other matters outside of my business)

7 Dimensions of Learning

Some Things That Could Go Wrong

When companies report a less than successful result on the business challenge(s), they usually mention the following:

- Lack of clarity by senior executives, and lack of alignment with participants on the business challenge and the expected deliverables by executives and participants.

- Participants who were not appropriate for the business challenge: usually too junior, inexperienced, or chosen for the wrong reason (for example, as a reward for their previous performance or length of service), or they were not able to understand the business challenge and lacked the business acumen needed to solve the problem or challenge.

- Dysfunctional teams working on the business challenge that were not able to reach agreement and to work together.

- Some teams lacked the courage to say what they really thought about the business challenge and hence their recommendations lacked depth and clarity, and their presentation was unpersuasive.

BDAL Success Factors and Lessons Learned

Successful BDAL interventions share several common characteristics. Some of the most important ones are listed below.

- *The "right" organizational culture is required for BDAL.* In closed, very controlling cultures, it is difficult to design and implement BDAL correctly, let alone in a manner optimizing and integrating all the seven component parts. Senior leaders who act as sponsors of BDAL programs must trust their people and trust the process.

- *The active support and participation of top executives is essential.* It's important to remember that the business challenges that are being addressed arrive from top executive teams. In turn, senior executives must appreciate that BDAL is more than just a taskforce: It integrates business challenges and personal challenges. Senior executives must actively engage on several fronts: by selecting strategic business challenges or opportunities with clear outcomes and follow-up; by participating in the selection of participants to help set the right business focus, and by directly engaging in the program (as leaders teaching leaders) or in a BDAL learning intervention.

- *The best senior executive sponsors are those who understand that there can be no action without learning, and no learning without action.* The ideal sponsor should ensure and allow a balance between action and learning in a BDAL program and not just a focus on business results.

- *The program manager/director is very important.* This should be someone who is well connected to the top leadership and is seen as a business partner. This helps in aligning roles and processes, and content in a way that is constructively challenging.

- *Company-wide support.* Mobilize internal stakeholders who know, care, and can do something about resolving the business challenge.

- *The involvement of key stakeholders outside the company can help with clarifying and resolving the business challenge.* This can include customers, suppliers, best practice companies, subject-matter specialists, thought leaders, government representatives, and others.

- *Information capture and knowledge sharing can be magnified through a collaborative website.* A website can leverage the processes and expand the learning to other parts of the company.

- <u>*BDAL is more than just a program.*</u> The follow-up component of the program is as important as the program or event. This includes following up on business challenge recommendations by senior executive BDAL sponsors, on the outside-in participants, personal challenge development, action and learning commitments, and the details of how and when. Many organizations do not spend much time nor devote enough resources to this aspect of BDAL. Those that do find that there is an easy transition to an appreciation that BDAL can be used in on-the-job contexts, with intact business teams, and in helping boards make decisions on such things as strategy and investment decisions.

requires follow-up!

- *From initial discussion or exploration of the idea to implementation BDAL programs takes <u>approximately two years</u>.* After building support for the work, the actual planning and preparation for the first BDAL program takes about six months.

- *Failure can also be a powerful learning experience.* A failed BDAL program with mediocre recommendations on the business challenge often results in great learning; but a company and its leadership must be prepared to tolerate perceived shortcomings. They can take the opportunity to develop leaders and develop themselves.

- *The results from work on the business challenges are usually positive.* For many companies, there is no need for an ROI (return on investment) analysis of a BDAL program because the results are so obvious. In the opinion of one very successful practitioner in Asia: "If there is a request for an ROI on a BDAL program, either there is lack of trust in the process or the people involved."

Resources

Boshyk, Y. (2000). *Business-driven action learning: Global best practices*. New York-London, UK: Macmillan Business.

Boshyk, Y. (2012). What is business-driven action learning today? In M. Pedler (Ed.), *Action learning in practice* (4th ed.) (pp. 141–152). Aldershot, UK: Gower.

Boshyk, Y. (2012, August). Understanding the many varieties of action learning. Presentation at the MIT Action Learning Conference, Sloan School. http://video.mit.edu/watch/2012-mit-sloan -action-learning-presentation-by-yury-boshyK–12301/

64

Action Learning with Community-Based Nonprofits

Lynn Fick-Cooper and Shera Clark
Center for Creative Leadership

I N AN INCREASINGLY complex and fragmented U.S. health system, community-based non-profit organizations provide critical support for millions of underserved Americans. These organizations encounter growing demand for services at the same time that their financial resources are decreasing. The impending exodus of senior nonprofit leaders due to the retirement of the baby boom generation exacerbates the challenges of developing leaders for nonprofit organizations. According to Tierney (2009) by 2016 the nonprofit sector will need approximately eighty thousand new senior managers each year. To address these obstacles, nonprofits need to develop new leaders who can create innovative, client-focused practices, manage day-to-day operations, and serve as visionary catalysts for systemic change.

The Robert Wood Johnson Foundation (RWJF) partnered with the Center for Creative Leadership (CCL) to create a fellowship program that would develop the next generation of community health leaders and equip them with the skills needed to lead their organizations in the future. After conducting ten months of field research to fully understand the needs of the emerging leaders now as well as what would be expected of them in the future in more senior leadership roles, we developed a sixteen-month curriculum including face-to-face classroom-based programs, action learning projects, individual coaching, and

Figure 64.1. Design of Ladder to Leadership Program

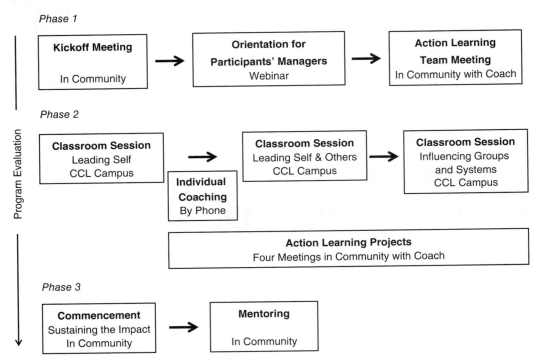

mentoring (see Figure 64.1). We learned from the hundreds of people we surveyed and talked to in both focus groups and interviews that the leadership competencies deemed most necessary were collaborative leadership skills, political savvy, influencing skills, networking skills, the ability to work across boundaries, systems thinking, visionary thinking, and time management skills.

Developing the curriculum was both an exciting and daunting endeavor. RWJF was willing to invest in a comprehensive process to develop these emerging leaders and equip them with long-lasting skills and behaviors in all of these areas. Designing and delivering such a curriculum was very exciting in a time when many organizations were looking for faster, cheaper solutions. It was equally daunting; however, because we knew the best methodology to truly develop all of the competencies noted above was action learning. To our knowledge at that time, action learning had not been tried within a community setting where there was no hierarchy or centralized leadership to determine the strategic projects and form cross-functional teams. How would we form community leaders into teams and what would they work on? To whom would they be accountable and what would we do about the traditional team sponsor role?

Our Approach

To develop collaborative leadership and networking skills—two of the top-rated competencies noted during the field research—we decided to implement the program using a community-based strategy, rather than creating a national program with participants from different communities. With this design, participants would be practicing collaboration and networking skills while actually building the local collaborative networks that would serve their work beyond the program. In other words, the program would provide a collaborative network-building experience from which they could enhance their skills and have immediate benefits for them in their leadership role. With RWJF we selected thirty emerging leaders in each of the eight different communities across the U.S. in which we implemented the program. As part of their application process, the leaders were asked to tell us what they thought were the most pressing health challenges facing their community and why, which gave us data about the community health challenges the applicants shared in common.

Once selected, the thirty emerging leaders started the action learning process before they ever participated in a developmental program. We conducted a kick-off event in their community during which they formed themselves into teams using an open space process (Owen, 2008). We started the open space process by reflecting back to them the top ten community health challenges they shared in their applications—a starting place for areas in which they already had shared passion and interest. They could add to or redefine the ten topics posted on flip charts around the room as they saw fit. They were given five criteria for team formation:

- A minimum of five and a maximum of seven people per team

- Select a health challenge for which you have genuine passion (primary importance)

- Select a health challenge that will help your organization (secondary importance)

- Consider the objectives of the action learning process itself (e.g., Which of these would be most developmental for you?)

- There must be five different teams at the end of the process

Within ninety minutes all thirty people had formed themselves into five different teams meeting the aforementioned criteria. They voted with their feet and engaged in dialogue with each other at the different flipcharts to understand each other's interest areas and thoughts about those health challenges. They were assigned an action learning coach and a team sponsor and they had their first meetings that same day.

They worked together in their action learning teams for a month before they attended the first classroom-based program. Then they attended a program every four months for a year. Each program had a different focus: individual leadership, team leadership, and systemic leadership. The content of each program was directly applied to their action learning teams and projects, which allowed the action learning process to serve as a real-time learning laboratory for their development (see Exhibit 64.1). The action learning coaches met face-face with their respective teams a minimum of nine times throughout the sixteen months. The teams met more frequently than that to accomplish the projects they chose and sometimes the coach was on the phone for those additional meetings.

Exhibit 64.1. Module Content

Teams applied much of the content in each program session to the work of their project teams. Following are examples of what they were asked to do based on that session's theme:

Individual Leadership

- After receiving their individual Myers-Briggs Type Indicator results, teams engaged in an activity that helped them understand how much time each team member would typically spend on the four different aspects of problem solving—gathering data (Sensing), exploring possible solutions (Intuitive), deciding on a course of action (Thinking), and determining the impact of the decision on people (Feeling). They were asked to discuss the implications of this knowledge for team meetings and processes.

- They were taught the Situation-Behavior-Impact (SBI) tool for giving feedback to other individuals and asked to practice using this tool with their fellow team members.

Team Leadership

- Teams were asked to assess which stage of Tuckman's model of team development applied to them at that moment and what they needed to do to move to the next stage.

- They were given the Fundamental Interpersonal Relations Orientations–Behavior (FIRO-B) instrument, which measures the degree to which we express and want three different interpersonal needs—Inclusion, Control, and Affection, as a way to deepen their understanding of team dynamics.

- Participants were taught a variety of tactics for more effectively managing conflict with others and then were video-taped in conflict role plays applying those skills.

- Teams were also exposed to Peter Block's Stakeholder Analysis model and asked to apply this model to the stakeholders of their project.

Systems Leadership

- Participants were taught a variety of influence tactics and boundary spanning leadership tactics that they were asked to put into practice during a simulation that required the entire cohort to collaborate to solve a community health problem. They were encouraged to think about how those tactics could help them with the implementation of their team project.

- They were taught storytelling techniques and required to apply them to the final presentation they were due to make at their commencement event. They were given class time to begin crafting their stories.

Given the lack of accountability to an organization's senior leadership team or CEO, we expected certain deliverables along the way. Each team was required to create a team charter, which forced the team to have a discussion early in their process about how they were going to work together, resolve conflict, and hold each other accountable. They had to create a logic model (or theory of change) for their project and write an impact statement to explain what they planned to accomplish, or what impact they intended to have on the health challenge they sought to address. These were due mid-way through the process. At each face-to-face program session the teams were required to present their progress—both what they were accomplishing with the project and what they were learning as individuals and as a team—to the entire cohort and faculty. Finally, at the commencement event conducted in their community, each team had to prepare a ten-page paper outlining the results they had achieved and perhaps more importantly, they had to present their results using story-telling techniques to 100+ members of their home community, including colleagues from their respective organizations, family members, their mentors, and many of the stakeholders of their project. The combination of their own personal desire to actually effect change in some meaningful way on the health challenges they chose to address and the deliverables and expectations we had of them as requirements for their sixteen-month fellowship proved quite effective in holding the teams accountable. See Table 64.1 for some examples of successful team projects.

Lessons Learned

Key Success Factors

Although multiple factors contributed to the success of the overall initiative and specifically the action learning process, two factors stand out: individual choice and a focus on learning. Without these, we might not have achieved success.

Table 64.1. Successful Project Examples

Community Problem Being Addressed	Project Summary
Increasing the engagement of some of the community's most vulnerable citizens	The team partnered with the administration, facilities staff, medical personnel, patients, and community members of the hospital located in the most vulnerable part of the community to create a community garden on hospital grounds. The patients and medical and administrative staff co-own the development and maintenance of the garden and tend it side-by-side. This has improved patient-staff relationships and has given purpose to many of the most disenfranchised patients. One gentleman, who never left his house before this, now takes the bus twice a day to tend the garden.
Improving the health education of teens	The team worked directly with teens to develop a Health-E-Teen website that partners teens with medical personnel to host online discussions and craft texting campaigns that educate teens about critical health issues. The team even generated grant funding for the development of the website.
Childhood obesity and food deserts	The team partnered with a Village Market store and an elementary school in a neighborhood where no fresh vegetables and produce were available and created a "Kids Corner" with healthy snack options that kids create themselves using healthy fruits and vegetables.
Obesity and diabetes	The team partnered with a national grocery store chain to bring online grocery shopping to disenfranchised citizens in a housing project for a reduced fee, allowing these residents to have fresh vegetables and produce delivered to their neighborhood. The project included education sessions with residents on healthy food choices and how to use the online shopping tools.

At every step of the way, the participants had a choice about their involvement or commitment. There was no boss, HR executive, or CEO requiring their participation in the fellowship or their presence on a team. Their own personal commitment, passion, and desire to succeed in their organization and community brought them to the program initially and also kept them engaged and committed throughout the sixteen months. In addition, they had complete choice about which project team they chose to join. It was their passion to effect change in the chosen project area and their desire to develop long-lasting collaborative relationships in their own community that sustained them through the difficulties involved in this kind of collaborative work.

One benefit of not having a centralized hierarchy to which we were accountable in each community was the freedom to truly focus on the learning happening during the teams' project work. While we wanted the teams to achieve meaningful outcomes for their community (and they did in most cases) and we had stakeholders invested in the success of their respective projects, one organization's "bottom line" was not the primary focus. The building of sustainable individual capacity for collaborative work was our primary focus and the projects were a means to develop those skills. The action learning teams provided live laboratories to practice those new skills. We promoted a focus on learning from projects by:

- Having each fellow identify and track progress on leadership development goals;

- Spending time during class sessions and in team meetings processing each personality assessment at the team level—asking themselves about the implications of their diverse styles on their group dynamics;

- Embedding time for individual and team reflection on their learning during meetings with their coaches throughout the process; and

- Requiring deliverables—both oral and written reports—that included a section on what they were learning from the process at the individual and team level.

Traps to Avoid

The flip side to the freedom provided by the lack of a centralized hierarchy is the lack of any real accountability for the project results. Their personal desire to complete the fellowship (and to earn the *RWJF Fellow* designation) provided enough incentive for the fellows to *complete* their project, but didn't necessarily result in successful or highly impactful project outcomes in every case—success was left open to interpretation of the team with some guidance from their coach and sponsor. To encourage excellence, we provided teams with a list of criteria they could use to evaluate their choice of project (see Exhibit 64.2), we provided an influential community member as their team sponsor, and we held a public commencement event where teams had to present their work to 100+ members of the community.

Exhibit 64.2. Criteria for Selecting Appropriate Projects

- Focuses on either a community health system concern or a significant community health issue that is relevant to each Fellow's home agency/organization

- Is within the team's sphere of responsibility and does not compromise similar efforts in the community

- Provides an opportunity for each Fellow to build or strengthen at least one personal leadership skill

- Requires outreach to other community leaders or partners

- Requires leadership to be successfully implemented

- Focuses on a problem or challenge that is complex in nature without one obvious solution

- Has support from each Fellow's organization and from the team's sponsor

- Will likely progress at a rate which will allow the Fellows time to build skills and acquire new knowledge

- Will be completed even if the implementation and follow-up must continue past the time of the program

The selection of the team sponsor was somewhat tricky. In this context, the team sponsor was an experienced community leader who had a desire to mentor and advise emerging leaders in their community to the ways of collaborative change efforts. Their role was to be a resource, a connector, a champion where needed within the community, but not to direct or lead the process for the team. This was challenging for the sponsor and often served as a developmental assignment for them because we selected community leaders who are known for their ability and expertise in "getting it done." Taking a back seat to their less experienced team members was not easy. Consequently, we learned it was important to choose sponsors who are non-judgmental, listen well, and see multiple possibilities to any challenge. They needed a fairly evolved emotional intelligence, including the ability to be fully present in the moment and ask powerful questions; think and act systemically; and live comfortably with paradox and ambiguity to be most successful. These were not easy people to identify and recruit. We left it up to the team and the sponsor to negotiate how much time they spent together, but in hindsight the most successful teams were those that met regularly with their sponsors—e.g.. monthly.

Design and Delivery of the Initiative

Key lessons learned about the design and delivery of the initiative included: (1) the importance of ensuring all parties involved accept the learning focus as a priority over the project outcomes; (2) the need to let the teams move at their own pace in the Tuckman (1965) model of team development (forming, norming, storming, and performing); and (3) the need to be somewhat flexible with the curriculum design given the variations of each community in which we implemented it.

While RWJF and CCL staffs were fully committed to a learning focus, we engaged collaborative partners in each community to help us implement the program. These partners were typically community based health oriented foundations. The local partners had more of a vested interest in the project outcomes for their community than did RWJF or CCL, so finding partner organizations that were supportive of a stronger focus on learning than on project outcome was important. The same is true for the team sponsors we recruited in each community. These individual community leaders had to be supportive of our focus on learning as the main priority. Otherwise they might have driven the team (e.g., directed the team's work) to ensure a certain community outcome versus allowing the team to learn from their own work, regardless of the outcome.

The curriculum was paced such that the content we provided at each face-to-face program session largely mirrored the teams' development, but not in every case. As faculty, we needed to remain patient and let the teams develop at their own pace, which required a level of patience we didn't always naturally possess. And while most of the communities in which we implemented the LTL program were facing the same community health challenges, there were some key differences among communities that required us to be flexible with our program content. We were able to adjust for the most part, but didn't always meet the customized needs of every community context. For example, some communities were dealing with more diversity among their citizens than others. Subsequently, the need of the community health leaders in those areas to develop awareness of the many individual and systemic issues of racism that impact leadership became more critical than in other communities. By the time we realized this in some cases, it was too late to fully change the curriculum to meet their needs.

Coaching Action Learning Teams

Four primary lessons learned about action learning coaching were: (1) the importance of understanding the role of the action learning coach, (2) the importance of establishing a relationship with the team sponsor, (3) the importance of creating a network of action learning coaching support, and (4) how to help the teams strike the appropriate balance between learning and taking action.

The first lesson learned for the action learning coaching role is to understand the skills required and the experience needed to serve as an action learning coach. The goal of the action learning coach is to teach the team how to ask powerful questions and challenge assumptions by modeling that behavior and providing just-in-time tools that help the team improve their group process and support their learning objectives. Ultimately, if the action learning coach is successful, the team becomes independently capable and no longer relies on the coach to engage in these behaviors. With traditional team coaching, on the other hand, the coach remains in the facilitation role throughout the process and the team relies on the coach to ask powerful questions and help the team learn. The action learning coach must be clear about the role and avoid stepping into a facilitator role by lecturing and injecting his or her personal views. While this is true of any action learning coach role, it was particularly important in this context because the participants were emerging leaders with varying degrees of experience and ability to run effective meetings, facilitate group process, or create a project plan. Thus, it would have been tempting to step into a traditional team coaching or facilitation role.

Different than an organizational context, the action learning coach in the community setting has a greater responsibility to establish a relationship with the team sponsor early in the action learning process. Forming this relationship sooner than later will lessen the confusion about the action learning coach role and the team sponsor role. Also, this relationship between the action learning coach and the team sponsor provides a consistent message for the team. Another lesson learned for the action learning coaching role is creating a learning coach network for the action learning coaches. This community of practice offers an opportunity for the coaches to share best practices and to serve as learning partners with one another.

Finally, it is critical for the action learning coach to strike the appropriate balance between the learning experience for the team and the work they are doing for the project. While all action learning teams struggle with this tension between learning and action, in this context the project is not part of any team member's paid job. While they have opted into the fellowship and thus the action learning process, they are less tolerant of the time it takes to complete a project that is outside of their day-day work when the coach continually stops their work to inject time for learning and reflection. Thus, the team is often engaged in the project development more than they are in the learning process. Therefore, the pressure on the coach to identify the appropriate tools that will help the team pause and reflect on the process and help the team to identify the lessons they are learning—all in ways that add value to the actual project—is heightened (see O'Neil & Marsick, 2007, and Rimanoczy & Turner, 2008, for examples of useful tools and strategies to encourage just-in-time reflection in action learning teams).

Summary

Action learning can be an effective method for developing leaders in a community context. It provides a real-time learning laboratory for community leaders to experience and learn from the collaborative process necessary to effect change in complex social problems. If implemented in conjunction with teaching self-awareness, team and systems content, along with the support of both team coaches and sponsors, the learning and project possibilities are endless and new collaborative capacity can be developed within the community.

References

Owen, H. (2008). *Open space technology: A user's guide* (3rd ed.). San Francisco, CA: Berrett-Koehler.

O'Neil, J., & Marsick, V.J. (2007). *Understanding action learning.* New York, NY: American Management Association.

Rimanoczy, I., & Turner, E. (2008). *Action reflection learning.* Mountain View, CA: Davies-Black.

Tierney, T. (2006). *The nonprofit sector's leadership deficit.* Boston, MA: The Bridgespan Group.

Tuckman, B. (1965). Developmental sequence in small groups. *Psychological Bulletin, 63,* 384–399.

65

Better Together: Building Learning Coalitions Across Organizations

Jan Wilmott
Royal Bank of Canada

WELL BEFORE THE beginning of the new century, many large international companies began awaking to the demands of a global market. Looking back over my twenty-plus years in senior leadership and organization development roles at Royal Bank of Canada, UBS, McDonnell Douglas, and The Boeing Company, I find a number of striking similarities. Focused almost exclusively on domestic and overseas sales, product quality, and improving production rates, corporate leaders were (and in some cases still are) just beginning to recognize the need to integrate global resources into all parts of the value stream, including the need to create global leaders.

Although it has become clear that companies need leaders who understand the challenges of globalization, you can't develop experienced and effective global leaders in an isolated U.S. classroom, even a classroom as nice as the Boeing Leadership Center in St Louis, Missouri. For The Boeing Company to become a "Global Enterprise" it has had to adopt a new focus on executive leadership development and new methods of executive education. My experience at The Boeing Company illustrates the lessons I have learned over the years in how to build a strong learning community that extends beyond an organization's boundaries.

In the summer of 1999, Boeing's first Global Leadership Program (GLP) was launched. GLP was the Boeing Leadership Center's initial step in the quest for developing leaders with a global "brain." This program was designed to help create the global mindset required of 21st century executive leaders. GLP, a thirty-day, business-driven, action learning program, provided the opportunity for twenty-seven Boeing executives to gain insight into the history, culture, politics, business practices, and societal norms of a strategically relevant region of the world. Not only did the participants learn from the experience, but the enterprise as a whole gained valuable information and insight. Over the next four years, the GLP team and I led global programs across Northern Europe, Spain, Japan, Italy, China, Australia, Germany, Korea, the United Kingdom, India, Turkey, and Brazil.

Although the externally focused GLP was a fabulous learning experience tied directly to Boeing's global strategy, the organization's executives were still missing the broader perspective gained by day-to-day interactions with senior leaders with a different set of international experiences. It was necessary to mix these executives with leaders from other countries and companies. It became clear that the development of a multicultural experience is crucial for understanding different ways of thinking and doing business. What was needed was a learning consortium created specifically to address these needs.

Developing the Consortium

Educational consortiums have been around for a long time, but they are usually run by individual business schools or for-profit consultancies. And participating companies often have to settle for faculty and curricula that already exist as part of the program. I wanted a game changing development experience that was both cost-effective and strategically focused to Boeing's business needs and the development needs of its top succession candidates. The design had to serve the needs of a very specific population of executives and be easily aligned with Boeing's business priorities. To be impactful, this level of executive development also had to have the visible support (and involvement) of the CEO and executive council. Additionally, Boeing wanted to develop its own high-powered and carefully targeted curriculum and to handpick top faculty, industry thought leaders, and consultants from around the world.

It was decided to create an executive education partnership between a number of like-minded international companies that were business peers and had equal sophistication and maturity in their ideas about leadership development. What was needed was firms similar in size and scope to Boeing—the world's largest aerospace firm—with solid financial performance and a global presence. These businesses should come from diverse regions of the world, represent multiple industry segments, and should not be a significant portion of each other's value streams. Boeing wanted to collaborate with them to jointly create and deliver an exceptional global leadership development experience for a subset of its high potential senior executives.

The next step was to identify partners and sell the idea both internally and externally. The engagement strategy called for each partner to have a representative serving on the steering committee. Conversations were held among ABN Amro Bank, a large banking institution headquartered in The Netherlands; Asea Brown Boveri (ABB), a strong Swiss industrial process engineering, consulting, and supply firm; Broken Hill Proprietary (BHP), an Australian-based mining and minerals company; and Boeing. All three firms Boeing spoke with were well-established international firms that were growing through mergers and acquisitions. And all were keenly interested in having senior executives develop far more global savvy.

The heads of leadership development for ABN Amro, BHP, ABB, and Boeing quickly formed a joint steering committee and agreed to share costs and hosting responsibilities.

Design Considerations

The steering committee quickly came to the conclusion that in order to effectively launch a program of this magnitude, it would be necessary to enlist the aid of an experienced action learning practitioner. Yury Boshyk, director of the Global Forum on Action Learning, had coordinated similar programs at GE's Crotenville and seemed to be the perfect choice as a coordinating partner and lead designer.

The design team agreed that each company would send six to eight participants selected from their executive high potential pools (succession candidates), individuals currently operating at the executive level. It was understood that to be successful the participants must be peers. Ensuring that all participants are high potential senior executive talent, each having similar breadth and depth of leadership and business experience, as well as P&L responsibility, is crucial to successful engagement of program participants.

The four companies agreed to participate actively in the design, delivery, and implementation of events. And as the companies tried to create the best of all possible experiences for global leadership development, it was agreed that action learning was the only way to go.

In the International Consortium Program (ICP), a team of eight to ten executives from each company is given a significant business challenge by their CEO. After four months of interaction and research, they present the results of their work along with recommendations for next steps to their respective executive councils. In programs like this, there's a real relevancy between the content, the problem, and the participants' implementation of a solution. It's leveraging learning and application of learning in real time.

Each company sends an executive team to the three-part program, providing participants with an opportunity to interact with leaders from other companies and gain their perspectives on some of the global issues they're dealing with. One of the interesting things discovered was that an aerospace company, a bank, an industrial products company, and a natural resources company are all too often dealing with the same problems at the executive leadership level. It doesn't seem to matter what industry a company is in. Companies are all dealing with the similar problems:

- Managing through business cycles—aligning people, resources, stakeholders, and ever-changing business plans
- Setting and communicating strategic priorities and context
- Motivating and engaging teams and individuals, engaging key stakeholders
- Seeing and understanding the disruptors of business strategy, be they competitors, technology, geopolitical changes, or financial markets
- Finding effective leadership that can articulate a vision and create followership

As only six or eight executives from each of the partner companies participated in each of these courses, by the end of the fourth year, fewer than fifty Boeing leaders had been through the program—a small portion of the number required to lead Boeing into a successful global future. However, providing deep experiences for the right people was more important than having broad but shallow learning for a broader population. Because of the consortium model and action learning, the experiences of these leaders have been profound.

Many courses are designed for volume, to train large numbers of people quickly, but developing globally savvy leaders is not something that can be rushed. The changes in perspective and understanding must be both deep and broad, and these changes must be practiced in real time to be internalized in a way that changes leadership behavior. It is these changes in behavior that work to change the culture and direction of a company.

The six months of intense teaming with fellow Boeing executives across organizational and regional boundaries also seems to carry a power of its own—one that solidifies and reinforces their own learning and spreads it through connecting organizations. The participating leaders served as catalysts and role models for other leaders in the organization.

Action Learning

There was no doubt that action learning would provide executives with the real experience of what it takes to run a successful global business. It was also a necessity. No one could give nice neat lessons in this new and challenging arena. Global business is the quintessence of an adaptive challenge, which means there are no tried-and-true formulas. In remarks to the initial gathering of the first participants at the Boeing Leadership Center in St. Louis in June 2001, Boeing President and CEO Phil Condit said:

> There are no signposts. There is nothing telling us where the answer lies. So my goals for this class are to give you: (1) a chance to get in there and rummage around in something pretty big and learn from that activity; (2) a chance to learn from each other, to learn what's working, what might work, and to imagine what could be; and (3) a chance to share back and forth inside the group. This class is clearly an experiment. We've not done it before.

But participants were not dropped into the sea without some charts, lifeboats, and swimming lessons. The curriculum was carefully planned, and the first week in St. Louis provided an intense academic but practical set of activities to level set, provide an overview and context for the course, share specific information about each company, and introduce some of the issues and considerations they must engage in the global business arena.

Action learning requires a business relevant focus. To drive this home, the team projects were put before participants during the first week. Perhaps one of the most exciting things about this kind of a program is the way the projects are devised. In conjunction with the CEOs of the four companies, a common theme or organizing focus is devised. Then each CEO or executive committee identifies a related specific business issue for the company's participants, something the company needs top thinkers to devote significant effort toward. The tasks are relevant projects of strategic importance. The program participants become a sort of "red team" focusing their nonpartisan best efforts to address an enterprise-wide issue critical to the future of the company. And they do it in concert with colleagues who bring a wide variety of diverse cultural, industrial, and business perspectives and experiences to the table. The ICP theme for the first program was to create customer value through e-business. No small charge! But one that was relevant to each member company. My bet was that they could, as they participated in a leadership development experience, contribute real business results to their respective companies. (See Exhibit 65.1 for a typical ICP curriculum outline.)

What the Participants Learned

Participants of ICP have said that the program helped them become newly capable in the global world of e-business. They reported that the value came because they were able to share issues and best practices, and acquire a much larger and more complex picture of the world of global international business. As they gained a better understanding of what globalization means, some discovered that Boeing wasn't quite as global as they had thought. Many realized that core leadership challenges seem universal, but how to operate globally is very different depending on where you're working. Some said the challenges facing other companies often put their own into perspective, and the issues of other industries shed light on their own. Many testified to the importance of their increased cultural understanding, for personal growth and for doing business and creating business relationships in other parts of the world. In addition, many developed an increased awareness of and sensitivity to the potential impact of economic growth on local cultures, thinking about ways to grow economies without ruining cultures.

The greatest gain, in the words of many, was the appreciation of multiple points of view, and these multiple perspectives were directly applied to the real business tasks at hand. All spoke to the value of increasing their network of colleagues, both at Boeing and worldwide.

Exhibit 65.1. Typical ICP Curriculum Outline

Three five-day sessions spread over five months:

Module 1: United States–St. Louis

- Growth challenges worldwide and for the Americas
- North America and its political economy
- Creating shareholder value
- The war on talent
- Company best practices in the Americas
- Latin American crisis and the global impact

Module 2: Europe–Zurich

- Key issues and business challenges in Europe
- Leadership, culture, and business challenges
- Europe and the global economy
- Sustainability and growth
- Global leadership
- Company best practices in Europe, Middle East, and Africa

Module 3: Australia–Melbourne

- Key issues and business challenges in Asia and Australia
- Implementing change
- Company best practices in Asia
- Pulling it all together

What the Developers Learned

Creation of the ICP was definitely an assignment as challenging to its developers as the tasks assigned by their C-suite bosses were to the participants.

Some people may think creating and maintaining leadership development consortiums is pretty much like dealing with any other type of leadership program, but anyone holding that view will quickly change his or her mind once the challenge is taken on. Consortiums constitute a distinctive breed of cat, and keeping everyone headed in a common direction sometimes feels like herding the proverbial felines. Selecting the right partner companies and keeping them actively engaged is beyond difficult. You are dealing with very diverse company partners with potentially different interests and priorities, and their involvement is voluntary; other than personal relationships, you have little real leverage.

Boeing was asking its partners to come together from their various organizational worlds to create and implement a common vision of leadership development—and to trust the process, which is difficult for many large organizations. To hedge the bet, Boeing researched best practices for what makes successful consortiums before beginning this program. It was quickly learned that consortiums make a high demand on resources and that they need to be extremely well defined and process-driven. The partners jointly developed guidelines around participant demographics, project quality, curriculum design and delivery, and CEO/executive group involvement to ensure both program and participant quality.

I believe that the most distinctive thing about Boeing's experience is that this consortium partnership between international companies was being created. Consortiums are challenging, even when they are between fairly homogenous partners on a U.S. college campus; when you add the complexities of international partners, the challenges definitely escalate. It took much of my time and taxed many of my stakeholder management skills to keep the consortium on track.

This journey has been an adaptive challenge in its own right, requiring continual leadership development to produce impactful learning experiences and real business results. The degree of success experienced with this program was a bit of a surprise. I sometimes feel as if we were riding as much as shaping a wave of innovation. But it's hard to argue with success, and the future of long-term strategic programs like this looks just as bright as the faces of the participants when they reflect upon their personal growth. Participants left the program with a network of not just peers but international friends and contacts, which they pass on to their own colleagues as wisdom dictates, again widening the spread of global understanding.

For anyone considering setting up an international consortium to carry out a leadership development effort, I would emphasize the following points:

- Find the right partner companies. Successful consortiums require significant time, energy, flexibility, and, most important, commitment. Like any relationship, you and your partner(s) have to be in it for the long haul.

- Be clear about the makeup of partner companies. For the ICP, Boeing wanted large multinationals from different geographical regions, companies that were noncompetitive, had engaged CEOs, and had a mature, established executive development practice.

- Ensure top management buy-in. CEO and executive group support is essential to ensuring you get the "right" participants, projects, and strategic alignment.

- Even though consortiums are a partnership, someone has to take a leadership role (it might as well be you). Being the glue that held the partnership together for three years was a hugely rewarding experience for me.

- Hire experts to help design the action learning content, manage "outside-in" benchmarking meetings, coordinate outside faculty, and so on.

- Ensure level and span of responsibilities of program participants are as similar as possible. Senior leaders have to be in the classroom with peers.

- Do not underestimate the amount of time, energy, and effort that goes into the design, development, and ongoing administration of a complex program like ICP.

- Trust the process. Well-designed and managed programs can have a huge impact.

66

Communities of Practice: Building and Sustaining Global Learning Communities

Yury Boshyk
The Global Executive Learning Network

THE ANNUAL GLOBAL Forum on Executive Development and Business Driven Action Learning is a worldwide community of practice that has been in existence for eighteen years. The longevity of the Global Forum attests to its effectiveness as a learning community; thus, I describe its origins, structure and operating guidelines, and meeting content and format for those who would like to develop and sustain their own communities of practice.

Origins

The Global Forum was the idea of company representatives from General Electric (Stephen Mercer), Johnson & Johnson (Ron Bossert), IBM (Herwe de Schepper), and Yury Boshyk, at that time a faculty member of IMD in Lausanne, Switzerland. In 1995 we came together at the IBM Learning Center in Armonk, New York, to share best practices in action learning. A key driver for this meeting was a desire at Johnson & Johnson to design and implement an executive program based on action learning principles in use at General Electric and IBM. After a very stimulating meeting, we decided we wanted to share and learn from others about their action learning and management education initiatives. We felt that action learning was the wave of the future—today action learning is used by many companies throughout the world.

A year later, the first Global Forum took place with a group of about thirty action learning practitioners from the international business community. Our focus was on action learning initiatives in major corporations. Companies represented included the core group—General Electric, IBM, and Johnson & Johnson—as well as Fiat, Philips, and about twenty-five others. Little did we realize that this meeting would prove to be the foundation of the Global Forum on Executive Development and Business Driven Action Learning, a worldwide community of practice that has met annually ever since (www .globalforumactionlearning.com).

Structure and Operating Guidelines

The Global Forum is very practitioner-oriented, with a clear focus on participants from its desired constituency—major global business organizations. The emphasis is on sharing learning from practical experience and not on exploring theory. In fact, one academic once turned down an invitation to participate because she felt that the Global Forum was "not theoretical enough."

Participants include senior executives and professionals in leadership and development, human resources, and other functions. The guidelines for attendance were set by the core group of participating companies and by a steering committee comprised of community members. One such guideline is that consultants who are invited are asked to bring along a client. "No selling" is another stipulation and, on occasion, some participants were not invited to return after crossing the line in this matter due to the rule of "one strike and you're out." Thought leaders, business school representatives, international organizations such as the World Bank and the World Council of Churches, national public service, government leaders, and some non-governmental organizations (NGOs) also take part.

The Global Forum meets annually and attendance is by invitation only, with no media allowed, and with no more than one hundred participants. This is deliberate in order to ensure the right mix and composition of participants, genuine interaction, confidentiality, and a more open and intimate setting for discussions. Community members must be willing to learn and share. The Global Forum is not for profit, meaning that all participants cover their own travel and accommodation and the meeting expenses are paid at cost by all, including the organizers. To ensure its global character, the group meets yearly on a different continent than the previous year, thus also engaging an ever wider community of practitioners.

For the first nine years or so, companies from the community hosted the Global Forum at their leadership centers, which were often situated outside the main business districts of cities. In time, however, Global Forums came to be organized in venues in downtown districts to facilitate the organization of so-called "outside-in" meetings and discussions with

Exhibit 66.1. Retrospectives Exercises

1. Self-Reflection

   - What did I enjoy?

   - What made the greatest impact?

   - What actions shall I take personally as a result of this experience?

2. In Rotating Table Groups

   - What did you learn during these days?

   - What surprised you?

   - What still puzzles you?

   - What will you do differently as a result of this experience?

   - What will you carry back and to whom?

   - What should we include in the next Global Forum?

major local companies and leaders in the location, which is an important part of the Global Forum.

The organizing team for each Global Forum usually consists of the small core team and community members from the location. This core team looks after all logistics regarding location selection and program details. The wider community members also contribute topics and themes they would like to see on the program through a "retrospectives exercise" (see Exhibit 66.1), introduced to the Global Forum by Intel, at the end of each annual meeting that formulates suggestions for topics to be covered at the next Global Forum.

Content and Format

Over the years the fundamental content has evolved from (1) show and tell presentations on what your company or organization is doing, why it is doing these things, lessons learned from these experiences, and next steps to (2) much more interactive and PowerPoint-free discussions on dilemmas and issues that are being tackled by attending organizations. Today, there are far fewer plenary sessions than in the past. There is also a general guideline that "the first time you participate, the next time you present," thus ensuring active sharing by all community members.

The format lends itself to interactive discussions and is varied to cater to all learning styles. A predominant format is what is referred to as the "galleria walk" and can best be described as follows:

There are usually three presenters per session over a period of two hours in a large room. Each presenter is in a different part of the room with a table, some chairs, and a flip chart. No computers or projected slides are allowed; however, slides are sent in advance and can be uploaded by participants for study before the Global Forum. In each session, presenters interact with three different groups of participants for thirty-five minutes each, followed by a fifteen-minute wrap-up in plenary on what was discussed and what each presenter learned in their discussions. It is not unusual for there to be around twenty sessions with about sixty-five presenters over the course of the four-day Global Forum meeting.

The content of the Global Forum is related either to what organizations and businesses are doing in the field of executive development and leadership or to business driven action learning initiatives. As many are aware, the house of action learning has many doors and the Global Forum has always had, and continues to have, participants representing the many varied approaches to action learning. The content is therefore diverse but inclusive.

Every year about 30 percent of participants are new due to changing locations and generational turnover including retirement. To introduce the concept and variations of action learning to new Global Forum members who may not be that familiar with action learning, there is always a preliminary session or workshop that provides a roadmap to various action learning principles and practices. This session also includes an update on the latest developments in the field.

Post–Global Forum Community Collaboration and Cooperation

There are many opportunities for community members to network and collaborate after each Global Forum. This is, of course, done informally and also in a more structured way. When appropriate, companies share experiences and dilemmas in formal meetings that are part of regional or local gatherings. The Global Forum website serves as a resource center for the community. Here members can find Global Forum presentations, photos from the gatherings, as well as extensive resources, including links and references to primary and secondary materials, videos, news, articles, and other relevant items. Over the years, community members have also contributed to several publications on action learning and executive and organization development.

In the end, it is a committed core group that, despite changes in composition over time, makes the difference. Through its motivation, dedication, ecumenical inclusivity, transparency, and curiosity, this group creates a welcoming spirit that helps nourish and sustain a community of trust that in turn inspires learning and sharing in our community of practice—the Global Forum.

67

Succession Planning: Developing General Managers Through Experience

Mary M. Plunkett

LEADERSHIP DEVELOPMENT AND succession management processes should include a focus on critical organizational positions. These are roles that are essential to the organization planning, designing, delivering, or managing essential products and services. When they are left vacant or when the work is left undone, for whatever reason, the organization will not be able to meet or exceed customer expectations, confront competition successfully, or follow through on efforts of crucial long-term significance.

It is important to build a pool of capable succession candidates for the 15 percent of top and senior management positions to ensure effective succession management, including correct percentage of coverage in the short, medium and long term and succession pools with the right balance of internal and external talent. All positions within the organization are important; however, some of them are so central to the strategy and require such specialized skills that they require extra attention.

The criteria for identifying key positions can vary slightly per function and may change over time depending on the business goals and functional agenda. Positions should be evaluated on a regular basis (i.e., six months prior to a change of incumbent of the position).

Exhibit 67.1 includes guiding questions to determine key positions.

Across industries, general management or business unit leader roles are frequently identified as critical to the achievement of strategic and operational business objectives. These individuals have profit and loss accountability and are responsible for planning, delegating,

Good Qs to ask about positions in org.

POINT!

Exhibit 67.1. Identifying Key Positions

- Is the position a direct contributor to the organization's key priorities or must-win battles?

- Is the position key to delivering strategy, leading projects, or activities that drive the functional agenda?

- Is the position key in mobilizing the organization to deliver the company or functional strategy and/or agenda?

- Is the position difficult to fill due to talent shortages or specialized skill requirements?

coordinating, staffing, and decision making, in order to attain desired organizational targets. Senior functional manager roles can also sometimes be critical (e.g., marketing in a consumer products company or software engineering in an IT company). However, general manager roles are always critical because they oversee all functions as well as day-to-day operations. The framework outlined below will describe how to incorporate experience requirements as a key criterion for identifying potential general managers.

Create Taxonomy of Critical Experiences

The first step is to understand and articulate a common language taxonomy of critical experiences that will best develop required skills and capabilities for effective general managers. Begin by identifying high potential general managers in your organization and understanding their career paths. You will likely see commonality among the types of roles they held, and the time in their careers when they held such roles. As you are building your experience taxonomy, you should consider the key experiences that have continued to consistently emerge as the most critical in the development of leaders since the publication of the *Lessons of Experience* (McCall, Lombardo, & Morrison, 1988).

Combining science and practice, create a taxonomy in language that is relevant to your business. Ensure a focus on future requirements. For example, it may be the case that your current high potential general managers did not have early experiences related to mergers or acquisitions; however, strategic acquisitions are key to your current strategy.

Following the creation of a draft set of key experiences, begin to share them with executive committee members and other high potentials in the organization. Include HR professionals as key stakeholders in this engagement phase. Incorporate feedback and modify language to ensure relevance. Ensure executive committee agreement on the taxonomy, and ideally introduce its usage at pivotal points such as annual succession or management review discussions to begin to foster a common language.

Develop a Talent Review Template

Incorporate the experience taxonomy, as well as general requirements (such as performance, mobility, and aspiration) and competency requirements (such as leadership and functional skills, strategic thinking, and business acumen), into a simple template that can be used during talent review discussions. This template should be useful for business unit reviews as well as functional reviews. See Exhibit 67.2 for a sample template.

Provide guiding questions that will enable productive dialogue among key stakeholders during the review process in order to identify potential general managers. Ensure a focus on demonstrated behaviors related to general, competency and experience requirements. See Exhibit 67.3 for examples of discussion questions.

Once a pool of potential general managers has been identified, offer relevant and targeted development opportunities incorporated into quality personal development plans and proactive career management. Continue monitoring and developing the individuals within their functional disciplines as well as offering assignments and programs supporting general management capability development.

Development of general management talent pools should occur at the local, regional and global level. At the local level, line managers play an important role in building stretch opportunities into current assignments, and providing ongoing feedback and coaching. It is important that local HR be equipped to partner with and support line managers in their role as talent developers. At the regional level, involve the potential general manager talent pool in programs and activities focused on developing emerging leaders. Globally, ensure opportunities for potential general managers to interact with each other and senior business leaders; consider an action learning program focused on leveraging potential GM talent against strategic business challenges.

Lessons Learned
Invest in Engagement

Ensure a thorough understanding of the strategic business drivers and engage a diverse group of stakeholders in discussions of key experiences that would best prepare future general managers. The stakeholder group should include executive committee members, current high potential general managers, high potential management team members, and HR professionals. Don't oversell or use a heavy handed approach when introducing the experience taxonomy; instead, allow the relevant experiences to emerge from the conversations.

Partner with Line HR Professionals

Align closely with HR professionals in the business to ensure understanding and commitment to the process of identifying and developing potential general managers. The line HR

Exhibit 67.2. Talent Review Template

A. General Requirements

☐	Performance	Consistent high performance; three-year performance track record (with consideration for the impact of new/ challenging roles)
☐	Potential	High and Promotable potential, through leader judgment and information from management review process.
☐	Adaptability	Ability to adapt across cultures, at work, and with people
☐	Mobility	Readiness to move across countries, internationally mobile
☐	Aspiration	Individual career desires: aspirations as stated in personal development plan
☐	Language	Ability to communicate fluently and transact business in English

B. Experience Requirements (Breadth plus number 2 or number 3)

☐	1. Breadth of Experience (three different jobs)	Variety of jobs held within and outside the company and/or functional discipline. At least one line management experience.
☐	2. Previous general management or management team experience OR 3. At least one critical experience	General management or management team experience before joining current company Candidate has successfully participated in at least one critical experience: • **Strategic Assignments:** career opportunities where direct, short-term application of specific skills are required, e.g., M&A assignment, innovation assignment • **Joint Venture:** working within JV partner operations • **Start-up:** setting up a new business, function, or department • **Fix it:** turning around an underperforming business, function, or team

C. Competency Requirements

☐	Leadership Skills	Ability to lead and develop others
☐	Functional Skills	Ability to demonstrate outstanding functional performance
☐	Strategic Thinking Skills	Ability to take planned and calculated risks in order to achieve business objectives
☐	Collaborative Skills	Ability to establish, develop and nurture long term relationships in the interest of the business
☐	Business Acumen	Application of the knowledge and ability to make effective (e.g., profitable, sustainable) business decisions

Exhibit 67.3. Talent Review Discussion Questions

1. From this person's experience, when, where, and how did the person best demonstrate the capabilities to become a successful general manager?

2. Is this person able to move or adapt to different cultures?

3. In which cultures or countries can this person be most successful?

4. Is there any reason why this person should not be considered for international assignments?

5. Has this person consistently demonstrated the ability to drive high performance?

6. Has this person consistently exhibited the ability to develop and inspire others?

7. Has this person demonstrated the ability to take calculated risks?

8. Is this person able to develop relationships and collaborative networks with others?

9. Has this person demonstrated the ability to share a vision and get others to work with the vision?

10. Does this person understand the key drivers of the business?

professionals will be responsible for facilitating talent reviews and introducing the business case and criteria to line managers. Importantly, these HR professionals will also be directly involved in the ongoing development and career management of individuals identified as potential general managers.

Reach Deep into the Talent Pipeline

In order to develop a strong bench of general managers, identify individuals as early as possible who could potentially become general managers. This is often difficult for organizations to do. In two organizations where this framework was applied, more than 40 percent of the initial pool of potential general managers were placed in general management roles within six months. In essence, these individuals were "ready" general managers, and once roles became available they were placed. The framework was useful for identifying the talent pool in a consistent manner, but did not always allow sufficient time for targeted development actions. Look for ways to introduce the framework into high potential programs or make it available to the larger organization.

Reference

McCall, M.W., Jr., Lombardo, M.M., & Morrison. A.M. (1988). *The lessons of experience: How successful executives develop on the job*. Lexington, MA: Lexington Books.

68

Building Breadth and Depth Through Experience

Jennifer Kennedy Marchi
Sonos, Inc.

MONITOR IS A strategy consulting firm that must bring to bear a corps of consultants who have the wisdom and expertise to help our clients with their toughest strategic problems. During my thirteen years working there, our goal as an organization was to motivate a workforce comprised of young, ambitious, well educated people who have many options and are prepared to exercise them. As leaders and coaches of hungry, talented employees, we endeavor to create a top-tier work environment that helps elite employees thrive and entices them to stay.

In the interest of finding and retaining great talent and building exceptional leaders, Monitor invested heavily in understanding the "anatomy of a star"—the exercise of identifying and understanding the professional DNA of the people who excel at their jobs and are a natural fit in the organization.

In the interest of finding and retaining great talent and building exceptional leaders, Monitor invested heavily in understanding the "anatomy of a star"—the exercise of identifying the professional DNA of the people who excel at their jobs and are a natural fit in the organization.

We learned that our stars had a set of unique characteristics, including:

- Exceptional academic records and a similar set of UG and MBA concentration areas

- Exceptional analytical capabilities

- A bias for action

- Strong interpersonal skills and receptivity to feedback and coaching

- A leadership track record

- Intense intellectual curiosity

- A need for new challenges at frequent intervals

We also learned that our stars and other successful employees are motivated by mentoring, coaching, mobility, and training. When we cultivated our stars, we found that they had longer tenure, and tended to progress more quickly into leadership roles.

For example, Juan, a first-year undergraduate from Harvard, quickly emerged as a star in our system. Right out of the gates he had tremendous impact. His manager loved him, and he delivered great work for the team. And Juan was happy every day. Why rock the boat?

We rock the boat because we know that Juan's long-term value for the firm is not as an undergraduate analyst. Breadth and depth is a critical component of our talent management strategy because it is motivating to young stars, extending their average tenure and helping them grow into future leaders of the firm. For Monitor, breadth and depth lies directly at the intersection of where our most promising employees find energy and commitment and where our clients find value.

We achieve success building depth and breadth through a variety of organizational systems, including targeted staffing, local training events, apprenticeships, and long-term project allocations. This approach and the talent outcome are unique in an industry where practice areas and office driven P&Ls foster depth, but often constrain breadth.

By investing in the breadth of skills as well as depth and content expertise, we equip our consultants to inspire clients with novel thinking and perspectives, and we provide truly unique and compelling insights and advice. By laying the foundation for breadth, and building depth over time, we groom our leaders to sell more complex projects which can be scaled across organizations (see Figure 68.1). We also equip the members of the project teams at each level to work across those scaled projects, increasing efficiency and building high-impact, lasting relationships within client organizations.

Building Breadth

Our approach to building breadth includes three critical complementary elements; staffing, training, and mentoring.

Early in a consultant's career we aggressively push breadth—strategically staffing younger consultants (one to two years post-undergrad) across a series of projects that expose

Figure 68.1. Building Breadth and Depth

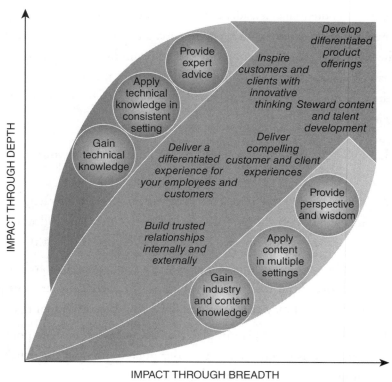

them to a variety of content and industries. We also offer them access to formal training, exposing them to our marketing, finance, and organizational IP (among other content). And we match them with a career advisor who provides mentoring and coaching throughout their early years, and serves as the advocate and voice of the employee with the human assets team.

Staffing for Breadth

Our workforce is extremely talented, driven, and motivated to excel. Pushing breadth aggressively helps keep them motivated and lays the groundwork for a leadership track. But it is not easy to achieve breadth through staffing.

Moving someone like our superstar Juan, sometimes against his preference, will be painful and will create work for managers and HR leaders. He will need to be replaced in his current role, a replacement will need to be trained, and he will need to be transferred to a new project where he will need more training. Leaving him where he is feels like a much easier, more efficient solution for all parties.

But look ahead six months, and then jump ahead five years. Leaving Juan in his first role will undoubtedly lead to boredom over time and will most likely not allow Juan to reach his full potential as a leader at the firm. More concerning, Juan is limiting his learning to one project, one content area, and one manager. To become a trusted and capable leader in the company, and to remain motivated and committed, the right thing to do is to invest in Juan's broad development. Allowing him to gain this experience early is a low cost risk for the firm, and has tremendous upside for Juan and for the firm over time.

How is it done?

1. Have an open discussion with Juan's manager about your motivation for the switch.

2. Be open and honest about the reasons for a breadth strategy, sharing examples of how employees with breadth can add value over time (ideally by citing names of more senior and respected colleagues who possess breadth).

3. Ask for and listen to her concerns. Are these issues you are prepared to address? If so, move ahead with the conversation. If the concerns are a surprise, this is good learning and may cause you to adjust your breadth building timeline.

4. Have a succession plan in place, and be prepared to share potential replacement names. This demonstrates that your organization has the bench strength to support a breadth program.

5. Have a training plan in place for the successor and offer to provide additional support during the transition. If necessary and feasible, make this extra support cost-neutral to the manager or department.

6. Be a partner to the manager throughout the transition. Demonstrating commitment and collaboration will be critical to the future of a breadth program.

7. Ideally, create a system where managers can both deposit into and withdraw from the program.

Training for Breadth

Create formal training programs that complement staffing and rotation programs. These can be content trainings or job-specific trainings, depending on job types and organizational specifics.

For example, if Juan were part of a financial planning and analysis team, he may rotate through a series of roles in the organization to maximize his impact. For example, accounts payable, accounts receivable, sales, customer service, and budget groups might be places where Juan could build valuable breadth. Gaining experience in these domains will help Juan develop a deeper understanding of the company as a whole, a leadership profile across multiple departments, and insight into the impact of the FP&A group's work across the company.

In order to add value throughout these rotations, Juan will expect and require training. Depending on the role, this training may happen on the job, may come through a workshop series, or may come through a multi-day internal or external formal program. Have a training plan in place, but be open to adapting it (especially early in a depth program). Good training programs evolve over time as companies understand the needs of their employees and the appropriate learning environment for learning needs.

Mentors and Advocates for Breadth

Because active breadth building early in a career is not common, it is important to invest in programs that orient employees to the concept and help them understand the end game. In an organization like Monitor where depth is an accepted part of the culture, the end game is clear throughout the recruiting and orientation process. But for companies embarking on a targeted breadth and depth program for the first time, launching a campaign is critical.

How is it done?

- Clearly state your goals and logic for a depth and breadth program:
    - How does it tie into the company's strategy?
    - How will the employees grow and add impact over time?
    - How will this affect retention and recruiting efforts?
- Share goals and logic with key stakeholders in the organization.
- Find leaders who believe in the concept and are willing to act as mentors for the participants.
- Ideally, launch a pilot in partnership with a group or manager who believes in the value of breadth.
- Learn from the pilot, adjust, and build upon the success.

Stakeholder advocates will be important champions for the program and will have strong voices with their colleagues. And mentors will act as coaches for the participants and ears on the ground for you as you monitor the success of the program.

Building Depth

By not allowing for affiliation until later in the career path at Monitor, we encourage exploration and avoid the "siloing" effect that often happens in professional services environments. As they become more senior, employees have the opportunity to specialize and usually obtain advanced practitioner status (advanced expertise) in at least one domain.

Our organically grown partners have been exposed to a breadth of IP, industries, and geographies. Complementing this breadth are one or two practitioner level areas of expertise and one area of advanced expertise. At Monitor, as in many organizations, depth is easier to achieve than breadth. The art of layering depth *over* breadth is what leads to a differentiated skill set and resource. As employees gain perspective through the breadth building programs, we more actively encourage building depth. In our organization, this is most efficiently and effectively achieved through apprenticeships, longer term project allocations, and targeted mentoring and coaching relationships.

We see depth along a spectrum of capability, illustrated in Figure 68.2. Practitioner status is achieved as an individual gains domain expertise and demonstrates mastery of industries or content areas.

Depth Through Apprenticeships

We define apprenticeships as six- or twelve-month opportunities to work with a group of thought leaders or industry experts to learn about a specific practice area. This is a fantastic introduction to the content with hands-on coaching, often leading the apprentice to achieve practitioner status. We recommend that our employees experience at least two apprentice-

Figure 68.2. Depth Through Apprenticeships

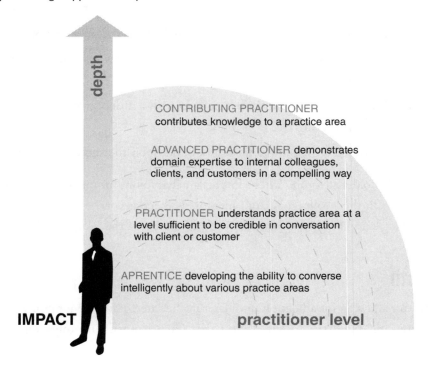

ships and aspire for our senior managers to have two practitioner designations before election to junior partner.

Depth Through Targeted Allocations

As opposed to an apprenticeship, the learning acquired through a targeted allocation is centered on delivering work to a client and gaining deep knowledge of the client's industry and business issues. Longer term project assignments (six to twelve months) can result in practitioner status in an industry or content area.

Depth and Mentoring and Coaching

As with breadth, mentoring and coaching are critical to a depth program. The role of the coach or mentor is to help the employee make choices about where to focus and to provide coaching and guidance during the journey. The mentor may act as an agent for the employee during apprenticeship conversations or during conversations about longer term allocations.

The result of this layering of breadth and depth is that partners "raised" at Monitor are truly fungible strategists who are equipped to tackle problems across a range of industries in multiple strategic domains. The yield is a differentiated product for our clients, an interesting group of colleagues to work with and learn from, and a compelling career path for an intellectually curious and highly motivated talent pool.

Through many years of trial and error, we recognize both the art and the science of building these skills in the field. Before embarking upon this process, be sure that there is a real value proposition for your company. Test your hypotheses with potential opponents, and use their differences to strengthen your argument. Find one or more champions and lean on them to spread the word about the merits of the program, but also build collateral that clearly explains your goals and logic. And finally, start small. The most effective change may come in waves, and the program will evolve and improve as the company evolves and as you learn about what works in your organization.

69

Profiles for Success: Building a Framework for Internal Transitions

Tanya Boyd
Payless Holdings, Inc.

PAYLESS HAS DEVELOPED "profiles of success" at each level of the organization as well as for specific roles across the organization. These profiles include the attributes, knowledge, experiences, and competencies that have been determined to contribute to success for that particular level/role.

- Attributes are personal characteristics that define who you are (example: energetic).

- Knowledge describes what you know (example: knowledge of shoe construction).

- Experience describes what experiences you need to have in order to be successful (example: working in a variety of factories, or going through an entire product life cycle).

- Competencies are the behaviors that are necessary for success (example: decision making, driving for results).

These profiles serve as the foundation for selection, development, and management, providing a common reference point and language for associates and managers about what

Exhibit 69.1. Sample Leadership Profile

Leadership Success Profile

Attributes	Enablers • Balance of Strategic and Pragmatic • Even-tempered, Calm in a Crisis • Independent Thinker/Strong Decision Maker • Open to change/Differences	Derailers • Difficulty Building Trust • Indecisive • Micro-manager, Controlling • Poor Interpersonal Relations • Resistant to Change
Knowledge	• Metrics & Reporting • Markets: Domestic & Global • Basic Budgeting • Basic Human Resources	
Experience	• Management/Leading a Team • Project Management • Cross-functional Experience • Exposure to Senior Management • Hiring/Firing/Performance Management	
Competencies	• Customer Orientation • Driving for Results • Building Organizational Talent • Cross-functional Collaboration • Communicating with Impact • Operational Decision Making	

is necessary for success (Exhibit 69.1 provides an example of a Leadership Profile). Associates interested in what is essential for success in their current role or for a potential future role can look at these profiles and use the associated self-assessment tools to determine their own levels of fit for a particular role as well as areas they may want to focus on for development.

Payless partnered with an outside vendor to develop the initial profiles for success and involved many associates in determining how to populate the profiles. (See Figure 69.1 for the four steps to developing the experience component of the profiles.) We involved senior leaders, as well as individuals in each role and the managers of individuals in each role, to determine the requirements for success through a guided interview process. Focus groups narrowed down the content, and broader surveys allowed input and confirmation of the profiles by all individuals involved with the roles.

The experiences component explores what experiences a person should have coming into a role in order to be successful. In some instances, we divided this category into experiences that are critical to have *prior* to entering a role and other experiences that are important but which can be gained while *in* the role. This information is very helpful both for hiring managers for selection purposes, and also for associates. As an associate considers taking on another role, they can see what they need to have experienced beforehand, and what they

Figure 69.1. Steps to Determining Experiences

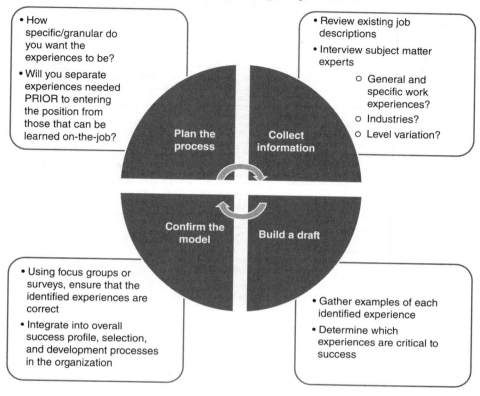

Steps to Determining Experiences

Plan the process
- How specific/granular do you want the experiences to be?
- Will you separate experiences needed PRIOR to entering the position from those that can be learned on-the-job?

Collect information
- Review existing job descriptions
- Interview subject matter experts
  - General and specific work experiences?
  - Industries?
  - Level variation?

Confirm the model
- Using focus groups or surveys, ensure that the identified experiences are correct
- Integrate into overall success profile, selection, and development processes in the organization

Build a draft
- Gather examples of each identified experience
- Determine which experiences are critical to success

should work with their manager to build into their job early on once they are in the new role. Exhibit 69.2 illustrates a sample self-rating form.

The biggest benefit that we have realized from this tool is having a common language across the organization to talk about what is required for success at any particular level or role across the organization. This information is easily available on our intranet, so associates can view it and use the information to build development plans for themselves. The biggest challenge that we face is deciding how granular to be with these profiles for success. We have developed profiles that apply across all functions for individual contributors, managers, and directors and VPs, with a slightly different model for senior leaders. However, it is also easy to imagine that a director in IT may require different experiences than a director in HR in order to be successful. By the same token, even within a function like HR, a director of compensation could require different experiences than a director of recruiting. We have chosen to lean toward a general description. By keeping the experiences fairly general, we have identified some that do apply across the organization at each level, but to really be of

Exhibit 69.2. Example of a Success Profile

Rating Description			
3-High: Have a sufficient amount of this knowledge/experience			
2-Moderate: Have some of this knowledge/experience but more would be beneficial			
1-Little To None: Have a significant need for more of this knowledge/experience			

<table>
<tr><th rowspan="9" style="writing-mode:vertical">Knowledge Areas</th><th></th><th>Self-Ratings</th><th>Immediate Mngr Ratings</th><th>Comments</th></tr>
<tr><td>Metrics and Reporting</td><td></td><td></td><td></td></tr>
<tr><td>Markets: domestic and global</td><td></td><td></td><td></td></tr>
<tr><td>Basic budgeting</td><td></td><td></td><td></td></tr>
<tr><td>Basic Human Resources</td><td></td><td></td><td></td></tr>
<tr><td>*Job Specific Knowledge Areas:*</td><td></td><td></td><td></td></tr>
<tr><td></td><td></td><td></td><td></td></tr>
<tr><td></td><td></td><td></td><td></td></tr>
<tr><td></td><td></td><td></td><td></td></tr>
</table>

<table>
<tr><th rowspan="9" style="writing-mode:vertical">Experience</th><th></th><th>Self-Ratings</th><th>Immediate Mngr Ratings</th><th>Comments</th></tr>
<tr><td>Leading a team–Has led a team; has experience setting and promoting a vision, building collaboration, and promoting teamwork</td><td></td><td></td><td></td></tr>
<tr><td>Project Management–Has managed a function–wide project from start to finish, including setting and tracking metrics for success.</td><td></td><td></td><td></td></tr>
<tr><td>Cross-functional experience–Has been a part of a cross-functional team or task force; has experience working with others who have different priorities and motivators.</td><td></td><td></td><td></td></tr>
<tr><td>Exposure to Senior Management–Has worked with and presented to senior management.</td><td></td><td></td><td></td></tr>
<tr><td>Hiring/Firing/Performance Management–Has selected and built talent, and addressed poor performance efficiently.</td><td></td><td></td><td></td></tr>
<tr><td>*Job Specific Experiences:*</td><td></td><td></td><td></td></tr>
<tr><td></td><td></td><td></td><td></td></tr>
<tr><td></td><td></td><td></td><td></td></tr>
</table>

the most benefit to the individual associate, a more specific list would be beneficial. We are slowly working through functions and developing more specific profiles for success with the experiences and knowledge relevant for particular roles, but this takes time to develop, update, and maintain. We are still working to find the optimal balance between general and specific, recognizing it is an ongoing challenge.

70

Hot Jobs-Hot People: Sharing Leadership Talent Across Organizations

Jeffrey J. McHenry
Rainier Leadership Solutions

SEVERAL YEARS AGO, I was approached by the president of the international division of the company where I was then employed. This individual believed that strong leadership was the key to sustained business success. At the top of his organization, he needed seventy-five to one hundred savvy general managers who could run end-to-end, multifunction, and often multi-country businesses. He knew that the best way to develop general managers like these was by providing them with a series of challenging, diverse job experiences. But he was stymied about how to make this happen:

> We do a great job identifying our high potential future leaders, but we aren't developing them. We know they need the right job experiences to develop into general managers. Every one of my vice presidents has at least one to two high potentials who need a new job experience, but my vice presidents aren't helping because they don't know of any appropriate job openings.

> What's ironic is that every one of my vice presidents also has job openings that they are struggling to fill. They tell me they can't find any qualified candidates. But part of the problem is that they are reluctant to hire people they don't know well because they are worried that they will end up with another VP's reject.

It seems that we ought to be able to match up our high potentials with our job openings.

Can you help me?

We had been tinkering with an approach we called Hot Jobs-Hot People for several years. The goals of this approach were perfectly aligned with what our international president wanted to achieve: developing high potentials by providing them the job assignments they needed to continue their leadership development, and filling critical leadership positions with qualified candidates to enable sustained business success.

Hot Jobs-Hot People is, in some ways, the final step in the succession-planning process. It draws on succession plans to identify the optimal candidates for open (or soon-to-be-open) leadership positions, taking into account candidate qualifications, candidate availability, and candidates who will benefit most developmentally from a job.

One of the best things about Hot Jobs-Hot People is that much of the work is done by the senior executives themselves in a relatively brief workshop (typically two to four hours long). It builds executives' leadership assessment, development, and talent planning skills.

During the next month, we refined and launched Hot Jobs-Hot People to our international division. The approach was so successful that we later extended it to many other business units. It proved particularly effective in organizations in which many leadership job changes occur in conjunction with a business cycle (for example, a product cycle, a fiscal cycle).

In this contribution, I will describe how Hot Jobs-Hot People works and offer some tips on when and where to use it successfully.

How It Works

The Hot Jobs-Hot People process includes seven steps. Following is a brief description of each step.

Step 1: Identify a Job Domain

The starting point is to identify a set or domain of jobs across organizational boundaries that have common requirements.

In the case of the international division, the domain of jobs included country VP/ managing director, plus senior sales, marketing, and consulting roles. This was about 150 jobs total, although at any point in time no more than 20 to 25 percent of these jobs were open or about to come open. The international president noted that all of these jobs had core requirements in common, and it was common for leaders in the general management and sales/marketing career paths to move between these jobs over the course of their careers. This made it sensible to discuss these jobs (and relevant job candidates) together. There were some leadership jobs in the international division outside this domain (for example, senior-level jobs in finance, human resources, and law/corporate affairs), but we agreed to omit these because they required specialty skills. We wanted a sharp focus to our discussion.

Within the international division, there was a strong preference to sync leadership transitions with the fiscal year. New leaders tended to start their jobs at the beginning of the fiscal year, so they could be involved in business planning and target setting. Departing leaders tended to exit their jobs at the end of the fiscal year, so they could see execution through to the end of the business cycle. We timed the first discussion for four months before the end of the fiscal year. At that point, most of our executives were pretty clear on which leaders would be ready to move at the end of the fiscal year and which jobs they would need to fill.

During our first Hot Jobs-Hot People workshop, we only discussed jobs in international. But we expanded subsequent discussions to include senior sales and marketing jobs in several other business units. We had just two simple requirements: first, that the leaders of those organizations had to be open to hiring from and sharing talent with other business units and, second, that their cycle for making leadership job changes needed to align reasonably well with international's cycle. This added fifty to seventy-five jobs to the job domain we were discussing, which was manageable. It also meant that we had multiple organizations involved in the process. This created some wonderful opportunities for cross-organization job moves.

Step 2: Identify Workshop Participants

As we shall see, Hot Jobs-Hot People culminates in a workshop in which participants match open jobs to people wanting a new role. We have found that the workshop is most productive when participants are peers in terms of job level/scope of responsibility (plus the sponsor or co-sponsors, who may be more senior level), head up the organizations with open jobs, and are very knowledgeable about potential candidates for the open jobs.

To illustrate, when we ran the workshop with the international president, we included all of his VPs responsible for large sales regions and the VP responsible for sales and marketing strategy; their organizations contained the jobs we were trying to fill and most of the candidates we were trying to place. We also included the VPs of several staff functions (finance, human resources, and legal) because they knew most of the candidates we were trying to place, and a handful of these candidates currently worked in their organizations. We excluded a couple director level staff people who reported into the international president (for instance, his business manager) because we would be discussing candidates who were at their job level and felt it would be inappropriate for them to participate in the conversation. When we expanded the meeting the following year, we insisted that additional participants must be VP-level, similar to the international president's direct reports, and they must meet the other criteria. This resulted in a rich, open discussion of jobs and candidates.

Step 3: Create a List of Job Openings (Hot Jobs)

As noted previously, it's helpful to focus on a domain of related jobs (that is, the jobs have common core requirements, and leaders within a career path such as general management or sales/marketing leadership often move between these jobs as they are advancing in their careers).

It's also important to focus on an appropriate range of job levels (or job grades) that will be discussed. The range of job levels should be based on three considerations: first, the number of job openings and the time available for discussion; second, the familiarity of workshop participants with the jobs and potential candidates; and, third, whether participants believe it would be a good use of their time to discuss jobs at a particular job level. As a general rule, we find participants are able to have very good discussions about jobs that report directly to them or one level below them.

Our international president had conducted in-depth talent reviews with each of his direct reports one to two months prior to our first workshop. We created an initial list of job openings based on the talent reviews. We included all jobs that were currently open or projected to come open within the next three to six months. We then asked each workshop participant to confirm the list for his organization. This was extremely efficient. But we have also run workshops when we've generated the list of job openings from scratch, usually by working with each participant and his or her HR business partner.

If possible, we recommend pooling jobs that are essentially identical (that is, same title, same scope/level, but different organization). For example, in our first international workshop, several participants were looking for an enterprise sales director for a large geography (more than $200 million in sales), so we pooled these jobs together, reasoning that a candidate who was qualified for one job would likely be qualified for the others. In another workshop we ran for the finance organization, several businesses with revenue ranging from $5 to $10 billion were all looking for a CFO, so we pooled those jobs together.

Step 4: Prepare Slates of Job Candidates (Hot People)

The next step is to generate a slate of potential job candidates for each job pool. Many companies maintain a succession plan for key company positions. This is an excellent starting point for preparing candidate slates. During the talent reviews that took place prior to our first international workshop, our executives had updated the succession plans for their organizations, so we had a great list of potential job candidates from the talent reviews.

Many companies also identify and track their high potentials. They often designate the likely career path(s) or track(s) for each high potential (for example, general management, finance, manufacturing, and operations). We recommend using some simple decision rules to generate potential job candidates from the high potential list (for instance, appropriate job level, appropriate job family/career path, at least two years in current role). This can be compared with the succession planning list to ensure that no strong candidates are missed.

Of course, some high potentials were credible candidates for several different job pools (that is, they could run a marketing organization or a sales organization), so we made sure that every high potential was on every appropriate slate.

One decision we had to make was whether to include job candidates who might not be mobile, especially given that the jobs we were discussing were located all around the world. I have found that what people tell you about their willingness to relocate is not always the same as their actual willingness to relocate. One American colleague insisted his wife would never move, but two months later he was sitting at his new desk in the United Kingdom, and his wife was even more enthusiastic about the move than he was. Another colleague had told me repeatedly that he would be open at any time for an assignment outside his home country, but in consecutive years he turned down assignments to Singapore, the United Kingdom, and the United States (none of them hardship locations). In the end, we decided not to eliminate anyone from our candidate list based on mobility, but we came prepared to discuss possible mobility issues for each candidate.

We ask each workshop participant to validate the list of potential candidates from their organization. This helps ensure they are not surprised by anyone who is presented at the workshop. We invite them to add or subtract candidates from the list we've prepared. One concern is that some participants will be talent hoarders—they will subtract their top talent from the list we present them and add some employees who are not performing well that they would like to move out of their organization. Our solution has been to tell participants that the Hot Jobs-Hot People sponsor (for example, this was the international president in our first workshop) will review and approve any changes they make to their lists. We often have some debates with executives about their candidates the first time we run Hot Jobs-Hot People, but we find that they become much more willing to share the right talent after they've gone through the process once.

Step 5: Prepare Workshop Materials

Given how participants are selected, it's expected that all will come to the workshop with a solid understanding of the open jobs that will be discussed, but they will likely not know some of the candidates well.

It's helpful to prepare two documents for participants in advance of the workshop. The first is a simple table that lists each job pool, the open jobs within the pool, and potential candidates (see Table 70.1 for an example). This will guide the discussion and serve as an agenda for the workshop. In addition, we strongly recommend providing a one-page biography of each individual. This might include a photo, education, job history, recent performance ratings, strengths and areas for development, experience gaps, and ideal next assignment. Data for this can often be drawn from an organization's HR systems or succession-planning tool. We typically compile these in alphabetical order in a binder for easy reference.

Table 70.1. Example of a Hot Jobs-Hot People List

Job Cluster	Job Titles	Job Candidates
Vice President, Large Geography (≥$500M)	VP France, VP Asia Pacific, VP Middle East and Africa	Robert Beauclaire, Sanjay Ghopal, Jimmy Lee, Karl Reichert, Heidi Roberts, Inge Swansson
Managing Director, Medium Geography ($250–500M)	MD Australia, MD Switzerland	Gunther Burkhalt, Willem Kuyper, Anna Meyer, Richard Schmidt
Enterprise Sales Director, Large Geography (>$200M)	ESD UK, ESD Asia Pacific	Mohamad Badawi, Ian Carter, Walid Halaby, Betty Lin, Anna Meyer
Enterprise Sales Director, Medium Geography ($100–200M)	ESD Netherlands, ESD New England, ESD SE Asia, ESD Poland	Tomas Bocek, Holly Carter, Kyoko Kamura, Ronan O'Connor, Kai Wenstrom
Marketing Director, Large Geography (≥$500M)	Mktg Dir UK	Holly Carter, Charles Hsu, Katrina Kieffer, Ronan O'Connor, Raj Singal
Marketing Director, Medium Geography ($250–500M)	Mktg Dir Switzerland, Mktg Dir Middle East, Mktg Dir South Asia	Christian Andersen, Holly Carter, Jila Patel, James Wu

In addition, we prepare some information for behind-the-scenes use by the facilitator, including: (1) three to four developmental lessons that each job may teach (for example, how to lead a turnaround, how to lead a high-growth emerging market, how to run an end-to-end multifunction business, and how to operate a business in a country where the company has a poor reputation); and (2) additional intelligence on the job candidates, including major recent accomplishments (or struggles), career aspirations, optimal timing for job transitions, likely openness to relocation, and any other information that might be useful in evaluating their suitability for potential new jobs.

Step 6: Facilitate the Workshop

We recommend beginning the workshop with a *very brief* review of the job candidates. Typically, the facilitator simply reads through the list of candidates in alphabetical order as participants leaf through the binder that contains candidate biographies. Occasionally, participants will offer a couple of comments about the people in their organizations who are being offered as job candidates.

We then spend the vast majority of time talking about top candidates for each job pool. Participants typically need little prompting to engage in conversation. Those with open jobs usually have lots of questions about the proposed candidates, and those who know the candidates usually have lots of comments and insights they're eager to share. Workshop participants may suggest additional candidates for some pools. Conversation and debate ensue. Ultimately, the goal of this discussion is to agree on the top candidates for each pool.

One of the roles the facilitator can play is to help ensure that participants are providing useful information about candidate qualifications during the discussion. Specific accounts of the candidates' actions and accomplishments are helpful (for example, "When the economy became sluggish and sales were behind plan, this candidate rallied the team and agreed on an action plan that enabled the team to meet its sales goals"). If participants offer vague, general statements about the candidates (for instance, the person is a "good guy," "really smart," or a "go-getter"), the facilitator should insist on examples and detail. (For outstanding tips on how to do this, see Sorcher and Brant, 2002.)

Another key role for the facilitator is to make sure that placement decisions take into account the development needs of the candidates. For example, assume there are two open positions in the same job pool. One of them requires a turnaround, the other does not. The facilitator should press hard to consider candidates who need turnaround experience for the turnaround position, even if the executive who has the open position prefers someone with proven experience. The facilitator should continually remind participants that one of the goals of the exercise is to match high potentials to jobs that will provide them with development opportunities. It is wasteful to assign high potentials to jobs where they will not gain new experiences that teach them new leadership lessons because it will not build the organization's leadership capability.

At the end of the workshop, the facilitator should review the top candidates for each open position. The facilitator also should lead a discussion about the follow-up plan for each job candidate. At my previous employer, job candidates were first contacted by the workshop participant (executive) in charge of the organization where the candidate currently works. The workshop participant told the candidate that his or her name has been surfaced for an open (or soon-to-be-open) position (or, in some cases, for two or more positions). This gave the candidate an opportunity to learn a little about the position and prepare for the initial conversation with the hiring manager. The workshop participant then contacted the hiring manager to let him or her know that the candidate could be contacted. At that point, it was up to the hiring manager to oversee the hiring and interview process. Regardless of what process your organization adopts, it's vital that all workshop participants leave with a clear understanding of next steps.

Step 7: Follow Up on Potential Placements

For the facilitator, the most critical part of the Hot Jobs-Hot People cycle is *after the workshop*. There is a natural tendency for the facilitator to focus all of his or her energy on the workshop itself to make sure it's a very productive two-hour or half-day workshop for the ten to fifteen participating executives. The fact is that the topic is so engaging for most executives that the workshop practically runs itself. Where it often breaks down is during follow-up. The facilitator must continue operating in high gear.

As soon as possible following the workshop, the facilitator should send an e-mail that summarizes agreements and decisions made at the workshop (that is, top candidates for each job, the process that will be used to follow up with candidates, and so forth).

The facilitator then should make sure that all candidates are contacted promptly, meetings with hiring managers are set up, interviews happen, offers are extended, and so on. This may sound like babysitting, but if it doesn't happen, all the effort that went into preparation and the workshop may be wasted. The line HR organization can be a key partner for the facilitator during follow-up. It can make sure that meetings are scheduled, counsel candidates and hiring managers behind the scenes, and oversee the interview process.

It's also useful for the facilitator to provide regular status reports on where the organization stands in filling the open positions. Often the job conversations and interview process continue for several months. Workshop participants generally have a pretty good sense of where they stand in filling the open positions in their own business, but they often are unsure what is happening to the high potentials who had been identified as candidates for jobs outside their businesses. The status reports help keep them informed.

Emphasizing Some Tips

I have given some tips and pointers throughout this article on how to achieve the most value from Hot Jobs-Hot People. Three stand out as particularly important.

First, keep in mind that Hot Jobs-Hot People is designed to help achieve two goals: developing high potentials by assigning them to jobs that provided great learning challenges, and filling critical leadership positions with highly qualified candidates who can achieve great business results. There is some tension between these goals. The best-qualified candidate for a job is one who has done the job very successfully before and has mastered all the job challenges, but of course that candidate will learn very little from doing the job again. The facilitator must help balance this tension. In general, most high potentials perform well and learn a great deal when they are placed in jobs that involve one or two new developmental challenges (for example, a significant increase in scope and a first international assignment). The facilitator may have to prod some executives to be open to candidates who are missing one or two critical experiences but who need those experiences for their development. At the same time, the facilitator must recognize that a few jobs may be so "mission critical" to the organization that executives cannot take big hiring risks.

Second, it's critical for the facilitator to follow up after the workshop and make sure that candidate meetings are happening, interviews are being scheduled, and so on. Facilitators should not think that their jobs are finished when the workshop is over.

Finally, make sure to keep workshop participants apprised of progress. In fact, it may be useful to track some key metrics and report them back regularly to participants during the follow-up step. I did not do this after our first workshop with international. The executive participants had left the meeting very excited about the process. During the following weeks, almost every executive filled at least one key opening based on the discussion, and several filled two openings. As I stood back and watched all this happen, I was pretty excited. We ended up filling twenty leadership jobs, which was a pretty good return on investment for a two-hour meeting involving thirteen executives. In addition, conversations took place with at least twenty additional high potentials. Even though they were not hired into any of the open jobs, they were thrilled to know that their names had surfaced in executive conversations and that the organization was paying a lot of attention to their careers. So I was shocked when I spoke with a couple executives a few months after the workshop and they told me that they had enjoyed the conversation but weren't sure that much had resulted from it. All they knew about was the one to two hires they had made, and maybe one or two of their high potentials who had landed new jobs. That didn't seem like much to them. So we asked for a few minutes at a staff meeting about four months after the workshop to share the total number of hires and contacts. They were surprised and very enthusiastic. Subsequently, we kept a running tally of hires and contacts, which we distributed to workshop participants bimonthly for three to four months after the workshop (during the follow-up step). The result was strong executive support for running Hot Jobs-Hot People on a continuing basis.

In summary, Hot Jobs-Hot People is an outstanding way to engage executives in leadership development. It helps place qualified candidates in key leadership roles, ensures that high potentials are receiving the job experiences they need to develop their leadership capability, and enhances the commitment of high potentials to the organization.

Reference

Sorcher, M., & Brant, J. (2002). Are you picking the right leaders? *Harvard Business Review, 80*(2), 78–85.

71

Multicultural Women in the Pipeline: Finding Hidden Treasure

Ella L.J. Edmondson Bell
Tuck School of Business and ASCENT—Leading Multicultural Women to the Top

ALL COMPANIES HAVE processes for identifying, developing, and preparing their most talented managers. Those managers, who reveal the best skills, show commitment, reflect the company's values in their managerial style, bring innovative ideas to the table, offer solutions that enhance the bottom line, are the managers who are listed on the succession pipeline plans, slated to senior positions in upper management, and considered for key executive roles. While the process for creating these plans is exhaustive and inclusive, too often just the opposite is true. The percentage of women, especially multicultural women, is far less representative in such high potential pools. I begin by discussing the reasons why multicultural women are not adequately represented in managerial and executive pipelines and then provide eight suggestions on how organizations can create a more inclusive pipeline.

One of the things that intrigues me in my organizational work with Fortune 100 companies is when I ask corporate executives and designers of succession plans about the female representation on their high potential list, because they are quick to point out an increasing number of women included. Their response also reveals a sense of confidence for doing the right thing. Their approach is working and overall they have a sense of progress. Then, I ask them the curve ball question: "What do the women in your high potential pool look like, in terms of their race and ethnicity, or their global representation?" Now the response changes—often it is more of a blank facial expression than a verbal response. When they dig a bit deeper, the women identified on their pipeline are mostly white. And, while their numbers are still lacking when compared to white men, the representation of multicultural women—Hispanic, African-American, Asian, Native American, and immigrant women— are woefully lacking. I should also mention that men of color are usually low in numbers, too. But for this contribution, I am going to focus on the dearth in the number of multi-cultural women found among high potential managers.

According to a 2011 report from Catalyst's Overview of Women in the Workplace, women made up 46.6 percent of the labor force. Women comprise a slight lead over men in managerial and professional positions at 51.4 percent. At first glance, it would appear that women are succeeding in shattering the glass ceiling. But when you unpack these numbers, you find a very different picture. Only 5.3 percent of women working in the managerial and professional occupations are African-Americans. After this racial ethnic group, the numbers only go lower: Asian-American women comprise only 2.7 percent; and Latinas only slighter higher at 3.9 percent. There were no statistics for Native American women. The total number of multicultural women is 11.9 percent in a society that is rapidly increasing in its racial, ethnic, and cultural diversity.

In my book *Career GPS: Strategies for Women Navigating the New Corporate Landscape* (Bell & Villarosa, 2010), I wrote about the critical implications of the dearth of the number of multicultural women being groomed and positioned to assume leadership positions in corporate America. I labeled it "Storm Warning," and I described it this way:

> It's a storm already defining your workforce. If you are not paying attention, this storm will create huge gaps in your succession plans. This storm is going to trump your ability to hire the best and brightest talent. This storm is going to take away your ability to sell your products not only here in the United States but everywhere else in the world as well. . . . The person you pass the company baton to may not be Jack, Hugh, Paul, Bob, or Richard. It may well be Carla, Kusum, Akeisha, Usha, or Masoko, but only if you respond to the changing weather. From all current indications, too many corporations still have a very long way to go to get their houses in order. (p. 220)

Causes for the Pipeline Void

Why are multicultural women missing in managerial and executive positions? Your company is, after all, presumably hiring them. Based on my research and the research of others, there are several reasons why multicultural women are not being represented in your company's talent pool. First, these women are often left out of both the formal and informal networks where employees and managers have an opportunity to build important relationships. Far too often, they are not invited to participate in high level networks, especially where senior executives are involved. Their white peers and colleagues can exclude them from informal networks. Plus, they often exclude themselves from such groups, feeling it is more important to concentrate on their assignments. Multicultural women tend to believe performance alone will be the magic for advancing to the executive suite. Too often, they shy away from participating in a company's informal activities. Here, it is important to note that, for this population, performance alone is never enough. It must be coupled with having authentic relationships with colleagues, managers, and executives. Corporate and professional networks are where such relationships are made.

Senior executives and managers must have a sense of their employees: their work ethics, values, managerial style, commitment, and contributions, before they are placed on succession plans. An employee's manager, mentor, or sponsor typically conveys the work ethic, values, managerial style, commitment and contributions. Colleagues, administrators, and team members can add to the "buzz" surrounding a potential high pool candidate. Good "buzz" such as that she is a good team player, she brings solutions to the table, or she really knows how to connect with clients, gets the attention of key decision-makers. But one cannot generate good buzz without first having critical relationships at work. Too often the "buzz" surrounding a multicultural woman lacks luster.

In addition, multicultural women are often uncomfortable showcasing their successes. In their cultures, boasting about their achievements, especially to a manager or an executive, can be considered prideful or arrogant. When a woman has an opportunity to socially interact with senior executives, she will be silent about her achievements, thereby reinforcing the blank slate surrounding her.

Another critical issue for multicultural women is a lack of sponsors. A sponsor is "a powerful person in your organization who uses his or her social capital to help you advance. A sponsor stands behind you, attaches his or her name to you, and provides connections, visibility, exposure, and coaching. Sponsors also offer protection." An article in *Diversity Primer* adds: "Nearly all people in executive ranks have had someone help them along the way, someone who can speak on their behalf at meetings or guide them through the corporate maze of managerial development." The "someone" they are referring to is a sponsor. The article concludes by stating: "If a woman of color is not in the pipeline to be recognized, she won't be."

Without sponsors, plus low or no participation in formal and informal networks, these women miss out on high visibility assignments. These are the assignments where a woman can truly prove herself by showcasing her skills, tenacity, and leadership and make a difference to the company's bottom line. Having a developmental assignment is usually the first step for preparing a woman for the high potential pool. Multicultural women have such opportunities less frequently than their white male and female counterparts. Often they have to work twice as hard just to prove their worth before even being considered for one. In *Our Separate Ways* (Bell & Nkomo 2001), Stella Nkomo and I found in our research that "many of the African-American women interviewed believed they were held to a higher and often different standard than their white colleagues, even when their credentials were extraordinary. Sixty-five percent of the African-American women managers who participated in our national survey believed they had to outperform their white colleagues for the same rewards."

The Hidden Jewels: Multicultural Women

Multicultural women are the hidden jewels in our corporate workforce. Consider the fact that women will be entering the workforce in greater numbers than white men in the next ten years. Consider also that the greater percentage of these women will represent a broad range of multicultural backgrounds. It is fair to say that within the next decade women, especially multicultural women, will represent the backbone of the American workforce. They will be in greater numbers both in managerial and executive positions. They will bring a unique perspective, or what I call a "special spice," to leadership positions. Their life journeys have been shaped by their gender, race, ethnicity, social status, immigrant status, and religion. Some represent the first generation in their family to be employed in the corporate world in professional positions. Consequently, they are able to question old paradigms.

Their unique brand of spice can help your company be on the cutting edge in this age of global competition. Multicultural women can transcend global borders. Their vision and cultural flexibility is an asset when it comes to marketing not only within American borders, but also in the rest of the world. Their innovation can only be a plus when it comes to creating new products. Their cultural savvy can only be a benefit when it comes to identifying new stakeholders, partners, and allies for your company. In this day and age, how can a company not afford to develop these women and to ensure they are fully represented in the company's high potential pool?

Creating a More Inclusive Pipeline

Creating a diverse talent pool in a company is not rocket science; however, it does require an expanded approach to the ways you identify and develop your company's talent pool. Below are eight suggestions for building an inclusive talent pool in your company:

1. When hiring a multicultural·woman who is considered a potential high flyer, discuss her career plans early on in her tenure. Keep your communication lines to multicultural women flexible and open.

2. Sponsor multicultural women for external developmental activities, including top tier executive education programs in leadership or executive MBA programs. Too often these perks are primarily awarded to white men. Also, offer developmental programs designed for these women. Such opportunities broaden a woman's network and can decrease her sense of isolation.

3. Talk with executives of color to help identify talented and younger multicultural women who are aspiring to climb the corporate ladder. Very often these women reach out to senior managers they feel a connection with because they possess similar identity traits. Along the same lines, if your company has affinity groups, collaborate with the leaders to identity high potential women.

4. Monitor high potential multicultural women throughout their tenure, paying attention to their assignments, managers, and performance. Another approach is to track their SAR (succession, advancement, and retention). Be prepared to question what appear to be stagnations in their career advancement, and intervene if necessary. Most importantly, make leaders accountable for their advancement.

5. Ensure multicultural women are given challenging developmental assignments enabling them to gain visibility and to build a solid track record.

6. Establish initiatives enabling women to network with senior executives and other company leaders, to meet potential sponsors, and to build potential allies. The idea is to give women exposure to the leaders of the company.

7. Hold executives and managers accountable to both sponsor and mentor high potential multicultural women.

8. When discussing and making decisions about the company's high talent pool, ask the hard questions: Where are we missing representation and why? If your answer is, "We don't have a star in any one particular group," you should go back to the drawing board. Be aware of star syndrome, the belief that there can only be one woman who will fit the build.

While these eight items are not exhaustive, employing them will create broader opportunities for women of color in your company. It will facilitate their advancement into senior management and executive positions, and will help to position your company to be more competitive and innovative in the global marketplace.

References

Bell, E.E., & Nkomo, S.M. (2001). *Our separate ways: Black and white women and the struggle for professional identity*. Boston, MA: Harvard Business School Press.

Bell, E.E., & Villarosa. L. (2010). *Career GPS: Strategies for women navigating the new corporate landscape*. New York, NY: Amistad.

Diversity Best Practices. (2010, November). *Five barriers to advancement for women of color at work: Diversity primer*. New York, NY: Diversity Best Practices. http://diversitybestpractices.com/publications/diversity-primer

Section 4

The Organization: Enabler of Experience-Driven Development

Solutions to Specific Obstacles

Section Introduction

Many aspects of an organization—its shared values, the behaviors and perceptions of its employees, its processes and routines—can either support experience-driven development or get in its way. For example, experience-driven development will more likely flourish in an organization whose members strongly believe that leaders are made rather than born, where there are fewer barriers to moving across organizational boundaries to gain needed experience, or where employees see personal benefits in pursuing on-the-job development. The thought of trying to change organizational values, beliefs, and expectations can be daunting; however, the journey toward experience-driven leader development inevitably includes this question: *How can you influence the organization more broadly to enable rather than inhibit experience-driven development?* In this section practitioners and thought leaders provide tools, frameworks, practices, processes, and advice for encouraging more widespread and sustained support for experience-driven development in organizations.

First, contributors offer frameworks for assessing the organization and its practices. Systematically evaluating an organization on multiple relevant dimensions sparks conversation among leaders, generates compelling data, and often produces momentum to improve. Contributors pose key questions for evaluating the value that an organization places on employee development (see *Organizational Climate for Development*) and the central practices for making leadership development strategic (see *Creating the "and" Organization: Seeing Leadership Development as a Key Strategic Issue*). Assessment is an important first step in stimulating organizational change.

A second set of contributions share how the design of on-the-job-development (OJD) tools and interventions themselves can increase their widespread use in an organization. In *Leading from Where You Are*, the authors describe five design elements that make employees want to use these tools and pass them on to others. *My Needs Their Needs: Designing High-Value Development Tools* illustrates how a development tool can be crafted to not only meet the needs of the organization but also the needs of individual leaders. And *Built to Last: Sustainable On-the-Job Development Interventions for the Entire Organization* describes the characteristics of OJD interventions that generate the level of organizational alignment and support needed to become self-sustaining, persisting well beyond the influence of the original designers.

In a third set of contributions, authors share effective approaches for directly influencing the beliefs and values of organizational leaders. They describe how one-on-one conversations and coaching can help leaders see their work as a central source of learning opportunities for themselves and others (see *Building Support for Experience-Based Development*) and how storytelling can better connect leaders to the power and possibilities of learning from experience (see *The Power of Stories in Leadership Development*). Sharing data that demonstrates the consequences of learning (see *Assessing Learning's Impact on Careers*) or of failing to learn from experience (see *Teaching Senior Leaders the Dynamics of Derailment*) is another strategy for obtaining the attention and support of organizational leaders.

Two final contributions focus on solutions for overcoming often-cited organizational obstacles to experience-driven development: constrained mobility in organizations (see *Strengthening Executive Mobility*) and a limited supply of high-impact developmental assignments (see *Talent Ecosystems*).

All efforts to develop leaders happen in a broader context that can hasten or hinder those efforts. The earlier sections of this book point to best practices in creating more developmental experiences for more people in the organization, equipping individuals to more readily learn from their experiences, and shaping HR processes and systems to support on-the-job learning. However, without working to also influence organizational values and beliefs associated with learning and leadership development, these practices run the risk of being short-lived and limited.

72

Organizational Climate for Development

Cynthia McCauley
Center for Creative Leadership

HR PRACTITIONERS ARE well aware that their efforts to enhance experience-driven leader development in an organization can be boosted or thwarted by the degree to which organizational members see learning and development as a worthwhile activity that produces useful outcomes. How much value an organization places on learning and development is reflected in its climate for development. The climate for development is established and reinforced through six organizational processes:

1. *Priorities of top management.* One of the most consistent findings in studies of organizations that are effective at developing leaders is the commitment and involvement of senior management (APQC, 2006; Hewitt Associates, 2007). Top management commitment is reflected in their efforts to examine the implications of organizational strategy for leader development, in their engagement in succession management and talent review processes, in the time they devote to coaching and teaching organization's leader development initiatives, and in the attention they give to leader development in their own units.

2. *Recognition and rewards.* To generate a climate for development, organizations reward several types of outcomes through their performance management and compensation systems and through formal and informal recognition. They reward effective leadership performance, an individual's enhancement of

his or her leadership skills and abilities, and a manager's attention to developing others.

3. *Communication.* What an organization values is also revealed in what it spends time communicating about. Organizations with a strong climate for development use formal communication channels to publicize the organization's development initiatives, share best practices, connect people to resources to use for their own learning, and talk openly about mistakes and lessons learned. Organizational members also express their belief in the importance of development, for example, when managers share their development goals with their teams or when co-workers encourage each other to take on stretch assignments.

4. *Efforts to track and measure.* Efforts to measure and track leader development at the individual and intervention levels are hallmarks of a development climate, for example, tracking individual progress on development goals, tracking the improvements in leader competencies over time, and evaluating the impact of formal development initiatives.

5. *Resources.* Organizations put more resources into activities on which they place high value. However, budgets for formal development initiatives are only one type of resource for development. Other resources include such things as employee time (for example, to engage in development activities or to coach fellow employees) and the use of some jobs and assignments for development (rather than always maximizing job-person fit).

6. *Skilled employees.* An organization that values development attracts, recruits, and retains employees who are skilled at learning and development. Such employees recognize when new skills or behaviors are called for, accept responsibility for their own development, engage in activities that provide the opportunity to learn and grow, and reflect on their learning processes.

Just like any aspect of organizational functioning, the first step in enhancing an organization's climate for development is to encourage key stakeholders to examine the current state of their climate. This examination can range from a facilitated discussion among a group of senior executives, to data that is systematically collected (for example, through focus groups or online surveys) and fed back to key stakeholders (for example, the organization's leadership development council or the steering committee for leader development initiatives in the organization).

Exhibit 72.1 provides basic questions that my colleagues and I have found to be helpful in guiding a reflective discussion with senior teams, in collecting input via interviews or focus groups, or in designing survey questions for collecting broader input on the experienced climate for development in an organization. The specific questions used need to be customized based on what the responder can reasonably answer. For example, senior managers may

Exhibit 72.1. Evaluating Climate for Development

How strongly does the organization demonstrate that it values leader development and sees it as a competitive advantage? Is this value reflected in:

Top management support?

- In what ways are senior managers involved in leader development in the organization?

- How much of senior management's time is spent in leader development?

- To what degree is the development of people a key element in discussions of organizational strategy?

Recognition and reward systems?

- In what ways does the organization reward people who develop the talents and skills needed for effectiveness in the organization?

- In what ways are people recognized for expanding their leadership capabilities?

- To what degree are managers rewarded for developing their employees?

Communication processes?

- To what extent can people readily access information about developmental strategies and opportunities in the organization?

- In what ways do channels for formal internal communication highlight leader development opportunities and achievements?

- To what degree do people express a belief that individuals can develop and an expectation that they will develop?

Tracking and measurement systems?

- To what extent do performance management systems track individual progress on development goals?

- What type of metrics does the organization have in place for tracking whether it is developing the leadership talent it needs?

- In what ways does the organization evaluate the effectiveness of its leader development initiatives?

Resource allocation?

- In what ways is the organization investing in leader development?

- When resources are tight, to what degree does the organization protect resources for employee development?

- To what degree do short-term business pressures interfere with the development of people in the organization?

The skills of employees?

- To what extent does the organization's "employment brand" emphasize development?

- In what ways does the organization seek evidence of the ability to learn during the hiring process?

- To what degree does the organization focus on retaining its exceptional learners?

be the only group that can reasonably assess how much of their time is spent in leader development, whereas almost anyone in the organization could provide perspective on the ways people are recognized for expanding their leadership capabilities. In utilizing these questions, it is always useful to ask for concrete examples of what has been observed in the organization related to each question.

These questions can start the discussion and provide some common reference points for evaluating the organization's climate for development. Identifying elements of the climate that could be improved (and crafting action plans for improvement) is one possible outcome of such discussions; however, the intent may be to simply raise awareness of the concept of a climate for development in order to pique the interest of key stakeholders in the ways in which they can strengthen the climate in their organizations.

References

APQC. (2006). *Leadership development strategy: Linking strategy, collaborative learning, and individual leaders*. Houston, TX: Author.

Hewitt Association. (2007). *Top companies for leaders 2007*. Lincolnshire, IL: Author.

73

Creating the "and" Organization: Seeing Leadership Development as a Key Strategic Issue

Stephen R. Mercer
SRM Consulting, Ltd.

THE ORGANIZATIONAL PREOCCUPATION with growth, competition, globalization, and corporate responsibility can often mask the most important factor in continued business success—constructing a pipeline of leaders capable of sustained execution. It's generally accepted that leaders need to manage for and deliver results in the short term. At the same time, leaders have to be cognizant of and instigators of change to keep their organizations functioning for the long term. The challenge embedded in those expectations can be framed as the difference between building "and" organizations and "or" organizations. Organizations with the "and" perspective balance short- and long-term results with flexible strategies and develop adaptable leaders who can implement them. In contrast, an "or" business mires itself in tradeoffs and sacrifices that pit short-term concerns against long-term visions and often don't achieve either. One of the first and most important steps toward creating "and" organizations is to see leadership development as a key strategic issue. Leaders at all levels of your business must involve themselves in developing the pool of talent the organization will require in the future. They are essential pieces to building a best-in-class leadership development system.

Three Vital Components

Does your organization see leadership development as a key strategic issue? To gauge your answer to this question, examine the degree to which your organization makes use of three vital components of best-in-class leadership development:

- Intentional selection of assignments to develop leaders according to their individual goals *and* the organization's need to deliver results;

- A succession planning system that carefully matches individuals and assignments, thus assuring a future pipeline of leaders qualified in the business and capable of seeing the relationship between results *and* sustainability; and

- Action learning grounded, business focused, and evidence-based formal development experiences.

Intentional Selection of Assignments

Developmental assignments, especially "trial by fire" experiences that push a leader to the edge of his or her comfort zone, create rich experiences that can yield important lessons. The Waypoint Project at the Boeing Company represents a strategic approach to selecting suitable developmental assignments. The project identified the key experiences that serve as catalysts to spur potential leaders toward developing the capabilities the company believes are critical to its success. For each type of key experience, the project identified the lessons learned, competencies developed, situations factors, and personal success strategies. (For more details, see *Leadership Maps* on page 25 of this book.)

Succession Planning with an Emphasis on Development

An organization needs a disciplined succession planning process to create a leadership pipeline that identifies the leaders of the future and their developmental needs. An illustrative example is the annual human resources review at the General Electric Company, which has run for decades and encompasses the entire professional population of the company. GE's annual process begins every January and culminates in a full-day review by the CEO with each business unit that covers the key leadership talent in that business and a development plan for everyone identified as a high potential.

At Boeing, the centerpiece of the succession plan is the "Green Room," a special room set aside at its world headquarters in which succession planning and career development are carried out on behalf of the executive population. Similar rooms exist at each of the individual business units and focus on their specific executive populations.

The walls of these rooms are decorated with executive level organization charts, with each executive represented by a chip that shows a brief description of that person. Each chip is also accompanied by a detailed leadership profile form. A succession plan for each chip includes both an upward path or lateral moves. Each plan carries a set of developmental assignments and educational experiences and a list of people who can fill the executive's role, each of which also comes with a set of developmental assignments and educational experiences that would qualify him or her to take the position. The experiences identified for the backup candidate are not designed to fully qualify him or her. Each assignment is selected to be a stretch opportunity that presents that person with a chance to learn and grow into the new job.

Formal Development Programs as Practice Space

Although the best developmental assignments are trial-by-fire experiences, failure in those situations can threaten a career. To mitigate that threat, organizations can provide practice space to allow leaders to develop the capabilities needed to be successful. Experiential methods create practice opportunities where developing leaders can test new and different—even radical—ideas. Within the safe haven of risk-free experimentation, leaders have freedom to fail without fear of reprisal or damage to their personal records. The only failure is the failure to learn from mistakes. Lessons can be reinforced using after-action reviews, a method piloted by the United States Army (see *After-Event Reviews* on page 221 of this book).

Experiential learning is at the center of best-in-class executive development programs. Markers of these programs are the use of real business problems, an extensive use of simulations, a philosophy of leaders teaching leaders (every participant assumes a dual role, as a student and as an instructor), mentoring that occurs not just from the top and downward, but also from below to the top and from side to side among peers and colleagues.

Some companies use a trickle-down approach to leadership development. They focus on the top level and expect that the concepts will disperse down through the organization. This flawed approach misses the opportunity to drive development through the entire organization. A simultaneous push at all levels ensures that there is a constituency for change in the organization, and it enables the leadership at the top to count on a group of allies throughout the organization.

Assess Your Organization

Use the questions in Exhibit 73.1 to assess your organization's leadership development system against best-in-class practices. And use it to generate discussion, reflection, and action among your leadership development colleagues. development that ensures the best chance of continuing success.

Remember that a careful and considered approach to executive development that combines intentional assignment planning, rigorous succession planning, and experiential, business-driven educational programs can address the continuing need to grow leaders at all levels. These are the kind of tested methods that make it possible for an organization to emerge from uncertainty or to pursue sustainability.

Exhibit 73.1. Strategic Leadership Development: A Best Practices Checklist

Assignment Selection

❑ Have you identified the key capabilities that drive success in your organization?

❑ Have you identified the key experiences that have been proved to develop the key success capabilities?

❑ Have you established a set of competencies associated with success?

❑ Are the competencies distinctly associated with key functional areas, as opposed to being generally applicable to all areas?

❑ Have you identified situational factors that are associated with the key developmental experiences?

❑ Have you determined the personal strategies that have aided leaders to succeed in coping with the key experiences and situations?

❑ Can you construct a series of matrices of this data to aid as tools in assignment planning?

❑ Have you made the data and tools available to potential leaders as well as to management so that people can be proactive in taking responsibility for their personal development?

❑ Do you schedule rigorous and candid developmental reviews at all levels?

Succession Planning

❑ Do you have a rigorous annual succession planning process?

❑ Does your process apply to all levels of your organization?

❑ Does your process involve a series of upward cascading reviews ending at the CEO level?

❑ Does your process require a specific development plan for everyone who is identified as having high potential?

❑ Do you subsequently review development plans to confirm that they have been implemented

❑ Are the people on the succession plan for each position qualified enough that a name can be drawn at random from the succession list to fill a vacancy?

❑ What percentage of vacant positions is filled by a person not on the succession plan? If more than 10 percent, the validity of your succession plan is in doubt.

❑ Do your succession plans include lists of developmental assignments for each candidate?

❑ Have you identified the developmental "stretch" elements of each future assignment for each candidate?

Formal Developmental Experiences

❑ Are your formal developmental programs planned for key transition points in a leader's career?

❑ Do your programs focus on real business issues?

❑ Do your programs allow for and encourage the formation of cross-functional and cross–business networks?

❑ Is your formal development process based on experiential learning approaches?

❑ Do you make good use of realistic business simulations?

Exhibit 73.1. Strategic Leadership Development: A Best Practices Checklist (*continued*)

- ❏ Do you create realistic practice fields?
- ❏ In your programs, will teachers learn as much as students?
- ❏ Do your programs include multidirectional mentoring?
- ❏ Do your programs focus on all levels of the organization and not just on senior executives?
- ❏ Are your programs safe havens for experimenting and learning from failures?
- ❏ Is there real-time feedback on performance and interpersonal skills?
- ❏ Do you use after-action reviews?
- ❏ Do you use creative approaches such as live role play, interactive theater, and leadership dilemmas?
- ❏ Do you have a learning accountability approach?

Leaders who see "and" instead of "or" develop that capacity on the job in structured encounters that also move them into position along the organization's pipeline. A focus on growth, competition, globalization, and corporate responsibility is without doubt an important strategic requirement—but it's leader development that ensures the best chance of continuing success.

74

Leading from Where You Are

Paul Yost and Emily Pelosi
Seattle Pacific University

Y OU ARE AN HR leader who is committed to making on-the-job development (OJD) a core element in the way that people are developed in your organization. You have several ideas about how you can leverage programs that you are leading to make OJD a foundational part of your organization's talent management system. Unfortunately, you are not in charge. You are, as they say, "stuck in the middle." For example, you may be in charge of a new mentoring program, a job rotation program, or a high potential program in one of the business units. These programs can be impactful and integral to your organization's overall mission, but they are not currently on anyone's radar. *You* need to be the catalyst for change if it is going to happen.

Don't give up. OJD initiatives that are built from below can be more sustainable over time. In fact, we propose that leading an OJD initiative from the middle of the organization is a gift in disguise because it forces you, as the initiative leader, to think like an entrepreneur. You are not only going to need to build an OJD initiative that people *want* to use but one that has the potential to gain energy over time. The experience of most HR professionals is that any initiative that survives longer than two years should probably be considered a success. I (Paul) have been part of six OJD initiatives that have lasted more than ten years and gained in momentum over time (and have been part of several that never lived up to their potential). The successful initiatives include three OJD processes (an executive assessment and development process; a certification program for people transitioning to first-level management; and a global leadership development program) and three OJD tools (a card-sort exercise on leadership competencies and derailment, a checklist called "Development Plans that Aren't a Waste of Time," and a set of leader self-assessments to accelerate on-the-job development). All of these not only survived, but their use spread throughout the organization. They gained momentum over time.

Five design elements were essential to their success, and each element prompts an important question that OJD initiative owners should ask themselves:

1. *Strategic.* How can you craft the OJD initiative so that it aligns with and directly supports the business strategy?

2. *Systemic.* How can you build the OJD initiative so that it complements and enhances other business and HR initiatives in the organizations?

3. *Simple.* How can you craft OJD processes and tools in a way that makes them so accessible and useful that it would be crazy for leaders not to use them?

4. *Sneeze-able.* How can you build the OJD processes and tools in a way that people will naturally want to pass them on (sneeze them) to others?

5. *Sustainable:* How can you design the OJD initiative so that it will not only endure but also grow in momentum over time?

These five design factors are discussed in more detail below. Table 74.1 provides an expanded list of the questions that you, as an HR professional, should ask in order to build an OJD initiative in alignment with the five elements. We will use an executive mentoring program to illustrate how an HR professional can use the design elements to build a strong OJD initiative. Specifically, we will discuss how an HR professional can build a mentoring program in one part of the organization that could become a catalyst for mentoring in the rest of the organization.

Strategic

Any OJD processes or tools that are built to last should be linked to the business strategy. Strategically aligned initiatives are significantly more likely to be picked up by other processes because they naturally help the organization reach its goals. The key message to communicate to organizational leaders is that using the OJD system will: (1) make the organization more successful and (2) help leaders grow and develop their potential.

For example, in the case of an executive mentoring program, one of the key messages should be that mentoring will help the organization develop the next generation of leaders. In your mentoring guidelines, you might want to include sample conversations that mentors and mentees can have about the business. For instance, mentors might describe key challenges that they think the business will face in the next five years and the skills and experiences that future leaders will need to possess in order to meet these challenges. To further ensure that the mentoring program is aligned with the business strategy, recruit a senior executive to champion and sponsor the program or recruit a handful of executives to serve as a steering committee. Look for ways to link the program to other business processes. For example, use the mentoring program to expose aspiring leaders to executives in other business units.

helpful chart.

Table 74.1. Building Viral OJD Initiatives

Design Dimensions	Questions to Ask Yourself
Strategic	What are the current business priorities in the organization?
	How can the OJD initiative be designed to help leaders execute the business and develop themselves at the same time?
	How does the OJD initiative build more effective leaders for the organization? Is it obvious or do you find that you have to explain how important it is to other people in the organization?
Systemic	What are the other high-visibility business and HR processes that could pick up the initiative and how can you craft your work in a way that will naturally be picked up by them?
	How can you craft the OJD initiative in a way that will complement and enhance other talent management systems?
	What is the language that you can use so your processes will naturally apply to *all* of them?
Simple	What OJD processes and resources can you provide that are so accessible and useful that it would be crazy for leaders to not use them?
	Does your OJD initiative make the leader's job easier?
	Would you want to use it? Are you using it?
Sneeze-able	How can you build the OJD processes and resources so that people will want to pass them on to others?
	Are all of the processes and tools self-contained or do they require the user to understand other systems?
Sustainable	How can you design the OJD initiative so it will last ten or more years?
	How can you design the initiative so it can adapt to changes in the business and new realities?
	How can you build the OJD initiative so it is scalable; that is, how can you build it so you can serve more people without increasing costs?

Systemic

Build the OJD initiative in a way that complements and enhances other business and HR processes. This requires you to think about the other talent management processes that could pick it up. You then have to build the tools in a way that will easily integrate directly into other programs to enhance their effectiveness. This is no easy task. For example, imagine writing mentoring questions that apply equally well to different business units, to different functions, and to different management levels. The work, however, is worth it because narrowly focused OJD systems and tools will become stuck in the system where they were created.

Simple

The tools created in OJD initiatives should be as lean and as simple as possible. You want them to be so good that leaders would be crazy not use them. Create visuals, checklists, and diagrams to help make resources more readable and attractive. For example, for the mentoring program discussed above, you might produce several one-page guidelines on topics that will be immediately relevant and useful to participants: how to find a mentor, what should happen in the first mentoring meeting what to discuss and when to discuss it, and mentoring dangers to avoid. These tip sheets should be written as simple, stand-alone "job aids." Any tools produced should make the mentoring process easier! You will know you have arrived when you can say, "This makes the leader's job easier, leaders *want* to use it, *I* want to use it, and I *am* using it in my own development."

Sneeze-Able

The best OJD systems and tools are the ones that people want to pass on to others. We call these tools *sneeze-able* because they have three qualities: They are popular; they are self-contained; and they encourage people to pass them on.

Popular ("sticky") systems and tools, are simple, useful, and fun. They are written in the language of their end-users. Unfortunately, OJD resources and tools are often written in HR jargon that does not resonate very well with business leaders. (Of course, the same criticism can be made of tools coming out of IT, engineering, and other technical functions). A typical old school HR tool announcing the new executive mentoring is provided in Exhibit 74.1. Exhibit 74.2 provides an alternative example with language that is more sneeze-able.

Sneeze-able tools are also self-contained; that is, they do not rely on understanding other organizational systems to use them. Tools that do not stand alone are not passed on. Unfortunately, there will always be pressure to create HR systems that are "integrated" with other HR systems. HR processes and tools that are dependent on understanding other HR systems feel like instructions on how to fill out a tax form. For example, how many development planning systems include the phrase "Please consult the organizational leadership competencies that are listed and defined at _____). In contrast, OJD processes and tools that gain momentum are independent; that is, they might reference other systems and tools, but they are not dependent on them. Think of good OJD initiatives as Lego blocks—independent pieces that can be joined and combined in a variety of configurations, but each block can also stand on its own.

Exhibit 74.1. Example of a Typical HR Tool

Mentoring Program Guidelines

Thank you for your interest in participating as a mentor in the Executive Mentoring Program. Before participation in the program, please answer the following questions, which were designed to help you prepare for your role as a mentor. Return the completed Executive Mentoring Profile (EMP) to your department mentor program supervisor (DMPS), who will provide you with the next step for your assigned protégé. Please review the EMP with your protégé at your first meeting.

1. What leadership competencies, knowledge, skills, and abilities do you possess that will make you a good mentor? (Please refer to the Leadership Competency on the HR website.)

2. What knowledge, skills, and abilities do you hope to develop in this relationship?

3. Have you included the mentoring relationships in your Individual Development Plan (IDP)?

Please review and initial each statement in the blanks below.

As a mentor, I know that I am responsible for:

Determining goals to achieve in tandem with my protégé _____

Dedicating time each week to meet with my protégé _____

Maintaining confidentiality with my protégé _____

Signature: _____   Date: _____

Exhibit 74.2. Example of a More Viral HR Tool

Executive Mentoring Program: Getting Started

Thank you for participating in the Executive Mentoring Program! Starting off right is one of the best predictors of a successful mentoring relationship. Begin thinking about the following questions before you meet your mentee for development:

1. What skills and experiences will be most critical for future leaders in this organization?

2. What are the skills and knowledge that you are most excited to share with your mentee? (For example, what skills, job-related knowledge, or abilities have been most important in your development as a leader?)

3. How do you want to develop yourself as a leader in this mentoring relationship? What do you want to learn from your mentee?

These are important elements to discuss at your first meeting with your mentee. Please sign below and return this to your program coordinator, who will send you information about next steps.

Signature: _____   Date: _____

Finally, OJD systems and tools should be built in a way that encourages people to pass them on. Ask yourself whether you can build a community of practice where people share best practices and lessons learned (for example, imagine mentoring best practice groups). Can the tools be designed in a way that encourages people to obtain feedback and have conversations with each other using the tools that you have provided?

Sustainable

A final challenge is to create an OJD process or tool that will survive over time. One way to promote sustainability is to ask, "How can I design the OJD initiative in a way that will be around ten years from now?" For example, think about the logistics—can the software, data, and other materials you need be used again in the future, and for how long? The resources should also be designed in a way that will require minimal ongoing maintenance. In dynamic organizations, new priorities will emerge every year. Projects with high ongoing maintenance costs are always vulnerable. Look for ways to design the system so it is self-sustaining. In our mentoring program example, can the process and guidelines be built so that mentors and mentees can set up and manage the relationships without any HR support? Can the mentoring guides be made available online?

This brings us to a key characteristic of sustainable programs: scalability. Can the OJD resources be designed in a way that can be easily used by ten, a hundred, or a thousand people? For example, the executive mentoring program might be designed for a small sub-group of people, but the mentoring guides and resources could be posted on the organization's intranet for anybody to access and written so people can proactively create their own mentoring relationships.

Finally, look for ways to ensure the process is self-adaptive; that is, it should be built in a way that can adjust to ongoing changes in the environment. Avoid referring to specific departments or companywide programs that are likely to change. Build feedback into the OJD processes so the process can self-correct and self-adapt over time. For example, in the executive mentoring program, build in feedback loops so participants self-assess what is working, what is not working, and why. Build processes into the mentoring system to track overall program goals and find ways to improve the process. Then experiment with new ideas going forward.

Final Thoughts

Building OJD initiatives that last is never easy. There will always be pressure to pick up the latest talent-management fads. New senior leaders will bring new priorities. There will always be pressure to integrate and create dependencies. It is hard for any function to break out of the typical language and paradigm. The following are some final thoughts about leading from where you are.

1. Designing strategic, systemic, simple, sneeze-able, and sustainable OJD initiatives will increase the probability of success but won't guarantee it. You might do all the right things and the OJD system will still fail. Business markets can change and other priorities can crowd out your work. Despite this, it beats the alternative—an OJD system or tool that is unlikely to survive because it becomes stuck in a small corner of the organization with little chance of being picked up by others.

2. Experiment and see what sticks. Any entrepreneur knows that nothing is ever perfect. A good market strategy is to test new ideas and find out what works and what doesn't. Look for the unexpected successes and failures and change your direction. Be adaptable. The people who have made a difference in the world are not necessarily the ones who had the perfect idea from the beginning, but the ones who persisted and were resilient in the face of difficulty.

3. Look for your traveling companions. Look for partners. The journey is a lot more fun with others along. Build a network of people who are equally committed to making a difference in the organization. In the end, the relationships that you build might last after the program is gone. Perhaps that is what really mattered anyway.

Resource

Yost, P.R., McLellan, J., Ecker, D., Chang, G.C., Hereford, J., Roenicke, C., Town, J., & Winberg, Y. (2011). HR interventions that go viral. *Journal of Business and Psychology*, *26*, 233–239.

My Needs, Their Needs: Designing High-Value Development Tools

Rob McKenna
Seattle Pacific University

Mary M. Plunkett and Kayode Adeuja
Heineken International

THE OLDEST CHALLENGE many practitioners in the field of learning and development face is building tools that will connect a person's development to the strategic needs of the organization. We repeatedly see leaders who invest in personal development tools they themselves would not use. In these cases, individuals risk seeing these tools as just one more thing that human resources is asking them to do. Why do leadership development professionals continue struggling with this same challenge?

The fact is, it's much easier to build tools that are either valuable to the individual and miss the needs of the organization, or are focused on the organization's needs alone, and provide less obvious benefits (if any) to the individual. Because organizations are paying for these tools, it is easy to focus on the organizational need first. However, such a narrow focus may be one of the most significant barriers to offering resources that people see as valuable for their personal development.

How can you begin to rethink the tools you offer to employees, the assumptions behind these tools, and the rules for engagement with them? In an attempt to meet the needs of the individual leaders in their organization and the needs of the business, Heineken

International faced this challenge head on, providing a tool known as the Heineken Personal Development Assessment, the HeiPDA, to its employees. This tool was built with the assumption that it would be owned by the individual employee, with an intentional linkage to the personal development plan (PDP) currently in place within Heineken.

The HeiPDA generates a personalized feedback report for each person who takes the the assessment. The feedback highlights the following for an individual:

1. Key experiences in the past, and relevance in the present and future.

2. Lessons learned from past experiences, current learning, and desired future learning.

3. Self-ratings on the Heineken leadership competencies.

4. Functional competencies the individual is targeting for learning that are specific to his or her job.

5. Current career satisfaction, learning adaptability, and career aspirations.

The purpose of this contribution is to highlight the process of constructing and delivering the HeiPDA as a tool intentionally built to meet the needs of Heineken, as well as the needs of the employees who use it. The emphasis on providing a developmental tool that satisfied both of these needs not only impacted decisions about what would be included in the tool, but also the website infrastructure used to contain and deliver it.

While the content within the HeiPDA is not new, the way that it asks questions and the basic assumptions it makes about how to use the tool were different from many other developmental processes. The following questions provided the foundation upon which the tool was built. These questions are framed in the perspective of the employee because we are committed to building development tools that are relevant to the needs of the person, while satisifying organizational needs in the process. As professionals, we are better at providing tools from the perspective of our organizations. More challenging, however, is thinking of the needs of the individual user first, and then creating the infrastructure to meet the needs of the broader business.

Who Owns My Information?

Anyone invested in purchasing or building a personal development process for their employees should begin by answering the question of who will ultimately have access to individuals' provided data. Succession planning systems are an example of processes where this question is omitted. Succession planning systems provide organizations with the data necessary to track the high potential leaders within the organization. The challenge is that this data is provided by employees, and concerns about privacy and ownership may hinder the amount of information they share regarding their learning and growth.

From the beginning, Heineken made a commitment to the idea that an employee should be the one with ownership of his or her development. For that reason, Heineken used an external provider's online assessment feedback portal that gives employees the opportunity to take assessments, receive feedback reports, and set, share, and track developmental goals. The key to this tool and the system within which it is delivered is that employees know that any information they provide will only be shared with their managers at their discretion. While we strongly encourage employees to share this information, it is the individual employee who makes that decision. Not only are employee responses kept confidential, but they are maintained through a website that is external to the Heineken business. While this arrangement may not always work, it has increased the sense of individual ownership we wanted to encourage.

While individual responses are not shared with the organization, the organization can aggregate information from individual responses to generate organization-wide analyses of the developmental profile of those using the tool. Therefore, the benefit to the wider organization is still there, but employees are encouraged to bring their honest feelings and perceptions to the process.

Where and How Am I Learning?

When you think about your own learning and development, what percentage of experiences and lessons did you gain outside of your current business? What percentage of your most critical advising, mentoring, support, and feedback network exist within the boundaries of and walls of your current organization? And finally, to what extent is your career identity connected to your current organization? While there are people whose networks, identities, and learning are mostly contained within the realm of their current organizations, many individuals have career and vocational identities beyond their current jobs. Their networks span across many organizations, industries, and business types, and individuals learn in all of those places. For that reason, we designed HeiPDA as a process that encourages people to think across these boundaries.

Two particular processes encourage each person to think in a more integrated way about his or her learning. First, the tool includes statements of learning and career satisfaction that transcend the individual's current job, and encourages him or her to think about critical experiences in the past, present, and future, inside and outside of Heineken. Second, the integrated goal setting process allows a person to invite feedback on goals, and this feedback network can include anyone the individual chooses, regardless of their direct association with the Heineken business.

While giving individuals an opportunity to think beyond their organization's boundaries may not appear to be a significant innovation, many organizations are not willing to offer this. Other organizations may view such a tool as reckless because of the threat of losing talented people to the competition. Increased employability is a noble goal, but a goal that is in direct tension with retention. And yet, organizations that fail to provide this infrastructure are in danger of missing the reality of what it means to invest effectively in the development of its employees.

How Much Is Too Much?

Each individual is connected to a broad base of lessons, experiences, and people in his or her life and work, and those connections run very deep. The challenge with offering employees a tool designed to support learning is deciding how much information to include, and how much reflection individuals can take before they are overloaded and lose interest.

From the beginning, we designed HeiPDA as a comprehensive development tool. Our choices of what it would contain included the usual suspects of experiences, learning agility, lessons, competencies, and career satisfaction. Because we made this commitment, we knew it was necessary to be intentional about the way we presented this information. We created a one-page overview that provides each person with a "snapshot" of his or her development to date. The snapshot includes the following quick reference metrics, with more detailed information for those who are interested in going deeper in certain areas:

- *Personal learning profile:* Self-identified learning targets that include things such as understanding how others see you, having a mentor, executing goals, and time for reflection.

- *Career learning profile:* Quick reference indices that provide a metric for how an individual perceives his or her level of learning, adaptability, and career satisfaction.

- *Past, present, and future experiences:* Experience breadth and depth indices based on the individual's perceptions of having had a certain number of experiences and the relative richness of learning from each experience.

Leadership and Functional Competencies

Competencies can be tricky because of perceptions that individuals complete competency ratings in the service of the business, and may or may not reflect competency in their current roles, or as personal to them. For that reason, we chose to include competencies that have direct relevance to the Heineken business, while giving each person the opportunity to identify job-specific competencies we call "functional competencies." This benefit to Heineken is twofold because this data, reported in the aggregate, provides the business with an overall audit of self-rated competence, as well as data to understand the set of day-to-day competencies critical to running the daily operations of the business.

From Questions to Strategies

The questions we highlighted emerged from our ongoing efforts to create a developmental tool that is useful to the business and valued and owned by the individual. The questions are straightforward, but executing a strategy similar to the one we have described can be challenging. While it may be easy to answer the question of who will own the data, gaining buy-in from senior executives can be more challenging. Based on our experiences with this tool and other similar processes, we offer the following steps that may help to guide your efforts.

Strategy 1: Think About the Experiences People Value and What the Business Offers

Identifying unique learning opportunities within your organization might seem simple, yet people often make the mistake of believing that all learning environments are the same and that they can offer tools without thinking about the learning that is available right now. For that reason, benchmarking what other organizations are doing can be a blessing and curse, because you can be romanced into believing that because Company X did it, you should do it, too. Instead, what if you thought more deeply about the experiences and the lessons to be learned within your organization? Thinking about available experiences also opens up other possibilities because you aren't compartmentalizing experiences into specific jobs. While a hiring manager may not have the job an individual would like next, the manager may create the job if he or she understands the work experiences an individual desires.

Strategy 2: Leverage Information About Learning and Development from the Outside

We built the assessment and associated feedback tool by integrating existing tools from an online leadership development process, past research on how leaders learn from experience, and the customized experiences, lessons, and competencies available at Heineken. While the tool includes generalizable questions and feedback based on substantial research in the areas of on-the-job development, the process requires the identification of Heineken-specific competencies and experiences and the customization of learning feedback to fit the needs of leaders within this specific context. The result is a deeply personal tool, relevant to the needs of the business, which provides the opportunity to set development goals and receive customized advice for learning on the job.

Business Implications

While self-assessment and feedback mechanisms provide individuals with insights necessary to develop specific leadership skills and competencies, HeiPDA also has systemic organizational impact. The tool allows for the introduction and/or reinforcement of the organization's leadership competency framework in a practical and meaningful way; individuals move from knowledge of the competencies to assessing their strengths and gaps and linking competencies to real experiences. The aggregate data from the assessments provides a snapshot of leadership strengths and gaps as well as a collective experience profile. This information allows the organization to proactively evaluate the depth and breadth of experiences provided to its leaders in order to strengthen succession management and resourcing.

Individual Implications

Learning and growth in a person is rarely about one thing. Focusing on experiences or competencies oversimplifies what is taking place in each individual. Providing a more comprehensive way to view one's career, knowledge, and increasing competence, HeiPDA connects the pieces in a way more closely aligned with the way individuals think about their careers. At the same time, individuals must understand the wealth of assessment data in relationship to their career trajectories, while the assessment itself helps to connect the pieces together.

Our overarching goal has been to create a high stretch, high performance culture by putting development in the hands of the individual leader, giving leaders the opportunity to reflect on their learning, competence, and careers in a holistic way, and connecting the individual's developmental needs and wants with the strategic needs of the business. We conclude with several lessons we have learned along the way about designing development assessment tools that meet the needs of individual leaders in organizations and the needs of the business.

Lessons Learned

- Allow individuals to self-assess competence and compare it with their own perceptions of the necessities in the job.

- Include questions and advice that are specific to the immediate business, but also generalizable questions that transcend the boundaries of the organization or the present needs.

- In some cases, avoid the temptation to use personal development processes to look over the shoulders of individuals. We know their answers change when managers are watching, so provide at least one space for a person to bring honest answers and receive personalized feedback without fear it will be used for other purposes.

- Make the connection between business and personal needs explicit and clear.

- Assess experience, competencies, and learning in one assessment in order to create a comprehensive learning map for a person, as opposed to a one-off tool that is focused in a narrow area.

- Provide a quick snapshot for a person. Too much data at once can be overwhelming. Providing simple indices and scorecards is useful for those with little time and valuable for those who will read feedback reports from cover to cover.

76

Built to Last: Sustainable On-the-Job Development Interventions for the Entire Organization

Paul Yost and Emily Pelosi
Seattle Pacific University
Sierra Snyder
Slalom Consulting

WHAT DO YOU do to accelerate the development of leaders throughout the organization? Many rookie race car drivers are surprised to learn that the most effective way to steer the car is by using the pedals rather than the steering wheel. While the steering wheel does serve a directive purpose, expert drivers will tell you that "looking where you want to go" and leveraging the weight of your vehicle will get you to the finish line faster than any other technique. Leading an organization-wide on-the-job development (OJD) intervention or initiative can be like driving a race car: to successfully manage your way around sharp twists and challenging turns, you must learn to leverage the entire organization and continually look in the direction in which you want to go.

Keeping this in mind, you should give some thought to ensuring that you are building an OJD initiative that will last. In our work, we have interviewed and surveyed several senior human resource leaders, organization development practitioners, and industrial-organizational psychologists to hear about some of their greatest successes and worst failures. We asked them to describe HR initiatives that had lasted ten or more years, and ones that should have succeeded, but never reached their potential. We also reviewed the latest research on the factors that are most predictive of successful strategic HR interventions. In the end, a subset of critical success factors emerged as fundamental in building HR initiatives that could stand the test of time. They fell into three broad categories: characteristics of the organization, characteristics of the intervention, and characteristics of the intervention leader. The factors are summarized in Exhibit 76.1. Before you read any further, take a few moments to think about a leadership development intervention that you are about to launch or one that is just getting underway. Rate yourself against each of the dimensions to identify what you are doing well and areas where additional work is needed.

Exhibit 76.1. Built to Last: HR Initiative Critical Success Factors

Directions: Think about an on-the-job development (OJD) initiative that you are leading. It might be a succession management system, a high potential program, or a leadership development program. Consider the following questions: What is the purpose of the initiative? What are your overall goals? In one year, how will you know you have been successful? Now rate the extent to which the (OJD) intervention contains the following elements.

1 = Not at All   3 = To a Moderate Extent   5 = To a Great Extent

Organizational Characteristics

Business Strategy Alignment: The goals of the intervention address the business needs of the organization; there is a compelling business case for the initiative.   1 2 3 4 5

Top Management Support: Top management supports and values the intervention; the initiative directly supports their priorities for the organization.   1 2 3 4 5

Key Stakeholder Support: Key stakeholder groups (e.g., business unit leaders, HR leadership, line managers, and initiative end-users) support the initiative. They are communicated with and involved in key decisions where their insights are needed. There is a compelling business case (i.e., what's in it for me?) for them to actively participate and support the initiative.   1 2 3 4 5

Cultural Alignment: The goals and the initiative implementation are consistent with the organizational culture.   1 2 3 4 5

A Compelling Story: A sense of urgency is created that can only be addressed by adopting the initiative. A story has been crafted that includes the challenge being faced and builds an emotional case for the work.   1 2 3 4 5

Talent Management Alignment: The intervention is integrated with and complements other HR processes in the organization.   1 2 3 4 5

Budget/Resources: The initiative is well-managed and cost-effective. Adequate budget and resources are acquired to carry out the initiative from beginning to end. The initiative is implemented on schedule and at cost.   1 2 3 4 5

IT Support: IT experts and resources are available and willing to fully support the intervention.   1 2 3 4 5

Exhibit 76.1. Built to Last: HR Initiative Critical Success Factors (*continued*)

Intervention Characteristics

Champion: A champion, usually a senior leader within the organization, sponsors the intervention, providing energy and "air cover" for the work.
1 2 3 4 5

A Well-Managed Project: The initiative's objectives and expectations are clearly laid out with a well-developed project plan. The project plan includes measures of progress and impact. Short-term goals and progress are celebrated and made known. The initiative is kept at the forefront of people's minds. The initiative implemented on schedule and at cost. Milestones and progress are celebrated and communicated.
1 2 3 4 5

Simple and Useful: The initiative makes work easier for the people affected by the work. Communications are simple and in the language of the target audience.
1 2 3 4 5

Fair: The initiative is perceived as fair and transparent, built on a foundation of communication, stakeholder input, and the involvement of key stakeholders in the process.
1 2 3 4 5

Research-Based: The goals, methods, and implementation of the initiative are grounded in research-based practices.
1 2 3 4 5

Integration: The initiative is embedded within other business and HR processes to increase its longevity.
1 2 3 4 5

Leader Characteristics

Top Management Engagement and Communication: As the leader, you are communicating with and involving top management to build for the initiative.
1 2 3 4 5

Stakeholder Engagement and Communication: As the leader, you actively involve key stakeholders in the initiative by gathering their input and taking their needs into consideration to resolve any potential conflicts/confusion.
1 2 3 4 5

Trusted Credibility: You have a reputation as a credible and trusted expert based on your content expertise or experience/reputation in the company.
1 2 3 4 5

Drive for Results: As a leader, you have built a reputation as someone who "gets things done." You hold yourself and others accountable to deliver high-quality projects, on schedule, and at cost.
1 2 3 4 5

Organizational Characteristics

Two organizational dynamics are especially important: alignment and support. Ensure that your OJD intervention directly supports the business strategy and that the connection is obvious (for example, how does the OJD intervention develop leaders to meet future business challenges?). Create a sense of urgency—why is this OJD initiative needed now? Engage top management in the process. The OJD initiative is more likely to succeed if it is owned by the business, and not just by a support organization like HR. Look for opportunities to engage key stakeholder groups as you are building the process and rolling it out. Some of the key groups to consider include business unit leaders, HR leaders, line managers, and, of course, the target users. Who has the most power in the organization? Which business units and/or functions are most valued? Which leaders are most respected and have a reputation for developing their people? Can you partner with them to pilot the work? As the OJD initiative is being rolled out, ensure that it is aligned with the organizational culture and that it is built in a way that is integrated with, complements, and enhances other talent management systems in the organization.

Structural support is also important. Lobby for adequate budget and resources to ensure the initiative's success. It is easier to acquire resources at the beginning of the program than it is to request more later. Interestingly, several senior HR leaders identified IT support as particularly important. When priorities are in conflict, HR processes can fall to the bottom of the queue if you do not secure IT support ahead of time.

Intervention Characteristics

The structure, design, and implementation of the intervention can also significantly impact its effectiveness. First, the intervention should have a senior leader who will champion or sponsor the OJD initiative. The champion should be an influential senior leader who can promote the program with other top leaders in the organization, remove obstacles, and provide political "air cover." Consider building an executive steering committee composed of several senior leaders. Basic project management practices are also critical. The initiative should have clearly defined objectives, a schedule, clear roles and responsibilities, and a comprehensive budget.

Other intervention characteristics that were named as critical by the senior HR, OD and I-O leaders included keeping the initiative simple, ensuring that it was useful (e.g., it was seen as valuable by the end-users), and ensuring that the process was perceived as fair. Finally, remember that the intervention has the best chance of achieving the desired impact if it is built upon research-based practices. We know a lot about how people learn and develop from experience, so make this evidence the foundation of any OJD program.

Leader Characteristics

The initiative leader also plays a critical role in the project's success. For example, top management support doesn't just happen. The initiative leader must actively communicate with senior leaders as the initiative is launched and continue to engage the senior leadership team as the work is rolled out. The leader also must ensure that he or she is actively engaging the other key stakeholder groups. None of the characteristics listed thus far occur spontaneously. These characteristics happen when an OJD intervention leader is proactive and drives for results.

Final Thoughts

We end with a few words of wisdom from the senior HR, OD, and I-O practitioners we interviewed. To begin, they advise: even if you do everything right, even the best planned initiatives can fail. Success is never guaranteed. The organization's priorities can change. Top management can change. HR leadership can change. You can't guarantee a program's success. What you can do is increase the *probability* that the OJD initiative will be successful. For example, rather than relying on a single person, work to build a broad coalition of support across multiple business units and functions; build the initiative into HR systems and processes that are embedded in the organization; and ensure the processes and tools you create are aligned with the long-term success of the organization and valuable for the people using the them.

Second, in a dynamic organization, you will never do everything right. As soon as you do, things will change. Look for the elements where you do have control and do them very well. Your goal is to do everything else "good enough" so the things outside of your control don't get in the way.

Finally, remember that you are more than your job. Your value does not depend on the success or failure of any organizational initiative. Leading big changes is inherently risky and will bring both successes and failures. Surround yourself with people who will support you. Always consider your work in the context of the other important roles in your life. And, in the words of one senior leader, "This is good and exciting work, so don't forget to have fun."

77

Building Support for Experience-Based Development

Brad Borland
Kelly Services, Inc.

SEVERAL YEARS AGO the Talent Management and Leadership Development team at Kelly Services set out to build broader support for experience-based development (EBD) in the organization. One obstacle we encountered was the long-held belief many leaders have that development and work are separate and that development is not really happening if there isn't a class or a coach involved. Regularly challenging this belief as we worked with leaders one-on-one helped create a grassroots shift in how Kelly Services understands development. A second strategy we implemented involved incorporating EBD into our foundational practices for leadership development. Following are two examples that illustrate our approach.

One Leader at a Time: The Chance Encounter

A fellow leader and I arrived early for a meeting we were having with others. Before the meeting began and after the usual greetings and small talk, my colleague stated that she and other leaders reporting to her had really been struggling to find time [note her mentioning time] for development. She lamented that she had a lot to do and seemingly too little time [mentioned again] to get it all done well. I agreed that making time for everything was challenging for me, too. Our development conversation took shape when she asked, "How can I really attend to my own development, let alone helping my team of leaders, while spending less time [are you seeing a trend?], *away from work*?" I asked whether she would be willing to meet again to talk about how she most likely had more time for development than she thought. "Yes" was her almost relieved response.

I then asked what she would like to become better at doing, and she said she wanted to "commit to innovation and change leadership," which is an element of the Kelly Leadership Blueprint (our leadership competency model). Because this competency often results in groundbreaking and profitable deals with customers, she was eager to improve. I told her that at our next meeting, we would talk about what she was *doing* developmentally.

When we met again, we started discussing what she was doing developmentally to improve her ability to commit to innovation and change leadership. She discussed a typical set of tactics (for example, taking a class to better understand our solution set; shadowing senior, customer-facing salespeople and solution architects), all of which she described as "time-consuming and of questionable help." The issue, in my estimation, had nothing to do with her motivation (pretty high) or the set of tactics she had chosen. Rather, it had more to do with her view that development was time away from work. She did not recognize the value of the daily on-the-job activities that she would be doing anyway. I asked her to take a minute to think about how she had spent her time since we last met and how much time she dedicated to working on true priority issues. She searched her memory and scanned her PDA, rattling off a list of activities. What she actually revealed were great, yet unrecognized opportunities for development on an almost daily basis. Unbeknown to her, she had a treasure trove of development opportunity waiting to be unlocked in her daily schedule that if re-cast could provide an enhanced ability to "commit to innovation and change leadership."

I asked her to isolate what happened in a product review meeting she mentioned. She recounted that since the product was being changed slightly there was a "pretty robust review" of all of its new specifications. She also received a customer profile describing the type of customer who would most benefit from this product. I asked her what she learned, and she shared several details that seemed especially aligned with her development objective. However, because the learning was in the context of doing her job, she viewed it as "just another meeting" and as having no bearing on her development. I asked her to state again what "commit to innovation and change leadership" entailed. "Understanding products and their varied uses, in combination with others," was part of her reply. My clincher follow-up question was: "How can you use the product meeting information along with other product knowledge that you gleaned from similar meetings?" A smile followed by a rapid-fire response about how, through connecting one feature to another, she saw a fairly innovative hybrid solution that she never would have connected.

This is one brief story of how we are showing leaders—one at a time—that they can change their views about how the work they do each day is also a potential developmental opportunity. Similar conversations and guidance with multiple leaders over several development cycles helped turn this around and create a grass-roots EBD campaign.

Succession Planning as an EBD Opportunity

I received a call recently from a longtime friend and former colleague. He left our company and was taking on some new responsibilities. He called to compare notes and hear my ideas on approaches for driving development of successor candidates. He asked me, in a frustrated tone "What are you doing about successor development? Nobody here cares much about it after the lists are made." I told him that, while it still is a challenge, we had tried a few new things. I briefly shared a little information about our efforts, and he became greatly interested in our talent summits.

I explained that a talent summit featured a leader presenting to fellow leaders a summary of a person's career aspirations, strengths, gaps, and especially *development commitments* that the presenting leader was making to help the person. I stressed that the summits had a "real development" focus. The "real development" phrase grabbed his attention. He asked, "Are you doing these everywhere?" I told him that we were and offered that initial summits globally were "mostly polite exchanges with no real development teeth" but were "getting better." "How?" was his natural, next question.

I shared honestly that we "got a little lucky" when several opportunities arose to empha- size EBD. Specifically, it came about in summits when leaders regularly called out a person's "time in role." He replied, "That's good. At least people aren't being rushed into new jobs ahead of being ready." I agreed, saying, "It would have been really good if we could have convinced people sooner that development would not just automatically occur by staying longer in a role." I also cautioned that we had tried and failed several times before getting it right. He followed up with, "What can you tell me that I might want to do or avoid?"

I described several early attempts we made in trying to help leaders use EBD and the "time in role" assertion. Our emphasis took a dual view that in order for time in role to produce development, two things were needed: (1) an ability to specify the actual develop- ment target and commitment and (2) asking: "When we get back together at the next summit, what will this person be doing better?" Neither of these was meant to stump the leader, but they created positive leverage and accountability to begin thoughtfully planning real development with an earnest focus on EBD. (A little competition among leaders was also unintentionally created. Each of them wanted to share a high-impact development/ growth story about the leader he or she managed at a future summit.)

My friend asked, "So how long did it take for summits to catch on?" and "What turned things around?" I stated that it took a few summit cycles for "time in role" to become rel- evant. His predictable response, which I was glad he asked, was quite simply, "How?" I went on to describe that the key was to agree with leaders, in and out of summits, that:

- Time in role was and could be valuable.

- Another year of doing the same job in the same way was not likely by itself going to spur the growth desired or anticipated.

- Planned EBD was ripe for the taking.
- EBD could be planned.

The idea that EBD could be planned became the beginning of a development partnership between Kelly Services' Talent Management and Leadership Development team and HR, in which HR helped guide leaders to create better development plans that actually produced development. The additional high-touch, consultative work performed ahead of summits, while time-consuming, was quite necessary. We discovered that people just did not know how to create and execute meaningful EBD-driven or other development. The one-to-one sessions were both educational and productive and seemed to be a breakthrough.

I also described to my former colleague several other EBD sales and marketing tactics that we tried. Some were more successful than others. They included:

- *Being rational.* We cited studies depicting EBD as the most impactful form of leader development. Citing studies wasn't enough to persuade the organization to wholly adopt EBD, but the information we shared began to create awareness about its use and its effectiveness.

- *Soliciting testimonials.* We asked in assorted venues (instructor-led courses, during the hiring process, and so on), "What is one of your most important development lessons, and how was it learned?" This was a more highly engaging tactic, as people liked telling their stories and hearing others.

- *High-touch one-to-one development planning.* When helping a leader design a development plan, we imposed EBD as a preferred method. This is where truly enabling conversion of leaders began, as most leaders care about their career growth.

- *Development support tools.* Within our performance management process, we made special mention of and created examples of development that was heavy on EBD. Because not enough leaders in our organization knew how to create real development, this was a useful means to help leaders build capability.

- *Commercials.* We mentioned the range of methods for driving real development with an EBD emphasis in our online learning portal, web articles, and instructor-led courses. These were easy-to-do activities that drew favorable attention.

EBD is an acquired taste, and it can be hard to implement. But with ongoing, dedicated attention and by using a range of means, EBD can become a foundational element in nearly any leader development planning initiative or process. We found it was well worth the time we spent to embed and emphasize EBD, especially when we measured year-over-year growth of successors and other leader talent.

78

The Power of Stories in Leadership Development

Paul Yost and Jillian McLellan
Seattle Pacific University

THE FOLLOWING EXPERIENCE illustrates the power of stories in leadership development work:

At Boeing, I (Paul) was part of a leadership initiative that followed the ongoing development of 120 executive, mid-level and first-level leaders in the company. We were interested in identifying the key experiences in their development and what they were doing to build their leadership skills over time. Three months into the project I made my first presentation of the results to senior leaders in the company. I began with a slide that captured the first interview question we asked the leaders we were following—a slightly modified version of the question used in the original lessons of experience research:

When you think over your career as a leader, certain events or episodes probably stand out in your mind—things that led to a lasting change in your approach to leadership. Jot down some notes for yourself identifying at least three "key events" in your career— things that made a real difference in the way you lead others.

I read the question aloud, and when I turned around I saw that I had lost my audience. They were distracted. They weren't paying attention to anything I was saying. They weren't looking at me. They weren't looking at the slides. Their eyes were vacant or they stared at the stack of papers on the table in front of them.

I struggled valiantly in the next few minutes to be funny, to be clever, to explain the business strategy and the importance of leadership development. I got nothing from them. Out of desperation, I stopped and asked, "Any questions?" One of the executives sitting at the back of the room spoke up. "I remember my first job was working under a tyrant. I swore I would never be that leader and started keeping a list of things I would never do when I became a boss."

Then the room exploded with conversation. Another leader started talking about one of his first jobs. Other leaders ignored him and started talking to each other. I lost control of the room for the next five minutes. But then I realized that the distracted looks that preceded the mayhem was not from boredom, but from these leaders reflecting on their own leadership stories. I had connected with them on a deeply personal, emotional level. I also had their commitment to the project, which continued for the next six years.

After that experience, I learned to pause after introducing the topic of key events to allow time for my audience to reflect on their own stories. I knew that if I didn't create the space, the people in the room would take it from me. From then on, those of us managing the development initiative included stories and quotes in all of the work that we did, and we challenged leaders to reflect on their own stories.

One of the reasons experience-driven development is so powerful is because it connects with leaders on a personal level. In this contribution, we will discuss why stories and quotes are important in leadership development, provide examples of how other practitioners have used stories and quotes in their work, and provide some sample stories and quotes that you can use in your own work.

The Power of Stories and Quotes

Incorporating stories and quotes into leadership development is powerful because they tap into and trigger leaders' own stories. In addition, stories and quotes can connect with leaders on an emotional level. Stories capture the complexity of leading in a way that a summary of facts and data cannot. For example, one of our favorite quotes to use when talking about experience-driven development comes from one of the managers in our research: "The most developmental jobs I had were the ones where I felt excited and scared at exactly the same time." Sometimes we begin a program with a quote from the *Dilbert* comic strip: "Change is good—you go first." Stories and quotes can capture what it *feels* like to be in the middle of a challenging experience and they remind leaders that other leaders have been through the same thing.

Using stories also helps leaders put the current challenges they face into a larger context. The anthropologist Joseph Campbell noted that a common theme that crosses cultures is what he called "the hero's journey." This common story arc starts with someone who leaves home and encounters new challenges in the wide world that continue to build until he or she reaches a great challenge or faces a monster that has to be overcome (often requiring the hero to overcome a weakness in himself or herself). When the hero reaches the goal of his journey, he finds himself, not at the end but at the edge of a new horizon with more adventures ahead. Such stories help leaders reframe the situations that they face, and they can be an important source of encouragement during difficult times. Rather than problems to be endured, challenges become a path that a leader needs to push through in order to develop. Current challenges are but one part of a bigger life journey.

How to Use Stories and Quotes

Stories are not always valuable. They can be distracting. Quotes can be misused. How can you use them effectively?

- Consider beginning a presentation by asking leaders to reflect on the key experiences or turning points in their own development. For example, in a workshop on career transitions, we begin with a brief summary of Joseph Campbell's idea of *the hero's journey* and ask participants to reflect on a time in their careers when they "left the village" and what they did to navigate successfully as they made their way into an unknown future.

- Ask senior executives who are presenting in a leadership development program to share some of the key experiences in their development. Encourage them to focus on stories that are related to the strategic topic at hand. For example, if the business is facing a downturn, ask senior leaders to discuss times in their career when they faced similar challenges. If the company needs to go in a new direction, ask senior leaders to talk about times when they took a team into the unknown. It's helpful to interview the senior leader in advance to identify relevant stories. The stories are especially powerful when they include the uncertainty, risk, and fear that the leader felt in those circumstances. Stories become emotionally powerful when they include vulnerability, courage, and resilience.

- Video record leadership stories to use in leadership development initiatives. A clip of senior leaders talking about key events in their development is useful when introducing a new topic in the program.

- Incorporate stories and quotes into your own work. The use of stories and quotes in your materials can help leaders connect their experiences to something meaningful and larger than themselves. In training programs and presentations, quotes can be used after a break to bring people back together.

- Stories and quotes can be used to obtain buy-in for a change initiative by increasing understanding, meaning, and motivation around the change effort. In a world of information overload, stories and quotes can cut through the facts and data to get at the essence of the message. Success stories about other change initiatives in the organization can increase feelings of possibility and can communicate organizational and personal values. Stories that illustrate an alternative future can increase understanding and motivation by creating creative tension between where the organization is now and where it needs to go.

- Focus on successes and failures. Look for opportunities for leaders to share the challenges that they have faced. Many leaders don't like to talk about vulnerability, but they are often willing to talk about the courage that is required in the face of adversity. They are also often willing to share failures they made and lessons they learned when they were younger. A story of resilience in the face of hardship or failure and the lessons learned from the experience can lessen the insistence on having all the answers to any situation. Sometimes, a leader has to move people forward without a full idea of what lies ahead.

- Add some humor. Sometimes stories and quotes are a great way for leaders to laugh at themselves and to recognize their foibles.

There are also some things you should avoid when using stories and quotes:

- Don't use generic stories or parables when real ones are available. Use stories about actual leaders, preferably from within the organization. Or find a way for people to talk about and share their own stories.

- Don't spend so much time on stories that you lose the opportunity to apply the ideas embedded in them. Encourage people to turn a story's ideas into specific ways they can implement them in the future.

- Don't use copyrighted materials without permission from the creator. Check with your legal department if you have any questions about the use of materials. Avoid putting yourself or your company at risk.

Think about and document some of your own stories that relate to experience-driven development topics. Think of how you might use those stories in your work.

79

Assessing Learning's Impact on Careers

Richard A. Guzzo and Haig R. Nalbantian
Mercer

L EARNING CHANGES INDIVIDUALS, and learning in organizations can be affected in several ways such as through formal educational programs, relationship-based coaching and advising, and by direct experience. The changes that occur due to learning have further consequences, both for the individual (e.g., their career attainments) and for the employing organization. Indeed, the best way of understanding how the consequences of learning play out, over time, for individual and organization is the central concern of this contribution. The framework that we find most useful for this understanding is that of the internal labor market. Nalbantian, Guzzo, Doherty, and Kieffer (2004) provide a thorough exposition of the internal labor market (ILM) framework, a few highlights of which are summarized here.

Internal Labor Markets

Imagine that every large employer has a unique combination of processes for hiring, placing into positions, retaining, managing, motivating, developing, and valuing the talents of their members. These processes, in aggregate, fuel the internal labor market dynamics of an organization, influencing such things as who stays with an employer and who leaves; who moves into new roles or careers, who is promoted and how financial rewards are allocated. Learning is a process that influences these outcomes, and it is one process in a larger system of processes. "Systems" and "systems thinking" are hallmarks of the internal labor market dynamics framework. For example, one feature of systems thinking is that multiple factors can influence the same outcome, as when the ascendency of certain individuals into positions of leadership is driven simultaneously by factors related to the person (e.g., his or her assessed capabilities), to the job (e.g., the extent to which it naturally feeds into or networks with other jobs), and to the organization (e.g., the complexity of the business units in which the person has worked).

Another feature is that a single event or process—such as learning—can influence multiple outcomes. Interdependencies also are a core feature in the approach. That is, the effects of a process in one organization should not be expected to be the same as in another because the contexts in which that process plays out differ. Guzzo, Nalbantian and Parra (in press) illustrate this in their finding that, for all the popular emphasis on pay for performance, the actual impact of variable compensation on employee turnover varies considerably across thirty-four organizations, with more organizations actually experiencing no or negative impact of variable pay on retention than a positive impact. Such contextually sensitive findings are not unexpected from a systems thinking perspective.

A further illustration comes from a well-known consumer goods company that implemented a leadership development program centered on internal mobility, exposing leaders in the making to broad swaths of the business by moving them into different functions, businesses, and geographies. Although it was considered at the time to be a "best practice," this program failed to account for critical contextual factors. For example, a long product development cycle meant that frequent moves distanced leaders from the consequences of their decisions, destroying accountability along with the opportunity to learn from mistakes. Further, the company heavily emphasized filling job openings from within and so each internal move that was orchestrated to grow leadership capability cascaded into a series of other moves that destabilized certain critical parts of the enterprise (e.g., product launch teams) and undermined the development of technical expertise in those areas where truly developmental experiences required more time. Such unintended negative consequences arising from a failure to take a systems view of this leadership development program diminished its effectiveness and led to major changes in program design (Nalbantian & Guzzo, 2009).

An internal labor market (ILM) *analysis*, then, is a systematic approach to understanding any one organization's ILM dynamics. The analytic approach is data-rich. It takes advantage of the extensive information in databases now routinely maintained by employers. Examples of such databases include those that are a part of the core human resources information system (HRIS), those in learning management systems (e.g., LMS, which captures facts about who experienced what training and development activities), employee survey databases, and databases generated by applicant tracking systems that can provide extensive facts about an employee's prior experience.

Indeed, a comprehensive set of facts about internal labor market dynamics over time often can be quickly amassed from several sources, and those facts are essential to understanding how learning influences outcomes such as individual performance, career advancement, turnover likelihood and other outcomes.

A first step in the analytic process often is a basic description of how talent flows in an organization (e.g., incidence of lateral moves, promotions, and exits). Such descriptive information can itself be quite illuminating. It may show where the "holes" are in the pipeline of talent being groomed for future leadership positions, as indicated by excess attrition rates at certain career stages, for example, or by a dearth of promotions in some parts of an enterprise. But the greatest power of an ILM analysis comes from applying statistical modeling processes to identify causes and consequences. That power comes from two sources. One is temporal ordering. That is, the analysis tests the extent to which current processes (e.g., learning experiences) reliably relate to subsequent outcomes (e.g., promotions). Causes must, of course, precede their consequences.

The second source of power is the capacity to account for other influences on the outcomes of interest. For example, the impact of learning on promotion is assessed after accounting for other plausible factors influencing who is promoted (e.g., such as the business unit in which one works, the tenure of the person promoted). Modeling also can identify and measure interactions with those other factors that either expand or limit the impact of learning. The results of applying statistical modeling to better understand internal labor market dynamics are very practical. Those results supply strong evidence—the business case—about what is really driving important workforce outcomes and thus what processes must be changed or maintained in order to for the organization to achieve the most desired outcomes. Moreover, because the results are quantified, they permit assessments of the return on investment in learning. Given how quick organizations are to cut back on investments in talent development in tough times, one cannot overstate the importance of being able to estimate the consequences and determine whether and to what extent such decisions may be self-defeating.

Case Example: Learning in an ILM Framework

A case study illustrates the application of the ILM framework to learning's impact. The organization is a large global energy company headquartered outside the United States. It engaged in an ILM analysis to better understand and improve its talent management practices generally and to help formulate an effective talent management strategy. Consequently, talent management practices other than learning were also addressed. The company has a long history of emphasizing the importance of learning and talent development and it makes huge investments for these efforts. Those investments include maintaining a substantial training function that delivers company conducted training programs, sponsorship of employees' pursuit of university and other external instruction, job rotations to enhance employee capabilities, and extensive use of overseas (expatriate) assignments to develop capabilities regarded as essential to successful leadership in the global enterprise.

Table 79.1   The Impact of Learning on Careers

Learning Experience	Percent Change in Probability		Percent Change in Amount	
	Promotion	Voluntary Turnover	Performance Rating	Total Pay
Overseas Assignment	49%	41%	6%	28%
Certification Program	47%	−89%	No Influence	No Influence
Degree Program	65%	No Influence	2%	−4%

Table 79.1 presents results from the ILM analysis for approximately fifty thousand salaried employees during a four-year period. Three forms of learning are depicted: completion of an overseas assignment, completion of a university-based degree program, and the completion of a program yielding a certification in function- or occupation-specific areas of expertise. Also shown are the influences of these forms of learning on each of four career outcomes: promotion, turnover, performance, and pay. Promotion and turnover are discrete variables, that is, either they happen or they do not in a given year, and the results show the change in probability of an individual being promoted or voluntarily quitting in the year following the completion of a learning event.

Performance (measured here as a rating on a 9-point scale) and pay are continuous variables. The figure shows the change in the value of the variables in the year following the completion of the event. For all three types of learning the results are "all else equal." That is, the results answer the question of the extent to which a learning experience influences an outcome after accounting for many other individual, organizational, and external market factors influence that same outcome, including factors such as employee tenure, work location, type of job performed, organizational unit, time since last promotion, and so on. "No influence" in the figure indicates the absence of a statistically significant effect.

As Table 79.1 shows, the three types of learning have substantial influences on individuals' careers. There are, however, important differences in their impact.

Overseas assignments are a classic example of learning by experience. In this energy company individuals are 49 percent more likely to be promoted in the year following completion of an overseas assignment relative to others who did not complete one, all else equal. Further, in the year following the assignment, their performance is more highly rated and their pay is greater. These outcomes clearly point to the positive benefits of experience-based learning through an overseas assignment. Note, however, that those who completed such assignments also are 41 percent more likely to leave the employer voluntarily in the year following the assignment, a startling finding given the prominence of this employer in its home country, region, and industry. From the organization's point of view, this increased attrition means that it will not reap the full benefits of the learning and development that it funded through these assignments and prior learning investments in these employees. Rather, some other employer will collect those benefits. It also signals that the strength of its employment brand may not be as strong as thought.

The figure also directly compares overseas assignments to two more traditional, structured types of learning, earning a certification and earning a degree. Here we see that the structured learning programs, like overseas assignments, also enhance the likelihood of a promotion in the following year. But they are not associated with talent loss. This may be in part because of how pay is managed. It takes time for those who leave for degree programs to have their pay catch up with that of their counterparts who stay on the job (note the negative impact of completing a degree program on pay). In effect, those who avail themselves of the opportunity to enhance their capabilities and knowledge participate in the funding of their development; specifically, they don't reap the full rewards until they begin to deliver results to the organization.

Finally, there seems to be a retention effect uniquely attributable to completing a certificate program, although neither on-the-job performance nor pay is significantly influenced by certifications.

Conclusion

When applied to learning—whether it occurs through experience, traditional coursework, or other means—the internal labor market framework is quite valuable, for these reasons:

1. It properly locates learning as one influence in a system of influences on behavior, thus allowing the impact of learning to be assessed vis-à-vis other influences, including comparing forms of learning to each other.

2. The data-rich, statistical modeling approach intrinsic to ILM analysis explicitly accounts for the impact of many other such influences—individual, organizational, contextual—when assessing learning's impact, thus providing a powerful business case for the unique value of learning outcomes important both to the individual and the employer.

3. The framework emphasizes observable events as consequences of learning—for example, who stayed with the employer, who was promoted—and thus the framework offers a potent complement to approaches that rely on, say, personal recollections and interpretations when assessing learning's impact on organizational life. Studying for a certification or a degree probably does not lead to as many vivid memories or dramatic life encounters as does experience-based learning. But that difference in intensity of experience during the process of learning should not be taken as a sign that one form of learning is therefore always more the powerful influence on behaviors and careers.

4. The framework simultaneously illuminates how the interests of the individual and of the organization are served—or not—by different forms of learning. In the best of all worlds, outcomes materialize that are good for employee and employer, but as case examples here illustrate, the ideal is not always the real world.

References

Guzzo, R.A., Nalbantian, H.N., & Parra, L.F. (in press). A big data, say-do approach to climate and culture: A consulting perspective. In B. Schneider & K. Barbera (Eds.), *The handbook of organizational climate and culture: Antecedents, consequences, and practice.* London, UK: Oxford University Press.

Nalbantian, H.R., & Guzzo, R.A. (2009, March). Making mobility matter. *Harvard Business Review, 87*(3).

Nalbantian, H., Guzzo, R.A., Kieffer, D., & Doherty, J. (2004). *Play to your strengths.* New York, NY: McGraw-Hill.

80

Teaching Senior Leaders the Dynamics of Derailment

Cynthia McCauley and Sylvester Taylor
Center for Creative Leadership

SENIOR EXECUTIVES PLAY a critical role in the development of high potential managers in organizations. They control access to key assignments and decide when a manager is ready for a job move. They can provide or withhold feedback, advice, and encouragement. They serve as role models (positive and negative) for those who aspire to higher levels in the organization. How can you encourage senior managers to be more actively involved in an experience-driven approach to the development of high potentials? A first step is to help them understand the dynamics of executive derailment—including the real costs to the organization—and what they can do to reduce derailment in their own organizations.

The Dynamics of Derailment

Derailment is the label that McCall and Lombardo (1983) gave to a phenomenon all too common in organizations. Highly successful managers in the middle ranks of organizations are identified as having high potential to move up and eventually take on top-level positions. Yet there are those who don't live up to that assessment of their potential. They plateau below their expected level of achievement or they reach higher levels only to fail miserably, resulting in being demoted or fired. For these managers, their careers have derailed from the track to the top that their organizations had expected them to follow. McCall and

Exhibit 80.1. Characteristics of Derailers

1. Problems with interpersonal relationships

   - Insensitivity to others

   - Abrasive and bullying style

   - Aloofness

   - Arrogance

2. Difficulty leading a team

   - Trouble identifying the right talent for the team

   - Over-managing the team by failing to delegate

   - Failure to manage conflict on a team

3. Difficulty changing or adapting

   - Unable to change behaviors that are no longer effective

   - Over-reliance on a core strength

   - Failure to adapt to a boss with a different style

   - Unable to shift from tactical to strategic thinking

4. Failure to meet business objectives

   - Poor performance

   - Ambitious plans without follow-through

   - Failure to meet obligations to the organization

5. Too narrow of a functional orientation

   - Unable to manage work outside of one's function

   - Trouble taking a whole system perspective on organizational issues

Lombardo's research (as well as subsequent studies) pointed to common "fatal flaws"—characteristics that play a central role in a manager's derailment. These flaws include problems with interpersonal relationships, difficulty leading a team, difficulty changing or adapting, failure to meet business objectives, and too narrow of a functional orientation (see Exhibit 80.1).

The research also uncovered some major difference between those who derailed and those who arrived and excelled at top levels of the organization:

- *Track records:* Derailed executives were successful, but in a series of similar jobs. Arrivers had more diversity in their track records; they had faced a variety of leadership challenges and had managed them well.

- *Composure:* Arrivers maintained their composure under stress. Derailers were moody or volatile under stress.

- *Handling mistakes:* Those who excelled in executive positions handled mistakes in ways derailers did not. They admitted the mistake, alerted others, then began analyzing and fixing it.

- *Going after the problem:* Although both groups excelled in this area, arrivers were particularly single-minded in the face of challenging problems. Derailed managers were more likely to be pursuing their next positions rather than worrying about their current jobs, and they had a less extensive network of contacts, narrowing their problem-solving resources.

- *Interpersonal style:* The arrivers had the ability to get along with all types of people. Derailers were more likely to be seen as too political or too tactless.

The learning-from-experience deck was clearly stacked in the favor of those who eventually achieved success in executive positions. They had more diverse leadership experiences and broader networks; and due to their composure, the way they handled mistakes, and the way they focused on solving problems, they were better equipped to learn from those experiences.

Getting the Attention of Senior Leaders

Getting senior leaders to focus on the potential derailment problems in their organizations requires engaging them in discovering the truths about derailment from their own and their peers' experiences, providing frameworks for organizing and confirming their discoveries, and then asking them to diagnose the costs of derailment and the role that their own behaviors play in the dynamics of derailment.

We begin these types of discussions by asking the executives—just as the executives had been asked to do in the derailment research—to identify two high potential leaders they had worked with during their careers: one who went on to be highly successful at the senior levels of the organization and one who had derailed (that is, was demoted, fired, or plateaued below what his or her earlier potential had predicted) and to jot down some notes in answer to these questions: In their estimation, what factors contributed the most to the success of the first leader? What factors played the biggest role in the derailment of the second leader? When comparing the two, what stands out? We asked the senior leaders to share their cases with one another in pairs or in small groups looking for similarities in their experiences. The example cases come easily to mind for the leaders and the ensuing discussion is always lively.

Next, we briefly share the derailment research findings, pausing after describing each fatal flaw or derailer-arriver differentiator to see how many of their cases reflected that particular flaw or differentiator and asking for some examples. We have yet to experience a group that does not verify the research findings from their own cases.

The next step is to have the senior leaders think about the cost of derailment to the organization. Their initial focus is typically on the lost investment in the high potential manager who derails (because it is common for organizations to pay these individuals more and give them more perks). There are also financial costs when someone is demoted or fired (for example, severance packages, search firms to find a replacement, potential relocation costs). But the conversation quickly broadens to human costs, particularly the damage to morale, motivation, and productivity of individuals who work with or for someone with one or more of the fatal flaws. And there's also the cost of losing the talents of a person whose development did not keep pace with his or her rise in the organization. We ask that they return to their own derailment examples and estimate the cost of those derailments to the organization.

The final step is to examine what senior leaders can do to prevent derailment of high potentials in their organizations. When asked what they can do (and are doing) to prevent derailment, they quickly point to the obvious implications of the research and the themes in their own cases: give people a more diverse set of experiences, help them broaden their networks, be available to coach, advice, and mentor them. But we ask them to dig deeper and see whether they have ever engaged in any of these practices that can contribute to derailment:

- *Moving high potentials too quickly through the ranks.* The danger here is that there is not enough time for the individual to learn from his or her experience in each position. The consequences of actions and decisions are not experienced. Deeper relationships are not built—relationships in which there is enough trust to give the individual tough feedback. Quick upward movement also reinforces the bad habit of thinking ahead to obtaining the next job rather than mastering the current one.

- *Failing to coach high potentials about the shift in roles and expectations at the executive level.* The strengths that put them on the high potential track may not serve them as well at senior levels, for example, they have to leave operational and technical details to others and focus more on strategic issues. There are also often unspoken rules at the top about how executives are expected to conduct themselves and interact with others.

- *Testing high potentials by giving them tough assignments and then leaving them to fend for themselves.* This sink-or-swim approach reinforces the high potentials' tendency to focus on demonstrating how well they can perform rather than on how they can grow from the assignment. It also denies them access to individuals who could support their learning from the experience.

- *Bringing high potential direct reports with you as you move into a new position.* Having trusted talented individuals to rely on might help a leader hit the ground running in a new position, but one dynamic of derailment is staying with the same boss too long. High potentials can become over-dependent on a powerful boss, not developing their own perspectives and not learning from exposure to different styles or approaches.

- *Not sharing with high potentials your own ongoing learning processes.* This includes mistakes and how they were handled; assessments of one's own strengths and weaknesses; and struggles to learn, grow, and change. Senior managers can be powerful role models for continuous learning.

- *Ignoring signs of interpersonal problems displayed by high potentials.* How a high potential is behaving toward those higher in the organization is not always the way they are interacting with others in the organization. It is important to seek out information about individuals' leadership styles and their impact on others. Tolerating bad behavior in a person who is prized for delivering results is perhaps the most common way senior leaders contribute to future derailments.

We close the exploration of derailment by asking the senior leaders to think about a high potential manager they work with or mentor who might be showing some early signs of derailment risks and commit to action steps to put the individual's career back on track.

Although teaching senior leaders about the dynamics of derailment focuses them on the critical role they play in the development of high potential talent in the organization, it has the added benefit of stimulating broader thinking about how their own behaviors and practices set a tone for learning throughout the organization.

Resources

Chappelow, C., & Leslie, J.B. (2001). *Keeping your career on track: Twenty success strategies.* Greensboro, NC: Center for Creative Leadership.

Gentry, W.A. (2010). Derailment: How successful leaders avoid it. In E. Biech (Ed.), *The ASTD leadership handbook.* San Francisco. CA: Berrett-Koehler.

Lombardo, M.M., & Eichinger, R.W. (1989). *Preventing derailment: What to do before it's too late.* Greensboro, NC: Center for Creative Leadership.

Reference

McCall, M.W., Jr., & Lombardo, M.M. (1983). *Off the track: Why and how successful executives get derailed.* Greensboro, NC: Center for Creative Leadership.

81

Strengthening Executive Mobility

Nora Gardner and Cameron Kennedy
McKinsey & Company

S TRONG LEADERSHIP HELPS companies achieve their financial goals, social-sector organizations deliver against their missions, and government institutions fulfill their duties to the public. One leadership development technique that many organizations have used effectively is mobility: requiring leaders or aspiring leaders to change jobs regularly during their careers. Doing so enables leaders to develop an organization-wide perspective, build networks, learn from others, and take on new challenges outside of their comfort zones.

The U.S. federal government recognized the benefits of mobility when it created the Senior Executive Service (SES), the cadre of career civil servants who hold the top managerial and policy positions in federal departments and agencies. Established by the Civil Service Reform Act of 1978, the SES was meant to be a corps of leaders who would periodically move within and across agencies and sectors to gain an enterprise-wide perspective. The authors of the 1978 law believed mobility among members of the SES would create seasoned managers, not technical experts, and in the process help the government build a more capable and cohesive leadership system that would better meet the nation's challenges.

More than three decades later, however, the government's original vision of SES mobility has not materialized. Today, almost half of the U.S. government's 7,100 senior executives have stayed in the same position in the same organization their entire SES careers. A mere 8 percent have worked at more than one agency during their SES tenure. Even fewer have worked outside the federal government, whether in state and local government, nonprofit organizations, or the private sector.

In 2011, we at McKinsey & Company worked with the Partnership for Public Service to investigate the benefits of executive mobility within the federal government, the extent to which it is used, and the barriers hindering its broader adoption. We studied all forms of executive mobility—from short-term intra-agency rotations to longer-term assignments requiring geographic relocation. Our research included interviews and focus groups with more than ninety political leaders, senior executives and government personnel from thirty-nine federal agencies and organizations. This work culminated in the report, "Mission-Driven Mobility: Strengthening our Government Through a Mobile Leadership Corps" (Partnership for Public Service and McKinsey & Company, 2012). This article provides a summary of our findings and potential options for increasing executive mobility across the federal government. Although our focus is on the U.S. government, the lessons are relevant for any organization that aspires to boost its leadership capacity through mobility.

The Benefits and Current Use of Mobility

One of the strongest rationales for executive mobility is the government-wide impact it can have. Recent events like the Gulf of Mexico oil spill and Hurricane Sandy have brought to the fore the need for government leaders to work together and to share information and resources across agencies and sectors. Executive mobility increases the government's ability to fulfill cross-agency missions.

It also allows individual agencies to build executive managerial skills, fill vacancies strategically, and infuse new thinking into the organization. Furthermore, mobility benefits the senior executives themselves: It helps them learn how to overcome new challenges, hone their leadership skills, and gain exposure to a broader network.

One example of a major cross-agency mobility effort for U.S. government executives is the joint-duty program within the intelligence community. The Office of the Director of National Intelligence (ODNI) established a system whereby each agency within the intelligence community nominates candidates for, and creates positions for joint-duty rotations of twelve to thirty-six months for employees from other intelligence agencies. Lessons from this joint-duty program, as well as a similar program for the U.S. Department of Defense, should inform government-wide executive mobility, since they will test whether government leaders can make the profound mindset shift required of them: viewing executives not as agency-specific resources but as national assets.

Despite its benefits, executive mobility is underutilized in the U.S. federal government. Only slightly more than half of SES members have held different managerial positions within their own agencies. Very few have gained experience working in other agencies, and even fewer have ventured outside the federal government. Initiatives designed to spur executive movement have yet to make a government-wide impact. Some agencies encourage mobility among early-tenured employees through Candidate Development Programs

(CDPs) and other executive feeder programs, but the quality of such efforts is uneven across agencies.

Barriers to Mobility

Within the U.S. government, there are hindrances to executive mobility at the federal, agency, and individual levels. At the federal level, the absence of a government-wide system to facilitate mobility is the main impediment; executives have to rely on word-of-mouth to learn about executive-level opportunities.

On an agency level, a major barrier is some agencies' strong preference for technical experts; such agencies do not relish "loaning out" their technical experts or providing rotational opportunities for executives who may not have the right technical skills. They therefore hoard talent and make little effort to integrate incoming executives. (Part of the issue may be that some technical positions are misclassified as SES roles when they truly belong in other job categories.)

At the individual level, executives' negative perceptions of mobility—many see it as punishment or as an unrewarding career move—discourage them from seeking rotational opportunities. Furthermore, the lack of adequate financial assistance for geographic relocation is a deterrent—even though many, if not most, SES job assignments do not require moving to a new city.

Options for Increasing Mobility

Overcoming these barriers will help the government build a first-class workforce and deliver better results. We put forward five options to increase executive movement, which we believe are broadly applicable:

1. *Build mobility into executive selection criteria.* Employees who have been mobile before becoming executives are more likely to embrace mobility as leaders. Decision-makers could add a mandatory criterion requiring executive candidates to demonstrate multi-sector, multi-organizational, or multifunctional experience; stick with these criteria, rather than promoting technical experts into executive positions; and require regular reviews of positions to ensure they are suitable for executives with general leadership capabilities rather than technical experts.

2. *Test a variety of program designs.* Agencies should experiment with a variety of mobility program designs to find what works best for their particular needs. For example, they could try clustering opportunities by geography, function, or mission area and helping executives move within those clusters. By testing program designs in smaller units before establishing agency-wide, permanent

mobility programs, agencies can identify challenges, refine solutions, and define and track performance metrics.

3. *Create incentives (and reduce disincentives) for mobility.* Agencies and executives should know how they compare with their peers when it comes to mobility. The government could require agencies to report on their use of intra-agency and cross-agency mobility, and recognize the top "importers" and "exporters" of talent. The government could also take steps to ensure that executives who relocate receive adequate financial assistance. Other potential incentives to encourage mobility include access to mentorship programs, sabbaticals, networking opportunities, and financial rewards.

4. *Invest in early-tenure mobility programs.* Agencies should integrate best practices into the designs of their professional development and executive feeder programs. Our research shows that government best practices include executive-level rotational assignments of at least six months, mentors for participants and graduates, and mobility discussions to which employees' families are invited. The government should conduct annual evaluations of the effectiveness of their professional development programs and their alignment with succession planning in order to ensure that program graduates are considered a key candidate pool for executive positions.

5. *Centralize management of executive mobility.* If a single entity were made responsible for executive professional development, it could take the lead in communicating and championing the original vision for the SES and coordinating agencies' mobility initiatives. One important initiative that the government could undertake is the creation and maintenance of a central database containing contact information and performance records for all SES members, as well as all SES job listings and developmental opportunities.

Conclusion

The original vision for the SES as a mobile corps of leaders has never come to fruition. The federal government can revive that vision—not just to be faithful to the spirit in which the SES was founded but also to improve the quality of the government's leaders and, consequently, government performance. The options we put forward in this paper could constitute a promising start.

Although the options outlined in this article focus particularly on the U.S. government context, many organizations—including companies, nonprofits, state and local governments, and others—could apply variants on these options to encourage more mobility in their own organizations. They too could build mobility into selection criteria for their leaders, test multiple mobility designs to see what works, create incentives for mobility, encourage mobility at the pre-executive level, and establish a centralized hub to facilitate mobility. In so doing, they could better achieve their aspirations for having a leadership corps that has the skills and capabilities to meet the demands of today's world.

Reference

Partnership for Public Service and McKinsey & Company. (2012, February 29). Mission-driven mobility: Strengthening our government through a mobile leadership corps. Retrieved from http://ourpublicservice.org/OPS/publications/viewcontentdetails.php?id=172

82

Talent Ecosystems: Building Talent Through Strategic Partnerships

D. Scott DeRue
University of Michigan

LEADERSHIP SKILLS ARE primarily learned through experience. A lot is known about the types of experiences that are developmental—those that are novel, have high stakes, involve change, and require people to work across boundaries—and about how to help people learn from these experiences by supporting them with feedback, reflection, and coaching. But there is one question that every manager and talent professional struggles to answer: How can I create or find high-impact developmental experiences for every person who needs them? It seems impossible.

The demand for developmental assignments is high and growing as organizations shift to more experience-based talent development systems. Yet, the supply of these experiences can be low, especially for senior managers, for whom the options for moving up or across the organization are constrained by fewer positions. To maximize the value of experience-based leadership development, firms must address the limited supply of developmental experiences.

Firms have a common solution for other resource constraints, such as a shortage of operational expertise, distributional capabilities, or financial resources. They seek and form strategic alliances with partners who can provide the missing resource. Strategic alliances provide firms with access to a broader and deeper portfolio of resources. In the case of talent development, the resource in short supply is the developmental experience. My idea of a talent ecosystem offers a possible solution. It is a set of strategic partners who form a mutually beneficial alliance to share and develop talent. In the talent ecosystem, employees temporarily work inside a partner organization on assignments or in jobs that provide developmental experiences that are not available in their home firms. By allowing talent to gain access to developmental opportunities across firms, not only within firms, the talent ecosystem expands the pool of available developmental experiences.

The idea for a talent ecosystem dates back to the Talent Alliance, a nonprofit coalition of firms including AT&T, Johnson & Johnson, Kelly Services, Unisys, and UPS. These firms formed the Talent Alliance in the 1990s with the purpose of matching skilled talent with available jobs in other partner firms. The Talent Alliance, however, was not designed to be a vehicle for talent development. Rather, it was primarily meant to be a "strategic" job-matching program for employees who were being laid off due to restructuring, with the goal of maintaining employability in the U.S. labor market. More recently, firms such as Google and Procter & Gamble have taken this idea further by engaging in talent-sharing arrangements with employee development as the primary aim. Unfortunately, these arrangements were not designed within the framework of a formal strategic alliance and, as a result, ended with firms poaching top talent from other participating firms. These talent-sharing arrangements quickly fizzled, but there is a more effective way to build talent ecosystems.

Firms must address four key issues in order to design and manage an effective talent ecosystem:

1. *Partner selection and strategic alignment.* You must first assess the strategic fit of partnering firms. All firms participating in the talent ecosystem must commit to employee development as the primary aim of the partnership. In addition, partners must have access to the types of developmental experiences that employees need, and must commit to providing those experiences. If goals are misaligned or one firm cannot (or will not) provide the needed developmental opportunities, the partnership will not achieve its intended purpose. For example, effective partners could come from within your firm's own value chain. Partners within your value chain should have opportunities that are relevant to your employees' developmental needs, and these firms' goals are more likely to remain aligned with your own.

2. *Talent selection.* There are at least three important considerations when determining which employees to share with partnering firms. First, the needs of the employee must match the opportunities available within the partnering organization. Needs-supplies fit will be essential for securing a high return on the investment. Second, to ensure reliability within your own firm's operations, you must have a strategy for backfilling the employee's job while he or she is working in your partner organization. The person's absence will likely create a developmental opportunity for another employee within your firm (or for

another partner firm), but you need to have a clear back-fill strategy before committing an employee to a partner organization. Finally, the employee should be someone who will represent your firm with integrity. You should not expect this person to perform flawlessly—it is a developmental experience where setbacks and mistakes are likely—but the person is a steward of your firm within the partnership and must take this responsibility seriously.

3. *Partnership structure.* There are two essential considerations regarding partnership structure: (1) *incentive alignment* and (2) *governance structure.* With respect to incentive alignment, you need to define what each partner receives in return for investing in talent development and ensure all incentives are aligned with the development goals that each firm has for entering into the partnership. For example, if your development need is for employees to gain exposure to a particular functional domain that you cannot offer, you must ensure the rewards for your partner are aligned with exposure to that functional domain. With respect to governance structure, the talent ecosystem will most likely be a non-equity alliance that is held together via a contractual partnership. Ensure that the partnership contract specifies each partner's decision rights, expectations related to the flows of talent across organizations (e.g., how many, when, where, etc.), and the parameters and costs associated with exiting the partnership. Every effective talent ecosystem will have a prenuptial agreement.

4. *Performance metrics and partnership viability.* Most strategic partnerships fail to achieve their objectives. According to Accenture, only 10 percent of alliances implement meaningful performance measures, and of those that do, 80 percent of their executives deem them inadequate. For a talent ecosystem to thrive, you need to determine and secure partner buy-in on the specific metrics that will be used by each partner to evaluate success. Then you have to develop procedures for tracking goal progress, sharing feedback, and determining how changes will be made to the partnership based on the feedback. These metrics should be explicit, linked to specific goals, and shared in real time with all partners. Transparency is essential.

Talent ecosystems represent a new form of talent development. Managers have historically looked within their own organizations for opportunities to develop employees, but in a talent ecosystem, managers develop strategic partnerships in which employees move across organizations to gain access to a broader portfolio of developmental opportunities. It could be the future of a more fluid and more effective talent development system.

Conclusion

AS EDITORS, the task of producing this book was its own learning opportunity. We worked with a diverse array of authors, reading descriptions of their practices and lessons learned, asking questions and prodding them to share even more, and thinking about the best ways to organize and make sense of all they had to offer. Toward the end of our work, we decided that each of us should step back and reflect on this topic that we had immersed ourselves in, articulating concluding thoughts that each editor wanted to share about the practice of experience-driven leader development.

Cynthia McCauley: The Speed of Development

A question that my colleagues and I at the Center for Creative Leadership hear regularly from those responsible for leader development in organizations, both talent management professionals and senior executives, is this: How can we accelerate leader development? When I dig underneath that question, I often hear an assumption that there is something out there to discover about development—a new element that, if added to the mix, will speed up the process. Certainly, there is more to learn about leader development, but my response to those who ask the question is usually something like this: There's a great deal known about human development; the way to accelerate leader development is to more regularly put into practice well-established principles of learning—for example, the building of expertise through practice and the use of goals and feedback for changing behaviors. Accelerating leader development is an important aim, but no one needs to wait for new discoveries to achieve faster results. The authors of the contributions in this book have convinced me even more that wise professionals with the drive to find solutions will transform general principles into purposeful action.

In the contributions to the book, I found great examples of the application of adult learning principles to on-the-job leader development—for example, how to give people experiences that stretch their current capabilities, how to focus their attention on learning, how to manage the performance-learning tension, how to use relationships to enhance development, and how to shape an organizational context that supports learning. However, three key principles stood out to me—strategies that I'm going to emphasize when I hear the "How can we make it go faster" question.

The first principle is *customization*. This means being deliberate about providing experiences tailored to address the individuals' most pressing development needs, or to help them meet the role demands they are facing or will soon face. It also means putting the knowledge and tools for self-development in the hands of employees so they can customize development for themselves. Customization streamlines development for the individual, removing the unnecessary elements and thus speeding it up.

The second principle is *integration*. "Integrate work and learning" is a phrase I have used a lot. However, I now have a greater sense of how interweaving these two can happen in ways that create synergies and thus speed up each one. In addition to giving people real work that will stretch them in new ways (the strategy that I have focused on the most), there are also tools for making learning a part of day-to-day life and practices that integrate work and learning in the classroom (for example, bringing current work or organizational challenges into the classroom, making it a laboratory for testing out and refining concepts). And I particularly appreciated gaining insight into how learning and development professionals work to influence and partner with managers who are in charge of the work in organizations to make integration possible.

The final principle is *concentration*. Although learning is an ongoing, daily process maximized by individuals poised to take advantage of growth opportunities that they stumble upon or create, development can speed up when there are periods of concentrated learning. Concentrated learning is characterized by clear intentionality to master a particular task (or develop a particular capability) and by use of multiple tactics to realize those intentions (for example, practice, feedback, coaching, and training). A number of the authors illustrate how to put experience at the center of these concentrated learning periods, positioning training and formal coaching in support rather than central roles.

I have another reaction when people ask about accelerating leader development: Let's be realistic and perhaps even cautious. Although a leader might quickly learn a new skill that aligns with his or her natural talents, changing behaviors that are deep-seated (and often well-rewarded) is more challenging and thus takes time. Likewise, becoming an expert at complex tasks such as building effective teams or creating organizational change takes practice over time and across many situations. And there are downsides to trying to push the gas pedal too hard, like moving people from assignment to assignment without enough time to experience the consequences of their actions (and thus learn from them) or burning them out. Although people can be surprisingly resilient, there appears to be a limit to what they can absorb. Perhaps the growing edge of the practice of experience-driven development will rely on a deeper understanding of how to best pace interventions that aspire to speed up the natural experience-driven leader development that is happening all the time in organizations.

D. Scott DeRue: Taking Responsibility for Your Own Development

Based on research and my own personal conviction, I believe there are four universal truths of leader development. First, leaders are born and made. Second, every person can learn to lead more effectively. Third, to the extent that leadership is learned, it is learned through experience. Fourth, it is a moral imperative that we invest in leader development—as the fate of humanity is in the hands of those who choose to lead.

As evidenced by the contents of this book, many organizational practices exist for identifying leadership development experiences, enhancing people's ability to learn from experience, integrating experience-driven development into human resource systems, and building cultures committed to learning and development. Yet organizations cannot do it alone. A couple of years ago (2010), Sue Ashford and I wrote a paper titled "Power to the People: Where Has Personal Agency Gone in Leadership Development." In that paper, we called for individuals to take responsibility for their own development. I repeat that call here, but with even greater urgency. Imagine a world where every individual took responsibility for creating his or her own stretch experiences—where a person's comfort zone was the exception rather than the norm. Imagine a world where individuals committed to learning from their experiences, not just rushing from meeting to meeting or finishing the next task. Imagine a world where mistakes are treated not as performance failures, but rather as means to innovation and causes for celebration when the same mistake is not made twice. We cannot afford for people to wait on schools, organizations, or other people to anoint them as "gifted" or "high potential" status, or to affirm that they are somehow now ready for development. Rather, we need people to own their developmental journeys, to approach them with purpose and drive, and to commit to a lifelong, self-directed pursuit of leader development.

To excel at self-directed learning and leader development, individuals must learn to learn. Yet, for most people, their entire educational careers are spent learning known essentials—in other words, facts and figures. As children or adults, rarely is anyone actually taught how to learn. As Chris Argyris (1991) showed in his research on single- and double-loop learning, the result is a cadre of really smart, high-achieving people who do not know how to learn from experience. It is imperative that we begin to teach people how to learn from their own and others' experiences. In fact, rather than trying to teach people how to lead, it is quite possible that teaching people how to learn from experience is a more sustainable and effective approach. As the Chinese proverb says: *Give a man a fish and you feed him for a day. Teach a man to fish and you feed him for a lifetime.*

Paul Yost: What Is Holding Us Back?

In contacting people for the book, I was surprised and excited by how much is going on! We have come a long way over the past twenty-five years. I personally have introduced several conference presentations by stating that HR professionals might know that experience-driven leader development is important, but we haven't figured out how to make on-the-job development a foundational element in most talent management systems.

We are now at an important inflection point. Even though some new practices are being adopted, the ideas are not necessarily being shared so they can build on each other. This begs the question: Why not?

One of the root causes may be an organizational hesitancy to share ideas in an attempt to protect the corporation's intellectual property. Some great ideas were not included in this book for this reason. A second root cause may be that when ideas are shared with other professionals, they are typically communicated in conference presentations or in communities of practice (for example, executive development industry groups). The half-life of these ideas is fleeting, with the same ideas being discovered over and over again. The ideas don't build on each other. A third root cause is that little research is being done to evaluate the effectiveness of leadership experience interventions (especially when compared with research on training).

How can we address these challenges? I would like to propose two ideas to significantly advance the use of experience-driven leader development. First, one of the best ways to build momentum going forward might be for practitioners and researchers to look for more joint partnerships. Working together, practitioners can provide the practices to be studied and researchers can write them up. Researchers are rewarded for their work and practitioners are kept up-to-date on the latest evidence-based leader development practices.

A second way to significantly advance our work is to identify what should be studied. That is, what will provide organizations, researchers, HR professionals, and the field the biggest payoff in accelerating experience-driven leader development? I propose that one of the most significant advances we can make is to create an experience framework that cuts across organizations, industries, functions, and management levels. When industrial-organizational psychologists and HR professionals moved from job- and organization-specific Knowledge, Skills, Abilities, and Other Characteristics (KSAOs) to competencies, competency taxonomies became the de facto talent management integration framework. Similarly, an experience taxonomy could become an equally important pillar in talent management systems within organizations. Competency models have a common framework that can be tailored to different functions and job levels. We don't have anything analogous for experiences. Several contributions in this publication are moving in that direction, but we clearly aren't there yet. Significant obstacles remain. For example, how should experiences be operationalized at different management levels? How should organizations include business unit and functional experience in their experience taxonomies? Is there an optimal combination of experiences? Should some experiences come earlier or later in a leader's career?

Some great work has been done over the past twenty-five years. Now is the time to consolidate our wins and move experience-driven development to the next level.

Sylvester Taylor: Beyond 70-20-10

This volume offers an impressive array of specific suggestions for how experience-driven development practices can contribute to better leadership. There is little doubt that each can have an impact. I would like to urge you, however, as you consider these suggestions, to keep in mind the guiding principle that informs them all—enhancing the ability of people to learn from experience is the core element in developing leaders.

That principle has guided the Center for Creative Leadership and many other leader development practitioners for decades. It has played a significant part in the establishment of large-scale efforts to understand and improve leadership—from the creation of experience-driven learning frameworks, to the establishment of systems such as job assignments and coaching (and the tools and techniques that are used to accomplish these), to attempts to promote change in fundamental areas such as HR practices, climate, culture, values, and beliefs. And it has precipitated notable research regarding many aspects of leader development, including cognition and personality.

It should not be overlooked, however, that this principle can provide valuable guidance for any leader development effort, no matter what systems, practice, and processes are being employed or what beliefs and values support the activity. If you ask yourself, "What is it that will help people learn from this experience?" and then use your answers to augment it, you will increase the likelihood of development occurring.

For instance, consider the example of sending someone to a leader development program—the 10 in the 70-20-10 learning and development model (70 percent challenging assignments, 20 percent developmental relationships, and 10 percent coursework and training) that ironically often seems to receive about 90 percent of our attention. If you ask the question above, you should conclude that the person should be given support before, during, and after the program in order to increase the chances for effective learning. I am suggesting that you go even further: re-envision your role as that of enabling people to optimize their ability to learn from experience, regardless of the learning experience. This applies at all levels—individuals, groups, teams, and the organization. Practitioners should consider changing their mindsets regarding development to one of creating an environment in which experience-driven development becomes part of the individual and organizational DNA. This will lead to deeper questions regarding individual and organizational motivations, goals, propensities, obstacles, and enablers. Your answers will ensure that learners are systematically and proactively helped to prepare for programs, work assignments, coaching, and other development initiatives.

For example, you can provide tools to help clarify their expectations for what will happen during a learning experience, thereby enhancing motivation, perhaps by articulating how the experience will contribute to career and personal goals as well as to organizational effectiveness. You can help people to better participate throughout the learning experience (by providing tools and frameworks that aid reflection and learning). You can help people to practice and effectively incorporate insights gained during and after an experience with an emphasis on helping them to keep learning and maintain momentum. Finally, you can influence organizational and individual beliefs, behaviors, and practices to support a climate that embraces learning from experience as a core activity that permeates organizational life.

If you are guided by this principle in all of your leadership development initiatives and activities, as you adopt and adapt the practices described in this volume, I am confident that you will significantly enhance the probability that your efforts will have an impact for people and for organizations. Don't worry about 70-20-10. Develop leaders by helping them learn how to learn from experience.

References

Argyris, C. (1991, May/June). Teaching smart people how to learn. *Harvard Business Review*, pp. 99–109.

DeRue, D.S., & Ashford, S.J. (2010). Power to the people: Where has personal agency gone in leadership development? *Industrial and Organizational Psychology: Perspectives on Science and Practice, 3*, 24–28.

Contributing Authors

Olukayode Adeuja is a talent management consultant at Heineken International, where he has spent the past ten years in various operational, management, and specialist human resource roles in Nigeria and Amsterdam. Prior to joining Heineken, Adeuja headed a consulting firm subsidiary, Thomas International (WA) Limited, which specializes in psychometric analysis, behavioral profiling, and team building.

Nisha Advani is a senior principal in Global Talent Management and Development at Roche, where she is responsible for designing and driving talent management strategies across the global pharmaceutical medicines operating group. In her corporate career in market leading companies, she has designed and implemented leadership development solutions for high potentials as well as a variety of organization development initiatives.

Nate Allen is a colonel in the U.S. Army and is currently a faculty member at the National Defense University, where he teaches in the areas of leadership, organization development, and national security strategy. He has served in the Army for more than twenty years and is cofounder of CompanyCommand and PlatoonLeader, distributed professional forums for Army company commanders and platoon leaders.

Sally A. Allison is assistant director for Duke University recruitment and manager of the Professional Development Institute. Her career in higher education has included training and development with students, staff, and colleagues on a national level. She has been with Duke since 2002.

Susan J. Ashford is the Michael and Susan Jandernoa Professor of Management and Organization at the Stephen M. Ross School of Business, University of Michigan. Her research publications focus on personal effectiveness in organizations and leadership development.

Ella L.J. Edmondson Bell is founder and president of ASCENT–Leading Multicultural Women to the Top, as well as an associate professor of business administration at the Tuck School of Business at Dartmouth College. She specializes in race, gender, and class in the workplace. Her most recent book is *Career GPS: Strategies for Women Navigating the New Corporate Landscape.*

Joshua Bellin is a research fellow at the Accenture Institute for High Performance. His work has focused on international operating models for the future and on new imperatives for global leadership.

Eric Berg is cofounder, president, and CEO of LINGOs (Learning in NGOs), a consortium of humanitarian relief, development, conservation, and social justice organizations created to share learning resources and experiences across the sector. Prior to LINGOs, he was a serial entrepreneur in the private sector in the learning, software, and systems sectors.

Laurie Bevier has been in General Electric human resources for twenty years in human resource business partner roles and in organization and talent development. She currently leads the company's global development programs.

Anita Bhasin is an organizational and leadership development consultant for Sage Ways, an independent consulting practice. She applies more than two decades of internal experience as a business leader with high-tech companies to capacity optimization for individuals and groups through talent management consulting and forging new ground in innovative leadership development.

Elaine Biech is president of ebb associates inc, a strategic implementation, leadership development, and experiential learning consulting firm. She is an author, consultant, facilitator, trainer, entrepreneur, and mentor. She currently serves on the Center for Creative Leadership's Board of Governors and is the American Society for Training and Development's inaugural Certified Professional in Learning and Performance Certification Fellow Honoree.

Paul R. Bly is a talent and development leader at Thomson Reuters and previously worked for Personnel Decisions International. He supports talent management, talent acquisition, employee development, and performance management initiatives at both the business unit and company-wide levels.

Brad Borland is senior director of global leadership development and talent management at Kelly Services. He has worked extensively in roles that encompass leadership and organization development. He regularly coaches leaders on the planned and applied use of job-based experience development to spur personal and professional growth.

Yury Boshyk is chairman of The Global Executive Learning Network, an international association of professionals providing geopolitical and trend analysis, strategic action learning opportunities, executive leadership development, facilitation, and coaching for global organizations for more than twenty years. Since 1996 he has been chairman of the annual Global Forum on Executive Development and Business Driven Action Learning, a worldwide community of practice.

Marisa Bossen helps organizations maximize their employee health and well-being, effectiveness, and organizational loyalty. She has collaborated with health care and nonprofit organizations to find solutions that address their workplace opportunities and is currently pursuing a doctorate in the industrial-organizational psychology program at Seattle Pacific University.

Tanya Boyd is manager of organizational effectiveness for Payless Holdings, Inc. She is involved in assessments, talent management and succession planning, performance management, leadership development, employee engagement, and organization development and design. She has also taught at Seattle Pacific University and been an external consultant in the area of leadership development.

Kerry A. Bunker has more than thirty years of experience as a coach, facilitator, author, researcher, speaker, and adviser to senior executives. He is a founder and partner at MEM (Making Experience Matter) and a senior fellow, human capital, at the Conference Board. As a former senior fellow at the Center for Creative Leadership, he conducted formative research on learning how to learn.

James Chisholm is a founder and principal of ExperiencePoint Inc. Over the past fifteen years he has authored more than a dozen leadership simulations and worked with thousands of public, private, and government leaders around the globe.

Shera Clark is manager of leadership development initiatives for the nonprofit sector at the Center for Creative Leadership. Her experience includes business development, account management, and the design and delivery of customized leadership development initiatives for the corporate, education, and nonprofit sectors.

Kenna Cottrill is the program coordinator for curriculum and staff training at Leadership Inspirations and the organization development and diversity specialist at City of Hope in Duarte, California. Her passion is helping people work better together.

Maxine Dalton worked at the Center for Creative Leadership for fourteen years. She managed, trained, and developed materials for the Tools for Developing Successful Executives Program. She is now retired and lives in Spring Creek, North Carolina.

Ritesh Daryani is a senior manager in human resources at Expedia. He has more than fourteen years of work experience in the United States, India, and Singapore in a variety of roles in areas such as organization development, mergers and acquisitions, talent management, human resource transformation, and restructuring.

D. Scott DeRue is a management professor and director of the leadership initiative at the Stephen M. Ross School of Business, University of Michigan. Reported by CNN/Money to be one of the top forty business school professors under the age of forty, DeRue conducts research and teaches in the areas of leadership and team development. He focuses on how leaders and teams learn, adapt, and develop in complex and dynamic environments.

Nicole Dubbs is vice president, special projects, and formerly vice president, organizational effectiveness, at Teach For America, where she has been responsible over the past six years for overseeing the organization's leadership development system. She previously worked at The Monitor Group, Archstone Consulting, and as a faculty member at Columbia University, where she helped clients address a range of talent management and performance effectiveness issues.

Lynn Fick-Cooper is the lead faculty member at the Center for Creative Leadership for many grant-funded initiatives designed and delivered for nonprofit or community leaders. Her work often focuses on developing the collaborative leadership abilities of leaders at all levels within health and health care.

Nora Gardner is a partner in McKinsey's Washington, D.C., office and a leader of its human capital practice. She is one of the organization's most experienced facilitators and coaches and led development of McKinsey's Talent System Assessment Tool (TSAT).

Ilan Gewurz is executive vice president of Proment Corporation. He is an attorney, real estate developer, and educator and has designed and delivered executive training around the world focusing on leadership development, effective communication, and negotiations. He has a special interest in negotiations and the connection between the creation of meaningful spaces and personal transformation.

Maynard Goff is an executive consultant with Korn/Ferry Institute at Korn/Ferry International. He works with clients to design and execute research to inform talent and talent practice decisions. His research has focused on leadership assessment, using multiple methods, including self-report, business simulations, and 360. He regularly authors publications and presents at conferences.

Marsha Green is a senior writer at Duke University, working with Human Resources' Office of Communication Services. She has been working with internal communications at Duke since 1995.

Richard A. Guzzo is founder and co-leader of Mercer's Workforce Sciences Institute, where he consults on strategic talent management issues and has R&D responsibilities. Prior to joining Mercer, Rick was a professor for many years at both New York University and the University of Maryland. He has published dozens of professional papers and four books, and his research and publications have won several awards.

Kim Hayashi is owner and executive director of Leadership Inspirations, a leadership training organization whose vision is to inspire learning, leadership, and service. Her passion is working with students and educators, and she also serves as an adjunct professor in the Leadership Studies Department at Chapman University.

Joy Hazucha is senior vice president of leadership research and analytics for Korn/Ferry International. Her experiences in consulting, office start-ups in Europe, leading key parts of the business, and crafting client solutions help her to provide client-relevant research and thought leadership.

Joy Hereford is an organizational psychologist specializing in leadership and talent consulting. She has worked with local and global organizations in a variety of industries and currently works with Yost & Associates, Inc., which specializes in strategic talent management, leadership development, and transition management.

Claudia "Cori" Hill is global director of high potential leadership development at Korn/Ferry International. With more than twenty years of experience in education, Hill is an active researcher and author of many professional publications, including co-authoring *Action Learning for Developing Leaders and Organizations*. She is a noted expert in the area of leadership development.

Lori Homer currently works at Microsoft, where she promotes increased leader and organizational effectiveness through her work with executives. She also volunteers in an experience-based community leader development program and has served as advisor for over thirty leadership capstone projects within the Leadership Executive MBA program at Seattle University.

Jennifer Jaramillo is a management consulting executive at Accenture, where she has experience in high-risk, high-visibility transformation projects across the private, public, and nonprofit sectors. She is a co-creator of the RLIx leadership development program at the Stephen M. Ross School of Business, University of Michigan, where she was a recipient of the Frank S. Moran Leadership Award.

Claudy Jules is a senior principal and executive coach at Accenture, where he works with CEOs and top teams to tackle their most pressing organizational challenges. He specializes in the areas of large-scale change, executive leadership, global operating models, organization design, and top team effectiveness.

Dana Kendall is an assistant professor of industrial-organizational psychology at Seattle Pacific University. She is committed to discovering practical ways to maximize the potential and effectiveness of mentoring relationships in the workplace.

Cameron Kennedy is senior manager of McKinsey's public-sector practice and an expert in public-sector organization issues. She helps federal clients address critical managerial problems such as creating alignment between headquarters and field organizations and acquiring and developing the requisite talent to fulfill their mission.

Robleh Kirce is an industrial-organizational psychology doctoral student at Seattle Pacific University, where he has conducted applied research in the area of leadership development. Robleh specializes in developing emerging leaders across a variety of industries ranging from health care to nonprofits.

Mark Kizilos is founder and principal of Experience-Based Development Associates, LLC, and FrameBreaking.com, where he helps individuals and companies leverage work experiences for leadership development. Over the past twenty years he has worked as a vice president of talent management at Thomson Reuters and as a consultant to major companies.

Shirli Kopelman is a negotiation professor at the Stephen M. Ross School of Business and a core faculty member of the Center for Positive Organizations at the University of Michigan, where she conducts research, teaches in degree programs and executive education, and writes theoretical, empirical, and practice-focused publications. She has developed expertise in strategic emotion management and leadership in cross-cultural business engagements.

Andrew K. Mandel has served as a leader of teacher preparation, support, and development at Teach For America for more than ten years. He is also a doctoral student in adult learning and leadership at Teachers College, Columbia University.

Jennifer Kennedy Marchi spent thirteen years with The Monitor Group, most recently as head of global talent management. She specializes in working closely with executive teams and employees to build human resource programs that drive engagement levels and is currently director of employee engagement and development at Sonos, Inc.

Cynthia McCauley is a senior fellow at the Center for Creative Leadership. She has been an active contributor for many years to the field of on-the-job leader development through her research, publications, workshops, and product development work.

Scott McGhee is manager of leadership and organization development at U.S. Cellular. He has broad responsibilities, including the design and management of leadership development curriculum and the application of organization development strategies to key leadership teams that drive U.S. Cellular's culture and business success.

Kelly McGill is vice president of global talent acquisition at Expedia, Inc. She has more than twenty years of diversified business and HR expertise developing scalable talent management infrastructures at several major companies, including Microsoft and T-Mobile. As an accomplished writer, an avid blogger, and a compelling speaker, she is passionate about guiding teams through transformational change in an inclusive way with minimal disruption to the business.

Jeffrey J. McHenry is principal and founder of Rainier Leadership Solutions, a consulting firm that specializes in leadership development, executive coaching and assessment, and leadership talent management. Previously, McHenry spent eighteen years at Microsoft working in a variety of leadership and organization development roles in the United States and Europe, culminating in the role of general manager, leadership development and recruiting.

Rob McKenna is executive director of the Center for Leadership Research and Development and chair of the Department of Industrial-Organizational Psychology at Seattle Pacific University. He is also president of Real Time Development Strategies, LLC. He works with a broad base of Fortune 500 and not-for-profit organizations, helping them design systems and processes for developing leaders in real time.

Jillian McLellan has worked for several boutique consulting firms in the areas of selection and 360-degree feedback systems. She is pursuing a doctorate in industrial-organizational psychology at Seattle Pacific University, where her research interests include on-the-job development, selection, and organizational change initiatives.

Stephen R. Mercer is former vice president of learning and leadership development at The Boeing Company. He came to Boeing from General Electric's Crotonville Leadership Center, where he and his team led business-driven action learning programs in more than fifty countries on five continents, as well as special executive programs for GE's global customers. He currently works at TRI Corporation, delivering experiential leadership development simulations.

Haig R. Nalbantian is a founder and leader of Mercer's Workforce Sciences Institute. A labor/organizational economist, he has been instrumental in developing unique capabilities to measure the economic impact of people practices. For over twenty years, he has deployed these methods consulting to many leading organizations around the globe. He is widely published in the field and is a member of the American Economic Association.

Luke Novelli, Jr., is president and founder of Leadership Development Resources Global and a former senior fellow at the Center for Creative Leadership. He specializes in design and delivery of leadership development initiatives, preparation of leadership teams and organizational systems for implementation projects, and organization learning–based program evaluation.

Sally Beddor Nowak works at Agilent Technologies, where her focus is on midlevel, senior, and executive leadership development globally. Her organization development and leadership experiences include health care, hospitality, academia, and private consulting.

Patricia M.G. O'Connor is general manager, leadership development and talent management, at Wesfarmers. She has more than eighteen years of global experience in the leadership field, with a track record of delivering results in corporate executive, consultant, coach, author, and speaker roles.

Patricia Ohlott works at OIC of America as an evaluator and project manager for workforce development initiatives. She has worked for more than twenty years in applied research and capacity building with organizations in the areas of program evaluation, leadership, and organization development.

Kristin Ohnstad is a senior member of the human assets team at Teach For America. She has contributed to the organization's evolving perspective on and approach to leadership development and has designed various leadership experiences and trainings for staff members.

Paul Austin Orleman is a member of SAP's global talent development team. He works with SAP's high potentials to provide experiential development opportunities linked to strategy execution.

Mathian Osicki has spent twelve years in various parts of IBM, including global workforce research; executive compensation; climate analysis in Bangalore, India; and a Corporate Services Corps assignment in Cross River State, Nigeria. Osicki's work in Nigeria provided her with the opportunity to help reduce the mortality rate of women and children across the state.

Emily Pelosi is pursuing her doctorate in industrial-organizational psychology at Seattle Pacific University. She is dedicated to improving organizational effectiveness through studying the design and implementation of effective organizational change initiatives.

Mary Mannion Plunkett has spent more than twenty years developing leaders and organizations across diverse industries and geographies. She has held senior roles at Boeing, BP, Heineken, and presently Carlson, Inc., a private, global hospitality and travel company that employs more than 170,000 people worldwide.

Laura Ann Preston-Dayne is a director for leadership development at Kelly Services, Inc. In this role she has provided leadership development support for Kelly's competency architecture, program design, assessment, succession planning, social media presence, talent segmentation, and workforce planning.

Eric Rait, principal at honeycombdevelopment.com, is a leadership and organization development expert. He led talent management, organization, and leadership development for Microsoft International for several years and has supported senior leadership teams across the engineering and the sales and marketing groups at Microsoft. Today he is focused on a variety of private-sector and NGO leadership and organization development efforts.

Lyndon Rego is global director of the Center for Creative Leadership's Leadership Beyond Boundaries initiative, an effort to democratize leadership development around the world. He writes and speaks on issues at the intersection of social innovation, complexity, and leadership.

Hilary G. Roche is pursuing her doctorate in industrial-organizational psychology at Seattle Pacific University. Her research areas include employee development, developmental networks, and work-life management. She has worked with Fortune 500 and nonprofit organizations to increase organizational effectiveness, manage transitions, and address team issues.

Peg Ross leads global human resources and serves on the executive leadership team at PCI, an integrated international development nonprofit based in San Diego. Prior to joining PCI, Ross was director of Grameen Foundation's Human Capital Center. She has spent more than twenty-five years building human resource functions that support strategy attainment and help navigate transformational change.

Marian N. Ruderman is a senior fellow at the Center for Creative Leadership, where she specializes in research on leaders and leadership. Her research findings have been developed into assessments, applied to interventions in organizations, presented to international audiences, and published in books, scientific journals, and the popular press.

Kristen Schultz is a cofounder of the RLIx leadership development program at the Stephen M. Ross School of Business, University of Michigan. Previously, she worked in Washington, D.C., as the fund-raising strategist for the political action committee EMILY's List. Schultz is starting as senior consultant in strategy and operations at a large international consulting firm.

Caroline Smee is an undergraduate student at Boston College. She is majoring in human development with a minor in organizational studies and human resource management. Most recently she worked as a client value intern at IBM, collecting and analyzing data on client satisfaction and employee climate.

Sierra Snyder is a member of the talent management team at Slalom Consulting, where she works to improve business performance and organizational effectiveness through advanced change management and talent management strategies.

Scott Taylor designs and facilitates leadership development programs at Teach for America(TFA) and helped pioneer the Leadership Journeys initiative. Prior to focusing on leadership development, Taylor worked as a senior managing director at TFA, supporting multiple teams across the western United States. He also has led experiential education programs and has supported nongovernmental organization development as a Peace Corps volunteer in Slovakia.

Sylvester Taylor is a director in the Research, Innovation, and Product Development Group at the Center for Creative Leadership. He has more than twenty years of experience researching, designing, and implementing leadership development projects, primarily helping organizations gain value from organizational and multi-rater feedback initiatives.

John Terrill is director of the Center for Integrity in Business at Seattle Pacific University. Prior to joining Seattle Pacific, he led InterVarsity's Professional Schools Ministries, served as a consultant with Hay Group, and worked as a commercial lender with NationsBank (now Bank of America).

Robert J. Thomas is global managing director of the Accenture Institute for High Performance, based in Boston. He is coauthor with Warren Bennis of *Geeks and Geezers* and author of *Crucibles of Leadership*. He writes and consults with global clients on leadership and transformational change.

Bela Tisoczki has held management positions at General Electric and at Swiss Re in human resource management, Six Sigma, change management, and organization development. He is also a doctorate researcher at Cranfield School of Management, focusing on rotational leadership development programs.

Norm Tonina has worked at Grameen Foundation since 2010 as both an independent consultant and its chief human resource officer. He spent more than twenty years at Microsoft and Digital Equipment Corporation in roles ranging from pricing and licensing to finance to culture and leadership. Tonina has also served as an adjunct lecturer at Seattle Pacific University and at the University of Washington.

Paul Van Katwyk is a vice president, consulting solutions, at Korn/Ferry International, where he has served as director for consulting solutions in the Asia Pacific region. In this role he has overseen the design of integrated solutions for key clients. His research has focused on measuring individuals' leadership experience. He is the leading author of the Leadership Experiences Inventory.

Vandana Viswanthan is a cofounder and partner at CoCoon, a design and consulting firm in India that works to strengthen leaders and organizations. At CoCoon, she leads work in the areas of leadership development and organizational effectiveness to drive performance and enable growth of organizations. She has worked over the past nineteen years in the areas of capability building and human resource strategy.

Shannon M. Wallis is principal and founder of Arrow Leadership Strategies, a consulting firm specializing in transformational change, leadership development, and strategic planning. Previously, she was global director of high potential leadership development at Microsoft, and she has consulted for and held management positions in businesses as diverse as Coca-Cola, Microsoft, Universal Studios, and Grameen Foundation.

Greg Warman is a cofounder and principal of ExperiencePoint Inc. He designs and delivers simulation experiences and believes passionately that digital games—if designed and implemented well—help learners bridge the gap between knowing and performing.

Andrew Webster is director of change and innovation solutions at ExperiencePoint Inc. He has contributed to the development and evolution of award-winning simulations and runs them for Fortune 500 firms around the world. He trains business school faculty in the use of simulations and consults on how to integrate them into executive programming.

Jan Wilmott joined Royal Bank of Canada in 2009 as head of leadership development. His global team's mandate is to build focus, alignment, and capability across RBC's executive, high potential, and emerging talent populations, leveraging their ability to execute RBC strategic priorities. Wilmott has more than thirty years of executive development experience at Fortune 100 companies, including McDonnell Douglas, Boeing, and UBS.

Jonathan Winter is founder and CEO of The Career Innovation Company, a think tank and design organization that has helped some of the world's best-known employers to inspire and engage their people. He has led the creation of research studies, publications, and software products and has spoken at events and on television and radio in many parts of the world.

Paul Yost is an associate professor of industrial-organizational psychology at Seattle Pacific University and principle and founder of Yost & Associates, Inc., which specializes in strategic talent management, leadership development, and transition management. He has worked at Microsoft, Boeing, GEICO, and Battelle Research in a variety of roles, including executive assessment, leadership development, and human resource research.

About the Center for Creative Leadership

Center for
Creative
Leadership
www.ccl.org

THE CENTER FOR Creative Leadership (CCL®) is a top-ranked, global provider of executive education that accelerates strategy and business results by unlocking leadership potential of individuals and organizations. Founded in 1970 as a nonprofit educational institution focused exclusively on leadership education and research, CCL helps clients worldwide cultivate creative leadership—the capacity to deliver results that matter by thinking and acting beyond boundaries—through an array of programs, products, and other services. Ranked among the world's Top 10 providers of executive education by Bloomberg Business-Week and the Financial Times, CCL is headquartered in Greensboro, NC, with campuses in Colorado Springs, CO; San Diego, CA; Brussels; Moscow; Singapore; New Delhi—NCR, India; and Addis Ababa, Ethiopia.

Its work is supported by more than 500 faculty members and staff.

Index

Page references followed by *fig* indicate an illustrated figure; followed by *t* indicate a table; followed by *e* indicate an exhibit.

HTX4